SACRED ALIGNMENT

A Message for Humanity

N. S. ELIJAH

DoctorZed
Publishing
www.doctorzed.com

Copyright © N. S. Elijah 2021

All rights reserved. No part of this book may be used or reproduced by any means, graphic, electronic, or mechanical, including photocopying, recording, taping or by any information storage retrieval system without the written permission of the publisher except in the case of brief quotations embodied in critical articles and reviews.

Copies of this book can be ordered via the author's website at www.thesacredalignment.com, booksellers or by contacting:

DoctorZed Publishing
10 Vista Ave, Skye,
South Australia 5072
www.doctorzed.com

ISBN: 978-0-6450656-8-8 (sc)
ISBN: 978-0-6450656-9-5 (e)

A CiP number is available at the National Library of Australia.

Because of the dynamic nature of the Internet, any web addresses or links contained in this book may have changed since publication and may no longer be valid. The views expressed in this work are solely those of the author and do not necessarily reflect the views of the publisher, and the publisher hereby disclaims any responsibility for them.

The author of this book does not dispense medical advice or prescribe the use of any technique as a form of treatment for physical, emotional, medical, or spiritual problems without the advice of a physician, either directly or indirectly. The intent of the author is only to offer information of a general nature. In the event you use any of the information in this book for yourself, which is your constitutional right, the author and the publisher assume no responsibility for your actions.

Printed in Australia, UK and USA

DoctorZed Publishing rev. date: 01/04/2021

"Your life unfolds according to the same principle that governs every other unfolding. You are rooted in the common ground of all creation. Being like everything else means that you are ordinary. Yet, consciously knowing that you are like everything else is extraordinary. And knowing how that universality works and having the sense to act accordingly is the source of your power, your endurance and your excellence. Consciousness or awareness, then, is the source of your ability. Learn to become increasingly conscious."

– Lao Tzu, Tao Te Ching, 5th Century BC

"Those who see a vision that is withheld from those lacking the necessary equipment for its apprehension are regarded as fanciful and unreliable. When many see the vision, its possibility is admitted, but when humanity itself has the awakened and open eye, the vision is no longer emphasised, but a fact is stated, and a law enunciated. Such has been the history of the past and such will be the process of the future."

– The Tibetan

CONTENTS

Acknowledgements vii
Preface ix
Introduction xii
List of Diagrams xxi

Chapter 1 The Light of Reconciliation 1
Chapter 2 The Key to the Mysteries Turned Seven Times 25
Chapter 3 Origins 71
Chapter 4 The Lost Books of Thoth 103
Chapter 5 Abraham 121
Chapter 6 Initiation 141
Chapter 7 The Road Less Travelled 175
Chapter 8 Exiting the Matrix – The Red Pill 199
Chapter 9 The Jewel of Great Price 273
Chapter 10 Blazing the Trail and Passing the Torch 331

Appendices 359
Selected Bibliography 365

"For all of humanity, may you rest and find peace in this knowledge and then set yourself to task, for the world needs you!"

– N. S. Elijah

ACKNOWLEDGEMENTS

This book could not have been written if not for the camaraderie, love, guidance, patience and sharing of life's lessons with the following people (some of which are still a part of my life and others are not – as the emanations and innumerable synchronicities of creation align us to walk side by side for a time and then move us on to other paths): Ava R, Adam M, Daniel C, Anna M, Susan M, Pauline N, Deb K, Bliss B, Brad P, Darren C, Rick D, Jessica C, Rishi A, Charlu M, Isaac S, My Mother, Father and siblings, Anthony C, Kevin R, Michelle M, Mark L, Michelle S, Cuinn W, Solara A, Dirk S, Rene S, Krista R, Honovi S and Pina D.G.

The graciousness of the Lucis Trust, The Urantia Foundation, Aurora Press, The Rishi Institute of Metaphysics, The Agni Yogi Society, The Academy for Future Science, Light Technology Publishing, AMORC – Ancient Mystical Order Rosae Crucis, The Order of Christian Mystics, Krishnamurti Foundation, Red Wheel Weiser, Penguin Random House UK, University of California Press, S.U.N.Y Press and Brien Foerster for permission to use their copyrighted works in the creation of this work before you.

The written instruction of spiritual teachers, light workers and fellow builders across time and space: His Holiness the Dalai Lama, Kalu Rinpoche, Madam Helena Blavatsky, Alice A Bailey, Carlos Castaneda and his teacher Yacqui Indian Don Juan, Elisabeth Haich, Drunvalo Melchizedek, J. Krishnamurti, Frank Homer Curtiss, Dwal Kuhl, Kuthumi, El Morya, Ptah-Hotep, Dr J. J. Hurtak, Dolores Ashcroft-Nowicki, Zecharia Sitchin, Robert Bauval, Graham Hancock, John Anthony West, Masaru Emoto, The 3 Initiates, Judith Page & Jan Malique, Solara Anra, Justin M Asar, Solara Anani, Manly P Hall, Swami Sri Yukteswar Giri, Kahlil Gibran, Caroline

Myss, Kaypacha, Robin Sharma, Paulo Coelho, Lao Tzu, Iamblichus and Hermes Trismegistus.

Every person that has crossed my path in this life has been a teacher and has added value; my grandparents, all of my cousins, and uncles and aunties and school friends, and university friends, and sports friends and co-workers and previous employers. The unseen guidance of the spirit world, the Masters of Light and Wisdom and the Angels in subtle and human form and my Star family that continue to grace my path and enrich my life's journey.

Thank you to all of you and to the light. And to my dearest son – a Grand Master soul that came in but for a short time and by his short life – helped me to open my heart wider and realign my bearing to my true purpose and to have the courage to follow it.

Blessings of Peace profound and the deepest Love to you all.

A special thanks for the cover art design image by Stefan Keller of Kelle Pics. And to Dr. Scott Zarcinas and team of editors and book design specialists at doctorzed.com that have helped me to shape this manuscript into its completed state – thank you for your patience and professionalism in seeing this come to light.

PREFACE

*"Take a simple idea and take it seriously...
Grab knowledge with full attribution plus extreme
reductionism where feasible."*

— Poor Charlies Almanack, **The wit and wisdom
of Charles T Munger**

The original source of the pages in this book that provide some of the lost teachings of the Book of Thoth is very ancient. The original account is thought to be attributable to Iamblichus of Syria; first rendered in ancient Greek that was later translated into French and then Dutch and then into English and is now out of print.

The chosen pieces of knowledge deemed fit for public consumption at this time, from the teachings of the Lost Book of Thoth, along with other ancient sources of instruction within these pages, will have a profound effect on your consciousness. So, it is indeed preferable to take it slowly.

Many thousands of years ago after long periods of purification and preparation and trials that could have ended in their death – the Initiate to the mysteries was taught the meaning of one sacred symbol a day, and then they had to let this understanding percolate in their consciousness in order to prepare them for the next symbol the following day. It is of course possible to read through this book in a few hours, however – pausing for at least a day after reading the teachings associated with each symbol of the Lost Book of Thoth is recommended.

This book contains four chosen symbols of the twenty-two symbols that comprise the summary of the Lost Books of Thoth. You can choose to read through this book in one sitting, however, you may lose the opportunity to allow time for the sacred teachings to take effect and work to unlock hidden aspects lying dormant within your consciousness.

On a different note, over time, the spelling of the names of some historical personages has changed. In the old language, Mohammad was spelled with an 'O.' However, today the consensus on the correct spelling is with a 'U' i.e. Muhammad. The reader will observe that quotes from older sources will be spelled as they were originally written with an 'O.' However, any reference to the Prophet by this author outside of quotations in the old spelling will be spelled 'Muhammad.'

It is also important to note that it remains inconclusive to scholarly consensus as to whether the first dynastic King of Egypt was known as 'Menes' or 'Narmer.' Some scholars conclude that they were the same individual and others conclude that they were two separate individuals. When mentioned in this manuscript they will be mentioned as being the same person, King Menes/Narmer.

Further, within these pages when I mention the 'Christing' of Jeshua Ben Joseph (Jesus), I refer to this deliberately as 'Christing' and not 'Christening' – in order to distance this significant event from the current normal application of the word 'Christening' used in ritual within the Christian Church.

Every effort has been made to check the validity of the interpretation of historical events and personages in order to present them in the light of greater truth.

The pages that follow are the result of dedicated endeavor for more than the last decade. I let this book go now on the mighty wings of the Divine Hawk – to carry the pages herein to the cosmic heart, to see if they will register in the consciousness of humanity, in the hope that they will serve to help to cause a remembrance in your own heart.

It is my hope that you read the following pages without bias and without any hint of animosity so that you to may start to see the vision of a united humanity and what this foundation will mean for steering the Earth and its people back to harmony.

INTRODUCTION

Greetings dear reader,

If we take a moment to look out at this world and the current state of affairs, we quickly see that something needs to be done about it, but where does one begin? I mean, why are there so many conflicts on Earth? Why are there so many religious-based wars? And is there anything that can be done that can steer our planet in a better direction?

I grew up listening to the feel-good tunes of the band – Credence Clearwater Revival. When I first heard John Fogerty's words:

> *"Long as I remember the rain's been comin' down*
> *Clouds of mystery pourin' confusion on the ground.*
> *Good men through the ages tryin' to find the Sun.*
> *And I wonder, still I wonder, who'll stop the rain?"*

They resonated very deeply with me for some reason. Little did I know at the time that it would be my life's work to alleviate the 'confusion on the ground' and stop the rain.

In a book called, '*Poor Charlie's Almanac: The Wit and Wisdom of Charles T. Munger, pages 428-429 Talk ten: USC Gould School of Law Commencement address,*' Charlie, the billionaire 84-year-old (at the time of writing this) business partner to Warren Buffett says that unless one is a genius like Einstein, then in order to solve a problem, one must use inversion. If we wanted to help India for example, Charlie suggests that we must invert the approach and ask, what is it that is causing the most damage in India? And then invariably from there we would be able to design an approach to work from those findings:

"Many hard problems are best solved when they are addressed backward." "The way complex adaptive systems work and the way mental constructs work is that problems frequently get easier, I'd even say usually are easier to solve, if you turn them around in reverse. In other words, if you want to help India, the question you should ask is not "how can I help India," it's "what is doing the worst damage in India?"

Similarly, if we want to help our planet, then we must invert the approach and ask: what is it that is causing the most damage in the world? Having spent many hundreds of hours deliberating on this, I have concluded that it is the current state of ignorance of humanity that is causing the most damage on the planet. This ignorance causes division, 'the confusion on the ground' that Credence Clearwater Revival referred to. And as long as those perceived differences remain, there will continue to be war and fighting and conflict. In my heart, I know that we as a species are capable of so much more.

However, in order for us to educate correctly and work to dissolve this ignorance; intellectual arrogance, as a current standard of the human condition, superiority and bias, needs to be dropped. Indeed, the cup must be emptied before it can receive revitalising elixir anew.

The time has come to unify the religions of the world and found the kingdom of God on Earth. For far too long there has been unnecessary misunderstanding that has kept humanity divided. There exists now and has since time immemorial – the most auspicious phenomenon called *'The Sacred Alignment.'* It is this sacred alignment that it becomes vitally necessary to accept collectively as our supreme potential. This sacred alignment is based upon a simple yet profound truth that once universally accepted will provide the simple foundation to reorient the societies of the world, and provide once and for all a sound basis for the foundation of an unselfish brotherhood and sisterhood in humanity. To that end:

This book has been written with a very specific and clear threefold purpose. The first is to identify, illustrate and explain the shared governing dynamics between all of the world religions – in order to unify them and end unnecessary division. The second is to provide mankind with a more

Introduction

accurate understanding and awareness of our true origins and highlight how we have been deliberately taught a false version of our history in order to keep us divided, powerless and controlled for the last 2,000 years (not to instil fear or anger into the population but simply to build awareness). And finally, the third is to identify, illustrate and explain how it is mankind can become more than man by way of achieving *The Sacred Alignment* – which is the underlying message preserved in the esoteric teachings and allegorically camouflaged verses of scripture passed down since antiquity that has been largely misunderstood.

This book will not resonate with everyone for it pushes the envelope of the accepted paradigm and is quite confrontational with the vision it paints regarding the true situation on Earth. I write from my personal experience and journey of revelations and strange experiences, over my almost 40 years living on this planet, in order to put forward a framework by which the distortions of history can be cleared up – to create a necessary bridge from science to spirituality.

Using lost knowledge of wisdom teachings of the Ancient Egyptian Mystery schools and the revelations of some of the content of the highly sought after most priceless seemingly lost works of the ancient world – *The Books of Thoth*; I tear asunder previous wrong assumptions of our forebears and prove that the same thread runs through all Abrahamic religions, proving the same point of origin – uniting the faiths of the true Christianity (not *Churchianity*), Judaism and Islam as well as the non-Abrahamic religions such as Buddhism and Hinduism and others.

To put the scope of this undertaking into perspective, I will quote the words of Jnanavatar Swami Sri Yukteswar Giri from the introduction of his 1894 book '*The Holy Science*':

> "*To show as clearly as possible that there is an essential unity in all religions; that there is no difference in the truths inculcated by the various faiths; that there is but one method by which the world, both external and internal, has evolved; and that there is but one goal admitted by all scriptures. But this basic truth is one not easily comprehended. The discord existing between the different religions, and the ignorance*

of men, make it almost impossible to lift the veil and have a look at this grand verity. The creeds foster a spirit of hostility and dissension; ignorance widens the gulf that separates one creed from another. Only a few specially gifted persons can rise superior to the influence of their professed creeds and find absolute unanimity in the truths propagated by all great faiths. The object of this book is to point out the harmony underlying the various religions and to help in binding them together. This task is indeed a Herculean one."

Like Sir Isaac Newton who stood on the shoulders of giants, I will stand on the shoulders of many that have come before me and connect the dots with Lost Knowledge, undertake this Herculean task and give a message (that has taken more than a decade to collate) that will iron out the creases and misconceptions to prove once and for all – the reality of the shared governing dynamics of the major religions on Earth. Thereby ending division and separation and providing a foundation from which we can build an unselfish brotherhood and sisterhood and unite based on recognition of sameness and interconnectedness. This realignment is vitally necessary for a spiritual and cultural transformation to positively alter the current trajectory of the Earth.

To put the importance of this message for humanity into perspective, I include the following words of scientist Gus Speth for your contemplation:

"I used to think the top environmental problems were biodiversity loss, ecosystem collapse and climate change. I thought that with 30 years of good science we could address those problems, but I was wrong. The top environmental problems are: Selfishness, Greed and Apathy – and to deal with those we need a spiritual and cultural transformation… and we scientists don't know how to do that."

It is evident therefore, that somehow, we must build a bridge

Introduction

from 'belief' to 'spiritual knowledge.' In order for us to achieve a spiritual and cultural transformation, somehow, we must succeed in bridging this gap. And to bridge it, I can tell you that the primary requisite is... Courage.

So, I ask you, are you courageous? Are you willing to be vulnerable right now? For it takes the greatest of a human being's courage to allow themselves to be vulnerable. Are you willing to let go of the reins of your beliefs that have carried you this far in your life and thus far given you your identity and from which you measured your place in the world – quantified and qualified your reality with? Can you do that? Can you, at least for the moment, loosen your hold on tradition and open your heart to the possibility that there may be more to learn?

Whether you identify as a Christian, Muslim, Jewish, Hindu, Sikh, Buddhist, Zoroastrian, Agnostic or Atheist (or other) – can you, right now, empty the cup that is your mind? Teachers come in many guises and truth may walk the Earth dressed as a fool. The ancient Chinese philosopher Lao Tzu says that 'a Journey of a thousand miles begins with a single step'... let us take a step now together.

"*I am a spiritual being on a human journey*" is a catch phrase that has gained in popularity over recent years as many souls begin to awaken to their true selves. Being one such soul, I feel compelled to share some insights of how we can approach this problem of ignorance, confusion and division and move forward as a united spiritual race on Earth.

C. S. Lewis points out quite poignantly in his 1960 book *The Four Loves* that when a man is led to the foot of knowledge through another man, a man may indeed reject the teachings out of jealousy:

> "*Sometimes a curious double jealousy is felt, or rather two inconsistent jealousies which chase each other around in the sufferers mind. On the one hand 'this' is 'ALL NONSENSE, all bloody highbrow nonsense, all canting humbug.' But on the other 'supposing- it can't be, it mustn't be, but just supposing there really were something in (this)? How, if the deserter has really entered a new world which*

the rest of us never suspected? But if so, how unfair! Why him? Why was it never opened to us? 'A chit of a girl' or a 'whipper-snapper' of a boy – being shown things that are hidden from their elders? And since that is clearly incredible and unendurable, jealousy returns to the hypothesis 'ALL NONSENSE.'"

Please do not reject the teachings in this book out of jealousy or deem it 'all nonsense', because you see, this new world is now being opened to you. The world has been under the control of a darker agenda and darker forces for millennia and they have grown fat from their ability to keep us – humanity – divided.

Mother Earth is crying out, peoples impoverished hearts are crying out, they are broken, confused, lost and in despair and therefore I write from a position garnered by extensive research and personal experience in order to put forward a framework in which the distortions of history can be cleared up – to help build a bridge from science to spirituality. Words that are written in the hope of being a soothing balm to peoples ravaged spirits.

Let us hope that the urgency of the hour for the state and fate of our planet is enough for people to take heed of these words and not dismiss them prematurely.

They say history repeats itself until needed lessons are learned. Noah was already choosing the most stalwart oaks for the construction of the Ark whilst the masses of humanity were getting drunk and making merry, oblivious to the impending doom fast approaching. So it is, the words in these pages are my chosen stalwart oaks – in the hope of building an *Ark of the Covenant*, to safely ferry lost souls (through the impending spiritual flood and forces bombarding the Earth at this time) to the entrance of the 5th Kingdom.

It is important that you read this book slowly without skipping ahead. This book has been specifically written by purposeful design to show you the clear progression of developed concepts and insights step by step. Each step is necessary to understand the step that follows it. You will perhaps be tempted to read fast and skip ahead, but if you do that, then your own bias and conditioning may cause you to gloss over and miss necessary links in the chain; because on the surface, they do not align to your current 'preference' of worldview and you will probably then dismiss them prematurely. Each step in the order presented will act to gradually dislodge any plaque in your mind.

For a seed to grow, it must be planted, watered, sheltered and given sunlight… similarly this book must be given time for the seeds to be planted into your consciousness and watered and then given light for understanding to grow.

The prevailing misconceptions that proliferate society today commonly held and generally accepted as the status quo, are likely so entrenched that you may more than likely encounter some resistance as your mind attempts to cling to its current level of understanding of this reality and our world as being what we have been incorrectly taught that it is. But, like the timeless wisdom of the ancient sages gently instructs us to do, I advise you to… let it go.

The ancient sage Lao Tzu, author of the masterpiece, *The Tao Te Ching* (The Book of the Way) wrote 2,500 years ago about the source of all things, what he called the Tao – pronounced 'Dao' – and how to live in harmony with it:

> *"Tao is as deep as the ocean. As high as the mountains. It permeates the universe. It circulates endlessly and resides in all beings. But, one cannot attain it by seeking and cannot describe it in worldly languages. Tao gives birth and nurtures Heaven and Earth. Yet it does not subside; it supports all creation yet it is inexhaustible. Heaven gets it and becomes vast; the Earth gets it and becomes strong; the Sun and Moon get it and go into motion; the four seasons get it and become orderly. All creation gets it and comes into existence…*
>
> *When one is rooted in the Great Tao he observes the origin of everything, life and death, right and wrong, the noble and the poor, glorification and humiliation. All are based on people's value system, which changes instantly. Tracing*

their origin they are all the same and indistinguishable. If one knows this great Tao he goes along with the change but is not attached at the heart."

Therefore, do not be attached to your current level of understanding. It is imperative that we are always moving forward and not plateauing out and remaining stuck where it is comfortable for us – as we do not want to go through the necessary period of discomfort to get to new comfort and new understanding. By its very nature, change of course can be uncomfortable and painful, but if you allow non-attachment then this journey does not have to be as painful.

If you remain non-attached at the heart, you will go along with the change just as a fallen flower's petal gently floats down the stream. There is an ancient Tibetan saying that comes to mind here as I write these words to you, to prepare you for the pages that follow, which I will paraphrase as this:

How do you stop a drop of water from ever drying out?
The answer is by returning it to the ocean.

So let us, you and I, journey back to the 'universal ocean' together. For humanity has been living in an isolated bubble of intellectual superiority and judgement and it is killing us. As we continue to strive for the greatest comfort at the expense of our moral integrity and at the expense of the planet – our most gracious host – we remain largely ignorant to the deeper relationship we have to the planet, to each other, and to something immensely greater than ourselves.

With an empty mind and an open heart, I invite you to read on and see where it leads you.

Blessings to all of you.

LIST OF DIAGRAMS

Figure 1:	Hermes Trismegistus
Figure 2:	Electromagnetic Spectrum
Figure 3:	Nature of Space
Figure 4:	Nature of Time
Figure 5:	Ages of the Earth Timeline
Figure 6:	The Four Yugas
Figure 7:	White Light through a prism
Figure 8:	The Seven Octaves of Vibration
Figure 9:	Meridians – Subtle Energy Body
Figure 10:	Energetic Potential of Mankind
Figure 11:	The Tree of Life
Figure 12:	The High Priestess
Figure 13:	Yin-Yang
Figure 14:	The Symbol of Sacred Alignment
Figure 15:	Knowledge of Divine Potential
Figure 16:	The Cube of Matter Unfolded
Figure 17:	The Divine Instrument on Earth – Horus and the Initiate
Figure 18:	Sri Yantra & Circumpunct
Figure 19:	The Secret Doctrine
Figure 20a&b:	The Sphinx and The Great Pyramid
Figure 21:	Paracas Skulls
Figure 22:	Akhenaton
Figure 23:	Nefertiti – Amarna
Figure 24:	Temple of Hathor Dendera – Ancient Lightbulb
Figure 25:	Mohs Scale
Figure 26:	Temple of Osiris – Osirian
Figure 27:	Unfinished Obelisk at Aswan
Figure 28:	Palette of Narmer

Figure 29:	The Magician
Figure 30:	The Emperor/Pharaoh
Figure 31:	Hidden Symbolism – The Emperor
Figure 32:	The Chariot
Figure 33:	Hidden Symbolism – The Chariot
Figure 34:	The Star of David
Figure 35:	The Hebrew Alphabet
Figure 36:	The Divine Feminine
Figure 37:	The Divine Masculine
Figure 38:	The Key of Solomon
Figure 39:	The Creator on His Throne
Figure 40:	The Law of the Triangle
Figure 41:	Sepher Yezirah – Star of David
Figure 42:	Sepher Yezirah – Dodecagon
Figure 43:	The Zodiac
Figure 44:	a) Divine Trinity b) Key of Solomon c) Staff of Hermes – Caduceus
Figure 45:	The Weighing of the Heart
Figure 46:	a) The Flower of Life b) The Tree of Life within
Figure 47:	Cross section of the Great Pyramid
Figure 48:	Kings Chamber – Separator
Figure 49:	Fibonacci Spiral/ Golden Ratio
Figure 50:	(a & b) Flower of Life Pyramid – sacred Geometry
Figure 51:	Ouroboros
Figure 52:	Weighing of the Heart
Figure 53:	Fixed Cross and the Heavens – Revelations
Figure 54:	The Four Faces of God – Revelations
Figure 55:	The Three Hallways
Figure 56:	The Mountain of Initiation – 7 Noble Gates of Virtue
Figure 57:	The Hall of Wisdom

LIST OF DIAGRAMS

Figure 58:	Gautama Buddha
Figure 59:	a) Jesus Christ – The Sacred Heart
	b) Mother Mary – The Immaculate Heart
Figure 60:	Rishis Institute of Metaphysics – Symbolic Diagram
Figure 61:	The Secret Doctrine
Figure 62:	The Fool
Figure 63:	Four Arcane Symbols – Lost Book of Thoth
Figure 64:	Krishna/Vishnu
Figure 65:	The Solar/ Planetary Hierarchy – The Great White Brotherhood
Figure 66:	The Solar/Planetary Hierarchy deciphered
Figure 67:	Divine Radiations
Figure 68:	The New Jerusalem
Figure 69:	Author Silhouette

Chapter 1

THE LIGHT OF RECONCILIATION

"We are all one – or at least we should be and it is our job, our duty and our great challenge to fight the voices of division and seek the salve of reconciliation."

– **Roy Barnes**

The Chair of the Divine

We are living at one of the most exciting times in known human history. A time where the gap between science to spirituality will once and for all, finally, be bridged. As you will discover in the pages that follow, we are that bridge. No longer will ignorance hold mankind back from the majesty inherent in our own design.

So, I invite you to journey with me now into sacred knowledge, to better understand who we are, where we come from, and where it is we shall go – as a species in the future.

What are the five major religions on Earth at this present time? In chronological order of the inception of each religion they are:

1. Vedic Brahmanism-Hinduism (approx. 900 million followers worldwide)
2. Judaism (approx. 14 million followers worldwide)

3. Buddhism (approx. 360 million followers worldwide)
4. Christianity (approx. 2 Billion followers worldwide)
5. Islam (approx. 1.3 Billion followers worldwide)

When were these five major religions formed?

1. Vedic Brahmanism-Hinduism: circa 3,500-4,000 years ago
2. Judaism: circa 3,300 years ago
3. Buddhism: circa 2,500 years ago
4. Christianity: circa 2,000 years ago
5. Islam: circa 1,500 years ago, although they profess to be the surviving link to the one true religion, dating back to Abraham, I have recorded this as 1,500 years ago as this is the time of their 'last' prophet.

So, the oldest religion is Vedic Brahmanism-Hinduism, which is at least 3,500 years old. Then comes Judaism, only about 200 years later, followed by Buddhism 800 years after that and Christianity 500 years after the establishment of Buddhism. Muhammadan Islam is the youngest religion out of the five and is a full 2,000 years younger than Vedic Brahmanism-Hinduism, 1800 years younger than Judaism, 1,000 years younger than Buddhism and 500 years younger than Christianity.

Who were the messengers these religions were built around?

1. Krishna/ Vishnu
2. Abraham/Moses
3. Gautama Buddha
4. Jesus Christ
5. Prophet Muhammad.

What was their message and how were their messages alike?

Please bear this next quote in mind as we progress through this discourse. I am teaching this out of service in the hope that a difference can be made in the raising of the prevailing level of consciousness on planet Earth. And in the hope of reconciliation through the correct filtering out of centuries of historical distortion that has caused unnecessary division and conflict.

> *"It is very difficult to serve the incredible species called man. Inform a man of a truth that would if accepted, alter his stereotyped way of life, and he will like as not condemn you as a radical; reason with him, and he will stubbornly insist on the primacy of his instincts; on the other hand, display indifference to his plight, and he will denounce you for being callous to his sufferings."*
>
> – Alice Bailey, The Labours of Hercules, page 133

Many guideposts of the stations of the spiritual path have been mapped out and left behind by the masters of wisdom that have come before us, but largely these instructions have been hidden (and remain hidden) in symbolism, in paradoxes, or in allegorical camouflage.

One of the points of explanation I have consistently fallen back on, with my instruction to others during my time on Earth this time around, is the use of the analogy of religion as being like a white chair in a circular golden room – the 'Chair of the Divine.' Depending upon where one positions oneself in the circular room, the appearance of the chair will be different. Yet we know it is the same chair that everyone in the room is looking at.

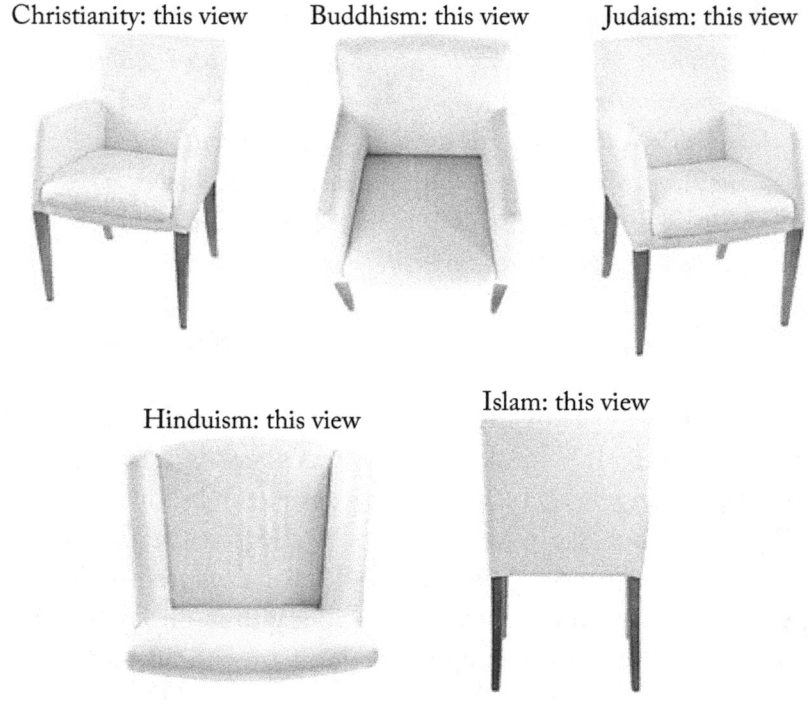

Atheist/Agnostic: this view:
(The perception that there is no chair)

But no matter what your point of view, it is the same chair. Why do so many religious leaders remain blind to this? 'What does the Chair look like?' is not the question that needs to be asked. Rather, the question needs to be 'What is the Chair made from?' Then there will be reconciliation. So, what is the Chair made from? Love? God? Light?

Throughout history there have been many messengers. The problem with humanity is that history shows mankind has the tendency to worship the messenger and forget the message... or grossly misinterpret it and then build a religion around it, totally missing the point. The message has always been the same, except each messenger was looking at the chair from a different angle, based on cultural influence, bias, and limitations of language, and delivered through the filter of their individual personalities and experience.

Human language is as limited as it is varied. If I was to ask you to describe to me the colour blue or orange or red, assuming I had not seen any of these colours before, and I had no point of reference, how would you succeed in doing so in order that I would understand exactly? You could not do it, right? So, if that is a visible manifestation and we cannot describe it adequately enough to bring on clear comprehension in our conscious awareness, then how much more difficult would it be to describe the invisible and the intangible? The answer is that it cannot be described, only known. This is the fundamental principle of Taoism, an ancient Chinese religion some 4,000 years old – that the Tao cannot be described, but the Tao (pronounced Dao) can indeed be known.

You can see why there has been and continues to be division, confusion, and misunderstanding. The question now becomes, how can we reconcile this and reach consensus? How can we as a world society, not just as individual countries following 'local religious heroes', start with the fundamental truth and build a new world, based on unity, brotherhood/sisterhood, and universality?

What was the primary message of these messengers? It was love. As human beings, when we say the word 'love', many things can come to mind, many different types of love. Love between a husband and wife, love for a son or daughter, brother and sister, friends, comrades and countrymen, love for animals, and love of nature.

In the Jewish religion there are eighteen different types of love. In Leviticus 19:18 in the Holy Torah of Judaism it says, *"Love your neighbour as yourself."* The ancient Greeks made the distinction of four different types of love: philios – friendship; storge – natural affection of a parent for their offspring; eros- romantic/sexual desire; and agape – charitable, selfless, altruistic, and unconditional love. Surviving in Buddhism we have the distinction of: kama – sensuous sexual love; karuna – compassion and mercy; and advesa – benevolent love. In Japanese again we find the distinction in the words: koi – romantic love; ren – benevolent love, ai – universal love; and a fourth combination called ren'ai – benevolent romantic love.

The apostle Paul wrote this of love:

> *"Love is Patient, love is kind, it does not envy, it does not boast, it is not proud, it is not rude, it is not self-seeking, it is not easily angered, it keeps no record of wrongs, love does not delight in evil but rejoices with the truth, it always protects, always trusts, always hopes and always perseveres."*

The apostle John wrote:

> *"Dear friends, let us love one another for love comes from God. Everyone who loves has been born of God and known God, whoever does not love does not know God, because God is love."*

In the mystical faction of Islam, Sufism, *"love is a projection of the essence of God to the universe."*

In 1960, C. S. Lewis distinguished four types of love in his book *'The Four Loves'* based on the four ancient Greek terms – affection (storge), friendship (philios), romantic love (eros) and charity (agape). The highest which Lewis proposed was charity, as this was the closest to divine love (agape) a man could get. He said that God bestows a grace to mankind and that this grace is a:

> *"Supernatural appreciative love. This of all gifts is to be the most desired. Here, not in natural loves nor even in ethics lies the true centre of all human and angelic life. With this all things are possible and with this, where a better book would begin, mine must end. I dare not proceed."*

And so it is fifty-six years on, I will take up that mantle: *'Supernatural appreciative love'* and the way in which it is bestowed unto man, why this was the foundation of the messages of the previous divine messengers, and how this has been distorted and misinterpreted through the ages.

To understand this, we must first understand the governing dynamics of this earthly reality that we find ourselves residing in as sentient beings at this time. This understanding will clearly show the sameness of the message that we have somehow managed to divide into separate understandings of the approach to 'God', from which we have built the five major world religions, and forged unnecessary wedges of division between people. Indeed, all world religions have their basis in the same governing dynamics – the revealing of how this is so will be the focus of this teaching.

It is a massive thing to ask a man or a woman to have courage to set aside a personal philosophy of religion so dearly held, for the prospect of gaining new knowledge. It is to be likened to walking to the edge of the cliff and having to take a leap of faith that you will not fall, but somehow you will be taken care of. It is when we have the courage to take that proverbial step off the cliff that our 'wings' appear.

So, let us delve further into what constitutes the building of a personal philosophy of religion and investigate the four phases in the evolution of a personal religious philosophy. I will draw upon the wisdom from a work known as *'Urantia'* pages 1113 -1114, first printed in 1955, to further explain the stages of evolution of a personal religious philosophy.

> *"The materials out of which to build a personal philosophy of religion are derived from both the inner and the outer environmental experience of the individual. The social status, economic condition, educational opportunities, moral trends, institutional influences, political developments, racial tendencies, and the religious teachings of one's time and place all become factors in the formation of a personal philosophy of religion. Even the inherent temperament and intellectual bent markedly determine the pattern of religious philosophy... The soundness of philosophic conclusions depends on keen, honest and discriminating thinking in connection with sensitivity to meanings and accuracy of evaluation. **Moral cowards never achieve high planes of philosophic thinking; it requires courage to invade new***

levels of experience and to attempt the exploration of unknown realms of intellectual living.

The great difference between religious and non-religious philosophy of living consists in the nature and level of recognised values and in the object of loyalties. There are four phases in the evolution of religious philosophy:

1. *Such an experience may become merely conformative, resigned to submission to tradition and authority.*
2. *It may be satisfied with slight attainments, just enough to stabilise the daily living and therefore becomes entirely arrested on such adventitious level.*
3. *A third group progress to the level of logical intellectuality but there stagnate in consequence of cultural slavery. It is indeed pitiful to behold giant intellects held so securely within the cruel grasp of cultural bondage for the materialistic fetters of a science, falsely so called.*
4. *The fourth level of philosophy attains freedom from all conventional and traditional handicaps and dares to think, act and live honestly, loyally, fearlessly and truthfully… The acid test for any religious philosophy consists in whether or not it distinguishes between the realities of the material and spiritual worlds while at the same moment recognising their unification in intellectual striving and in social serving. Philosophy transforms that primitive religion which was largely a fairytale of conscience into a living experience in the ascending values of cosmic reality."*

I think the biggest hurdle to overcome with helping people move from a 1st, 2nd or 3rd level of religious philosophy/belief into a 4th level, is that they tend to take only their religion's sacred texts as the 'authoritative holy word' and reject all other sources and scriptures. It is as though they are blind to anything that exists outside of the contents of their chosen religion's sacred books.

I will speak directly and plainly here, but my intention is not to be insensitive to your chosen religions, I am merely asking you to have an enquiring mind and follow what is said and see where this leads you. You may have a knee-jerk reaction and want to put the book down after the next few paragraphs, but I ask you to continue, at least until the end of Chapter 2.

It is difficult for many adherents of specific religions to look outside of the accepted 'holy word' of their chosen faith. Generally, either from inference given from the leaders of these faiths, tradition or within the pages of these holy works are expectations or statements that the contents are true and without error. For example, with the Holy Qur'an (Koran) of the Muslims, it says right at the beginning of the second surah: "*This is the book in which there is no doubt*" – Indicating that the words contained therein are beyond reproach.

And that may be true. However, the challenge and great risk lies with the fact that words and phrases can be subject to different ways and layers of interpretation and meaning. The hardest thing to overcome is misinterpretation of the original meaning.

The words in the holy pages may well be 'true and have no doubt' but what if, many hundreds of years ago, they were misinterpreted? What if the meaning which was intended to be conveyed was somehow twisted by the limitations in human comprehension? It would not be difficult for a person in a position of religious authority, with human fallibility, to misinterpret the meaning and convey that incorrect meaning to their followers and thereby shift the 'whole truth' by degree in which something was being represented.

Christians, for example, do not accept any literature from outside of the 'canonically accepted' scriptures in the Bible. They generally point-blank refuse to look at other sources such as the 'Dead Sea Scrolls' or scrolls found at Nag Hammadi that are two thousand years old, like the Gospel of St. Thomas, or recognise other sacred scriptures from older religions. They refuse to acknowledge that at some point the 'word of God' was decided upon as certain passages were accepted and others rejected with the result of the Council of Nicaea. Along with the Nicene Creed and the consequent alterations to the Bible, they also refuse to look at the limited and literal interpretation of the Papacy, or to acknowledge that priests are deliberately taught to interpret the meaning of these sayings and parables through a very selective lens – that Jesus Christ was the *only* Son of God – under papal decree of 1904.

The Holy Jewish Torah, the holy scriptures of one of the oldest religions on the planet, seems to be steeped in traditional understanding/interpretation of scripture, with strict observances in a very set, rigid way; according to them, that way must not be changed. And yet, what if they have somehow forgotten the original message of their founding patriarch Abraham or misunderstood the Law of Moses? What if through centuries of worship this human error factor has not been accounted for and resulted in massive misunderstanding from early on?

With the Hindus, who worship so many individual Gods – what if in the beginning their scriptures were written allegorically and those who came afterwards did not understand how to accurately interpret them? What if in the beginning the various Gods depicted were originally designed to depict various manifestations or aspects of one God? Or represented humans that reached a higher state of spiritual advancement? It takes courage to investigate this. If you are a Hindu, Muslim, Christian, Jew, Buddhist, or an Atheist or Agnostic reading this; I ask you just for the moment to have courage, have tolerance towards the information being presented before you, to let go of the tight grip you have on your beliefs and tradition and just see where this leads you.

With the goal being for us all to attain the fourth level of a personal philosophy of religion, surpassing stagnation and cultural bondage to tradition, our first step is to courageously explore the current definitions of different aspects of the prevalent faiths on Earth. The second step will be to go back as far as we possibly can through history to find the original teachers and teachings before they were misinterpreted and the original truth became altered – whether deliberately, through ignorance, or through an inability to accurately comprehend the original meaning.

The first step I have taken is to use the following definitions from the Oxford Dictionary. Let us take a snapshot of some aspects of 'faith' across the planet to help illustrate the foundation of the message of Krishna-Vishnu, Gautama Buddha, Jesus Christ, and the Prophet Muhammad (peace be upon him). According to the Oxford Dictionary, we proceed:

Hinduism:

Is a major religious and cultural tradition of South Asia, developed from the Vedic religion. Hinduism is practised primarily in India, Bangladesh, Sri Lanka and Nepal. It is a diverse family of devotional and ascetic cults and philosophical schools, all sharing a belief in reincarnation and involving the worship of one or more of a large pantheon of gods and goddesses including: Shiva and Vishnu, Kali, Durga, Parvati and Ganesh.

Vedic religion:

Is the ancient religion of the Aryan peoples who entered North Western India from Persia circa 2000-1200 BC. It was a precursor of Hinduism and its beliefs and practices are contained in the Vedas. Its characteristics included: ritual sacrifice to many Gods especially Indra, Varuna, and Agni; social classes (Varnas) that formed the basis of the caste system; and the emergence of the priesthood, which dominated orthodox Brahmanism from circa 900 BC. Transition to classical Hinduism began in about the 5th century BC.

Vedas:

Are the most ancient Hindu scriptures, written in early Sanskrit and containing hymns, philosophy, and guidance on ritual for the priests of the Vedic religion. Believed to have been directly revealed to seers among the early Aryans in India and preserved by oral tradition, the four chief collections are:

Rig Veda – From the Sanskrit Rgveda, from 'rk' (Sacred) stanza + Veda (Sacred) knowledge. The oldest and principal of the Vedas, a collection of 1028 hymns composed in the 2nd millennium BC in early Sanskrit.

Sama Veda – From the Sanskrit Samaveda, from Saman 'Chant' and Veda (Sacred) Knowledge.

Yajur Veda – From the Sanskrit Yajus 'sacrificial formula' and Veda (Sacred) Knowledge. One-of-the-four Vedas, based on a collection of sacrificial formulae in early Sanskrit used in the Vedic religion by the priest in charge of sacrificial ritual.

Atharva Veda – From the Sanskrit Atharvan (The name of Brahma's eldest son) said to be the author of the collection + Veda (Sacred) Knowledge.

Brahmanism:

Is the complex sacrificial religion that emerged in post-Vedic India (circa 900 BC) under the influence of the dominant priesthood (Brahmans) at an early stage in the development of Hinduism.

Brahma:

Is a member of the highest Hindu caste, that of the priesthood in Hinduism. Brahma means 'the ultimate reality underlying all phenomena.'

Judaism:

Is the monotheistic religion of the Jewish people (Jews). For its origins, Judaism looks to the biblical covenant made by God with Abraham, and to the Laws revealed to Moses and recorded in the Torah (supplemented by the rabbinical Talmud), which established the Jewish people's special relationship with God. Since the destruction of the Temple in Jerusalem in 70AD, the rituals of Judaism have centred on the home and the synagogue, the chief day of worship being the

Sabbath (sunset on Friday to sunset on Saturday) and the annual observances of Yom Kippur and Passover.

Kabbalah (Also: Kabbala, Cabala, Cabbala, Qabalah):

Is the ancient Jewish tradition of mystical interpretation of the Jewish bible (Torah), first transmitted orally and using esoteric methods (including ciphers). It reached the height of its influence in the later middle ages and remains significant today in Hasidism. From the Jewish Qibbel 'receive, accept.'

Esoteric:

Intended for or likely to be understood by a smaller number of people who have a specialised knowledge or interest.

Buddhism:

Is a widespread Asian religion or philosophy, founded by Siddhartha Gautama (known as Buddha), in North Eastern India in the 5th century BC. Buddhism has no creator god and gives a central role to the doctrine of Karma. The 'four noble truths' of Buddhism state that all existence is suffering, that the cause of suffering is desire, the freedom from suffering is Nirvana, and that this is attained through the eight-fold path of ethical conduct, wisdom and mental discipline (including meditation). There are two major traditions – Theravada and Mahayana.

Theravada – The more conservative of the two major traditions of Buddhism (the other being Mahayana), and a school of Hinayama Buddhism. It is practiced mainly in Sri Lanka, Burma (Myanmar), Thailand, Cambodia and Laos. From Pali – Theravada, literally 'doctrine of the elders', from Thera 'elder' + Vada 'speech, doctrine.'

Mahayana – One of the two major traditions of Buddhism, now practiced in a variety of forms especially in China, Tibet, Japan, and Korea. The tradition emerged around the 1st century AD and is typically concerned with 'altruistically oriented spiritual practice' as embodied in the ideal of the Bodhisattva. From the Sanskrit Maha – 'great', + Yana 'vehicle.'

Bodhisattva:

Is a person who is able to reach Nirvana but delays doing so out of compassion in order to save suffering beings. Early 19th century Sanskrit 'a person whose essence is perfect knowledge' from Bodhi – 'Perfect Knowledge' from Budh 'Awaken' + Sattva 'being, essence.'

Christianity:

Is the religion based on the person and teachings of Jesus Christ, or its beliefs and practices. Christianity is today the world's most widespread religion, with more than a billion members, mainly divided between the Roman Catholic, Protestant, and Eastern Orthodox churches. It originated among the Jewish followers of Nazareth, who believed that he was the promised Messiah (or 'Christ'), but the Christian Church soon became an independent organisation, largely through the missionary efforts of Saint Paul. In 313AD, Constantine ended official persecution of Christians in the Roman Empire and in 380AD Theodosius I recognised Christianity as the state religion. Most Christians believe in one god, in the three persons (the Father, the Son and Holy Spirit) and that Jesus is the Son of God who rose from the dead after being crucified. A Christian hopes to attain eternal life after death through faith in Jesus Christ and tries to live by the teachings as in the New Testament.

Gnosticism:

Is a prominent heretical movement of the 2nd century Christian Church, partly of pre-Christian origin. Gnostic doctrine taught that the world was created and ruled by a lesser divinity – the demiurge –

and that Christ was an emissary of the remote supreme divine being, esoteric knowledge (gnosis) of whom enabled the redemption of the human spirit.

Heresy:

Belief or opinion contrary to orthodox religious (especially Christian) doctrine.

Manicheism:

Is a dualistic religious system with Christian, Gnostic, and Pagan elements, founded in Persia in the 3rd century by Manes (circa 216-276AD) and based on supposed primeval conflict between light and darkness. It was widespread in the Roman Empire and in Asia and survived in Eastern Turkestan (Xinjiang) until the 13th century.

Cathar:

Is a member of a heretical medieval Christian sect, which professed a form of Manichean dualism and sought to achieve great spiritual purity. It comes from the mid-17th century medieval Latin 'Cathari' and from the Greek 'Katharoi' meaning 'The Pure.'

Islam:

Is the religion of the Muslims, a monotheistic faith, regarded as revealed through Muhammad as the Prophet of Allah (God). Founded in the Arabian Peninsula in the 7th century AD, Islam is now the professed faith of more than a billion people worldwide, particularly in North Africa, the Middle East and parts of Asia. The ritual observances and moral code of Islam were said to have been given to Muhammad as a series of revelations, which were codified in the Koran. Islam is regarded by its adherents as the last of the revealed religions, and Muhammad is seen as the last of the Prophets, building on and perfecting the examples and teachings of Abraham, Moses and Jesus. There are two major branches of Islam: Sunni and Shia.

Sunni:

Is one of the two main branches of Islam, commonly described as orthodox and differing from Shia in its understanding of the Sunna and in its acceptance of the first three Caliphs.

Sunna:

Is the traditional portion of Muslim Law based on Muhammad's words or acts, accepted (together with the Koran) as authoritative by Muslims and followed particularly by Sunni Muslims.

Caliph:

Is the chief Muslim civil and religious ruler, regarded as the successor of Muhammad. The Caliph ruled in Baghdad until 1258 and then in Egypt until the Ottoman conquest of 1517. The title was then held by the Ottoman Sultans until it was abolished in 1924 by Ataturk. Late-Middle-English, from old French 'Caliphe', from Arabic Kalifa meaning 'Deputy of God', from the title Kalifat Allah meaning successor (of Muhammad).

Shia:

Is one of two branches of Islam, followed especially in Iran, that rejects the first three Caliphs and regards Ali, the fourth Caliph as Muhammad's first true successor. Ali was the son-in-law of Muhammad.

Sufism:

Is the mystical system of the Sufi's. Sufism is the esoteric dimension of the Islamic faith, the spiritual path to mystical union with God.

Mystic:

Is a person who seeks by contemplation and self-surrender to obtain unity with or absorption into the deity or the absolute, or who believes in the spiritual apprehension of truths that are beyond the intellect.

Now we will look to what the Oxford Dictionary says about the divine messengers of these religions:

Krishna:

Is one of the most popular gods, the eighth and most important avatar or incarnation of Vishnu. He is worshipped in several forms: as the child god whose miracles are extolled in the Puranas; as the Divine Cowherd whose erotic exploits, especially with his favourite- Radha, have produced both romantic and religious literature; and the Divine Charioteer who preaches to Arjuna on the battlefield (Kurukshetra) in the Bhagavad-Gita.

Vishnu:

A god, originally a minor Vedic god, now regarded by his worshippers as the supreme deity and saviour, by others as the preserver of the cosmos in a triad with Brahma and Shiva. Vishnu is considered by the Hindus to have had nine earthly incarnations or avatars including Rama, Krishna, and the historical Buddha; the tenth Avatar will herald the end of the world.

Avatar:

Is a manifestation of a deity or released soul in bodily form on Earth, an incarnate divine teacher. From the Sanskrit Avatara 'descent', from Ava 'down' + tar 'to cross.'

Buddha – Siddhartha Gautama:

Is a title given to the founder of Buddhism – Siddhartha Gautama (circa 563- 460 BC). Born a prince in what is now Nepal, he renounced wealth and family to become an ascetic, and after achieving enlightenment while meditating, taught all who came to learn from him.

Jesus Christ:

Is the central figure of the Christian religion. Jesus conducted a mission of preaching and healing (with reported miracles) in Palestine in about 28-30 AD, which is described in the Gospels. His followers considered him to be the Christ or Messiah and the Son of God, and belief in his resurrection from the dead is the central tenet of Christianity. Christ is Old English, from Latin 'Christus', from Greek 'Khristos', noun use of an adjective meaning 'anointed', from Khrieiu 'anoint', translating from Hebrew 'Masiah' Messiah.

Muhammad:

(Circa 570- 632 AD) An Arab prophet and founder of Islam. In circa 610, in Mecca, he received the first of a series of revelations that, as the Koran, became the doctrinal and legislative basis of Islam. In the face of opposition to his preaching he and a small group of supporters were forced to flee to Medina in 622AD. Muhammad led his followers into a series of battles against the Meccans. In 630AD, Mecca capitulated (ceased to resist) and by his death Muhammad had united most of Arabia.

Some of these definitions are a little brief. To further show the scope of the mystical aspects of these faiths, I have included some extracts from Wikipedia.

The Kabbalah:

Is Hebrew for receiving – it is the mystical aspect of Judaism: esoteric teachings that explain the relationship between an infinite, eternal, and essentially unknowable creator with the finite and mortal universe of his creation. In solving this paradox Kabbalah seeks to define the nature of the universe, the nature of the human being, and the nature and purpose of existence.

Basic tenets:

Every idea grows from the foundation of God. "The foundation of all foundations and the pillar of all wisdom is to know that there is one God that brought into being all existence. All the beings of the heavens and the Earth and what is between them came into being only out of the truth of God being. The ten different ways that the one God reveals his will through the emanations. It is not God that changes but the ability to perceive God that changes:

1. Kether (Will)
2. Chochmah (Wisdom)
3. Binah (Understanding)
4. Chesed (Mercy or Loving Kindness)
5. Gevurah (Severity or Strength)
6. Tiferet (Harmony or Beauty)
7. Netzach (Victory)
8. Hod (Glory)
9. Yesod (Power / Foundation)
10. Malchut (Kingdom)

(Hinduism) Vedanta:

In Sanskrit Vedanta means 'the culmination of knowledge.' The Vedanta is a spiritual tradition 4,000 years old that is concerned with self-realisation, by which one understands the ultimate reality (Brahman). The Vedanta teaches that the believer's goal is to transcend the limitations of self-identity and realise one's unity with Brahman.

Basic tenets:

1. Human nature is divine
2. The aim of human life is to understand and realise that human nature is divine

The goal – a state of cosmic consciousness. Uttara Mimasa – 'higher enquiry.'

The Vedanta, or those that follow it, are known to follow what is known as Vedic philosophy. One of the key texts of Vedic thought is the Upanishads. The term Upanishad means 'the setting to rest of ignorance by revealing the knowledge of supreme spirit, knowledge of the self.' An excerpt – *"Whoever sees all beings in the soul and the soul in all beings… what delusion or sorrow is there for one who sees unity? It has filled all. It is radiant, incorporeal, invulnerable, wise, intelligent, encompassing, self-existent, it organises objects throughout eternity."*

The Tao (The Dao):

Often referred to as 'the nameless.' Neither it nor its principles can ever be adequately expressed in words. It is conceived with neither shape nor form, both perfectly still and constantly moving, as both larger than the largest thing and smaller than the smallest thing. Shape, movement, and size always create dichotomies and Tao is always a unity.

Basic tenets:

Whilst it cannot be expressed it holds that it can be known and its principles can be followed. The value of virtue. The uselessness of trying to control/understand the Tao. Often compared to water – clear, colourless, unremarkable, yet all beings depend on it for life and even the hardest stone cannot stay in its way forever. Indefinable, unlimited, and unknowable.

All phenomena are considered to be a manifestation of Tao, including people, societies, and structures they create – TAO is a constant active force in the universe. Because of this TAO is not a moral or ethical code, nor is it a set of ideals to be attained. Rather, it is a functional reality that is encountered on a daily basis.

Buddhism:

Buddha means 'The Awakened One.' He attained enlightenment at thirty-five years of age and died at the age of eighty in 483 BC.

The main tenet of Buddhism:

There is no such thing as 'the self' independent from the rest of the universe. There are two main schools:

Theravada – 'The School of the Elders' and **Mahayana** 'The Great Vehicle.' In Theravada Buddhism, the ultimate goal is the attainment of the sublime state of Nirvana, achieved by practicing the Noble 8-fold Path (the Middle Way). Thus, escaping what is seen as a cycle of suffering and rebirth (Samsara).

Mahayana Buddhism aspires to Buddhahood via the Bodhisattva path, a state where one remains in this cycle of (incarnation) to help other beings reach awakening.

Islam:

Translates to 'will of Allah be done.' Muslims believe that Islam is a faith that has always existed and that it was gradually revealed to humanity by a number of prophets. But the final and complete revelation of the faith was made through the Prophet Muhammad (peace be upon him) in the 7th century CE. **Last Prophet Muhammad:** The name of

Muhammad means 'Seal of the Prophets' and his message was oneness of God, worshipping of that one God, avoidance of idolatry and sin, and belief in the day of resurrection or Day of Judgement and life after death. In the Koran 48:29 Muhammad is considered in Islam to guide humanity the right way. Muslims believe that Muhammad is the final prophet sent by God. According to Muslims he was sent to restore Islam, which they believe to be the unaltered original monotheistic faith of Adam, Ibrahim (Abraham), Musa (Moses) and Isa (Jesus).

Huna Kalani:

>Translates to hidden secrets of the chiefs (Hawaiian).
>Basic tenets:
>Kahuna – Keeper of balance.
>Ho'omanama – Making of 'Mana' (Energy).
>Aloha – Love, Harmony (literally – We breathe together).
>Huna of Ku – Concerned with the power of emotions and wild places.
>Huna of Lono – Concerned with the power of the intellect.
>Huna of Kane – Concerned with the power of spiritual and community development. Three steps:
>
>1. The purity of your integrity
>2. The clarity of your intellect
>3. The application of your knowledge

The heart of Huna Kalani is to live in peaceful community, with love, joy, and in balance with nature.

These examples of differing schools of thought are only a small portion of the plethora of other examples we could look into across different cultures and across different times from Earth's history. Of particular interest are the startling similarities of the mystical aspects of these faiths:

Hinduism → Mystical inner teaching of Vedic Brahmanism.
Judaism → Mystical inner teachings of Kabbalah.
Christianity → Mystical inner teachings of Gnosticism/Cathars (despite being deemed heretical knowledge).
Islam → Mystical inner teachings of Sufism.

Basically, they are inculcating the same truth, just approaching it from a different background and cultural lens of perspective and using different ways of representing this. And just **'how this is the same truth'** will now be explained.

Governing Dynamics

Are there underlying governing dynamics? A point of origin, which all of these approaches to God share?

The answer is a resounding… YES.

Chapter 2

THE KEY TO THE MYSTERIES TURNED SEVEN TIMES

'The principles of truth are seven, and he that knows them is given the secret key to which all of the doors of the temple fly open!'

– Thoth

As we scan the pages of history for insight into the governing dynamics of this reality, if we go back far enough, we come across the name of Hermes Trismegistus. Hermes was a great teacher of man. He was known as Trismegistus as he was 'thrice great' being a scientist, philosopher and priest.

The Oxford Dictionary says:

Hermes Trismegistus

A legendary figure regarded by Neoplatonist's and others as the author of certain works on astrology, magic and alchemy. Latin 'Thrice Great Hermes' – in reference to Thoth (identified with Hermes).

Neoplatonism

A philosophical and religious system developed by the followers of Plotinus in the 3rd century AD. Neoplatonism combined ideas of Plato, Aristotle, Pythagoras, and the stoics with oriental mysticism. Predominant in Pagan Europe until the early 6th century AD, it was a major influence on early Christian writers, on later medieval and Renaissance thought, and on Islamic philosophy. It envisages the human soul rising above the imperfect material world through virtue and contemplation, toward knowledge of the transcendent 'One.'

It is from the teachings of Hermes Trismegistus that we have the surviving phrase '*hermetically sealed*', denoting hidden wisdom. As such, it is to him that we look to understand governing dynamics. He said:

'The principles of truth are seven, and he that knows them is given the secret key to which all of the doors of the temple fly open!'

Figure 1: Hermes Mercurius Trismegistus. Source: Historia Deorum Fatidicorum 1675. Reproduced from publisher of Manly P Hall, The Secret Teachings of All Ages.

Figure 1 (previous page) shows the oldest known surviving representative image of Hermes Trismegistus, from the 1675 *Historia Deorum Fatidicorum*.

In a separate work known as *'The Kybalion'* a book written by authors known only as 'The Three Initiates', the writers explain that:

> *"There is no portion of the occult teachings possessed by the world which have been so closely guarded as the fragments of the Hermetic Teachings which have come down to us over the tens of centuries which have elapsed since the lifetime of its great founder, Hermes Trismegistus, the 'scribe of the gods', who dwelt in old Egypt in the days when the present race of men was in its infancy.* **Contemporary with Abraham, and, if the legends be true, an instructor of that venerable sage,** *Hermes was and is the Great Central Sun of Occultism, whose rays have served to illuminate the countless teachings which have been promulgated since his time. All the fundamental and basic teachings embedded in the esoteric teachings of every race may be traced back to Hermes. Even the most ancient teachings of India undoubtedly have their roots in the original Hermetic Teachings."*

Like Jesus, who said, *"For those that have ears to hear,"* the ancient Hermetic aphorism: *"The lips of wisdom are closed, except to the ears of understanding"* shares a remarkable similarity. The foundations of the Hermetic Teachings are based upon seven principles or universal laws, and they are as follows:

1. **The principle of mentalism:** "All is mind, the universe is mental." (ORDER)
2. **The principle of correspondence:** "As above so below, so below as above." (COMPENSATION)
3. **The principle of vibration:** "Nothing rests; everything moves, everything vibrates." Differences between manifestations of matter, energy, and spirit result from different rates of vibration. (VIBRATION)

4. **The principle of polarity:** "Everything is dual; everything has poles, everything has it's pair of opposites; like and unlike are the same; opposites are identical in nature, but different only in degree; extremes meet; all truths are but half-truths; all paradoxes may be reconciled." (POLARITY)
5. **The principle of rhythm:** "Everything flows out and in; everything has its tides; all things rise and fall; the pendulum swing manifests in everything; the measure of the swing to the right is the measure of the swing to the left; rhythm compensates." (CYCLES)
6. **The principle of cause and effect:** "Every cause has its effect; every effect has its cause; everything happens according to the Law; chance is but a name for the Law not recognised; there are many planes of causation, but nothing escapes the Law." (CAUSE AND EFFECT)
7. **The principle of gender:** "Gender is in everything; everything has its masculine and feminine principles, gender manifests on all planes." (BALANCE)

These are the seven principles of 'truth' governing dynamics. Learn them, study them, and see how they apply to all workings of your life and your reality.

The reality is, what we think is real is only perceived as such within the parameters of our five physical senses. Our visual sense can detect visible light at a range of 380nm to 780nm, but as you can see from the diagram of the electromagnetic spectrum in Figure 2 (next page), so much more exists outside the frequency of visible light. Our aural sense detects vibrations in the range of 20 to 20,000 Hz (vibrations per second) and again this provides very limited access to sound, with much that exists in the acoustic spectrum beyond the range of human hearing.

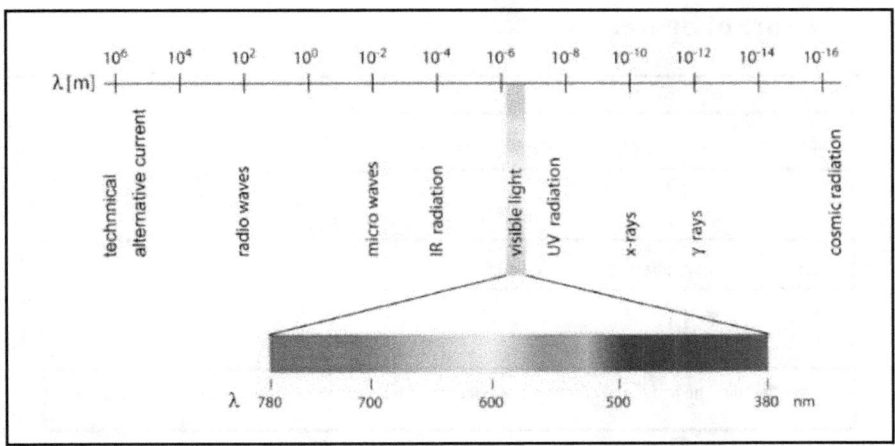

Figure 2: The electromagnetic spectrum

We must understand that everything we see is an illusion. It is not real. It looks real and feels real and seems to be immutable and solid, but in essence it is extremely malleable, non-fixed, and non-solid. Indeed, science, and breakthroughs in quantum mechanics have revealed that reality is indeed holographic and that consciousness seems to impact the state of reality. In a scientific principle known as the 'Observer Effect', the act of observing an experiment will influence the outcome of the experiment, which directly points to the unstable nature of reality and its ability to be directly affected by human consciousness.

The following diagram, Figure 3, is a chronological progression of prevailing scientific thought on the nature of space, extracted from Brian Green's 'Fabric of the Cosmos' video series 2015 (which was presented verbally). This is a summary of the evolution of scientific thought on Earth, with reference to the nature of time, space, and the beginning of life in the universe; from the first prevailing theory of 'known history', right up to the current general consensus of the scientific community in 2016.

The Nature of Space:

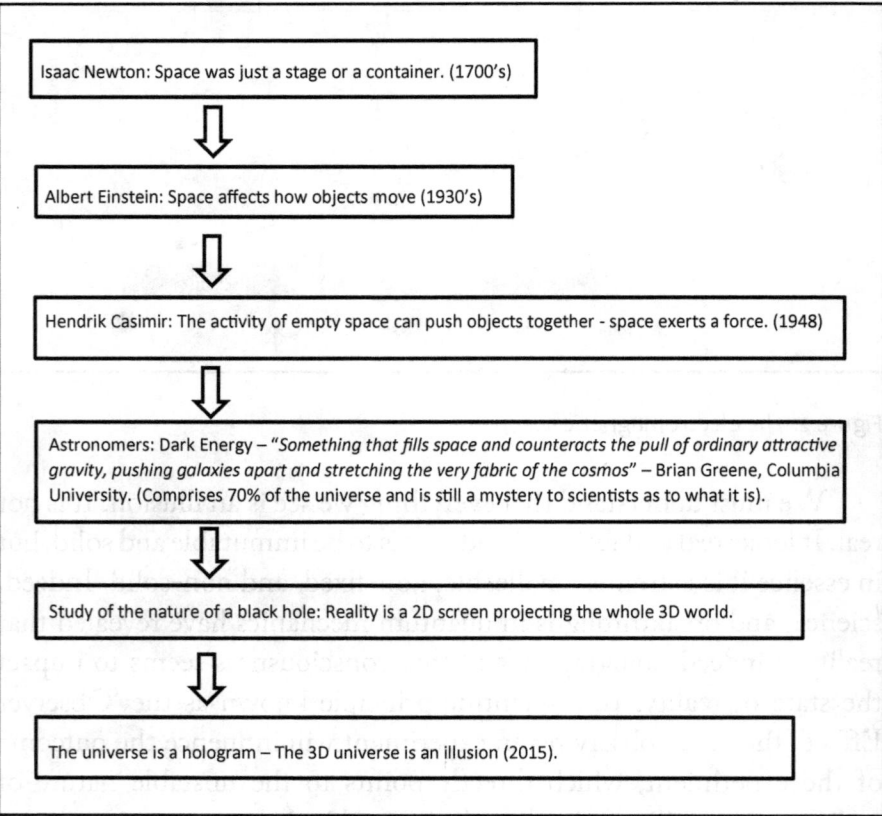

Figure 3: The progression of evolution of human thought on the nature of space.

In the same documentary, the evolution of the prevailing theory of the **nature of time** held on Earth shown in Figure 4 (next page) is as follows:

The Nature of Time:

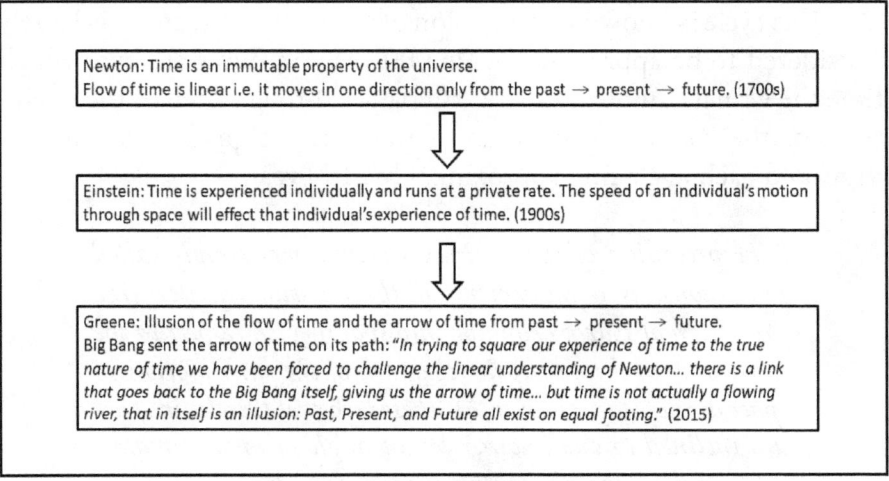

Figure 4: Progression of evolution of thought of the nature of time.

Brass Tacks – Progress Bias

A Progress Bias is a tendency, inclination or prejudice towards the idea that humanity has evolved in a linear fashion over time – from the distant past being the most undeveloped to the present time being the highest level of civilisation ever achieved on planet Earth.

The current accepted timeline of our history proposed with the progress bias is a lie. The 21st century version of human civilisation is not the greatest or most advanced civilisation that has ever been on Earth. Instead, the Earth goes through grand cycles of time – periods of ascending and descending ages. Ascending ages are typified by possession of a vast almost complete knowledge of the governing dynamics of the universe and grand examples of architecture and engineering. Descending ages are typified by an almost total darkness, where the light of knowledge all but dies out.

Right now, we are at a turning point from a descending age into an ascending one.

Precession of the Equinoxes

This cycle is known as precession of the equinoxes, and it is largely considered to be approximately 26,000 years in duration, over which time the vernal equinox of the Earth passes through each of the twelve signs of the zodiac. With each of the twelve signs constituting an 'Age' and each age being approximately 2150 years.

> *"The precession of the equinoxes (sometimes simply called precession), is a movement of the celestial equator (the projection of Earth's equator into space) with respect to the fixed stars and the ecliptic (the path of the sun's motion in space as viewed from Earth). These two great circles in space are inclined to one another by an angle of approximately 23.5°, called the obliquity. Their intersection defines the equinox. The equator moves from east to west – in the same direction as the daily motion of the sun – at a rate of about 50.2° per year."*
>
> – Encyclopedia.com

Many people hold the opinion that the Age of Aquarius will begin on the 21st December 2020 in alignment with the grand conjunction of Jupiter and Saturn, the likes of which the Earth has not seen for 400 years. And so it is this date that we will use for our calculations in this discourse.

Using the date of commencement of the Age of Aquarius as 21st December 2020 we end up with a proposed precession of the equinox timeline as follows in figure 5 below:

AGES OF ZODIAC – PRECESSION		
Aquarius	2020 AD	Now
Pisces	130 BC	2,150 years ago.
Aries	2280 BC	4,300 years ago.
Taurus	4430 BC	6,450 years ago.
Gemini	6580 BC	8,600 years ago.
Cancer	8730 BC	10,750 years ago.
Leo	10880 BC	12,900 years ago.
Virgo	13030 BC	15,050 years ago.
Libra	15180 BC	17,200 years ago.
Scorpio	17330 BC	19,350 years ago.
Sagittarius	19480 BC	21,500 years ago.
Capricorn	21630 BC	23,650 years ago.

Figure 5: Timeline of the ages of the Earth (Precession)

There is then a further split between those who calculate the precession cycle to be 25,920 years, which makes an age 2160 years in duration. Depending on which approach resonates with you, the year the ages began and ended will vary slightly. This is not that important. What is important is that we recognise a grand cycle like this takes place and has noticeable effects on the events playing out on Earth and on the consciousness of the beings existing on Earth at that time.

What is a Yuga? A challenge to accepted chronology

According to the Oxford Dictionary, Yuga is from Hinduism, and means *Any of the four ages of the life of the world*. So, what are the Four Ages of the Life of the World – or Yugas?

1. Satya Yuga, 2. Treta Yuga, 3. Dwapara Yuga, and 4. Kali Yuga.

These Ages are calculated as follows: One full cycle is known as the Electric Couple and lasts approximately 25,800 years (the same period of time as the procession of the equinoxes). The full cycle is comprised of two 12,900-year periods, known as Daiva Yugas. A Daiva Yuga is made of one Satya Yuga, one Treta Yuga, one Dwapara Yuga and one Kali Yuga, in a diminishing ratio. From Swami Sri Yukteswar Giri's 1894 book, *The Holy Science*, we have Figure 6 representing this below, based on the positioning of the Autumnal Equinox as follows. However, calculations were simplified to a 24,000-year cycle: Satya Yuga 4,800 years, Treta Yuga 3,600 years, Dwapara Yuga 2,400 years and Kali Yuga 1,200 years.

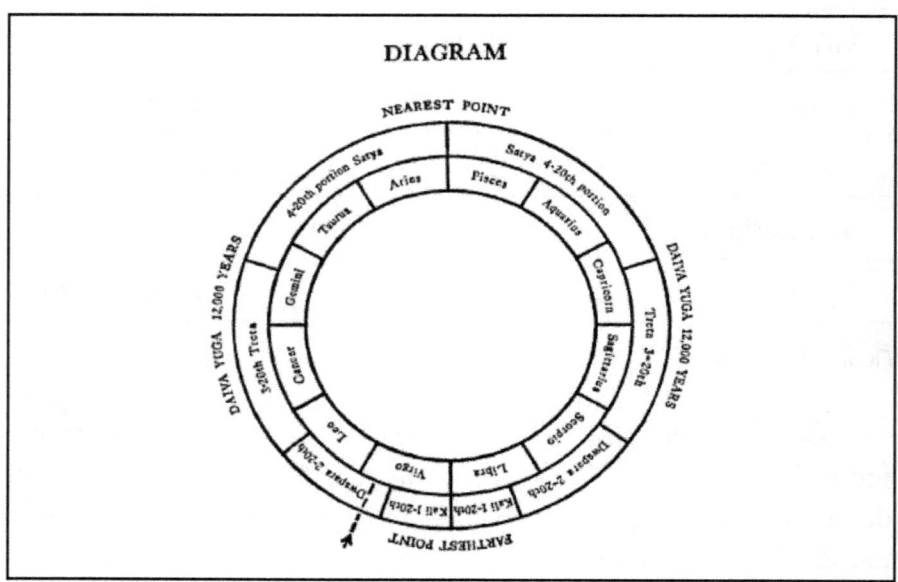

Figure 6: The Four Yugas, from Swami Sri Yukteswar Giri's 1894 book, The Holy Science, showing the 2 x 12,000-year Daiva Yugas comprising 1 x 24,000-year cycle. With alignments made to show Autumnal Equinoxes, and notice from Ptah-Hoteps teaching. (That will follow Shortly) about the precession of the vernal equinoxes that Scorpio is the opposite of Taurus.

Please be aware that we have two separate cosmologies at work on an approx 24,000 to 26,000-year cycle.

According to Swami Sri Yukteswar Giri when he published his book "The Holy Science" in 1894 we had already been in the dwapara yuga for 194 years, i.e with a commencement of 1700. However, in other theosophy teachings, there was an observable marker 'event that happened on Earth' in 1946 that indicated the beginning of the current dwapara yuga at that time. If we accept the theosophy teachings and also factor in the difference from the 24,000 to the 26,000 year models of the precession of Equinoxes cycles, for ease of calculation let us say that the current dwapara yuga commenced in approx. 1950. This was preceded by two Kali yugas of approx. 1300 years in succession. Taking all this into consideration then, we have cycles working within cycles – the ages of the Earth Yugas ticking by as the vernal equinox passes through the 12 Ages of the Zodiac.

According to some ancient mystical accounts there is right now an experiment unfolding in the genetics of mankind that is expected to culminate over approximately 13,000 years cycle (a cycle that is mirrored in the stars) – where man – without visible guidance will spiritualise the matter of their bodies and arise out of matter, this is what is known in certain New-Age circles today as 'The Ascension'. This will be revealed further in Chapter 6 – Initiation. For now, using the 12,900 year time frame we continue.

This current 12,900-year cycle began approximately in the year 10880 BC, when the Autumnal equinox was in Aquarius and the Vernal equinox was in Leo. Now, according to Swami Sri Yukteswar Giri, *'each period of 12,000 (12,900) years brings a complete change both externally in the material world, and internally in the intellectual or electric world.'* With the modified cyclical calculations of 12,900-years we continue.

The Kali Yuga, lasting approximately 1,200 to 1,300 years, is a period where, *'The mental virtue is then in its first stage and only ¼ developed. The human intellect cannot comprehend anything beyond the gross material of this ever-changing creation, the external world.'* Man is ¾ sin and ¼ virtue.

The Dwapara Yuga, lasting approximately 2,400 to 2,600 years, is a period where, *'The mental virtue is then in its second stage of development and but half complete. The human intellect can then comprehend the fine matters of electricities and their attributes which are the creating principles of the external world.'* Man is ½ sin and ½ virtue.

The Treta Yuga, lasting approximately 3,600 to 3,800 years, is a period where, *'The mental virtue is then in the third stage; the human intellect becomes able to comprehend the Divine Magnetism, the source of all electrical forces on which the creation depends for its existence.'* Man is ¼ sin and ¾ virtue.

The Satya Yuga, lasting approximately 4,800 to 5,200 years and known as the Golden Age, is a period where, *'The mental virtue is then in its fourth stage and completes its full development. The human intellect can comprehend all, even God the spirit beyond this visible world.'* Man is without sin and is completely virtuous.

If we apply this ancient knowledge of the Yugas to the anomalies that we observe in the level of sophisticated construction techniques, used by the ancients that have been mentioned in the works of John Anthony West's *Magical Egypt* and Graham Hancock's *Fingerprints of the Gods* etc., such evidence shows that these techniques seem to actually decline in complexity and mastery over time. The older sites are identified by a lack of hieroglyphic inscription on the stone. This may be due to the increased hardness of the materials used (namely granite), along with a loss of the knowledge of more complex methods of construction.

With an understanding of the phenomenon of the Yugas – the Four Ages on Earth – we start to see a very accurate picture of why this occurs. And we can better date the examples of architectural feats left behind, based on an understanding of this phenomenon **of the involution of the intellectual capacity of human beings – due to the effects on the Earth of the Vernal and Autumnal equinox and variations of radiations of the sun over 25,800 years.** The 25,800-year cycle is comprised of 2 x 12,900 arcs known as Daiva Yugas as previously mentioned.

This is the natural temporal progression unless mankind makes an unprecedented spiritual advancement. In which case the shift to the next golden age may be accelerated due to activation of dormant genetic coding (as we arise out of matter – explained further in this discourse).

Now the most widely held approach to calculating the length of the Yugas is what is known as the traditional Hindu Indian cycle, and the lengths of the ages are as follows: Satya Yuga of 1,728,000 years, Treta Yuga of 1,296,000 years, Dwapara Yuga of 864,000 years and Kali Yuga of 432,000 years. You will notice of course that this is considerably different to the system of Swami Sri Yukteswar Giri. This discrepancy was in fact accounted for by Swami Sri Yukteswar Giri, by explaining that errors were made in calculations at the time of the last descending Dwapara Yuga, and were not picked up at that time because of the darkening effect or involution of consciousness on man's intellect.

The interpreters of the ancient annals at that time introduced the concept of the Demi God Year or Divine Year, where one day of the demigods is equal to one human year, or one year of the demigods was equal to 360 human years, when this was never supposed to have been introduced. And so, it is that through observation of historical anomalies we can further verify the likelihood of the errors made in calculations by the interpreters of the ancient Vedic annals during the descending arc of the last Dwapara Yuga. We can thus accept the 25,800-year cycle as the better, more accurate, system for calculating Yugas.

This knowledge survives in many ancient cultures around the world – the Vedic Yugas, The Mayan Great Year, The Precession of the equinoxes etc. All we need to understand is that we are not the most advanced civilisation that has ever been on Earth and that when we possess the keys, we are able to unlock the doors of camouflage of the Ancient Knowledge and Wisdom of the Mysteries – to find the answers to the big existential questions of life that have eluded philosophers for millennia. Namely: Who are we? Why are we here? Where are we going?

Seven Octaves of Vibration

The first of the keys that I would like to share with you is the ancient knowledge wisdom of the seven octaves of vibration. This instruction applied to the evolution of mankind reveals the end goal – the answer to the 'Where are we going?' question is contained within its comprehension. So, how does this explanation help?

With human life, the challenge comes with the dichotomy of 'spirit' being contained within 'matter' or 'form.' The challenge comes from the resistance of matter. However, the challenge – the resistance – is the point of it all.

Without the resistance of matter, there would be nothing tangible for the subjective soul to experience. Therefore, resistance is purposeful. In the corpus of scrolls that were found in Nag Hammadi, Egypt, between 1942 and 1956, known as the '*Nag Hammadi Scrolls*', Jesus is purported as saying in the 'Gospel of Thomas':

> *"Blessed is the lion which becomes man when consumed by man and cursed is the man whom the lion consumes, and the lion becomes man."*

This is the dichotomy of man and spirit. As a human being, we are both animal and something more – a spirit, a soul. So, as a man or woman, there are two potentialities – : either the man takes his nature and puts it in the hands of his spirit to guide and, with discipline, lead it upward of baser desires and thus, becomes blessed; or the passions and lusts of the flesh are given free rein and the animal takes over the man, the spiritual essence, snuffing out the spiritual light and thus, becomes cursed... yet is still man.

The ancient Egyptian mystery schools, which were an offshoot of Hermes/Thoth teachings in the hidden teachings, taught that matter existed within seven gradations or octaves of vibration or consciousness. As the Jewish Kabbalists say:

"A man becomes a stone, a plant, an animal, a man, and finally a God."

Just as white light shone through a prism produces the seven-coloured rainbow, Figure 7 (next page), it is that the divine consciousness, as the pure white light, pours into the universe to manifest in myriad expressions of life.

Figure 7: white light through a prism. Demonstrating how the radiations of the Divine burst out into the universe in myriad forms of expression.

This is the very demonstration of Hermes' Second Principle of **Correspondence**: *As Above So Below, So Below As Above*. It is the cosmic universal law of the macrocosm being reflected in the microcosm. There are seven colours in the rainbow and seven notes in a musical scale; pay attention to the Law of Seven that permeates the mysteries of existence.

The Kabbalistic inner teachings survive from the Ancient Egyptian mystery schools (and this link will be further proven in Chapters 4 and 5). And the aforementioned Kabbalistic adage, *'A man becomes a stone, a plant, an animal, a man and finally a God'*, is known in the hidden teachings as 'The seven octaves of vibration or consciousness', being:

1. Mineral
2. Plant
3. Animal
4. Human
5. Genius
6. Prophet/Seer
7. God (God-man)/Divine

Man occupies four of these stations of consciousness: Human, Genius, Prophet/Seer and God (God-man)/Divine. At this point, you may be having some difficulty reconciling yourself to the idea that man can occupy the 7th station and become a God (Divine). In 1894, Sri Yukteswar Giri's book *'The Holy Science'* also hints at man's ability to progress through the seven levels or octaves of vibration or consciousness, which says:

> *"Such is the great influence of time which governs the universe, no man can overcome this influence except him who, **blessed with pure love, the heavenly gift of nature – becomes divine**; being baptised in the sacred stream Pranava (The Holy Aum vibration), he comprehends the kingdom of God."*

The adage, *'There is a difference between knowing the path and walking the path'* is incomplete. More accurately, it should be, *'There is a difference between knowing the path and walking the path… **and before one can walk the path, one must become the path.**'*

If this seems like a nonsensical statement, look deeper into the words to find the meaning. How can a man become the path? As Jesus said, according to Mark, *'I am the way (the path), the truth and the life, and none come to my father's kingdom except through me.'*

The meaning of this will now be revealed. The Ancient Egyptian mystery schools represented the knowledge of the seven octaves of vibration within the form of an equilateral triangle:

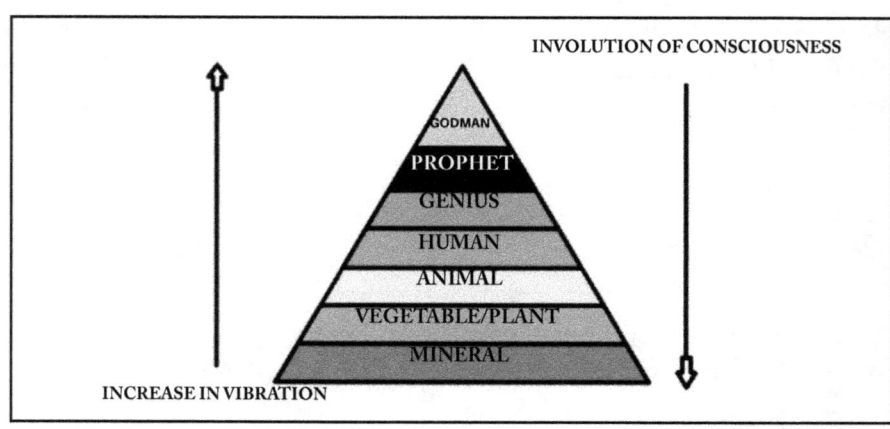

Figure 8: The Seven Octaves of Vibration. Copyright N. S. Elijah.

These octaves of vibration have a corresponding degree of consciousness. This degree of consciousness was also directly related to the glands in the human body that correspond with the subtle wheels of energy known as Chakras (see Figure 9).

Much has been written about the workings of Chakras in recent years, so I will briefly give you a quick summary from which to understand, then apply and move on to the next steps in learning.

Figure 9: Comparison of Nadis location and the ancient meaning of these energetic centres, represented symbolically in an ancient Hindu drawing. David V. Tansley, Subtle Body – Essence and Shadow, 1977 Art and Imagination Series, reproduced with permission (Thames and Hudson, London).

In Hindu teachings the subtle body or energy body is known as the Pranamayakosha. The Pranamayakosha or energy body is comprised of 3 primary energy channels that run from our coccyx all the way up our spine to the crown of our heads. They are the Ida and Pingala nadis intertwining around a central channel called Sushumna.

From these 3 primary nadis – Ida, Pingala and Sushumna – stem 72,000 lesser nadis. Nadis are the pathways or channels of Prana in our system. Prana is the Sanskrit equivalent to the Chinese Chi, Japanese Ki, Greek Pneumos, Hawaiian Mana, The Jewish Ruach, The English

Vital Life Force of the Rosicrucians. There are 7 primary wheels of energy located along the spine and up to the crown of the head, and these wheels of energy are known as Chakras: the base chakra – Muludhara, the sacral chakra – Svadisthana, solar plexus chakra – Manipura, heart chakra – Anahata, throat chakra – Vishuddha, 3rd eye chakra – Ajna and crown chakra Sahasrara.

The diagram on the previous page from David V. Tansley, *Subtle Body - Essence and Shadow*, 1977 depicts the Nadis or energetic pathways in the human body very well. And the clusters along the spine, depict the chakras.

This relationship can be directly mapped to the Staff of Hermes/Thoth which reveals the knowledge of the seven octaves of vibration as a foundation to the mysteries.

Sahasrara	*Crown*	7th Octave	*Godman*
Ajna	*3rd Eye*	6th Octave	*Prophet/Seer*
Vishudda	*Throat*	5th Octave	*Creative Genius*
Ana-hata	*Heart*	4th Octave	*Average Man*
Manipura	*Solar Pl.*	3rd Octave	*Animal*
Svadisthana	*Sacral*	2nd Octave	*Vegetative*
Muludhara	*Base/Root*	1st Octave	*Matter/Material*

Figure 10: The energetic potential of mankind, showing the real reason why the Caduceus Staff is the symbol of Medicine and how this correlates to the progression of consciousness through the seven octaves of vibration. © N. S. Elijah 2016

The Tree of Life

To further illustrate this, I will now bring to your attention the teachings of the Jewish Kabbalah, and show you how the origins of this predate the Jewish understanding and originated instead from Ancient Egypt. The origins of the Kabbalah are from the lost Books of Thoth, summarily represented in the 2nd symbol of the Major Arcana Tarot "The High Priestess." Firstly, let's take a look at the 'Tree of Life of the Sephiroth', which survives today in Jewish mystical teachings in the Kabbalah as follows:

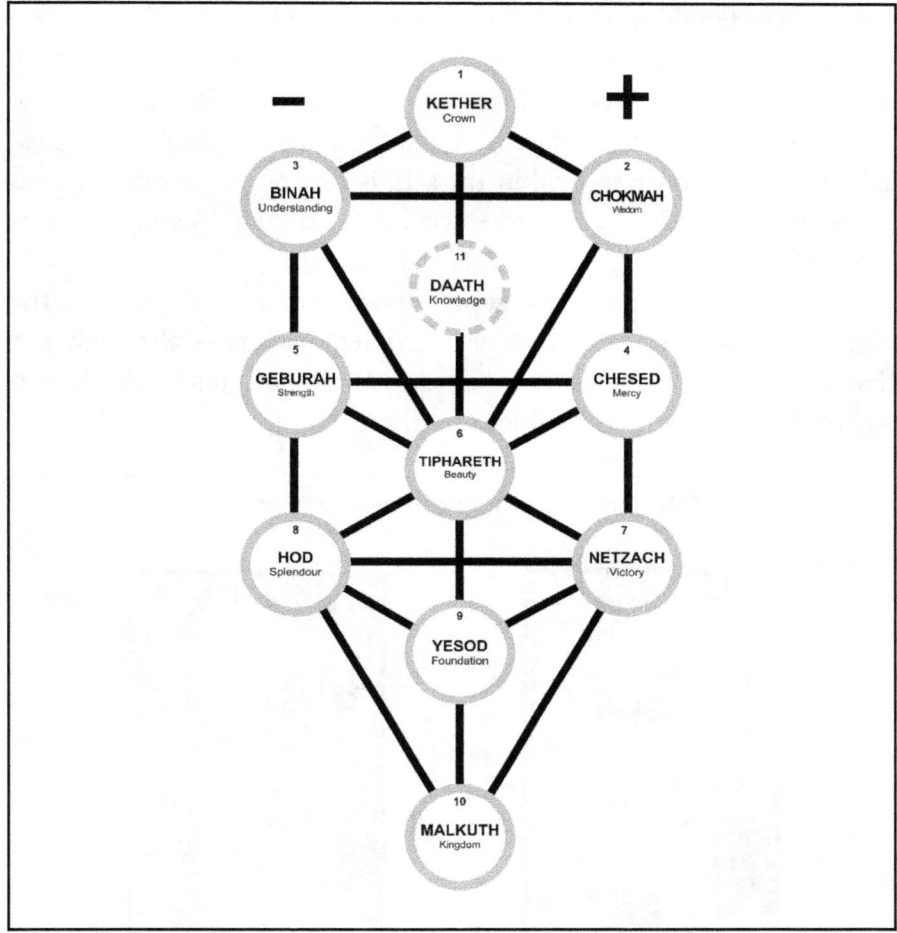

Figure 11: The Kabalistic Tree of Life. Source and Copyright: N. S. Elijah

The High Priestess

You will observe from the tree of life diagram, Figure 11 (above), that there is a negative column on the left and a positive column on the right. This is the representation of the **7th Principle of Hermes: The Principle of Polarity.** The crux of this teaching is that when a man/woman sits on the throne of wisdom within himself/herself, he/she has managed to balance the pairs of opposites within himself/herself. The subtle forces of the negative feminine vibration and the positive masculine vibration are not only recognised at work within the person, but balance and mastery of these forces is achieved. This truth of knowing God through the unification of the Divine Masculine and the Divine Feminine energies/aspects of consciousness, within the self, is part of the secrets depicted in the Major Arcana Tarot card – The High Priestess. A comparison is made of this in the diagram in Figure 12 (below).

You will see that if we superimpose the tree of life over the high priestess that a remarkable alignment occurs – although not that remarkable when we are clear on the true origins of the Jewish Kabbalah, that of the Lost Books of Thoth!

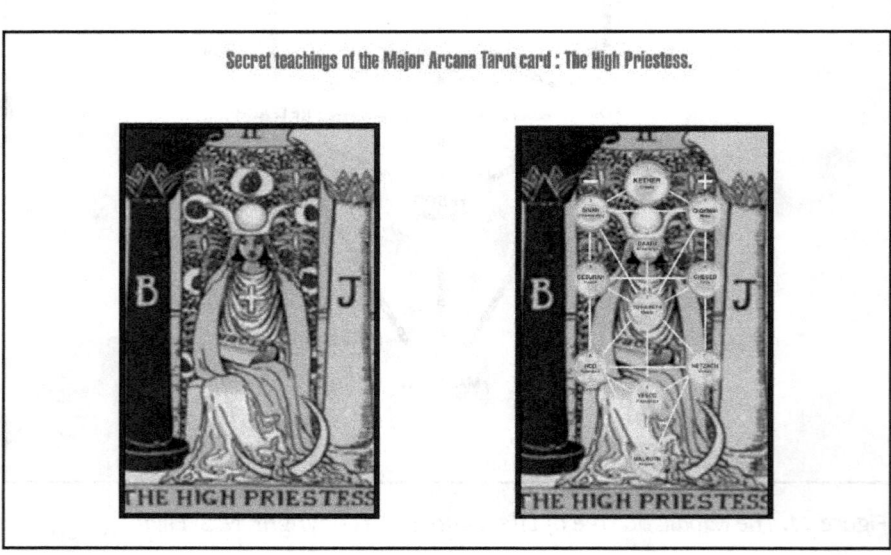

Figure 12: Comparison of the Major Arcana High Priestess and the Kabbalistic Tree of life. Source and Copyright (right-hand image): N. S. Elijah 2016

Allow me to interpret this diagram further. You can see behind the seated High Priestess several yellow circles with 'fruits' in them. Look at the triangular pattern of the top three; and see how if you superimpose the tree of life over this, they line up exactly. They are the fruits of the tree of life. Also, observe the illustration of the Universal Law of Polarity – one pillar Black (Boaz – feminine negative polarity) and the other White (Jachin – masculine positive polarity). Quite deliberately we see the High Priestess seated comfortably 'between the two poles' depicting thorough comprehension of this truth known by the ancient world. This is significant. To attain mastery, one must achieve balance – one must balance all the 'pairs of opposites' within themselves. In the Eastern mysteries this is represented in the Yin-Yang symbol, Figure 13 (below).

Figure 13: Yin-yang.

And so, it is that the human being is the visible half of their projected self (as we have noted, the current scientific understanding is that 3D reality is just a projection of an underlying 2D reality). The other half must remain behind, in the realms of spirit, in order for there to be a physical manifestation, otherwise the joining of the two halves physically would result in the destruction of the material form, and it could not exist on the material plane at the divine level of vibration – just look at what high voltage electricity does to the human body!

The human being, then, is a half – and so, by design, we seek our completion in another. And this coming together, this desire to be whole, leads to sexual union – in the search for completion. However, quickly after coupling we feel depleted, we feel somehow robbed of a promise of something greater, something that we cannot quite put our fingers on – a lasting union. This is the foundation of tantric practices and conservation of the sexual vital life fluids; their transmutation into higher energy to be used to attain higher experiences of consciousness and states of being.

The Law of Love

So, what do we mean by the Law of Love? At octaves 3 and 4, the animal and animal nature in man is led by its drives and passions and urges to perpetuate the species. The species' survival instinct is programmed into the body. The emotions and instincts belong to the animal or 3rd Octave of the animal nature. So, the following of these drives and passions is not the highest form of love.

In 1970, Krishnamurti explained very well what love is by first dismissing everything that love was not. He said that love is not based on ownership or possession of another or fear of losing security. Love is something much more than the puny thing we generally attribute it to be in the human condition and context. One of the main parts of my message to you is that love is God. Love is God at work – all encompassing, never taking, always giving.

In Kahlil Gibran's Islamic Sufi wisdom book *'The Prophet'*, he writes, *"When you love, do not say that God is in my heart, but rather I am in the heart of God."* When we do this for all of humanity and all nature and all existence, then we are awakening the love force necessary for evolution into a prophet/seer at the 6th Octave of Vibration/Consciousness, and we are on our way to the embodiment of divine man, such as Buddha, Jesus (Isa), Horus, and Krishna. It is at this level, before the shift to the 7th Octave of vibration when we are vibrating at the 6th Octave, that our love is not self-seeking or selfish, it is selfless. **A love exemplified in the life and teachings of the Prophet Muhammad, Christ, Buddha, Krishna, and Ptah-Hotep.** It is at this point that man becomes more than man. The illusionary nature of this world becomes glaringly and gloriously obvious and the 'reality' underlying it all is revealed. Paralleling this shift in consciousness is the Hindu teachings of Chakras (spinning wheels of energy) and the Kundalini (the risen divine force).

The High Priestess depicts union. The balancing of these pairs of opposites within oneself, the melding of the polar opposites into unity within oneself – just as she attained the union with her other half in consciousness. She is in command of the energies of her body and the forces at work magnetically seeking union outside of herself, and she understands very intimately her interconnectedness with all reality. She recognises that she is a part of a greater whole and this understanding is the force for the birth of altruistic divine love. A love not based on possession or desire, but a love based on sameness on recognising herself in every other outward manifestation – a supernatural appreciative love – and this is the basis for the spiritual brotherhood and sisterhood: the true Namaste, the true in Lakesh, the true Shalom.

It is the birth of this supernatural appreciative love which is the love of the prophet/seer, the love held at the 6th Octave of vibration. It is at this level that the 'Christ consciousness' has been born in the heart, the rose of the heart, the lotus of the heart. Listen. Understand. Be at peace.

What we need to understand is that what is known in spiritual texts around the world as 'The Fall' is just a veiled way of saying, 'A fall in consciousness, a separation from being one, consciously, with the creator occurred.' From this, we can see that in the beginning our consciousness was one with God, and in order for God to have an experience of experiencing itself subjectively as a creator, a separation occurred.

A break from the paradisiacal unity with the Godhead occurs, as the consciousness descends in to matter, to learn through suffering and experience over countless lifetimes, to remember, to come out of the amnesia; and with this consciousness attainment comes, one day the spiritualisation of matter of the body and then the soul progresses on to other worlds to learn other lessons. This is the foundation to the Buddhist teachings of the wheel of Samsara, the law of reincarnation. The eight-fold path of Theravada Buddhism is a mechanism to accelerate this spiritualisation of matter!

Knowledge of The Priests of Horus

The Priests of the Shem-shu-Hor (Priests of Horus) in Ancient Egypt, prior to the fall of the prevailing consciousness in 3100 BC, were living in divine union on Earth in their physical bodies. They understood in totality that divine potential laid dormant in mankind, so they left us coded messages of this truth of our potential which survive in the structure of the Pyramids of Giza on the band of peace.

The Pyramid is a shape, as you probably know, that has a square base and four equilateral triangles forming the sides. Whilst this type of pyramid is the perfect shape for conducting and channelling energy, it also is a coded message to mankind stating that through using the physical body a man can become divine.

Allow me to explain:

The triangle is the three in one and one in three – and represents divinity.

The square is the 'something added' to divinity (the extra line unfolding) and represents matter.

The four triangles forming the sides of the pyramid represent the four cardinal directions and also directly correspond to the four elemental triangles of the zodiac.

Each elemental triangle is comprised of three signs totalling the twelve signs of the zodiac:

The Fire Triangle: Aries, Leo, Sagittarius.

The Earth Triangle: Taurus, Virgo, Capricornus.

The Air Triangle: Gemini, Libra, Aquarius.

The Water Triangle: Cancer, Scorpio, Pisces.

These twelve zodiacal signs comprise the twelve tribes of Israel or Is- Ra -El (Isis, Ra, El – Of God).

So, the preserved message is that man, using the square base (the physical body) as a foundation, can raise up his consciousness from any sign in the zodiac, from any tribe of Israel, and can become more than man – can, in fact, become divine. The lost golden capstone!

Many thousands of years ago it was the responsibility of the High Priest in Ancient Egypt to oversee the initiations of the initiates.

The guardian of the secrets as Hierophant used to protect the sacred knowledge as:

Triangle = Divinity. Creation = Square. Eternity = Ouroboros (the snake eating its own tail forever) which we then further simplified as the circle.

We knew that the great secret upon which all of our sacred knowledge was based was that **divinity lay at rest for eternity within creation.** We knew how to awaken it and have it rise, fully conscious, whilst in the human body living on Earth. We represented this truth in the following symbol:

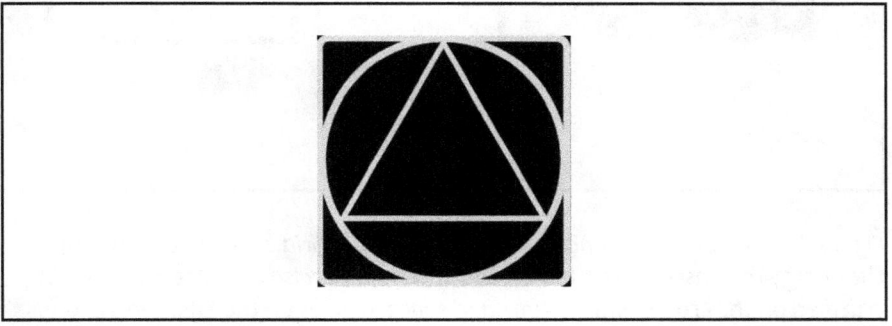

Figure 14: the ancient symbol representing divinity (triangle) at rest for eternity (Ouroboros – circle) within creation (square). Source and Copyright: N. S. Elijah

This is the foundation message I want people to understand from this discourse. We symbolised this penultimate achievement in human form by the pharaoh wearing the Uraeus. The Uraeus was the symbol of the awakened, raised, and achieved state of the divine consciousness whilst in the physical body – the manifestation of the 7th Octave of vibration. A being that achieved this state was known to be eating of the fruits of the tree of knowledge of life.

Knowledge of our Divine Potential: Surviving in Symbolism

Figure 15: The surviving symbolism of the ancient world of the knowledge of the energy of consciousness having the potential to raise awareness or remain crucified on the crossbeams of time and space. Uraeus on the Pharaoh's brow symbolises the achievement of divine consciousness, the Kundalini serpent energy rising. Serpent Tau symbolises the rising of the fallen divine consciousness within man on the crossbeams of time and space. Source and copyright: N. S. Elijah.

However, we also knew that the alternative was that the spirit of the divine could remain crucified on the cross beams of time and space, and if that consciousness identified itself as the body and not the consciousness within the body then that being would be eating of the tree of knowledge of death.

When you unfold the cube of matter, you get what? That's right; the cross, the crucifix.

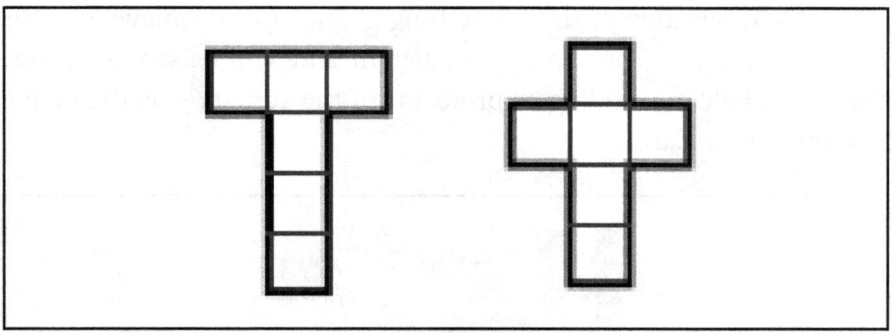

Figure 16: the cube unfolded is the true symbol of the cross or crucifix.

Now should be one of those moments for the reader to exclaim, 'Oh my Heavenly Days!' – and rightly so. Because now you should start to see the misconception perpetuated by the church for 2,000 years.

We do not need to be saved by an external divine being – that is the misconception that has kept mankind enslaved for 2,000 years. We have the potential through our inner divinity to save ourselves – that is the truth.

The raising from the dead and the transfiguration are not isolated miracles attributed to Christ as the 'Only Son of God.' They are manifestations of the potential of what happens when a man lives in accordance with the universal and divine laws and raises his consciousness from the 4th, through the 5th and 6th, and up to the 7th octave of vibration. The dormant codes in the DNA become activated and the overshadowing of 'something greater from somewhere else' occurs. This is known as the Christ.

Christ comes from the Latin word 'Christou' and means anointed. So, the personality is overshadowed by something greater from somewhere else. What happens is that the divine recognises itself within the created form and speaks forth. That is why the world teacher, the Christ, called himself the Son of God. For indeed, the human personality had been subjugated by the divine and the Christ being was the divine instrument on Earth. But he never said that he was the *only* Son of God (read the Bible). He only ever said that he was *a* Son of God – as indeed we are all sons and daughters of God!

This knowledge of the 'something greater from somewhere else' overshadowing the personality we taught and symbolised as Horus, the Great Falcon standing as protector of the Initiate – as the divine instrument on Earth.

Figure 17: This photo in its true interpretation depicts Horus (the something greater from somewhere else) overshadowing the Initiate, forming the divine instrument on Earth. Image interpretation copyright: N. S. Elijah

The Secret Doctrine

Whilst our history books may not present an accurate picture of chronology of our true origins, we can look to the preserved meaning of spiritual symbols left behind by our forefathers, in order to get to deeper truths as they left the knowledge of the true teachings preserved in symbols for us to discover. The circumpunct is the symbol of God that survives today. This is the circumpunct. ⊙ It also represents the Sun, a microcosmic manifestation of the reality of God. Why does the circumpunct represent God? Why did they use this symbol to preserve the meaning of God? How can a circle with a dot in the centre represent God?

The answer lies with a King James Bible verse:

"In the beginning was the word and the word was with God, and the word was God." What is meant by this ancient axiom? The Vedic – Brahman – Hindus understood this sacred truth and represented it in the Sri Yantra – see Figure 18 (below). From a singular nothingness, a singular point, a word, a vibration, a big bang, was sent forth in all directions and slowed down and became matter. That is what is depicted in the circumpunct and the Sri Yantra; a divine pulse sent forth, impregnated with the codes of creation, which cools and condenses into physical reality.

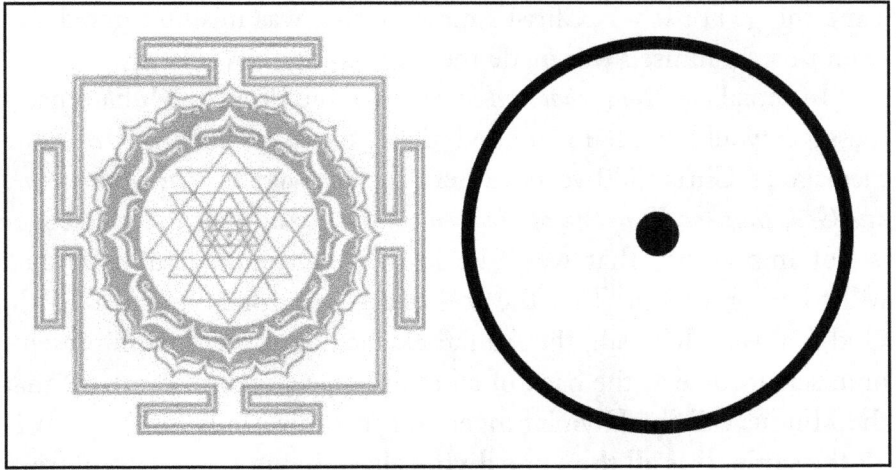

Figure 18: Comparison of the Sri Yantra (left) and circumpunct (right), showing the same principle. Association Source N. S. Elijah.

Throughout history there have been many personalities (aspects of the Godhead) that have come to Earth to guide man and their teachings hold similar undertones. These undertones are known as the wisdom religion or secret doctrine. This has been taught under various guises since time immemorial; the most recent proponent of this ancient teaching was Helena Blavatsky, the founder of theosophy in the 19th Century.

Before her, the most well-known was the Christ – Jesus or Isa (Islamic Koran). *"Take up the cross and Follow me,"* said Jesus and then we had the birth of the illiterate Prophet Muhammad (peace be upon him) who united the warring tribes in Mecca until his death in 632AD. Four hundred years later in 1095 AD, the Pope called for a crusade to 'rescue Jerusalem from the Muslims' and many a blood thirsty battle was fought, until 1127 AD when Saladin drove the Catholic forces from the Holy land.

Yet, if research had been carried out and the Qur'an translated and compared to the Christian Bible, they would have found startling similarities. Jesus is recognised as a divine prophet known as Isa. The mosques were built to show the glory of God Allah – the same God of the original Christians to which they built their churches to show the same thing. For it was Christ's message that was misinterpreted and from this, he himself was made the focal point.

In actual fact *'those that had ears to hear'* the Prophet Muhammad's message would have understood that he was delivering the same message as Christ 500 years earlier. The message is *that there is only one God, that the Kingdom of Heaven is near...* and that the messenger is not important. That we must learn to surrender our individual will to a higher will. That the message – the worshipping of Allah, God, Yahweh, Jehovah, the All father, the omnipotent, omnipresent, omniscient force at the back of all of existence, the same creator that the Hindus call the Divine Singer and the universe is his song, **'It is all the same. It is all the same divine chair, being looked upon from a different angle!'**

Political climate and hostilities at the time meant that the message was veiled in allegory.

When the world teacher, 'The Christ', 2,000 years ago, said, *"Take up your cross and follow me,"* he was not saying pick up your wooden crosses and use it as a justified banner to fight your bloody wars! He was not calling for a vicious hypocritical assault on innocent people carrying the cross, or having it emblazoned across armoured chests as they carried out gruesome travesties against fellow brothers in humanity with an evangelical agenda centuries later in his name through Holy War! I ask you; how can war be holy?

No, he was saying, 'Take up your consciousness off of the cross beams of time and space and follow me (live as I have shown you how to live) to the Heavenly Kingdom on Earth – because your potential is divine.'

This is the correct interpretation of those words: From Helena Blavatsky's Secret Doctrine: 1889

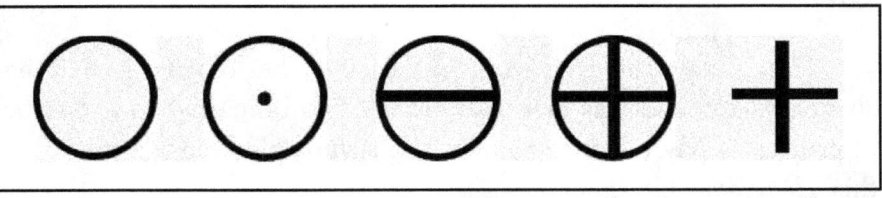

Figure 19: The Secret Doctrine, Helena Blavatskies, The Secret Doctrine.

1. *The one infinite and unknown essence exists for all eternity.*
2. *A disc with a point in it, the first differentiation in the manifestations of the ever-eternal nature, sexless and infinite, with the point in the disc being potential space within abstract space.*
3. *In its 3rd stage the point is transformed into a diameter, thus now symbolising divine mother-nature within 'the all', embracing absolute infinitude.*
4. *When the diameter line is crossed by a vertical one, it becomes the mundane cross and is the sign for human life to begin.*
5. *When the circumference disappears and leaves only + it symbolises that the 'fall of man' (from being conscious of his oneness with the absolute) into matter is accomplished.* And man's divine consciousness is crucified on a cross beam of time and space with the horizontal line – the wave of the spirit (time and space) and the vertical line being the force of life (the evolution of matter).

What Christ was saying when he said, "*Take up the cross and Follow me,*" was 'Pick up your crucified consciousness that keeps you crucified on the cross beams of time and space and remember that you are divine consciousness, not this crude matter, this crude body of bone and flesh!'

> *"And whoever does not take up the cross and follow me is not worthy of me. Those who find their life will lose it, and those who lose their life for my sake will find it."*
> – Matthew 10.34

This is also the true basis of Islam – the 'one faith that has always existed and was gradually revealed to humanity by a number of prophets.' My Islamic brothers and sisters, please pay attention to this. *Al-salamu alaykum.*

Christianity in its Gnostic pure form is a true way. It is the way, the truth, and the life, because the world teacher 'Christ' was love incarnate. His message, his teaching, was how to be the embodiment of love. Love is the strongest force in the universe, and so on the physical plane it is as strong as God and therefore it is divine; that is it. He said, *"these things I do you shall also do and greater"* – the message of Christ was that **'as you become love incarnate, you become divine.'**

But, for 2,000 years, the Church has twisted this simple message and unnecessarily positioned themselves as an intermediary to God. That is not necessary. And they know this. But because they want to maintain their position of power and control, they drip feed knowledge-lies to the spiritually thirsty masses and are therefore able to maintain their earthly power under a lie.

The knowledge required to correct this false indoctrination is available to us. If we have courage to let go of what we have been deliberately taught for fifty generations!

Where does the original teaching of this knowledge come from? The answer is Thoth.

Now, I know you may question the validity of an ibis-headed god actually being real. But the ibis head is symbolic of a manifestation of a quality and an emanation of the Godhead. Just as with Horus – the hawk-headed god; and Sekhmet – the lion-faced goddess. It is not literal, it is a symbolic representation, much the same as a bull is a symbol of strength, a lion is a symbol of courage, a human of intelligence, and an eagle of spirit. The Ibis head is a symbolic revelation of his essence – probing into governing truths underlying reality.

The same symbolism is used in the representation of many gods in the Hindu pantheon, with Ganesh the elephant god also representing wisdom and strength and being known as the 'remover of obstacles.'

If we investigate the Sphinx – Figures 20a&b (below) – it has a bull's body (strength), a lion's claws (courage), a human face (intelligence) and an eagle's wings (spirit). This is not a coincidence! It is a very powerful coded message surviving from antiquity about the nature of man and his potential to be more than man. It is based upon knowledge of the Ancient Egyptian mystery schools.

Figure 20a: Sphinx and the Great Pyramid at Giza, Egypt.
Figure 20b: The Sphinx, The Secret Teachings of All Ages, Manly P. Hall.

Thoth (Hermes Trismegistus) was the thrice-great master of masters. He taught in his fabled Emerald Tablets that we as human beings, *"Are the word of God, travelling through the eternal thought of God, that we are stars chained to a mountain."*

Take a moment now and get your head around that. *"In the beginning, there was the Word and the Word was God."*

We are the word of God travelling through the eternal thought of God! The only reason for 'time' to exist as a construct is so that events and people can be located within the 'eternal thought of God.' Einstein's relativity theory is only relevant to the material manifestation of reality, not to the unseen elements – namely consciousness or spirit.

Time has the illusion of flowing as a linear river from past to present to future. **Linear time exists as a notion, or a construct as a measure, to locate ourselves within the eternal thought of God.** Because of that, what we call time or linear time is just an illusion. There is no past or future, there is only ever now! And now! *And now!* Past-past, past-present, past-future, present-past, present-present, present-future, and future-past, future-present, future-future. And the reason for this is that the universe is holographic in nature. Every part is a part of every part. Separation is the grand illusion – everything is interconnected and has a divine design. The Ancients of Egypt understood this very well.

Ptah-Hotep

While researching and connecting the dots together from history, I discovered what is known to be the oldest surviving book in the world. It is a book known as the '*Instruction of Ptah-Hotep*' and is a 1906 translation by Battiscombe G. Gunn of the 5,500-year-old '*Prisse Papyrus.*' Today, the *Prisse Papyrus* is on display in the Louvre in Paris. Why is this book significant? In Gunn's words:

> "*The Prisse Papyrus which is well known by name... was acquired in Egypt by M. Prisse D'Avennes, a French archaeologist of distinction and published by him in 1847.* **Spread out flat it measures 23 feet 7 inches (wide) with an average height of 5-foot 7/8 inches.** *Which is about the average of papyri of the Eleventh and Twelfth Dynasties. It contains 18 pages of heavy and bold black and red writing in the so-called hieratic character. At first sight it appears to be in perfect preservation, being entirely free from the cracks*

*and decay which may mar the manuscripts of a far later date; but an examination of the contents shows **that an unknown quantity has been torn off from the commencement.** Originally the roll contained at least 2 books, of which we have the latter part of one and the whole of the other. Between these there is a blank space of some 53 inches!"*

Battiscombe G. Gunn goes on to say,

"With the book 'Instruction of Ptah-Hotep' – the author lived in the reign of king Isosi, Isosi ruled from about 3580-3536 BC, thus we may take about 3550 BC as the period of Ptah-Hotep."

Who was Ptah-Hotep? Well this is very interesting indeed. In Robert Bauval and Adrian Gilbert's 1994 book *'The Orion Mystery'* pages 35 - 36 we are told that the proposed date of the first dynasty of Egypt has, over the past couple of centuries, been a subject of contention among scholars:

"In the 1830s Champollion, the father of scientific Egyptology and decipherer of hieroglyphics, believed that the first dynasty began C.5867 BC. Later the German Egyptologist, Karl Lepsius, moved this to 3892 BC. Then Mariette, writing in the 1870's reverted back to 5004 BC. Finally, his colleague, Dr Brugsch, settled for 4400 BC... then in the 1940's, the dating of the first dynasty was again adjusted to C.3100 BC. This is constantly refined to 3150 BC, 3300 BC, 2900 BC and so on, leaving us confused about what system we are to consider definitive. In any event, it should now be clear that the science of Egyptian chronology is far from perfect."

According to the current prevailing understanding of Egyptology, Menes, aka Narmer, was the first dynastic king of Egypt c.3100 BC. According to the 5,500-year-old record in the Prisse Papyrus, Ptah-

Hotep was the vizier to king/pharaoh Isosi c.3550 BC, 450 years before the so-called first king/pharaoh of the First Dynasty – so we seemingly have an anomaly.

The history we are taught is actually in many important ways altered, and is the winner's account of events, skewed to support their own agenda and future designs.

Remember – knowledge is power. Ask yourselves, what could have happened to 53 inches of pages – 5 foot 7 inches high of the 5,500-year-old papyrus? How much was torn off from the unknown commencement? Why was this amount removed from the beginning and the centre of the oldest book on Earth, when the rest of the manuscript remains in near perfect condition? Then I want you to ask yourself, what could have been written there that required it to be removed? Because **remember – the rest of the manuscript is perfectly preserved!** Now, some of the translation of Ptah-Hotep's words of instruction will be given at the end of this chapter when we compare the words of the previous messengers/spiritual teachers of humanity and reveal their startling similarities.

Although the translation of the words of Ptah-Hotep, as they survive from the *Prisse Papyrus* in the Louvre today, will show you the level of refinement of ethics and civilisation at that ancient time which reflects some of the words of Christ in their selflessness and delivery, I want you to understand that the foundation upon which they are framed runs far deeper into ancient mystical knowledge – a knowledge so powerful in its entirety that it was deliberately removed from the *Prisse Papyrus* many centuries ago.

I mentioned before that the Earth is subject to vast cycles of time, known as Yugas, and the Mayan Great Year and Precession of the Equinoxes. It is upon this cosmology that we have the modern terms of the Age of Pisces or the Age of Aquarius. With precession, there are twelve signs of the Zodiac that the spring equinox of the Earth rotates through at a rate of approx. 2,150 years per zodiacal sign. The time of Christ was in the Age of Pisces, and we are now moving into the Age of Aquarius. Ptah-Hotep lived at the end of the Age of Gemini when the Earth was transitioning into the Age of Taurus.

In 1960 Erzebeth Haich, or Elisabeth Haich, wrote a book called *'Initiation'* in which she remembered being a neophyte of Ptah-Hotep in a previous incarnation; and with instruction, delivered in such a concise knowledgeable manner at the time when the Earth was moving into the Age of Taurus that unlocks many of the mysteries of the universe.

For those of you that do not hold the idea of reincarnation to be plausible, I ask you to set aside your prejudice for the time being, be open to the idea and see where this leads you. Jesus Christ advised his disciples that, *"Elijah again came and went as John the Baptist but was not recognised."*

The Dalai Lama is the reincarnation of the Bodhisattva of Compassion. The Hindus hold that Gautama Buddha was a reincarnation of Krishna/Vishnu. And in the same vein, Hermes Trismegistus was purported to be the incarnation of Thoth (The Egyptian God of Wisdom).

In Elisabeth Haigh's book *'Initiation'* there is a passage where she recounts the memory of being taught this ancient knowledge many thousands of years ago in a previous life by a being known as High Priest Ptah-Hotep. In ancient Egyptian 'Ptah' means 'God.' Remember, we have the 1906 translation of the *Prisse Papyrus* that Ptah-Hotep was the 'vizier/advisor' to Pharaoh Isosi – at a time when the vernal equinox of the earth was moving into the sign of Taurus, approximately 6,500 years ago.

If you are having a hard time reconciling that it is possible for a human being to have a clear memory of previous lives, I would like to direct your attention momentarily to the treasured centuries-old writings of Patanjali. The 'Yoga Sutras of Patanjali' explains to us how it is indeed possible for a 'Yogi' to attain special abilities known as Siddhis. One of these Siddhis is the ability to recall events and details of previous lives.

So, with open mindedness and an open heart please listen to the simplicity and certainty in this account by Elisabeth Haich from one of her former ancient embodiments, and then weigh its authenticity for yourself. The words that follow are the translated words she recalled of her instruction from Ptah-Hotep, at a time when the Earth was entering the Age of Taurus, before 4500 BC!

> *"The Earth and its inhabitants are not yet conscious of the forces which reach the Earth from out of the cosmos and maintain it. Consequently, the inhabitants of the Earth aren't able to control these forces and transform them at will. The Earth receives these radiations from out of the cosmos and is immersed and bathed in these waves of energy. Everything that happens on Earth is a direct reaction to the action of these radiations... a kind of resonance resulting from their interaction. The sun magnifies to a tremendous extent the radiations of the particular constellation in which it stands at any given moment as it radiates its force to the Earth, simultaneously with the radiations of the constellations concerned. This fact has a bearing in the way in which the four seasons have come into being.*
>
> *The material world has come into being because interferences have occurred in the divine creative radiations traversing cosmic space, and these interferences have caused condensations, solidifications, materialisations. If the celestial bodies were to receive pure, untransformed vibrations of the creative force, this would result in the immediate annihilation of all matter.*
>
> *The fixed stars – the suns – are the great transformers which convert the creative vibrations from all celestial bodies and transmit them in wavelengths and frequencies that are tolerable for the earth. The transformed rays reach us from the fixed stars which form the constellations of the zodiac.* **Thus when we want to represent the highest divine radiation of energy, we choose the symbolic form of the constellation with the strongest effect on the earth, and this is always the 'epoch-making constellation' through which the vernal point is moving at the time.**

> *"We are now living in an epoch in which the vernal point is moving into the constellation of the bull. God (Ptah) reveals himself to us in the radiation of this constellation, and that's why the divinity manifesting itself in the atmosphere of the Earth is represented in the form of a bull, in the form of the divine bull Apis. The complementary constellation of Scorpio-Eagle is represented as the temptress – a serpent crawling upon the earth – or in the form of the divine falcon Horus. You know that this energy, as long as it is earthly and expresses itself on the low plane binding spirit to matter, is the serpent luring man back into further incarnations. On the other hand when this force is spiritualised, it helps man to experience, while still in the body, the highest degree of spirituality... The initiate is thus an instrument of the divinity which reveals itself through the zodiacal sign of the bull. That's why in our epoch these animals are regarded as 'holy animals' throughout the entire world. Now you understand why the initiates change their representations of God to accord with the constellation in which the vernal point falls at any given time. Above and behind all these symbols, of course, there always stands the unmanifested First Cause – divinity resting within itself."*

As this knowledge begins to register with you, you will begin to see how much has been deliberately hidden from us because of its power to shape us.

But is this really all that far-fetched? All we know is what we are taught. The evidence survives in multiple examples around the world that the ancient cultures were in possession of remarkable cosmic knowledge.

Now in 1970, J. Krishnamurti gave a speech in San Diego under the title, '*Understanding meditation requires order*' where he outlined this and also the consequences of this conditioning/programming upon the human being and on our current civilisation and society:

> *"You are the product of your conditioning. You are the product of your society. You are the product of propaganda, religious or otherwise – for 2,000 years as in India 10,000 years or 5,000 years you have been told what to believe… what to think, you repeat what others have said. All your education is that… the repetition of what you have learned from a book and you are that. You are conditioned – you are not free, happy, vital, passionate human beings. You are frightened human beings and therefore second-hand. You're full of authority of others; of your own particular little authority of your own knowledge – you know something about something and you become an authority. So you are not free. Intellectually look, are you free? Not repeat what others have said, not what you have been taught in university or what you have learned in a book. And what you have experienced? You have experienced something that you will always recognise otherwise it is not experience. Therefore experience is always old, like thought is always old… because it is the response of memory. So you are second-hand human beings intellectually, emotionally, you go to places to learn how to be sensitive. Be taught by another how to think. So morally, intellectually, deeply you are not free."*

The teachings of Ptah-Hotep, not just a vizier to the Pharaoh, but actually the Egyptian High Priest/Hierophant of the Priests of Horus, explains, along with the instruction from hierophant to initiate in another ancient Egyptian record, that **all of their knowledge comes from Thoth and the Books of Thoth.** I will get to explaining that in just a short moment. However, first let us take a look at the previous messengers of love and then take a look at our true origins.

WORDS OF THE MASTERS

WORDS OF PTAH-HOTEP – HIGH PRIEST TO PHAROAH ISOSI – FROM THE PRISSE PAPYRUS, 3550 BC

1. "Follow thine heart during thy lifetime; do not more than is commanded of thee. Diminish not the time of following the heart; it is abhorred of the soul that its time be taken away. Shorten not the daytime more than is needful to maintain thine house. When riches are gained, follow the heart; for riches are of no avail if ones heart be weary."

2. "Be not proud because thou art learned; but discourse with the ignorant man, as well as the wise (sage). For no limit can be set to skill, neither to any craftsman that possesses full advantages. Fair speech is more rare than the emerald that is found by the slave maiden on pebbles."

3. "If thou be among people, make for thyself love the beginning and end of the heart. One that knoweth not his course shall say in himself (seeing thee), 'He that ordereth himself duly becomes the owner of wealth; I shall copy his conduct.' Thy name shall be good, though thou speak not; thy body shall be fine (vibration); thy face shall be seen among thy neighbours; thou shalt be provided with what thou lackest. As to the man that obeyeth his belly (animal desire); he causes disgust in place of love. His heart is wretched, his body is gross (vibration), he is insolent towards those endowed of God. He that obeyeth his belly (animal desire) has an enemy."

4. "If thou desire (spiritual desire) that thine actions may be good, save thyself from all malice and beware of the quality of covetousness, which is a grievous inner malady. It gathereth unto itself all evils; it is the girdle of all wickedness. But the man that is just, flourisheth; truth goes in his footsteps and he maketh habitations therein, not in the dwelling of covetousness."

5. "If thou be powerful, make thyself to be honoured for knowledge and gentleness. Exalt not thine own heart above others, that it be brought low. Be not silent, but be aware of interruption of words with heat (anger). Put it far from thee; control thyself. The wrathful heart speaketh fiery words; it darteth out at the man of peace that approacheth, stopping his path."

6. "If thou wouldest seek out the nature of a friend, ask not a companion of his; but pass a time with him alone, that thou injure not his affairs. Debate with him, after a season; test his heart on occasion of speech."

7. "As for the fool, devoid of obedience, he doeth nothing. Knowledge he regardeth as ignorance, profitable things as hurtful things. He doeth all kind of errors, so that he is rebuked therefore every day. He liveth in death therewith; it is therefore his food. At chattering speech he marvelleth, as at the wisdom of princes, living in death every day. He is shunned because of his misfortunes, by reason of the multitude of afflictions that come upon him every day."

WORDS OF JESUS CHRIST, APPROXIMATELY 34 AD

1. "A new command I give you: Love one another. As I have loved you, so you must love one another. By this all people will know that you are my disciples, if you have love for one another."
   – John 13:34-35

2. "Jesus said unto him, 'Thou shalt love the Lord thy God with all thy heart and with all thy soul and with all thy mind. This

is the first and great commandment. And the second is like unto it, thou shalt love thy neighbour as thyself. On these two commandments hang ALL the LAW and the Prophets.'"
– Matthew 22:37-40

3. "Jesus answered and said unto her, 'Whosoever drinketh of this water shall thirst again: But whosoever drinketh of the water that I shall give him (knowledge) shall never thirst; but the water that I shall give him shall be in him a well of water springing up into everlasting life.'"
– John 4:13-14

4. "Ye have heard that it be said, 'Thou shalt love thy neighbour, and hate thine enemy.' But I say to you, love your enemies and pray for those who persecute you, so that you may be sons of your Father who is in heaven; for he makes his sun rise on the evil and on the good, and sends rain on the just and on the unjust.'"
– Matthew 5:43-44

5. "And behold, I come quickly; and my reward is with me, to give every man according as his work shall be. I am the Alpha and Omega, the Beginning and the End, the First and the Last."
– Revelations 22:12-14

6. "If you bring forth what is within you, what you bring forth will save you. If you do not bring forth what is within you, what you do not bring forth will destroy you."
– The gospel of St. Thomas.

7. "Therefore do not be anxious about tomorrow. For tomorrow will be anxious for itself. Sufficient for the day is its own trouble."
– Matthew 6:34

8. "I am the Way the Truth and the Life. None come to the Father except through me (the overshadowing of something greater from somewhere else)."
– John 14:6.

WORDS OF LORD KRISHNA FROM THE BHAGAVAD GITA (Song of the Spirit), 3000 BC.

1. "He sees truly who perceive the supreme Lord present equally in all creatures, the imperishable amidst the perishing. He who is conscious of the omnipresence of God does not injure the SELF with self. That man reaches the supreme Goal."
   –Xiii: 27- 28.

2. "This self is never born nor does it ever perish; nor having come into existence will it again cease to be. It is birthless, eternal, changeless, ever-same (unaffected by the usual processes associated with time). It is not slain when the body is killed."
   –11:20.

3. "He who perceives Me everywhere and beholds everything in Me never loses sight of Me, nor do I ever lose sight of him."
   –VI:30.

4. "Brooding on sense objects causes attachment to them. Attachment breeds craving; craving breeds anger. Anger breeds delusion; delusion breeds loss of memory of the SELF. Loss of right memory causes decay of the discriminating faculty. From decay of discrimination, annihilation of spiritual life follows."
   –II: 62-63

5. "Lust, anger and greed – these constitute the threefold gate of hell leading to the destruction of the soul's welfare. These three therefore, man should abandon."
   –XVI:21.

6. "Just as an individual forsaking dilapidated raiment dons new clothes, so the body-encased soul, relinquishing decayed bodily habitations, enter others that are new."
   –11:22

7. "O Arjuna, as the ignorant perform actions with attachments and hope of reward, so the wise should act with dispassionate non-attachment, to serve gladly as a guide for the multitudes."
   –111:25.

WORDS OF SIDDARTHA GAUTAMA BUDDHA – THE DHAMMAPADHA, 500 BC

1. "All that we are is the result of what we have thought: it is founded on our thoughts and made up of our thoughts. If a man speaks or acts with an evil thought, suffering follows him as the wheel follows the hoof of the beast that draws the wagon. If a man speaks or acts with a good thought, happiness follows him like a shadow that never leaves him."
2. "Do not believe in anything simply because you have heard it. Do not believe in anything simply because it is spoken and rumoured by many. Do not believe in anything simply because it is found written in your religious books. Do not believe in anything merely on the authority of your teachers and elders. Do not believe in traditions because they have been handed down for many generations. But after observation and analysis, when you find that anything agrees with reason and is conducive to the good and benefit of one and all, then accept it and live up to it."
3. "Holding on to anger is like gripping a hot coal with the intent of throwing it at someone else; you are the one who gets burned."
4. "A man is not called wise because he talks and talks again; but if he is peaceful, loving and fearless then he is in truth called wise."
5. "As rain falls equally on the just and unjust, do not burden your heart with judgements but rain your kindness equally to all."
6. "There are only two mistakes one can make along the way to truth; not going all the way and not starting."
7. "What is evil? Killing is evil, lying is evil, slandering is evil, abuse is evil, gossip is evil, envy is evil, hatred is evil, to cling to false doctrine is evil; all these things are evil. And what is the root of evil? Illusion is the root of evil."
8. "The one who has conquered himself is a far greater hero than he who has defeated a thousand times a thousand men."
9. "When you come upon a path that brings benefit and happiness to all, follow this course as the moon journeys through the stars."
10. "The way is not in the sky, the way is in the heart."

WORDS OF THE PROPHET MUHAMMAD – THE QUR'AN, 1500 AD

1. "There is a polish for everything that takes away rust, and the polish for the heart is the remembrance of God."
2. "You will not enter paradise until you have faith. And you will not complete your faith until you love one another."
3. "The worldly comforts are not for me. I am like a traveller, who takes rest under a tree in the shade and then goes on his way." (Reincarnation).
4. "The greatest wealth is the richness of soul."
5. "Strive always to excel in richness and truth."
6. "The strong person is not a good wrestler. Rather, the strong person is the one who controls himself when he is angry."

Can you see the underlying truth now? Love is the primary message of all of the previous divine messengers. And they are divine because God has recognised himself/herself within manifested creation. The divine recognises itself within form and then speaks. It is the bestowing of the Christ Consciousness or, as Ptah-Hotep says, The Man of Peace. This is the true covenant of God with Abraham.

Let us now explore our true origins.

Chapter 3

ORIGINS

"A people without the knowledge of their past history, origin and culture is like a tree without roots."
— Marcus Garvey

For a very long-time humanity has been subjected to a very real and very sinister underhanded system of control. There are powers behind the curtain (as mentioned in the Zeitgeist film), such as the Bilderberg Group for example – a conglomerate of the world's richest and most powerful families – the world elite. They are pulling the strings of the visible world leaders to try to steer things according to their insidious designs. They orchestrate the periodic collapse of world markets and they fill the Earth with vibrations of fear. So, they can, under the guise of 'for our security and our safety', strip us more of our freedoms and power and maintain control over us.

Hidden agenda – disempower and control the people.

The Global Elite's most subtle means of control are through the deliberate presentation of a false history, and the strategic use of the mechanism of religion and its apparent divergences to keep us divided and controlled. For a couple of thousand years, this was done with fear of hell fire and sin and guilt and sexual repression. And if we turn our heads back to the Dark Ages, to the Spanish Inquisition, to the burning at the stake of pagans, and the torture of those who did not want to be converted to Christianity, you can see that the very message of Christ of **'loving your neighbour like yourself'** and **'thou shalt not kill'** was spat upon by a ruthless dark agenda hypocritically acting under the pathetic veil of the greater interests of Christ.

The historical travesty of the Albegensian Crusades (1209-1229) was a twenty-year military campaign initiated by Pope Innocent III to eliminate Catharism in Languedoc, in the south of France. The Catholic Church slaughtered the Gnostic 'Cathar' Christian community in France, as the Church was afraid of what this peaceful knowledge and way of life would mean for their grip on power, if this teaching was allowed to spread. Remember 'Cathar' comes from the Greek 'Katharoi' and means 'pure.' So, it was ruthlessly stamped out.

The indoctrination and the dogmatic literal interpretation of the Bible (the way the Papacy wanted it taught) meant that people looked at themselves as weak and gave away their power to something outside of themselves, whether that was a church intermediary who provided access to God or a figure on a cross – a man that died for our sins because we are apparently born into sin. But this was not the message of Christ. **Christ's message was so much more. It was a love message; it was a message of tolerance and loving one's neighbour as oneself, not from the position of ethics or morality, but from the understanding that we are ALL one under God and we are all interconnected at a very deep cosmic level.**

The Dead Sea Scrolls

Our accepted inherited world-view today is largely understood in relationship to one significant event in our history – the birth of Jesus Christ. Who was Jesus really? Was he in fact the only Son of God as the Church would like us to believe? Or was he just a man in whom the divine spirit had full control and showed forth through the medium of the human form?

Having the audacity to make this enquiry is probably enough

for some bigots entrenched and blinded by literal interpretation and teaching of scripture to put this book down in disgust. But if you do not want to categorise yourself as such, then I ask you to have courage and keep reading. In 1991, Michael Baigent and Richard Leigh, co-authors of the book, *The Deception of the Dead Sea Scrolls*, made some impressive ground through their meticulous research into the deliberate suppression of the Dead Sea Scrolls. What are the Dead Sea Scrolls, you may ask?

The story goes… In 1947, Muhammad Adh-Dhib, or Muhammad the Wolf, a member of the Ta'amireh Bedouin tribe, found the scrolls in a cave in the cliff face of Quamran in Jordan whilst searching for a lost goat. He tried to look inside but it was too dark, so he threw a stone which resulted in the sound of breaking pottery. In the first instance he found a number of large earthenware jars, about two-feet tall and ten inches wide, and inside were three leather-wrapped scrolls that had not seen the light of day for nearly 2,000 years. Over the proceeding ten years, excavations by various parties at locations of Qumran and Wadi Marabba'at would bare caches of around 1,000 scrolls of various import and various ages.

The mistreatment of the study and release of the findings is an academic, political and theological hot mess that basically resulted in the delay and suppression of the findings for nearly forty years, and is arguably the greatest academic travesty of the last couple of hundred years. In 1947, American scholars photographed some of the scrolls and sent a complete set of prints to an acknowledged expert in the field, Professor William F Albright at John Hopkins University. On 15th of March 1948, Professor Albright confirmed the importance of the discovery with a date a little older than they were in order to distance the find from the political landscape at the time of Christ:

> *"My heartiest congratulations on the greatest manuscript discovery of modern times! There is no doubt whatever in my mind that the script is more archaic than that of the Nash Papyrus… I should prefer a date around 100 BC… what an absolutely incredible find! And there can happily not be the slightest doubt in the world about the genuineness."*

I have selected various sections of the extensive research of the amazing book *'The Dead Sea Scrolls Deception'* by Michael Baigent & Richard Leigh, published by Jonathan Cape and reprinted by permission of The Random House Group Limited, and I have included them in the next couple of pages to depict the unfolding of circumstances, and key players around the delay of publication (see copyright permissions page 362 for page numbers).

By the end of 1954, there were two entirely separate groups of Dead Sea Scroll materials and two different groups of experts working on them. In West Jerusalem, there were the Israelis working on scrolls in the institution that they specifically established to house the scrolls called 'The Shrine of the Book.' And in East Jerusalem, at the Rockefeller Museum, there was a team of international scholars operating under the direction of the Catholic Priest, Rolland De Vaux. We proceed with passages from the book *'Deception of the Dead Sea Scrolls'*, to further explain:

> *"At the heart of Christian belief, history and theology are inextricably entangled. Each suffuses the other. Yet each, if looked at separately, is a potential threat to the other. It is therefore easier and safer to blur the demarcation lines between them. Thus for the faithful, two quite distinct figures are fused into one. On the one hand, there is the historical individual, the man who according to most scholars, actually existed and walked the sands of Palestine two thousand years ago. On the other hand, there is the man-God of Christian religion, the divine personage deified, extolled and promulgated by Saint Paul."*

> *"Those responsible for developing the consensus view of Christianity have been able to exercise a monopoly over certain crucial sources, regulating the flow of information in a manner that enables its release to serve ones purpose… Those purveying the 'party line' can bolster authority they arrogate to themselves by claiming that they alone have seen the relevant sources, access to which is closed to*

all outsiders... Thus most outsiders, in the absence of any access to the relevant sources, have no choice but to accept the interpretations of the 'party line.' To challenge those interpretations is to find oneself labelled at best a crank; at worst a renegade, apostate or heretic. Few scholars have the combination of courage, standing and expertise to issue such a challenge and hold onto their reputations."

"A cache of some eight hundred scrolls had been discovered in Cave 4 in 1952. To deal with the sheer quantity of this material, an international committee of scholars had been formed, each member of which was assigned certain specific texts for study, interpretation, translation and eventual publication... The committee in reality functioned under the virtually supreme authority of Father De Vaux."

The international team was comprised of: Father Roland De Vaux, Professor Frank Cross, Monsignor Patrick Skehan, Father Jean Starcky, Dr Claus-Hunno Hunzinger, Father Maurice Baillet, Father Josef Milik and John M Allegro. De Vaux was the director of the Ecole Biblique in Jerusalem from 1945-1965. In 1953, he was also president of the board of trustees of the Rockefeller Museum. He was a devout Catholic, anti-Semite, and hostile to Israel as a political entity.

"In 1971 on Father De Vaux's death, an extraordinary situation developed. Although he did not in any legal sense own the scrolls, he nevertheless bequeathed his rights to them to one of his (Catholic) colleagues, Father Pierre Benoit... for Father Benoit to actually inherit De Vaux's rights, privileges, and prerogatives of access and control was as a scholarly procedure, unprecedented... with De Vaux's behaviour as a precedent, other members of his team followed suit... Thus the Catholic Scholars at the core of the international team maintained their monopoly and control and the consensus remained unchallenged. Not until 1987 on the death of Father Benoit were their methods to be contested."

"The most significant material – the material found in the veritable treasure trove of Cave 4 – continued to be withheld from both the public and the academic community… It only took 3 years for the draft translation of Nag Hammadi codices to be in circulation. And the entire Nag Hammadi corpus was in print within 11 years. It is now approaching 38 years since De Vaux's team began their work and they have so far produced… less than 25% of the material in their hands… very little of it is the material that really matters."

"One of the international team members, Catholic Professor Frank Cross, wrote in 1958, 'Most of the scroll fragments that at the teams hands had been identified – had indeed been identified in fact, by the summer of 1956'… And according to John Allegro (The ousted agnostic member of the International Team), *writing in 1964, assembly and identification of all Cave 4 material was 'nearly complete' by 1960/61."*

"The Qumran texts are generally classified under two rubrics. On the one hand, there is the corpus of early copies of biblical texts, some with slightly variant readings. These are referred to as 'biblical material.' On the other, there is a corpus of non-biblical material consisting, for the most part, of documents never seen before, which can be labelled 'sectarian material.' Most outsiders, needless to say, instinctively assume the 'biblical material' to be of greater interest and consequence – the simple word 'biblical' triggers associations in the mind which lead automatically to such a supposition… The biblical material is perfectly innocuous and uncontroversial, containing no revelations of any kind. It consists of little more than copies of books from the Old Testament, more or less the same as those

already in print or with only minor alterations. There is nothing radically new here. In reality, the most significant texts comprise not the 'biblical' but the 'sectarian' literature.

*It is these texts – rules, biblical commentaries, theological, astrological and messianic treatises – that pertain to the 'sect' alleged to have resided at Qumran and to their teachings. To label this material 'sectarian' is to effectively and skillfully to diffuse interest in it. Thus, it is portrayed as the idiosyncratic doctrine of a fringe and maverick 'cult', a small highly unrepresentative congregation divorced from, and wholly peripheral to, the supposed mainstream of Judaism and early Christianity, the phenomena to which it is most pertinent. Outsiders are thus manipulated into accepting the consensus – **that the Qumran community were so-called Essenes and the Essenes... have no real bearing on broader issues. The reality... is very different and the perfunctorily discussed 'sectarian' texts... contain material of an explosive nature indeed.**"*

On 24th December 1957, John Allegro wrote to Frank Cross, **"From the way the publication of the fragments is being planned the non-Catholic members of the team are being removed as quickly as possible... a dangerous situation is fast developing where the original idea of an international and interdenominational editing group is being bypassed."**

Allegro continued to bring attention of the public to the delays in the publication of the scrolls. In 1987, a year before his death, he declared his former colleagues, for years, **"have been sitting on the material which is not only of outstanding importance, but also quite the most religiously sensitive... There is no doubt... that the** *evidence from the scrolls undermines the uniqueness of the Christian as a sect... In fact we know damn all about the origins of Christianity. However, these documents do lift the curtain."*

One of the scrolls found has become known as the 'Copper Scroll' being entirely made from copper. Father De Vaux lied about the findings of the translation of the copper scroll saying it was merely a collection of buried treasure legends; *"A collection of traditions about buried treasure."* With no mention of it actually being a list of the sacked Temple of Jerusalem.

"If the treasure were real there were theological grounds for concern. De Vaux and the international team had been intent on depicting the Qumran community as an isolated enclave, having no connection with public events, political developments or the 'mainstream' of 1st century history. If the 'copper scroll' did indeed indicate where the actual contents of the Temple lay hidden, Qumran could no longer be so depicted. On the contrary, connections would become apparent between Qumran and the Temple, the centre and focus of all Judaic affairs. Qumran would no longer be a self-contained and insulated phenomenon, but an adjunct of something much broader – something that might encroach dangerously on the origins of Christianity. More disturbing still, if the copper scroll referred to a real treasure, it could only be a treasure removed from the Temple in the wake of the AD 66 revolt. This would upset the safe dating and chronology **(which they wanted to be before the time of Christ)** *which the international team had established for the entire corpus of scrolls."*

In reality, the international team seemed to recognise accountability to no one, except the 'Ecole Biblique.' And to whom was the 'Ecole Biblique' accountable? Well, they were accountable to The Vatican! The authors explain that in the wake of Renan's famous published works in 1860 called *'La Vie de Jesus'* (The Life of Jesus) portrayed Jesus as a mortal and non-divine personage. In Charles Darwin's *'Origin of the Species'* and his 1871 *'The Descent of Man'*, there followed a great age of agnosticism. Along with Thomas Huxley, Herbert Spencer, Schopenhauer, and Nietsche, they were all challenging conventional Christian ethical and theological assumptions.

> *"And to counter the depredation being wrought on scripture by Renan and German biblical scholarship, the Church began equipping her own cadres of meticulous scholars – elite intellectual 'shock troops' who were supposed to confront Catholicism's adversaries on their own ground. Thus arose the Catholic Modernist Movement... The Modernists were originally intended to deploy the rigour and precision of Germanic methodology not to challenge scripture, but to support it. A generation of clerical scholars was painstakingly trained and groomed to provide the Church with a kind of Academic Strike Force, a corps specifically formed to defend the Literal truth... To Rome's chagrin and mortification, however, the program backfired... critical scrutiny of the Bible revealed a multitude of inconsistencies, discrepancies and implications that were positively inimical to Roman dogma. The modernists quickly began to question and subvert what they were supposed to be defending."*

> *"In 1904 the Pope issued two encyclicals opposing all scholarship which questioned the origins and early history of Christianity. All Catholic teachers suspected of 'Modernist Tendencies' were summarily dismissed from their posts."*

> *"1905 (former Italian Senator) Antonio Fogazzaro wrote: 'The Catholic Church, calling herself the fountain of truth, today opposes the search after truth when her foundations, the sacred books, the formulae of her dogmas, her alleged*

infallibility, become objects of research. To us, this signifies that she no longer has faith in herself."

"*In July 1907 the Holy Office published a decree officially condemning Modernists' attempts to question Church doctrine, Papal Authority and the historical veracity of biblical texts... less than two months later in September, Modernism was effectively declared to be a heresy and the entire movement was formally banned.*"

Back in 1890, Father Lagrange established a biblical school in Jerusalem. It was initially called the 'Ecole Practique d'Etudes Bibliques' and created for it its own journal 'Revue Biblique.'

Lagrange, "*Sought to imbue the new institution with an attitude towards historical and archaeological research... according to Father Lagrange, 'The various stages in the religions of history of mankind form a recit, a history that is directly and supernaturally guided by God to lead to the ultimate and definitive stage – the Messianic age inaugurated by Jesus Christ... The Orientation was clear enough. To the extent that Lagrange employed modern methodology at all, he would employ it to prove what he had already, a-priori, decided to be true – that is, the literal veracity of scripture. And the definitive nature of the New Testament and the events it chronicled rendered it effectively off limits to scholarly scrutiny... The Pope himself recognised that Lagrange's faith was still intact, and that his heart, so far as the church was concerned, was in the right place... Lagrange was accordingly made a member of the Pontifical Biblical Commission* **(Modern day version of the Inquisition)** *and his journal 'Revue Biblique' became the commission's official organ... The Ecole Biblique, originally created as a forum for Modernism, had now become a bulwark against it.*"

"Among the original team of international scholars assembled by Father Rolland De Vaux in 1953 was the late Monsignor Patrick Skehan. Father Skehan was head of the department of Semetic and Egyptian languages and literatures at the Catholic University in Washington. He was also later a member of the Pontifical Biblical Commission. And in 1955, he was director of the Albright Institute in Jerusalem. In this capacity, he was instrumental in the political maneuverings which established Ecole Biblique's dominance of the Dead Sea Scroll research...

"Father Skehan was among the few scholars to be entrusted with access to the scrolls themselves. His attitudes offer some indication of the orientation of the Catholic Scholars associated with the Ecole Biblique.

Writing in 1966, Father Skehan declared that the Old Testament was not 'a thumbnail sketch of history and prehistory of the human race... in the fullness of time, Our Lord came; and a proper part of the duty of every Old Testament scholar is to trace in sacred history the development of the readiness to be aware of Christ when he would come.' In other words, the primary responsibility of every biblical scholar is to ferret out from the Old Testament supposed anticipations of accepted Christian Doctrine. Viewed in any other way, the Old Testament presumably has scant value and relevance... Ultimately the biblical scholars' work should be guided and determined by Church doctrine and be subject always to the sovereign right of the Holy Mother Church to witness definitively what is in fact concordant with the teaching she has received from Christ... The implications of this are staggering – All enquiry and investigation, regardless of what it might turn up or reveal MUST be subordinated and accommodated to the existing corpus of official Catholic Teaching. In other words, it must be edited or adjusted or distorted until it conforms to the requisite criteria. And what if something comes to light which can't be made thus to conform? From Father Skehan's statements, the answer to that question would seem clear. Anything that can't be subordinated or accommodated to existing doctrine MUST of necessity be Suppressed!"

"...For years, most independent scholars were quite unaware of any such divine mandate having been possessed by the Ecole Biblique, or of the Vatican's wishful thinking on the matter. On the contrary, the Ecole Biblique appeared to be an impartial scholarly institution dedicated, among other things, to collecting, collating, researching, translating and elucidating the Dead Sea Scrolls, not for suppressing them or transforming them into Christian propaganda."

It is clear, from reading the preceding passages, that the delays of over forty years of the publication of the findings of the Dead Sea scrolls was deliberate; in order to be able to preserve the foundations of the beginnings of early Christianity as being what the Church has always taught them to be. The reality, on the other hand, is much more explosive.

We have evidence that the Vatican has deliberately attempted to suppress archaeological evidence that reveals the true origins of Christianity – origins that are completely different to what they say they are. Now, is it really that hard to believe that the Bible has not been altered over time? That people have not attempted to misrepresent the words of the apostles and of Christ, thereby giving the Church supreme authority as the only official intermediary between man and God? And what would be the most damaging ideology that they would need to remove all trace of? Reincarnation. Christ himself spoke of reincarnation being a fact when he gave what has become known as the parable of the growing seed. When they were altering the Bible to align to their chosen narrative, they missed that one! I have included it in the appendix if you are unfamiliar with it at this present moment so that you may familiarise yourself with it.

Current Situation

As the Earth is transitioning into the Age of Aquarius people are not as easily duped. Consciousness is evolving – more and more people are rejecting the dogmatic interpretation of the Bible or the Koran. Old souls are returning to the Earth in droves and we are one family, the Family of Light. We do not accept the ludicrous interpretation of how man relates to God and God to man as presented in these dogmatic interpretations. The stirrings of our soul's knowing drives us in the pursuit of truth and this has 'the powers that be' scared and shaking in their boots, as their masquerading agenda is about to fall. Indeed, we have already won and we are just cleaning up.

So, the dark forces behind the curtain are pulling out all the stops and trying to get us to kneel to fear. They are fabricating wars and diseases and lying about the real reasons for them, attempting to control and chemically alter our food supply, they are poisoning our water with fluoride that is supposed to be good for our teeth but it atrophies our higher senses, calcifying our pineal gland. And yes, the secrets of the pineal gland have been known and guarded by the papacy for a thousand years or more. That is what the big pinecone in the gardens of the Vatican represents – pinecone – pineal gland – higher human potential!

The powers that be are poisoning the air with chem trails and trying whatever they can to shut down our awakening DNA by forced administering of vaccines such as the MMR triple shot (see appendix) which poisons our children and induces autism. They are trying to control us through fear and terrorism and attempting to microchip the population because they fear us awakening and they do not want to surrender their dark thrones on the earthly plane to the returning children of light!

Many helpful texts of esoteric nature have been eradicated from mainstream availability. This repression of information is very deliberate. Instead, there is this drip feeding happening, gradually dumbing down the population with preoccupation of new technologies, bodily appearances, sex, and a cultural numbing to violence and sexual depravity with pornography being made readily available to minors on handheld electronic devices.

We have children in their early teenage years thinking they are supposed to have sex early – with all of the cultural pressures and conditionings, and the Earth seems to be spiralling out of control. The worst thing is that we are letting this happen, because we are in – and remain blinded by – our **comfort induced comas.** We want the latest gadgets and the biggest houses, the big bank accounts and the millionaire lifestyles so we can indulge in our endless sexual lusts and bodily pleasures. We are very quickly demonising the Earth with our worship of a material god that we have built. We elevate our individual intelligence to the position of our own god and then we reject the idea of God altogether, cutting ourselves off from grace. The underlying reason for this is because, deeply, we are not free and the only way we can be free is through sexual expression. That is why it has become so extraordinarily important and prevalent in our culture. As Krishnamurti continues in his speech in 1970:

> *"So deeply you are not free and therefore you are only free in sexual expression. And that is why it has become so extraordinarily important. There you are full, you are free – though it has its own problems and its own neurotic attitudes and actions. So sex becomes important when everything else becomes unimportant. When life, the whole of it not just sex – life includes living, life includes what love is, what death is, the whole movement of living when that has no meaning, then the fragment which you call sex becomes extraordinarily important and vital! When you are not passionate about freedom inwardly then you are lustfully passionate about sex, that's all. And with that you associate love, pleasure. And with that you associate tenderness, gentleness – you may be sexually very tender, very kind, considerate – but outwardly you destroy, you kill everything around you, animals to eat, to hunt. So your love is based on pleasure and therefore is it love? Love*

is something, surely none of all this. Compassion means passion for everybody, not to your particular little desire."

There is a culture of YOLO being created now, a sense gratification culture under the cries of 'you only live once.' Well I'm sorry to burst your bubbles but you don't. You see, because knowledge is power, the true knowledge has been kept out of reach of the common folk. What people do not understand is that this hedonistic culture takes away our spiritual light. With every indulgence in drugs or alcohol or sex without love, we poison our bodies and we decimate the holy temple, closing ourselves off from the higher guidance. In addition, these behaviours tear holes in the energy field of our bodies and this creates a whole other world of problems – which we will discuss in Chapter 8 – *Exiting the Matrix, The Red Pill*.

From the above quote, under the chapter title, you can see how important it is for us to have the correct knowledge about where we actually come from. Because without this knowledge, we are living our lives based on a lie. One of the things about our origins that we need to understand is that there is no missing link in the chain of evolution. There is only a link that has been deliberately buried because it directly opposes the version of history that the establishment wants us to accept about who we are and where we come from!

When I tear the veil asunder in the next few pages, your conscious mind is going to want to scream 'bullshit' because of the damage of the indoctrination over the past fifty generations. So, you will need to have courage now. I ask you to empty the cup that is your mind – filled with preconceived notions and ideas about reality – and be open and curious about what else there is to learn in regard to where we truly come from.

What we need to understand is that in our history within the last 10,000 years there was another race of superior beings in existence on Earth – known as the Sons of God. Physically, they were different to us and they had some specific identifying features that provided the necessary biology for superior intelligence.

The Sons of God

In Genesis 6:1 in the Bible, we have the first man Adam being 'created' from approximately 4124 BC or approximately 6140 years ago, if we take each year as being one year in the biblical chronology. And around 4000 BC, we have the Sons of God already on the Earth and it was at this time that the Sons of God mixed their blood with the Daughters of Men and created a mixed Sons of God/Sons of Man race: *"the **sons of God** saw that the men's daughters were very beautiful, so they married those they chose."* This is also accounted for in the previous life account in Elisabeth Haich's book *'Initiation'*, with instruction from Ptah-Hotep as follows:

> *"Look my child for you to understand many of the things here on Earth, you must first know something about the Earth's development. Just like all celestial bodies in the universe and like all the forms of life on these celestial bodies, our Earth is subject to the laws of constant change. The divinely creative forces radiate from the eternal infinite original source and in constantly expanding waves they penetrate the plane of matter. That is to say, matter is formed of these forces. This process reaches its highest point in ultra-matter, then automatically reverses itself. The process of spiritualisation begins again, and the matter is transformed into force. But this process takes aeons of time! The changes are going on regularly but so subtly and slowly that they cannot be noticed or observed in the course of human life. On the other hand, some changes, which require thousands of years of slow and unnoticed preparation, occur suddenly and visibly when the proper time has come. Right now we are living in such a period of transition in which changes are noticeable. One of these phenomena is evident in the fact that various races of people with roundish skulls are led and governed by rulers who are spiritually greatly superior to them and who are even different from them physically. They have a more graceful figure and an elongated cranium.*

Once there lived on Earth a race of people very different from the races living today. They manifested completely the law of spirit and not the law of matter like the races of people living today. These people were conscious on the divine plane and manifested God here on Earth without any admixture of the self-seeking characteristics of the body. In their divine purity, these people deserved the name the 'Sons of God.'

Their entire life was based on spirituality, love, and selflessness. And they had no physical appetites, urges and passions to cast shadows on the spirit. The members of this high race possessed all the secrets of nature, and as they were perfectly acquainted with their own powers and kept these powers completely under the control of the spirit, they were also able to control and guide nature with all of its tremendous forces. Their knowledge was boundless… they knew all the laws of nature, the mysteries of matter, the powers of the mind, and the secrets of their own being. They also knew the secret connection with the transformation of force into matter and matter into force. They constructed devices and tools with which they could store up, set in motion, and utilise not only the forces of nature but also their own spiritual forces. They lived happily and peaceably as the dominant race in a great part of the Earth.

At that same time, however, other creatures similar to the Sons of God were also living on the Earth, but with much more material bodies and on a much lower plane of development. Obtuse in spirit, their consciousness was completely identified with the body. They lived in primeval jungles struggling with nature, each other, and animals. These creatures were the ancestors of present day man. The race of the sons of men you see in this country represent a cross between these two races.

As I said a moment ago, the law of constant motion and change is at work throughout the universe. The Earth is now going through a period in which the process of materialisation is advancing. This means that the divinely creative power is moving farther and farther on into matter, and the power on Earth is gradually falling more and more into the hands of ever more material races of people who were once under the guidance of higher, more spiritual races. Little by little the higher race is dying out. They are withdrawing from the plane of matter to the spiritual plane and they will leave humanity alone for a period of time – as time is reckoned on Earth, many, many thousands of years – so that humanity may, without visible guidance, climb upward with its own power.

And so it has come about that this animal-like material race of cave men is experimenting in accordance with divine laws, growing mightier and more powerful until the time comes for it to begin ruling the Earth. Before leaving the Earth, however, the higher race had to implant its special powers in the lower race. Through the operation of the laws of heredity, this will enable the lower race – after a long, long process of development – to arise out of matter again. This is why many sons of the divine race made the great sacrifice of begetting children with the daughters of primitive man. Through this first crossing of the races there have developed new individual types and gradually new races of people.

The divine power of the Sons of God and the mighty physical powers of the daughters of men have produced different types of descendants. On the one hand, physical, and on the other, spiritual giants. There have also been physical titans who, from their mother's ancestry, have inherited primitive, undeveloped brains. In these persons, the spiritual power of their fathers, working on the material plane, created tremendously strong bodies. With their gigantic physical strength, these individuals have overcome weaker persons and, because of the animal appetites of their nature, they have become tyrants greatly to be feared.

But there have also been spiritual titans who have manifested their inherited creative power through the higher centres of their brain, rather than on the lower physical plane. These spiritual giants were assigned the task of leading and teaching for a time, the lower, animal-like, body – conscious race of humans, as well as the hybrid race which later rose through the interbreeding I have already mentioned. These spiritual giants have the task of teaching the people of these two races wisdom, sciences and arts as the basis of a higher civilisation, and of giving them a good example of divinely universal love, unselfishness and spiritual greatness. That is why there are some countries today where despotism and tyranny are dominant while others are ruled with love and wisdom. This will gradually disappear, and humanity will know the great initiates and their secret sciences only through historical records, tradition and legend. However, even in the darkest period of human development, by virtue of the laws of heredity, there will be the possibility that a Son of God may be born in a human body in order to show humanity the way out of darkness and misery."

We need to understand then, at that time, there were **two very different species on Earth.** The Sons of God were a different species to the Sons of Men. The Sons of God were the race of demigods of the land of Egypt prior to the 1st Egyptian Dynasty that were conscious on the divine plane, and they were called the Khemitians and the land was known as the land of Khem.

All over the world there is evidence of a lost ancient technology, and we need to understand that this technology belonged to beings that were a little different to us. The Sons of God or the Khemitians – had elongated heads, which gave them vast powers of intellect and allowed them to consciously manifest God on Earth in their person – as they were on the Earth from the time of the last Satya Yuga (approx. 13000 BC) a time characterised by people where:

> *"The mental virtue... then in its fourth stage and completes its full development... can comprehend all, even God the spirit beyond this visible world."*

In an article by April Holloway on www.ancient-origins.net, she mentions that in 1928, Peruvian Archaeologist Julio Tello discovered a massive graveyard in Paracas on the south coast of Peru. The graveyard contained more than 300 elongated skulls believed to date back around 3,000 years. In her article, April Holloway says that one of the ways elongated skulls can be explained is by deliberate deforming of the skull over a long period of time with the skull being bound. However, and this is important, this process **does not alter the volume, weight or other features that are characteristic of a regular human skull:**

> *"The Paracas skulls, however, are different. The cranial volume is up to 25 percent larger and 60 percent heavier than conventional human skulls, meaning they could not have been intentionally deformed through head binding/flattening. They also contain only one parietal plate, rather than two. The fact that the skulls' features are not the result of cranial deformation means that the cause of the elongation is a mystery, and has been for decades."*

The mystery is solved now. These are skulls of the 'Sons of God', the giants of intellect from Ancient Egypt and the origins of the oldest surviving constructions in South America that predate Inca and Olmec. To provide further evidence of this; an email received by Brian Foerster from a geneticist, who for privacy reasons can only be identified as 'Vladamir', reports that in preliminary DNA tests on one of the Paracas Skulls, the genetic analysis of the skull shows:

"It had mtDNA (mitochondrial DNA) **with mutations unknown in any human, primate, or animal known so far.** *But a few fragments I was able to sequence from this sample indicate that if these mutations will hold we are dealing with a new human-like creature, very distant from Homo Sapiens, Neanderthals and Denisovans."*

Just take a look at some examples of these Paracas Skulls in the next pictures, Figure 21, and see how the volume is far too great for a regular human skull? This could not be achieved through head binding.

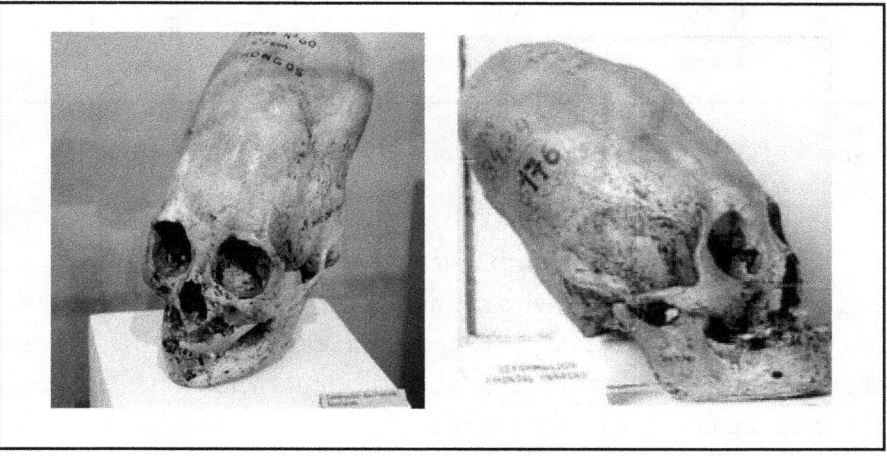

Figure 21: image courtesy of Brien Foerster: https://hiddenincatours.com/global-phenomenon-of-elongated-skulls/

You will notice the caption to Figure 21 says global phenomenon. That is because wherever there are traces of ancient high civilisation all over the world, these are the feats of the elongated skull race of beings, known in the hidden histories as the Sons of God. Figure 22 (next page) shows the Sons of God or Khemitian's – Akhenaton, his wife Nefertiti, and their children – with their elongated heads. An ancient depiction of their likeness which survives on the walls of the Egyptian temples:

Figure 22: Elongated heads depicted on ancient Egyptian temple. Association Source: N. S. Elijah.

Look at the children in the picture, the shapes of their heads are clearly visible and that is why the adults are wearing those elongated large hats. Underneath those hats are the elongated skulls that give them a greater intellect! And if you still doubt the elongated heads depicted under the hats, then look at Figure 23a (next page), an image of a statue discovered in Tel-el Amarna which was found with the more well-known bust of Nefertiti, Figure 23b (next page), that is on display in the Berlin Museum. Reproduced with permission of Light Technology Publishing from D. Melchizedek, *'The Ancient Secret of the Flower of Life – Vol. 1'*. (Please forgive the quality of these two images.)

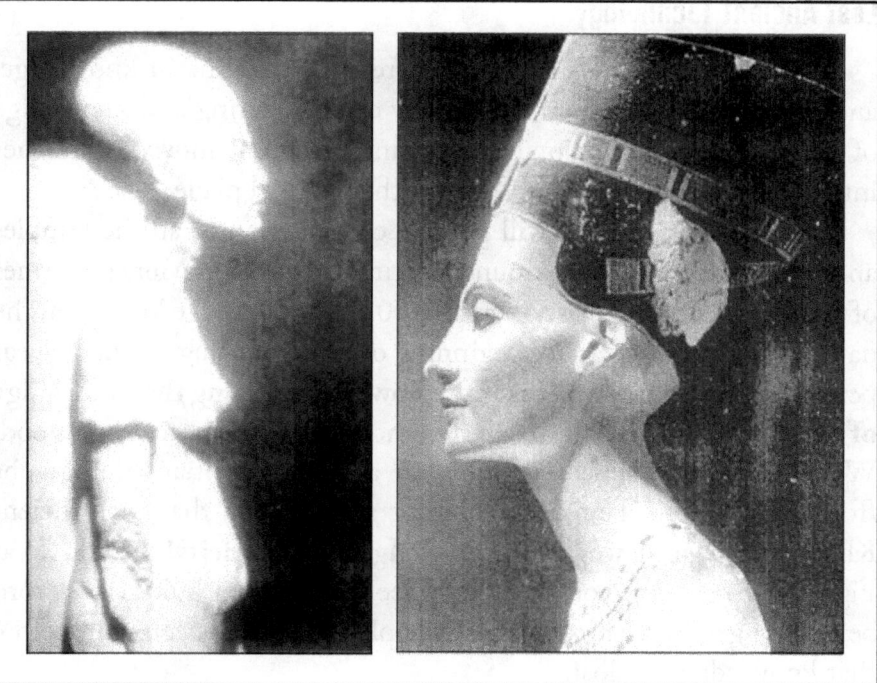

Figure 23: Figure 23a – (left) little known Statue of Nefertiti not wearing a hat, found at the same time in the same ruins as the more well-known bust of Nefertiti Figure 23b -(right), now in the Berlin Museum. Source: Figures 5.12 and 5.13 from D. Melchizedek – Ancient Secrets of the Flower of Life Vol – 1.

The cranial deformation practices of the native tribes of South America and Africa were developed because they were trying to mimic or emulate the giants of stature and intellect that came before them, the Sons of God that passed on such immense sidereal knowledge to them, such as the knowledge of the star Sirius being a binary star system; being passed on to the Dogon tribe for example.

Lost Ancient Technology

We need to understand that there was a decline in knowledge, and therefore, a decline in complexity of engineering and knowledge of methods of construction as the divine radiations moved on further into matter and the Sons of God left the physical plane.

Modern Egyptology will put the construction of all the temples and pyramids in Egypt to around the time of Pharaoh Menes/Narmer of the so-called 1st Dynasty – circa 3100 BC or later. We know that the date of 3100 BC is near the beginning of Dwapara Yuga, a 2,600-year period in which **mankind loses the power of grasping the knowledge of electricities and their attributes** and before the cataclysmic flood! We also have evidence surviving in ancient Egyptian hieroglyphs from the Ancient Temple of Hathor at Dendera, that the Ancient Khemitians **had a working knowledge of electricity!** Just look at Figure 24 (below) – you can visibly see a giant light bulb with a cord being plugged into a box, so these temples must have been built before that knowledge was lost.

Figure 24: Temple of Hathor at Dendera. Ancient image depicting a working knowledge of electricity. Source and Copyright: Mick Palarczyk. (reproduced with full permission).

As has been observed in this discourse, the further back in time, before 3100 BC, the more incredible are the examples of knowledge and feats of architecture and construction. In one of Brien Foerster's documentaries he mentioned that the book '*Giza Power Plant*', by engineer and author Christopher Dunn, puts forward a very strong case that the Great Pyramid was actually a power plant that generated electricity by splitting the hydrogen from the oxygen in the water molecule. I can tell you that, but it is only part of the Great Pyramid's purpose.

The Great Pyramid of Egypt is generally attributed to Pharaoh Khufu by conventional Egyptologists, all because they found a small cartouche with Khufus name on it. Now there is no other writing or hieroglyphics of any kind anywhere else in the structure and the cartouche can be explained by one of two reasons: either it is an academic forgery to deliberately misinform the people of its real purpose and ancient beginning or it was put there by Khufu himself as he wanted to claim construction of it himself as he did not want to be made to look small by the complexity of this accomplishment. Most likely, I think it is an academic forgery trying to uphold the narrative of the 'fake history' the powers that be wanted to plant into the consciousness of humanity in order to keep them controlled.

In Chapter 6, I will further explore the true purpose of the Great Pyramid in ancient Egypt on the Giza Plateau. But for now, suffice it to say that it was built before the beginning of the Satya Yuga approximately 13000 BC because its true function requires **full intellectual power to grasp spiritual knowledge!**

Granite has a hardness of around seven on the Mohs scale. Since 1812, we have used this scale to measure the hardness of one mineral in comparison to another. This is determined by the ability of one mineral to scratch other minerals. The image of the Mohs scale on the next page is modelled from the Indiana Geological Survey. The Mohs scale is as follows:

SACRED ALIGNMENT

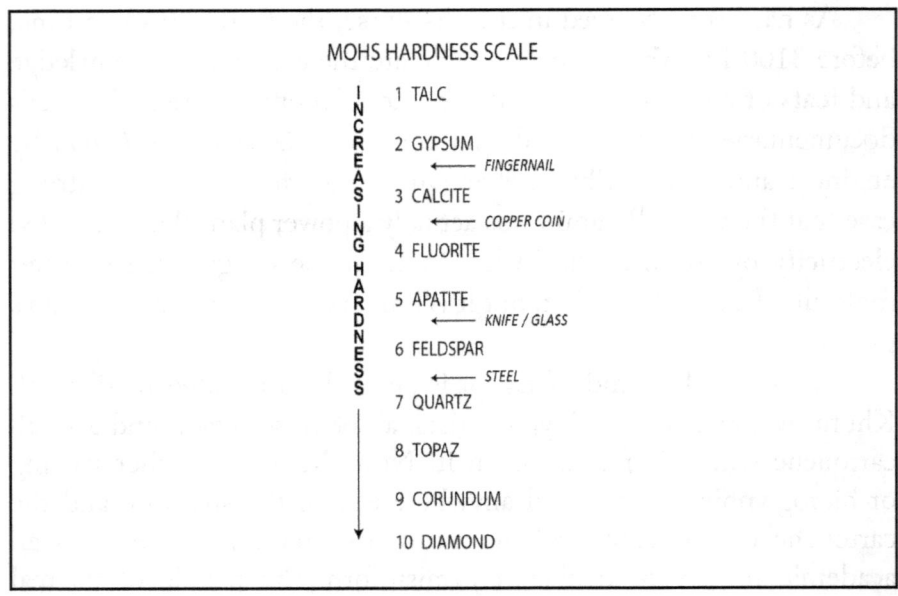

Figure 25: Mohs Hardness Scale, modelled from the Indiana Geological Survey.

In order to measure the hardness of granite we need to understand that granite is composed of multiple minerals. Typically quartz, feldspar and mica. However the hardness of granite is greater than many other rock types because of the interlocking mineral structure that causes the crystals to be interlocked tightly. And as such cannot be etched or inscribed by anything other than ruby, emerald (corundum) or diamond.

This picture to follow, Figure 26, is of the Temple of Osiris known as 'The Osirian', is found at the rear of the temple of Seti in Abydos Egypt. Of interesting note is the dovetail joints used in the granite blocks that weigh nearly 100 tonnes each. I have circled this in the picture over the page. In order to build this, these blocks would need to first have the dovetail grooves cut into the base and then they would have to be slid in place from the front and slid back to interlock. The stones could not be directly lowered with this type of dovetail joinery.

Figure 26: Temple of Osiris – Abydos Egypt. Image courtesy of Brien Forster.

The dovetail grooves cut into the base of the granite megaliths would have been engineered with a cutting technology and material greater than seven on the Mohs scale. Therefore, the only logical conclusion is that this example of lost ancient technology that exists at the Temple of Osiris, that is conservatively 6,000 years old, was done with the use of electricity and most likely diamond cut or machined. There is no way that stone hammers and copper chisels with a hardness of four on the Mohs scale could have even crudely shaped the stone, let alone been employed to achieve this level of precision!

The level of precision, which shows evidence of being electrically diamond cut into the granite or machined some 6,000 years ago, is something that defies our imagination, based on the current accepted version of our history, and yet the proof is there for all who care to not remain closed minded. The truth is that our real history is very different to the one that 'the powers that be' would like us to swallow and have been shoving down our collective throats for two thousand years. However, even the concept of electric diamond drilling is dwarfed in comparison to the evidence of a further, more advanced lost technology, when we look at the remaining traces of methods used to extract the unfinished obelisk at Aswan.

The next picture, Figure 27 (below), is a close-up of the unfinished obelisk at Aswan. You can clearly see the remaining evidence of the use of a lost technology that seems to have scooped out the stone like butter! This of course sounds ridiculous but if you look at the picture it is clearly evident that some kind of sonic wave technology was used to alter the molecular structure of the stone to extract it.

Now, as Brien Foerster explains in one of his documentaries, at this site 'the powers that be' have placed all these little stone diorite pounders which fit in the palm of the hand – and we are supposed to believe that the ancient Egyptians used these to cut the obelisk out of the ground. But just look at the picture and the effect on the stone. There is no way that primitive methods were used in extracting these obelisks from the bedrock. Some kind of cataclysmic event must have transpired to have them not finish the task.

The ancient Khemitian's were in possession of knowledge of not only remarkable technologies many thousands of years before the First Dynasty of Pharaoh Menes, but also were in possession of a remarkable and complete knowledge of **who man was, where he came from and**

Figure 27: Close-up of technology used at unfinished obelisk at Aswan. Image courtesy of Brien Foerster.

what he was capable of becoming. And the power of this knowledge was deliberately hidden from the populace of our modern day in order for 'the powers that be' to maintain their grip of control.

> *"The control of information is something the elite always does, particularly in a despotic form of government. Information, knowledge, is power. If you can control information, you can control people."*
>
> — Tom Clancy

The Palette of Narmer

Armed with a better understanding of our real history, let us look at just one example that I found where we can achieve better clarity of meaning. Remember how in Chapter 2 we mentioned the first Egyptian King Narmer, whom scholars think is the same person as Menes, and who lived circa 3100 BC? Well the consensus view is that the following picture of an artefact represents King Narmer uniting Lower and Upper Egypt circa 3150 BC. It is called 'The Palette of Narmer' and it is on display at the Museum of Cairo in Egypt.

Figure 28: Palette of King Narmer, from Hierakonpolis, Egypt, Predynastic, c. 3000-2920 B.C.E. (apparently), slate, 2' 1" high (Egyptian Museum, Cairo. Source: This is a faithful photographic reproduction of a two-dimensional, public domain work of art).

Scholars have looked at the headless bodies in the right-hand image and immediately assumed 'slaughter.' Then they have looked at the object being held in the king's hand resembling a mace and have immediately assumed 'mace', and assigned the entire interpretation of the depicted scenes to mean 'military conquest.' They have looked at the two figures at the bottom of the left-hand picture and immediately assumed 'two dead men', following the trend of the 'headless bodies' meaning 'slaughter.'

Then continuing with this theme, they assume that the bull on the right-hand side image represents 'the king in the act of military conquest killing a man' having crashed through a wall. Then they have looked at the differences of the appearances of the crowns being worn by the king and assumed 'unification of Lower and Upper Egypt.' They have no idea what the other aspects mean, and that is because the context they are interpreting the imagery in is completely wrong! This is what Charles T Munger refers to as being 'Extreme and counterproductive psychological ignorance.'

> *"If an academic maintains in place an ignorance that can be easily removed with a little work the conduct of the academic amounts to treachery"*
>
> *- Samuel Johnson*

This palette is depicting a time significantly earlier than 3100 BC and the images give us clues. Can you guess? Okay, let's work through this – firstly – who holds a mace near the top? If, as scholars say, this scene represents King Narmer about to cave a poor conquered person's skull in with a mace, it seems unusual to have the king hold the 'mace' so close to the top, and not use what appears to be the grip on the handle, right? Scholars have looked at the headless bodies and then looked at the mace-like object in the hand of the king and assumed – 'Mace' and 'military conquest.'

But they are wrong. **It is actually a scene depicting a prophecy of the changes of the Earth and the involution of the consciousness of man in the current Adamic race.** And now I will explain why. What is the astrological sign for Gemini? The twins, right? Look closely at the bottom of the left-hand photo – how much alike would you say those two figures are? In the language of symbolism in some respects they are a mirror image of each other – one light, one dark – one is one polarity and the other is the opposite (represented by opposite hands lowered and raised). And what is important is that they are facing us. This means that the scene taking place above is taking place during the age of Gemini.

Now, what astrological sign follows on from Gemini in the precession of the equinoxes? You guessed it… Taurus. And Taurus is represented by a Bull. So, on the right-hand image you have a clear indication of when the Earth is moving from the Age of Gemini (represented by only one of the twins facing away from us and the other has moved out of view – signifying that a significant passage of time of Gemini has passed) into the astrological sign of Taurus circa 6,000 years ago. It is not a stone wall that the Bull is crashing through but rather a field of stars. This clearly indicates that the scene being depicted on this side of the palette is at a time when the Earth is moving into the constellation of Taurus – and thus, the two sides represents two different time periods and two different kings!

With this clearly established we can proceed. The mace is not a mace but a device of high technology that is used by the initiated to channel divine energy. The king is not holding a tuft of hair in preparation to bash in the person's skull, but rather the king is about to perform an act of bestowal of some kind of spiritual initiation on man. The man in supplication is on his knees ready to receive. And we have further evidence that this is the true meaning as we look at the breath of life being given from 'Horus' at the 7th Octave of vibration. There are six octaves which Horus is standing on, and then the seventh is represented by the human face (the breath of life being pulled from the nostrils by Horus). Further, above the man to the left of the king, you will find a seven-sided star or seven-petalled flower (7th Octave of vibration – divine radiation) during the age of Gemini, which begins circa 6500 BC or 8,500 years ago.

On the right-hand image, we note that the petals of the flower or sides of the star reduce to six, symbolising the beginning of the involution of consciousness and of divine vibrations moving further on into matter. This is backed up by the animals – whether lions or dogs – symbolising the animal nature of man being harder to control. What the scholars think are decapitated bodies as a result of a military campaign actually represent the 'passage of time mankind loses his divine state of consciousness' – loses his head – as the powers of intellect devolve from the Treta Yuga to the Dwapara Yuga.

Further, the figures at the top of the palette are what the Egyptologists call the cow god, Hathor. We know from Ptah-Hotep's instruction that the initiates used the symbol of the bull to represent the divine radiations when the Earth was moving into the age of Taurus. And the horns on the top of the Hathor simply represent initiated beings at a time when the Earth was moving into the sign of Taurus. Remember we have Figure 24, found in the Temple of Hathor, depicting a working knowledge of electricity, and we know from the studies of the Yugas that this was a time prior to the deluge. If you research a race of beings known as the Hathor's you will find some beautiful teachings on the use of sonic vibration for healing. The description to Figure 28 should more accurately read:

Misinterpreted by scholars. Depicts a prophecy for involution of human consciousness from the Age of Gemini through to the Age of Taurus. The beginnings of the 12,900-year plan for the current Adamic race and why the Bible and Qur'an put creation at 6,000 years ago. Source: This is a faithful photographic reproduction of a two-dimensional, public domain work of art.

This is just one artefact that I have chosen to decipher for you, to better show how the history that we are told is ours is a complete fabrication to keep us limited and controlled and will not have us question our education or our origins.

Chapter 4

THE LOST BOOKS OF THOTH

*"Deep are the mysteries around thee, hidden the secrets of Old.
Search through the KEYS of my WISDOM.
Surely shall ye find the way."*

– Emerald Tablets of Thoth

The Lost Book of Thoth – Arcane Knowledge

In order to further validate the truth of the secret doctrine, the tenets on which it is built and the true meaning of the words of Jesus Christ, I will reveal four of the twenty-two symbols from the Lost Books of Thoth. The first three now and the last near the end of this discourse. What is the 'Book of Thoth'? It is perhaps the most heavily guarded and highly sought-after source of knowledge and wisdom from the ancient world. Manly P. Hall in 'The Secret Teachings of All Ages', 1928 writes:

> *"While Hermes still walked the earth with men, he entrusted to his chosen successors the sacred "Book of Thoth." This work contained the secret processes by which the regeneration of humanity was to be accomplished and served as the key to*

his other writings. Nothing definite is known concerning the contents of the "Book of Thoth" other than its pages were covered with strange hieroglyphic figures and symbols, which gave to those acquainted with their use unlimited power over the spirits of the air and the subterranean divinities. When certain areas of the brain are stimulated by the secret processes of the mysteries, the consciousness of man is extended and he is permitted to behold the Immortals and enter into the presence of the Superior Gods. The Book of Thoth described the method whereby this stimulation was accomplished. In truth, therefore it was the "Key to Immortality."

According to legend, the 'Book of Thoth was kept in a golden box in the inner sanctuary of the temple. There was but one key and this was in the possession of the "Master of the Mysteries," the highest initiate of the Hermetic Arcanum. He alone knew what was written in the secret book. The Book of Thoth was lost to the ancient world with the decay of the mysteries, but its faithful initiates carried it sealed in the sacred casket into another land. The book is still in existence and continues to lead the disciples of this age into the presence of the Immortals. No other information can be given to the world concerning it now, but the apostolic succession from the first hierophant initiated by Hermes himself remains unbroken to this day, and those who are peculiarly fitted to serve the Immortals may discover this priceless document if they will search sincerely and tirelessly for it.

It has been asserted that the Book of Thoth is, in reality, the Mysterious Tarot of the Bohemians – a strange emblematic book of seventy-eight leaves which has been in the possession of the gypsies since the time when they were driven from their ancient temple, the Serapeum (according to the secret histories the gypsies were originally Egyptian priests). There are now in the world several secret schools privileged to initiate candidates into the mysteries, but in nearly every instance they lighted their altar fires from the flaming torch of Hermes. Hermes in his Book of Thoth revealed to all mankind the "One Way" and for ages the wise of every nation and every faith have reached immortality by "the way" established by Hermes in the midst of darkness for the redemption of humankind."

– Manly P Hall, The Secret teachings of All Ages, 1928.

Please take a moment now to take in exactly where you are. Ninety years on from when these words of Manly P Hall were written in 1928, a little more information of the Lost Books of Thoth can now be given!

Take a couple of nice relaxed deep breaths and allow a sense of immense gratitude to well up from the depths of your heart for the next step on your journey. For if you have been led to this book and made it this far, then it is safe to say that you have been seeking for some time and your mind is open and ready to receive the light of knowledge:

"Ask, and it will be given you; search and you will find; knock, and the door will be opened for you. For everyone who asks receives, and everyone who searches finds and for everyone who knocks, the door will be opened."
– Matthew 7.7

Find that place of gratitude in your heart, for I will share with you now some of the means of instruction from hierophant to initiate in the days of the Ancient Egyptian mysteries.

Do you understand the gravity of this moment? How many souls have searched for this wisdom throughout history and died broken and empty-handed? Indeed, it is a privilege to be able to receive this sacred wisdom. Many thousands of years ago, candidates for initiation into the entirety of this knowledge were tested very literally on pain of death if they did not display the necessary qualities to escape it.

As we are now transitioning into the Age of Aquarius, the sign of the water bearer, it is imperative that the *'waters of life'* be given to people, to quench their ancient spiritual thirst that neither dogmatic adherence to religious doctrine and tradition or the investigations of science have yet been able to fully accomplish.

So please sink into a state of reverence now, close your eyes, take a couple of deep breaths and centre yourself. And when you feel ready, awaken your eyes:

Welcome to the entrance of the sacred temple, please remember to take off your shoes and wash your feet. Do not dirty the steps! Here follows some of the undiluted teachings from the Ancient Mystery School of Ancient Egypt and a translated page of the highly sought after and ever elusive Arcane Book of Thoth. Indeed, the knowledge does survive in the Major Arcana of the Tarot of the Bohemians. However, the book is useless unless you have the Egyptian Mysteries* key to accurately decipher the symbolism in which it has been styled. The first symbol of the Major Arcana in the Tarot, **The Magician, is unlocked for you now** in Figure 29.

* See Bibliography

Figure 29: The ancient symbol of The Magician tarot card, Rider Waite Tarot Deck.

"The high priest addressed him as follows: "These pictures contain, in symbolic form, everything we know. Everything the gods wished to reveal, everything we mortals can understand, is contained in them.

"These pictures, which we call the Book of Thoth and which reflect a summary of the forty books of Thoth, God of

Wisdom, tell of the essence of the God we serve, of the world and its creation and the path humanity will follow. In this way they reveal the natural laws to which art, society, science and the entire universe are subject.

They contain infinitely more than you can imagine at this time. However, I will give you a key to enable you to read this book. In future you will spend many hours here to gain knowledge and insight from these symbols. At the appropriate time I will also tell you more about the relationship between these paintings. However, today I merely want you to realise that you can read about yourself in this wonderful book. Your entire development – in all your material lives and through countless centuries which you spent in the spiritual realms – can be found here, for you came from the lap of the Higher Being and you will return there.

Thought is the beginning of all things; everything was created from Divine Thought, observe the first Symbol: it represents the greatest God, the infinite, the eternal, unnamable, absolute active, never totally understood. It is not a representation of Osiris but a symbolic revelation of his essence.

You see a man in the raiment of a magician who knows and controls the eternal laws of nature, one who knows. Look at the position of his hands: He commands in heaven and makes things real on Earth. Thus he is a summary of the great principle, of the creator, by whom all things were created and to whom all things will return, whose hand reaches everywhere, whose eyes see everything, who is omnipotent and omnipresent. He is also the Lawgiver who in his wisdom, made the laws which allowed the creation to take place and continue. Mankind, the elements and natural forces, all life and all death are ruled by him. In front of him on the table there are four symbols: A staff, a goblet, a sword and a coin. They are symbols with many meanings. For today it will suffice if I tell you that they represent the human body and human society in various images.

"The staff represents the brain, which produces thoughts; the goblet stands for the breathing breast which allows us to live; the sword, which can change the circumstances of life, points to the stomach which digests the food that is eaten. The coin, the money that passes from hand to hand, represents the sexual organs and the creation of new generations.

At the social level, the staff represents those who testify to society – the poets, the artists, the inventors. The goblets show us the preservers – judges, scholars and collectors. The swords reveal those who reorganise, who are eager to fight, who strive for change and who change the forms and values of society. The coins represent the pregnant and productive members of society – the people who have many children and from which higher classes develop. Osiris is the Great One, who produces infinite series of numbers but is not descended from anyone himself. You come from him: Your spirit, the core of your personality is a spark of the primeval fire, a drop of the primordial sea and it is his will that you go through life along the great curve, up and down, back to him in a large circle – a snake eating its own tail.

Your spirit has a divine origin and has all the characteristics of the higher being, just as a drop has all the characteristics of the primordial sea surrounding the Earth. But your spirit is not yet active, it sleeps while you must develop it into a ruler. It is your body and its needs, and not the soul and its longings that must be the

> *decisive factor for you. Your spirit is that which makes you a Child of God.*
>
> *There is only one Creator and his children are a part of him. They are the 'Conscious', therefore listen: Men are Immortal Gods and Gods were immortal men. That is the goal to which you must aspire from this day forth. Now go in peace and return tomorrow morning early."*

Do you feel the simple truth of this? Has this recognition caused a remembrance? Are you feeling deep emotion in your heart? Has the weight you have been carrying for all this time on your shoulders, like Atlas carrying the world, been lightened now? Can you see more clearly? You should take a moment to process this and read it again, perhaps take the time to nurture yourself as you begin to remember. Maybe even take a day, to STOP and sit with this sacred revelation – reflect on what this means to your life and current trajectory. Because this book will reveal sacred knowledge that is very powerful and will have very powerful effects on your consciousness, it is okay to take it slow – and indeed preferable.

I hope you took my advice and took some time to meditate and reflect on the first unveiled symbol of the Lost Book of Thoth. Do you wish to know more? Then read on. You see, because we are consciousness, we must be vigilant with the children of our mind – our thoughts. Because we are creator beings, we must understand that we create our realities and we have the potential to be so much more than what we are traditionally taught.

Lost Book of Thoth – Arcane Symbol Two

In order to further demonstrate this gradation of consciousness within man (the 7 octaves of vibration) and also to further illustrate man's potential, with the Egyptian Mysteries* key, I will **reveal now the 2nd chosen Arcane symbol of the Lost Book of Thoth.** Again, please find that place of utter gratitude for being privileged to receive this ancient instruction that will serve to help you eliminate suffering. **It is the Major Arcana Tarot Card marked IV – The Emperor.** In its original form it was known as 'The Pharaoh' meaning 'Great House.' However, over time, it evolved into 'The Emperor.' You will note some of the primary symbolism remains preserved, and other symbolism has slightly changed, i.e. – the second sceptre is now represented as the golden orb in his left hand.

Figure 30: Major Arcana tarot card IV: The Emperor/ Pharaoh (in its original form). Rider Waite Tarot deck.

"On the fourth day, the high priest spoke these words, 'You are now standing my son, before a mural known as The Pharaoh. In the first mural, you saw the creative deity commanding the elements, and now, in this fourth one, you see the god who governs creation – the cube – by means of fixed laws.

"Laws govern the universe. No one can escape these laws. The two crowns on the head of The Pharaoh, and the two scepters in his hands, reveal that with these laws he governs both the world that is visible and those that are still invisible to us.

The universe which he governs is represented by a cube or die, for the law of fours is the basic law of creation; everything depends on the fourfold Law. The Deity is a trinity: Osiris, Isis, & Horus **(Father, Son, and Holy Spirit)**. *The eternal primeval beginning, the active principle, breaks away part of its self; the passive principle receives this part. In this way, a relationship is created between these two principles. The third, which develops from this, is not only the result but also the connection. That is why deity is always represented by a triangle.*

However if this deity, existing at a spiritual level, wishes to create a universe with thousands of solar systems and millions of stars, then the visible world is a fourth part. If a straight line is added to an opening triangle this forms a square.

And this mysterious law of fours does seem to dominate everywhere. There are four points of the compass: north, south, east and west; the universe consists of four elements; there are four seasons and the day is divided into four parts. We go from the cradle to the grave in four stages: child, youth, adult, greybeard. And you are composed of four parts, if you consider yourself carefully – body, life, spirit, and self... You have a material body and a life that shines softly for a seer, which penetrates and glows around the material body. After death these bodies dissolve in the impurities from which they were created.

For death is merely a loosening of the ties which bind together the four parts of which we are made up. Your spiritual body, the third part, which consists of a very fine material to which the impurities of the material body adheres, leaves a visible shell after death, at the same time as the self, the divine spark, the fourth part, passes through the realms of shadows and death. As you see the number four is a dominant factor also regarding the way in which we are composed.

Last of all, we will observe the position of The Pharaoh, The Law, The Will. It reveals yet another great truth expressed symbolically: the deity rules over 'his' creation. Note the position of the arms – together with the head they form a triangle, and the legs crossed together form a square. This can only be interpreted in one way: the deity rules over the universe. When you observe the universe and wish to understand more of the essence of God, you must first learn the laws with which deity rules over the universe. The Laws of God are the first thing the seeker will find on his way to truth. Now, go in peace and let this resonate in you."

* See Bibliography

Figure 31: Major Arcana tarot card IV: The Emperor with superimposed indication of hidden symbolism of deity ruling over his creation. Source and Copyright: N. S. Elijah 2016.

Which of course takes us back to the Seven Principles of Hermetic Philosophy. Indeed the 'laws of God with which deity rules over the universe', THE ALL In All and All in THE ALL and **THE ALL that is in you.** The Seven Principles:

I. The Principle of Mentalism **(everything is consciousness – the unified field)** [ORDER]

II. The Principle of Correspondence (COMPENSATION)

III. The Principle of Vibration (VIBRATION)

IV. The Principle of Polarity (POLARITY)

V. The Principle of Rhythm (CYCLES)

VI. The Principle of Cause and Effect (CAUSE AND EFFECT)

VII. The Principle of Gender (BALANCE)

And magically: 3 (sides of the triangle) + 4 (sides of the square) = 7, and the Seven Octaves of Vibration.

I hope that you are coming to realise that we are much more than the crude matter of our bodies. Who we are extends far beyond the confines of our physical body. We are consciousness. We are energy. And ultimately, we have the master controls of our vibrational frequency. Low emotions of guilt, blame, fear, anger, and shame result in the lowering of our vibrational frequency. High emotions of bliss, joy, contentment, happiness, and even unconditional love result in the heightening of our vibrational frequency. **In this understanding you will begin to see the subtlety of the mechanism of slavery inherent in the dogmatic interpretation, specifically of the Christian religion** – with all the emphasis on guilt and sin and repression which ensures your frequency is kept low, low, low!

For they, the leaders of the Church, prescribed a self-serving meaning to the words of our elder brother Christ, then glorified the man as the only divine son, different to you all, and twisted the meaning to evince an insidious design of control of all of you – by having you believe you were born in sin and live in the lowest vibration of guilt and shame and need to be saved.

Every thought and emotion we have, we hold in our auras (our energetic field – aura is Greek for light) and everywhere we go we imprint this on reality. It is like a pilot wave that is sent out that tells/instructs/programs the environment how to respond to you, and that then becomes your individual experience.

The great burden of humanity is that, generally, as a collective we hold deep beliefs that we are not good enough, that we are not enough, that we are undeserving. For many of you that are reading these words, these deep feelings are likely to be because you have been killed repeatedly for your cosmic knowledge and beliefs and attempts to live life differently to how 'the powers that be' wanted you to. And this soul memory penetrates your core and remains in your super-conscious mind, and manifests on this earthly plane as a deep fear of not being good enough!

Because we were made in the image of God – i.e. we are creator beings, we are so powerful – what happens is that our realities match the frequency at which we are vibrating. Einstein knew this when he said, "*It is a matter of physics. Match the vibration of what it is you wish to experience and you will attract it to yourself.*" So, pay attention – as the Buddha was purported as saying in the Dhammapada, "*Frown at the world and it will frown back at you, smile at it and it will smile with you.*"

So, turn off your TV and do not listen to the bullshit of fear and war. The media is controlled by those that are *very* aware of these universal laws and bend them to their own design, to keep the marvellous power of minds trapped in a fear loop, which creates what it collectively fears! It is this that, unchecked, perpetuates the tightening of the reins of control and a manufactured glamour that bewitches us into believing that the universal laws do not exist!

Lost Book of Thoth Symbol Three

You must understand that all of your religious dogma is deliberately misrepresented in order to control through fear. To provide this understanding I will now reveal to you another *Egyptian Mysteries** Sacred Arcane symbol of the Lost Books of Thoth, so again please take the time now to prepare a state of gratitude in your hearts for the imparting of this sacred knowledge: It is the Major Arcana Card number 7 "The Chariot" and it is unlocked for you now. Please turn over the page.

* See Bibliography

Figure 32: Major Arcana tarot card VII – The Chariot. Rider Waite Tarot deck.

"On the seventh day the High Priest spoke thus: The first thing we mortals will notice about this god, who treads such high levels that he is impenetrable and inaccessible to most people, is the existence of certain laws. However, laws evoke authority so that the divine plan can be achieved.

My son, you have been called to perfection in the divine plan. This means not only that you must destroy all that is bad and unworthy in yourself, and that you must develop higher and more refined skills, but also that you should seek insight into the broader lines of God's policy. Let us now take a closer look at today's mural. It can lead to all sorts of conclusions which provide a wealth of food for thought.

The Chariot of Osiris represents the realisation of the great plan. It shows a man standing up and driving a chariot. The crown on his head and the scepter in his hand reveal a relationship with the Pharaoh. Symbol 1 showed God, who created the universe **(The Magician).** *Symbol 4 showed the deity resting after creation* **(The Pharaoh/Emperor)** *and governing the world he had created with his laws. Symbol 7 shows God leading his creation toward perfection.*

The stars on the canopy of the chariot indicate that myriads of constellations are also involved in evolution. The winged disc also painted on the chariot means that Earth, like the rest of the universe, is moving towards ever-higher stages of development. The phallus on the front of the chariot reveals that generation follows generation, always improving, and the forms in which the spirit is embodied are becoming increasingly complete by means of education and instruction. Also note the scepter in the hand of the chariot driver. It consists of a triangle inside a circle surrounded by a square, which means: **'God is inside his creation for all eternity.'** *The eternal one is faithful. He will never abandon the work of his hands. Learn to find peace and trust in this certainty.*

The black and white sphinxes pulling the chariot represent the forces of good and evil, which, in serving the deity, contribute to the realisation of the great plan. The sphinx is an enigmatic creature; at times it is incomprehensible how the divine plan can be served by certain events. We must not allow this either to excite or irritate us, but learn to accept it with complete trust. After all, it would not be difficult for him to destroy evil with it, would it? However, this will never happen, because, apart from the fact that this would disturb the equilibrium, **evil is essential for the instruction of the Children of God. They must be able to encounter dissolution if the choice between good and evil is to be as meaningful as possible. They must be prepared to fight evil, and in order to acquire physical strength, they must practice.** *For if the black sphinx pulls the chariot harder, the white one will also have to accelerate. Everything serves the great plan, for everything comes from deity. He maintains everything, and everything returns to him. Now go and find peace in this knowledge."*

Sit with this for some time, and perhaps read it again. I have made some alterations to the surviving symbol to better depict the truth in this teaching above by the hierophant to an initiate. I have remade the staff with the symbol at the beginning of each chapter, and I have circled the representation of the symbolic phallus on the front of the chariot mentioned in the original instruction. Here is that altered image for you now in Figure 33:

Figure 33: Showing in red the change in symbolism from original teaching over time. Source: N. S. Elijah.

Chapter 5

ABRAHAM

"In... most occult and wonderful paths of wisdom did JAH the Lord of Hosts engrave his name."
– Abraham

Biblical chronology – when was the time of Abraham?

Now Judaism, Christianity, and Islam are Judeo-Christian religions and are also known to be 'Abrahamic Religions.' This is because they all share the same 'father' of their religion. A historical figure known to us as the patriarch Abraham. To give you the sequencing, in the Bible, from the first man Adam it is as follows:

ADAM → Seth → Enoch → Noah → Shem → Arpachshad → Shelah → Eber → Peleg → Reu → Serug → Nahor → Terah → **ABRAHAM** (had two sons, Ishmael and Isaac)

ABRAHAM → 1. Ishmael → Ishmaelite's (The Prophet Muhammad says all Arabs are descendent from Ishmael). → 2. Isaac → Jacob – Jacob was given a new name ISRAEL and had twelve sons. One of these son's was Joseph. Joseph gained favour with the pharaoh through his prophetic visions and ability to interpret dreams; and the other eleven sons of Jacob, and their families, came to live in

Egypt. → 430 years pass and all of the children of the sons of Jacob (the twelve tribes of Israel) are the slaves of Egypt → **MOSES** → EXODUS into promised land → Ten Commandments → Samuel → First King of Israel, Saul → King David (David and Goliath) → Solomon (Solomon's Temple) →

And at this point there is a split between:

→ The Tribes of Judah/Benjamin that became the 'House of Judah' – the Southern Kingdom with the capital Jerusalem. AND → the rest of the tribes that became 'The House of Israel' – the Northern Kingdom with the capital Samaria.

→ After the split we have → Elijah → Elisha → Isaiah → then around 700 BC the Assyrian Empire → Around 600 BC we have the Babylonian Empire under Nimrod → Daniel → Malachi → Then a period of around 400 years where there are no more 'writings of inspired divine nature' → Jesus (of the Line of King David – The Davidic Line).

As mentioned before, the three initiates say that **Abraham was a contemporary of Hermes Trismegistus** and that Hermes Trismegistus was the **teacher/instructor of Abraham**. If we are to prove this then we need to first determine the time of Abraham. So, when was the time of Abraham? According to the extensive research of Rhodes scholar, Dr Andrew E. Steinmann, Distinguished Professor of Theology and Hebrew at Concordia University Chicago, in his 2011 publication *'From Abraham to Paul* (FATP): *'A Biblical Chronology'*, the time of Abraham can be calculated from Exodus. Summarised nicely in a comprehensive book review from Rodger C. Young MA, in July 2012, on www.biblearchaeology.org:

> *"The crucial text here is Exodus 12:40, 41, where 430 years are given for the sojourning of the people of Israel who dwelt in Egypt ... by the most straightforward reading of the Masoretic text, the 430 years would start when Jacob, at the age of 130 years, entered Egypt (Genesis 47:9). This would mean that Jacob was born in 2006 BC, Isaac in 2,066 BC, and Abraham in 2166 BC. FATP accepts this so-called 'long sojourn' interpretation, which seems to be the majority opinion of conservative scholarship."*

Book review: From Abraham to Paul: A Biblical Chronology, by Andrew E. Steinmann. St. Louis: Concordia Publishing House, 2011. Hardback, 421 + xxxviii pages. Part II. – July 12, 2012 by Rodger C. Young MA.

http://www.biblearchaeology.org/post/2012/07/12/Book-Review-From-Abraham-to-Paul-A-Biblical-Chronology-Part-II.aspx#Article

Initially in the Bible, Abraham is called Abram, and it is not until he is 99 years of age – with his 'covenant with the lord' – that his name is changed to Abraham. If we can place the time of 'Abraham' to be 2067 BC, as per the scholarly efforts of Dr Steinmann, then that would mean that Abraham and Hermes Trismegistus must have lived approximately 4,000 years ago.

Foundation to Abraham's teaching – The Lost Book of Thoth

The Holy Jewish Torah, the Holy Scriptures of one of the oldest religions on the planet, Judaism, seems to be steeped in traditional understanding/interpretation of scripture in a very set rigid way, and according to them that way must not be changed. And yet, what if they have somehow **forgotten the original message of their founding patriarch Abraham, or misunderstood the full meaning of the Law of Moses?** What if through centuries of worship, this human error factor has not been accounted for, and has resulted in massive misunderstanding from early on?

The difficulty with people that are stuck in the 1st, 2nd, and 3rd stages of evolution of a personal religious philosophy (as explained in Chapter 1) is that they largely tend to remain satisfied with their religion. Perhaps on some level they like the separatist or perceived elitist aspect of belonging to some specific faith or tradition. The Jewish people, for example, seem completely satisfied with their religion of nearly 4,000 years, and show little desire to change. So, to help the Jewish reader understand the actual foundation of their religion – a foundation that the Rabbis themselves largely seem to have forgotten – we will start with an overview of their primary symbol for their religion: The Jewish Star or the Star of David, in Figure 34 (next page):

SACRED ALIGNMENT

Figure 34: The Star of David: the ancient symbol of the Jewish religion.

What does this symbol actually mean? Well, in simple terms, it is a representation of some of the divine laws of Hermes Trismegistus. The Hermetic Principles 2, 4, and 7. The principle of correspondence – *'As above so below'*, the principle of polarity, and the principle of gender – *'Everything contains the masculine and the feminine'*, where we have the masculine emanation represented as the phallic upward-pointing triangle, and the feminine principle represented as the womb shaped downward-pointing triangle intersecting; in that process, it becomes the Star of David.

There is also a hidden dimension to the symbol that will be revealed. In its correct application, the Star of David actually becomes the 'Key of Solomon.' The upward-pointing triangle represents the male phallus and thus the divine masculine principle. The downward-pointing triangle represents the female womb and thus the divine feminine principle. The unification of the divine feminine and divine masculine aspects of consciousness within an individual results in the finding of the Key of Solomon. It is the secret to the Mystical Kabbalah that results in the 11th sphere of (daath) knowledge, and is the truth represented in the correct understanding of Major Arcana Symbol II – The High Priestess (revealed in Chapter 2).

And the key is the Heart – Tiphareth, Anahata – and Beauty, unstruck. This is the birth of the Christ consciousness within man and the unfolding of the rose. When this happens, something extra is added to the Star of David – the divine consciousness (the point in the centre) creates the 'Key of Solomon.'

The esoteric instruction of the Kabbalah to the people of the Jewish faith, is typically reserved for those 50 years of age. I am unsure what the current reasoning is for there to be this age restriction in place for the conveying of this ancient wisdom. However, through the eyes of the ancient mystery school teachings, an interesting parallel can be drawn based on sacred numerology. 5 is the golden number, the number of man, and 10 is the number of completion. 5 x10 = 50 and thereby symbolizes the perfectment of man.

For generally it is not until a man is 50 years of age, can he be safely trusted with the responsibility and burden of knowledge. He must have had sufficient time to experience life and learn valuable lessons about the power and destructive forces flowing through him when misdirected – in order to in some small measure at least, minimise the harm that may be caused to himself and others through misapplication of the sacred knowledge.

We know that the ancient Major Arcana of the Tarot of the Bohemians is actually the pictographic representation of the Book of Thoth. And I have revealed to you three of these symbols thus far and given you the unlocked hidden meaning that hopefully has resulted in a humbling epiphany. If, perhaps, you still question this link to the foundation of Abraham's teaching and simultaneously all Abrahamic faiths, then read on.

To further verify the point of origin of the Jewish teachings of Abraham being from knowledge of the Book of Thoth, I will now explain the Hebrew alphabet and where this actually comes from. We know that modern historians study the evolution of language to deduce points and times of evolution of different peoples and track the migration of certain cultures on Earth. It is in a similar vein that I will proceed.

I will reference what is known to be the **oldest Jewish text** '*Sepher Yezirah*', which is a title meaning 'A Book on Creation', the English translation of which was published in 1877 by Reverend Dr. Isidor Kalisch, based on an earlier 1830 translation by Johann Friedrich Von Mayer. In his words in the preface, Reverend Kalisch says:

> *"The metaphysical essay called 'Sepher Yezirah' (book on creation or cosmogony), which I have endeavored to render into English... is considered by all modern literati as the first philosophical book that ever was written in the Hebrew Language... Tradition, which ascribes the authorship of this book to the Patriarch Abraham can be proved by many reasons."*

He then continues, further on in his preface, with something very interesting:

> *"A Christian theologian, Johann Friedrich Von Mayer, remarked very truly in his German preface to the book 'Yezirah' published in Leipzig 1830, 'This book is for two reasons highly important: in the first place; that the real Cabala, or mystical doctrine of the Jews, which must be carefully distinguished from its excrescences, is in close connection and perfect accord with the Old and New Testaments; and in second place, **that the knowledge of it is of great importance to the philosophical inquirers and cannot be put aside. Like a cloud permeated by beams of light which makes one infer that there is more light behind it, so do the contents of this book, enveloped in obscurity, abound in coruscations of thought, reveal to the mind that there is still more effulgent light lurking somewhere and thus inviting us to a further contemplation and investigation, and at the same time demonstrating the danger of a superficial investigation, which is so prevalent in modern times, rejecting that which cannot be understood at first sight."***

So, it is with humility and an open heart that I ask the Jewish reader specifically to weigh in their hearts the words and associations that follow, where I unmask the obscurity that Johann Friedrich Von Mayer describes in his 1830 works. That being said, all adherents of the Abrahamic religions – the original Christianity (not 'churchianity'), Islam, and even other faiths will prosper from the words that also follow.

The *'effulgent light behind the clouds'* is none other than the knowledge and wisdom of the lost Books of Thoth that were taught to Abraham by Hermes Trismegistus/Thoth himself, and now I will show you why.

As a starting point remember the first symbol, The Magician. In order to ensure it is fresh in your mind, go and read this again now please, followed by the second symbol, The Pharaoh/Emperor.

In 1877, Reverend Dr Isidor Kalish wrote of the Yezirah essay ascribed to the authorship of the patriarch Abraham:

> *"It teaches that a first cause, eternal, all wise, almighty, and holy, is the origin and the centre of the whole universe, from whom gradually all beings emanated. Thought, speech and action are an inseparable unity in the divine being. God made or created, is metaphorically expressed by the word: writing. The Hebrew language and its characters correspond mostly with the things they designate, and thus holy thoughts, Hebrew language and its reduction to writing form a unity which produce a creative effect.*
>
> *The self-existing first cause called the creation into existence by quantity and quality: the former represented by 10 numbers (Sephiroth) the latter by **22 letters**, which form together 32 ways of the divine wisdom. Three of the 22 letters, namely Aleph, Mem, Sheen, are the mothers or the first elements, from which come forth the primitive matter of the world: air, water, and fire that have their parallels in man (male and female): breast, body, and head, and in the year: moisture, cold and heat. The other 7 double and 12*

simple letters are then represented as stamina: from which other spheres or media of existence emanated."

Now for ease of understanding that passage I will include a picture, Figure 35 (next page), of the breakdown of the 22 letters of the Hebrew alphabet.

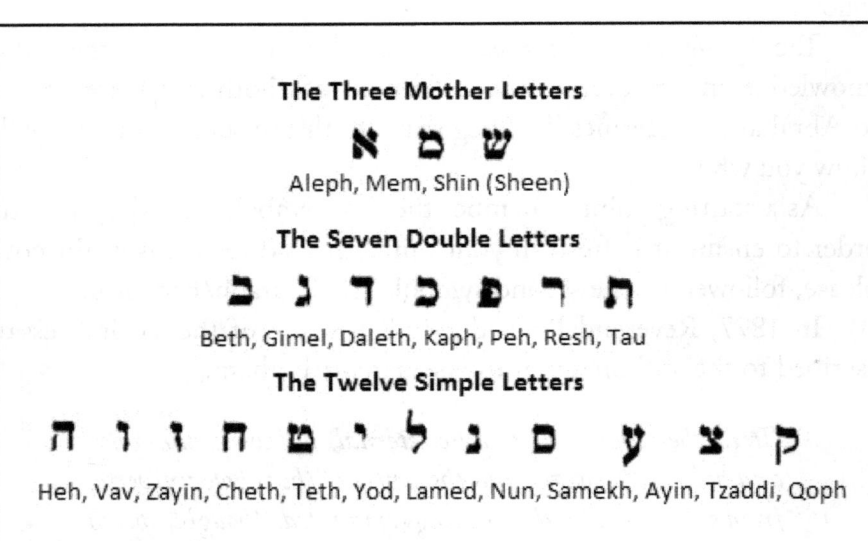

Figure 35: 22 Letters of the Hebrew Alphabet.

The first thing that you will notice is that there are twenty-two letters in the Hebrew alphabet and there are twenty-two cards in the Major Arcana in the Tarot of the Bohemians, The Book of Thoth. This is not a coincidence. Now, I will include some parts of the translation from the 1830 copy of the first known book written in ancient Hebrew, ascribed to the authorship of patriarch Abraham himself, from which **all Abrahamic faiths – Judaism, Christianity and Islam – stem! The point of origin!** And as we go, I will remove the obscurity that the authors of the 1830 and 1877 translations were confronted with. Every addition of my own will be marked by an asterix and italics.

CHAPTER IV

Section 1:

"The 7 double letters with duplicity of pronunciation aspirated and unaspirated serve as a model of softness and hardness. Strength and Weakness."

Section 2:

"7 double letters shall as it were symbolise: Wisdom. Wealth. Fruitfulness. Life. Dominion. Peace and Beauty."

Section 3:

"7 double letters serve to signify the antithesis to which human life is exposed.

The antithesis of: Wisdom is Foolishness, of Wealth is Poverty, of Fruitfulness is Childlessness, of Life is Death, of Dominion is Dependence, of Peace is War and of Beauty is Ugliness."

*(Hermes Key Principle 4: Polarity: "Everything is dual; everything has poles, everything has its pair of opposites; like and unlike are the same; opposites are identical in nature, but different only in degree; extremes meet; all truths are but half-truths; all paradoxes may be reconciled.")
(POLARITY)

Section 4:

"The 7 double consonants are analogous to the 6 dimensions: Height and Depth, East and West, North and South and the holy temple that stands in the centre which carries them all. The double consonants are 7 and not 6. They are 7 and not 8… reflect upon this. In fact inquire about it and make it so evident that **the creator be acknowledged to be on his throne again.**"

(*What does this mean?)

*Well if we list the 7 double consonants in the specific order written as:
1. Wisdom → Foolishness
2. Wealth → Poverty
3. Fruitfulness → Childlessness
4. Life → Death
5. Dominion → Dependence
6. Peace → War
7. Beauty → Ugliness.

Then the 'holy temple that stands in the centre that carries them all' is **4. Life → Death.**

Further, working with the law of the triangle, we have the feminine triangle making up the Star of David as in Figure 36:

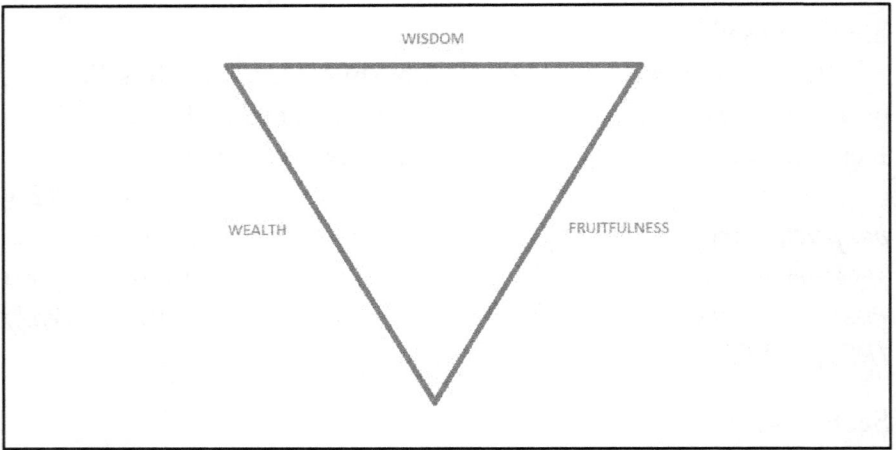

Figure 36: The ancient symbol representing the divine feminine. Source and copyright: N. S. Elijah.

And we have the masculine triangle making up the Star of David as in Figure 37:

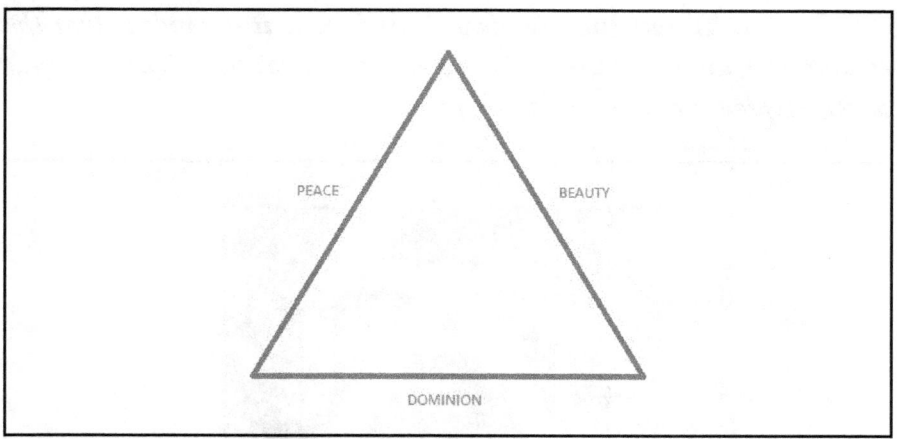

Figure 37: The ancient symbol representing the divine masculine. Source and copyright: N. S. Elijah.

And with the 'holy temple' that stands in the centre that carries them all, we have the Key of Solomon. 7 and not 6, 7 and not 8 – Figure 38

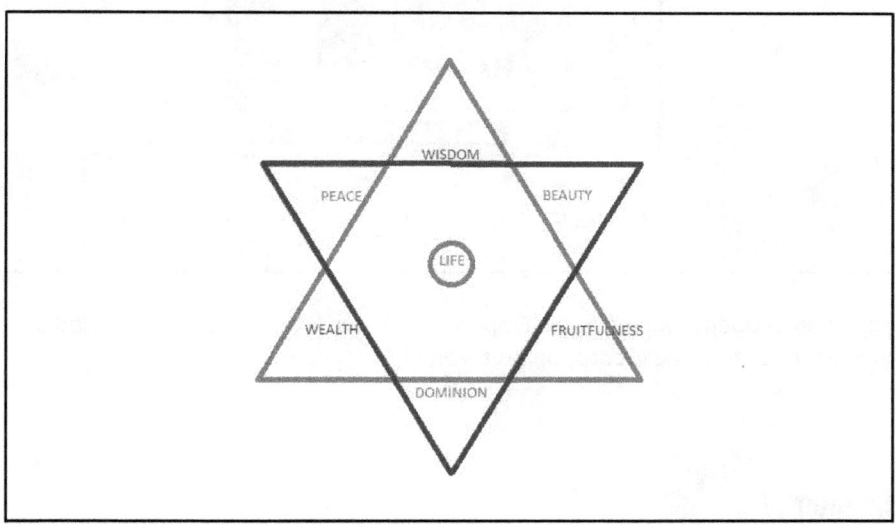

Figure 38: The ancient symbol representing the Key of Solomon. Source and copyright: N. S. Elijah.

Further: 'In fact enquire about it and make it so evident that the creator be again acknowledged to be on his throne': See Figure 39 (next page) – *reproduced from the last chapter.*

Figure 39: Hidden meaning in the Emperor Tarot card explaining lost knowledge in Sepher Yezirah. The Creator on his throne.

Chapter IV

Section 1:

"The 12 simple letters symbolise as it were – the organs of speaking, thinking, walking, seeing, hearing, working, coition, smelling, sleep, anger, swallowing, and laughing."

Section 2:

"The 12 simple consonants symbolise also the 12 oblique points: East Height, North East, East Depth, South Height, South East, South Depth, West Height, South West, West Depth, North Height, North West, North Depth. They grew wider and wider to all eternity and these are the boundaries to the world."

Section 3:

"The 12 simple letters stamina, having been designed, combined, weighed and changed by God, he performed by them: 12 constellations in the world: 12 months in the year and 12 organs (leaders) in the human body, male and female."

Section 4:

"The 12 constellations in the world are: Aries, Taurus, Gemini, Cancer, Leo, Virgo, Libra, Scorpio, Sagittarius, Capricornus, Aquarius and Pisces. The 12 months in the year are: Nisan, Iyar, Sivan, Tamus, Ab, Elul, Tishri, Marcheshvan, Kislev, Teves, Schevat and Adar."

CHAPTER VI

Section 3:

"The first elements (Aleph, Mem, Sheen) are Air, Water and Fire. Fire is Above, Water is Below and the Breath of Air establishes the balance between them."
*which can be represented as either: Figure 40.

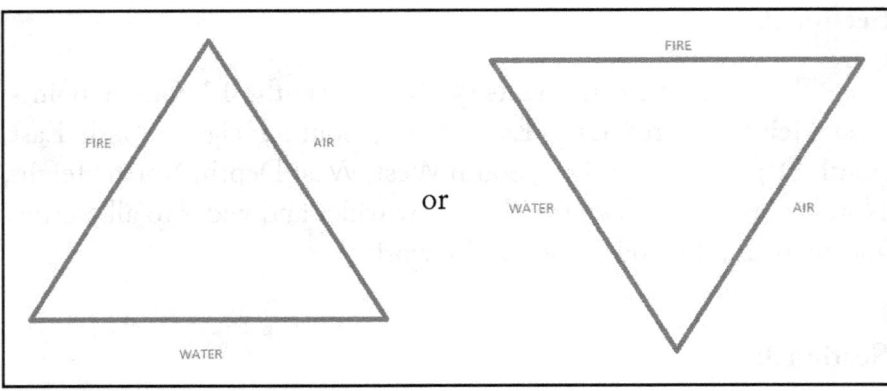

Figure 40: The law of the triangle. Source and copyright: N. S. Elijah.

Section 5:

"God has also set the one over against the other; the good against the evil, and the evil against the good; the good proceeds from the good, and the evil from the evil; the good purifies the bad, and the bad the good; the good is preserved for the good, and the evil for the bad ones."

> *See the 3rd symbol, The Chariot, given from the book of Thoth in the last chapter for further verification. See how this fits perfectly! For it is the one true source.*

Section 7:

"There are 7 of which three are against three and one places them in Equilibrium. There are 12 at which are all the time at war; 3 produce love, 3 hatred, 3 are animators and 3 destroyers."

> *The three against three and one places them in Equilibrium is: Figure 41.*

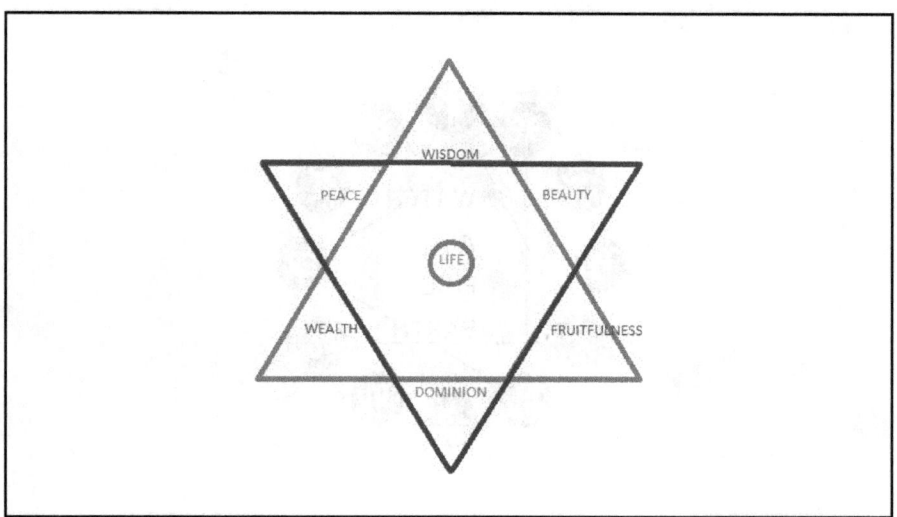

Figure 41: One places them in equilibrium: Source and copyright: N. S. Elijah.

What are the twelve that are all the time at war? It is the zodiac, twelve signs in a circle all facing each other as though they are at war.

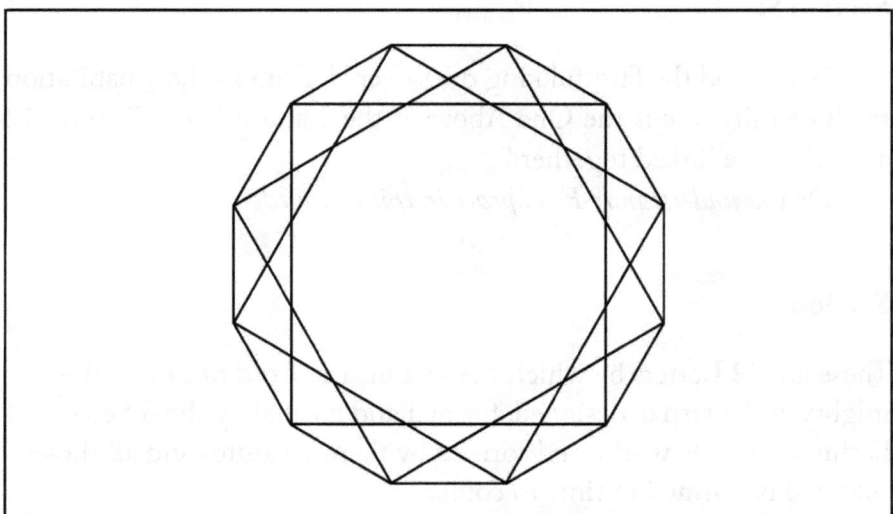

Figure 42: Twelve-sided shape: dodecagon comprised of three overlapping squares, but can also be represented as four overlapping triangles!

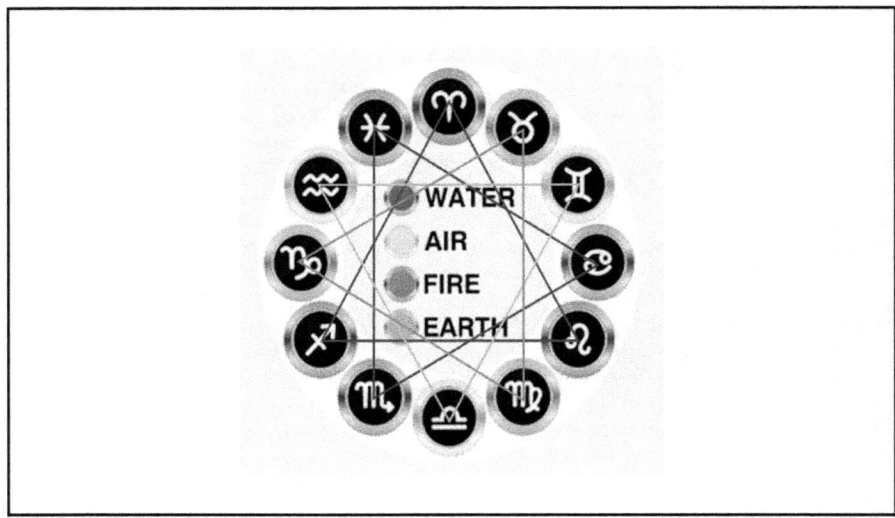

Figure 43: Twelve signs of the zodiac always at war, because they are all in a circle facing each other- opposing each other.

Section 8:

"And God the faithful king rules over all from his holy habitation to all eternity. He is the One Above 3, the 3 above 7, the 7 above 12 and ALL are linked together."

Do you understand? Find peace in this knowledge.

Section 9:

These are 22 Letters by which I AM Yah, The Lord of Hosts, Almighty and Eternal, designed, formed and created by the 3 Sepharim, his whole world, and formed by them creatures and all those that will be formed in time to come.

Section 10:

"When the Patriarch Abraham comprehended the great Truism, revolved it in his mind, conceived it perfectly, made careful investigations and profound enquiries, pondered upon it and succeeded in contemplations, The Lord of the Universe appeared to him, called him his friend, made with him a covenant between the 10 fingers of his hands, which is the covenant of the tongue, and the covenant between the 10 toes of his feet which is the covenant of circumcision, and said to him: "Before I formed thee in the belly I knew thee."

> *10 Fingers + 1 Tongue (law of silence/divine speech- covenant of the tongue) + 10 Toes + 1 phallus (symbolic of the spiritualisation of sexual energy or creative organ 'cleansed' – covenant of circumcision) = 22! With a specific focus of sacred numbers 3,7,12 =22.
>
> This is the same as the twenty-two cards in the Major Arcana in Tarot – the preserved three sacred intersecting paths of Osiris, Isis and Horus of seven cards each, plus the final card marked zero (which is later to be revealed as the fourth chosen symbol to unveil from the Lost Book of Thoth). Twenty-two letters in the Hebrew language. Who was the author of the Tarot? Thoth – lord of space and time. Who then was the contemporary of Abraham? Hermes Trismegistus, the reincarnation of Thoth, **the Lord of the Universe** that appeared to him and called Abraham friend.
>
> Further remember that the centre of the 7 was **4. Life and Death?** Also remember that the 4th Chakra, the centre of, 7 is the heart – anahata (meaning unstruck) – the key to life and death. Figures 44a, 44b and 44c.

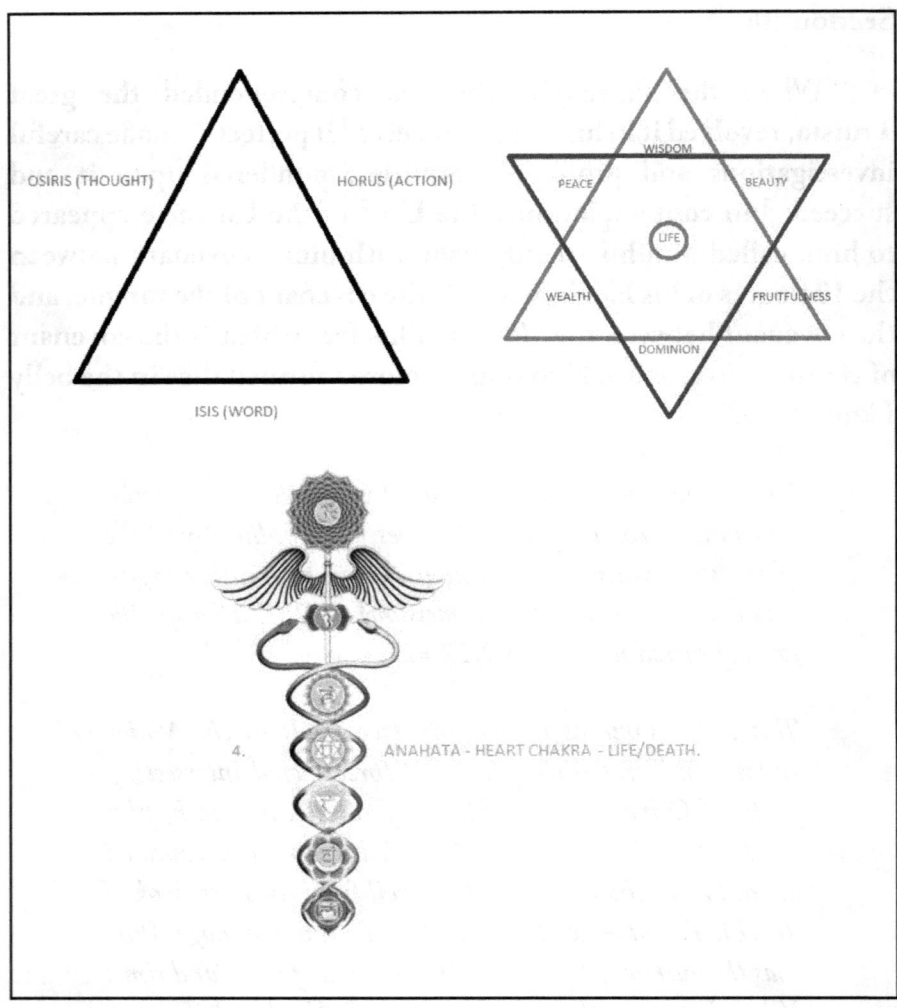

Figure 44: The Divine Trinity, 44b – The Key of Solomon and 44c – the staff of Hermes/Thoth. Source and copyright: N. S. Elijah.

The Key is the Heart

All masters and spiritual teachers of the past have taught that the kingdom of heaven can be contacted through communion with the higher self or spirit within. Now, science has looked at the achievement of spiritual states of being purely from the measuring of wavelength of brainwaves and classified them into four categories, and ascribed to them four letters of the Greek alphabet – Alpha, Beta, Delta and Theta.

Theta is the bandwidth of heightened states of meditation. Beta is your general day-to-day range of activity. In more recent times, there has been a catchphrase used to describe the achievement of desired state of theta brainwave function – 'Meditate deeper than a Zen monk.' This is the phrase people hear when they embark upon deep meditation exercise, indeed a Zen monk enters 'theta' brainwave state.

But you see, it is not just about the brain and the achievement of a certain brainwave frequency. The primary ingredient that is often overlooked and only looked upon from a physiological functionality is the heart. However, the heart is not just an organ that pumps blood around the body. It is also the generator of the largest magnetic field within the human body. This is what powers the aura. Recently, scientific instruments have only just become sensitive enough to detect these emanations, and this will be further explained in Chapter 8: *Exiting the Matrix – The Red Pill*.

You see, we have had it all wrong. The key does not lie with the mind, for as Helena Blavatsky accurately states, *"The mind is the slayer of the real."* Invariably, the key lies with the heart, and you don't need to look very far in order to see more of the underlying truth of this reality. Let us briefly investigate: heartache, heart attack, heart palpitation, bitter heart, cold hearted, loving heart, big hearted, broken hearted, warm hearted, and so on. So, what does this all mean?

We understand intuitively and unconsciously that the heart is *the* place. The heart is the portal for God emanations. Divine emanations are projected through the heart (and, to a lesser extent, the eyes). Remember, we are consciousness and the highest consciousness is unconditional love and it is good. Indeed, it is God. For God really is love. Love is the strongest force in the universe. Unconditional love is the strongest form of love and thus the strongest force in the universe, for it is as strong as God and God is omnipotent. Indeed, unconditional love *is* the power of God.

That is why human beings suffer heart attacks and heartaches. They harden their hearts to the world. They literally, through pain and suffering and bitterness and for many other reasons, close their hearts off to the world. The heart chakra – Anahata (unstruck) – the spinning wheel of energy, slows down and closes the gateway for the access to the God consciousness within. And as this closes, divine grace is blocked from simultaneously being expressed through you and experienced by you because there is a big 'Closed' sign on the doors of your heart.

We deeply know this to be true, don't we? But we instead, here in the West particularly, have the tendency to deny this existence of God or reject the idea of an external God separate from us or, worse still, make a false god out of our perceived powers of intellect; so we rationalise and rationalise, until eventually we shut ourselves off from feeling. Until we no longer are able to feel. We are then dead emotionally and blinded intellectually. Death – the antithesis of life.

It is extremely important that we attune our minds to the idea of symbolic representation of deep spiritual truths. Symbols can be pictures, such as previously shown, or they can be concepts such as mythological stories of legend.

And this leads us now to the spiritual concept of initiation. To understand it we need to accurately decode the symbolism left behind by the ancients, and this will be the focus of the next chapter.

Chapter 6

INITIATION

"We take spiritual Initiation when we become conscious of the Divine within us, and thereby contact the Divine without us."
— **Don Fortune**

Because deep spiritual truths have always been represented symbolically, I am aware that the true idea of initiation is something that might be quite alien to people. It is important to understand the difference between the initiations undertaken on the way to '*Christ consciousness*' or '*Buddha consciousness.*' And those of the lesser ceremonies and rituals conducted in various secret schools, or of elect secret societies bent on the misappropriation of power that are now unfortunately largely a misguided dim light of their forebears.

Spiritual initiation is the journey up the immense mountain, overcoming many snares and pitfalls to finally stand on the summit and come face to face with God. The oldest record of this process of initiation survives in ancient Egypt. The following frieze known as '*The Weighing of the Heart*', in its correct holographic interpretation depicts an aspiring soul (candidate dressed in white) going through the initiatory stages and testing's during life; and finally, if proven worthy, coming face to face with God/The Divine – represented as Osiris.

Figure 45: The Weighing of the Heart 'ceremony.' Ancient Egypt.

In Elisabeth Haich's book '*Initiation*', there is a previous life account where she was being instructed by the Hierophant or High Priest of the Shemshu Hor (Priests of Horus). The High Priest Ptah-Hotep gives the following instruction:

> "*We use the serpent standing erect as the symbol of initiation, as the mistress of the tree of recognition and knowledge. The initiate is the high-flying eagle who has spiritualised the serpent – the power of the instinctive urge – and manifests it as a spiritual power through his intellect.*" **(That is why as we have mentioned the pharaoh – divine incarnated – wore the uraeus, the raised serpent symbol on their heads)**

> "*Initiation means becoming conscious. You are now conscious to a degree corresponding to the resistance of your nerves and body. When a person becomes conscious to a higher spiritual degree, he automatically guides higher, stronger, more penetrating powers into his body. For this reason, he must also raise the level of resistance of his nerves and body.* **To achieve the supreme, divinely creative degree**

> *of consciousness, while at the same time increasing the resistance of the nerves to the supreme degree in order to be able to endure this divine condition without harm to the body* – that's what initiation means. Initiation also entails omnipotence and omniscience."

The most important thing mentioned in this account is: '*To achieve the supreme, divinely creative degree of consciousness, while at the same time increasing the resistance of the nerves to the supreme degree in order to be able to endure this divine condition.*' The reason this is the most important aspect is because it provides a clue as to how the ancient Egyptian priest-kings – 'Priests of Horus/Shemsu-Hor' of the time of the Satya and Treta Yugas, were able to achieve this.

In addition to accounts of many long years of training the individual, with exercises of consciousness and training the nerves and undertaking morning specific physical exercises, where they learn to direct consciousness into different parts of their bodies (which is where the yoga of India originates). The prepared candidate for initiation would also undergo a process of initiation, one that would immerse the initiate into specifically designed atmospheric conditions in order to radiate the body with certain particles, all to create the 'divine creative degree of consciousness experience' for them whilst in their body. That was the purpose of the specifically positioned large granite sarcophagus in the 'Kings Chamber' in the Great Pyramid.

The Flower of Life

The Flower of Life is a geometrical figure composed of multiple overlapping circles, arranged to form the pattern of a flower, with the centre of each circle being on the circumference of the surrounding circles. According to the writings of Drunvalo Melchizedek, the Flower of Life is the pattern of creation. It is said to contain all knowledge (male and female). Within the proportions of the Flower of Life can be found every single aspect of life. Every mathematical formula, every law of physics, every harmony in music (the ancient

Chinese sages used to say that geometry was 'frozen music'), every biological life form, every atom, every dimensional level – everything that is within this waveform universe.

As you look upon the images of the Flower of Life, in Figures 46a and 46b (below), you will notice that hidden within its geometry is the 'Kabbalistic Tree of Life.' Now I say 'Kabbalistic Tree of Life' because this is how I have introduced it to you in Chapter 2. However, as we are beginning to understand, the knowledge on which the Kabbalah is based goes back much further in time than Judaism.

In Chapter 3, as we were exploring the lost technologies of the ancients, I brought to your attention the ancient site known as 'The Osirian.' The Osirian, as we remember, is the older semi-submerged temple that is behind the temple of Seti, at Abydos in Egypt. It is at The Osirian that we find the oldest known example of the Flower of Life.

Figure 46a and 46b: The Egyptian Flower of Life showing the Tree of Life in its geometry.

Whilst the oldest known example of the Flower of Life is found in the Temple of Osiris in Egypt, other examples of the Flower of Life can be found in: The Forbidden City in China, the Masada in Israel, various temples in Japan, and the Harimarandir Sahib (the Golden

Temple) in India. Knowledge of the Flower of Life is important, in order to understand sacred geometry and the true purpose of the Great Pyramid in Egypt.

The Great Pyramid – Chamber of Initiation

As we look upon modern photographs of the Great Pyramid (or perhaps we may be blessed to travel there and see it in person), we are confronted with an image that does not do it justice. What we see today, whilst still breathtaking and awe-inspiring, is a far cry from its original majesty.

Many thousands of years ago, the Great Pyramid was significantly more impressive than it is today – for what we see as we look upon the structure today are the underlying sandstone building stones. According to many ancient accounts, in its original form, each of the four faces of the Great Pyramid were entirely covered with immensely beautiful white casing stones and the capstone was made of solid gold.

Over thousands of years, and the comings and goings of the various cultures that followed, the beautiful white casing stones were removed and used in other construction. Drunvolo Melchizedek suggests in his book *'The Ancient Secret of the Flower of Life Vol- 2'* that today one can see a number of these stones making up the glorious walls and ceilings of some of the oldest mosques in Arabia.

Contrary to what the Egyptologists tell us, the Great Pyramid of Egypt is not the tomb of Khufu. For starters, it is much older than Pharaoh Khufu. The granite sarcophagus in the King's Chamber is still there today and has not been stolen **because it is bigger than the doorway entrance to the chamber! A seemingly minor detail yet it is incredibly revealing as to the actual purpose of the Great Pyramid,** as Drunvalo Melchizedek explains in *'The Ancient Secret of the Flower of Life – Vol 2'*:

"The fact that this is an initiation chamber and not a burial chamber is pretty obvious for two reasons. The first has to do with the mummification process used in Egypt. Throughout early Egyptian history—for every known king, queen, pharaoh, doctor, lawyer or other special person who was ever mummified—the process was carried out the same way. They had a ceremony, took out the organs and placed them in four clay jars, then wrapped the body, known as the process of mummification, and placed it in the sarcophagus, sealing the lid. Then they carried the sarcophagus and the four jars to wherever they were going to bury them. There have been no known exceptions to this procedure… yet **in the King's Chamber the sarcophagus is larger than the doorway. They couldn't have carried it into the room because they can't even get it out. It's one enormous piece of granite. It had to have been placed in the King's Chamber during the construction of the pyramid.** *That's the only reason it's still there—otherwise it would have been stolen a long time ago and put in the British Museum or somewhere. The lid's gone because it could be taken out, but they can't remove the sarcophagus."*

If we look at a cross-section of the Great Pyramid, we will begin to see that it has a very specific design. What we need to do is look at this like a giant machine. Designed for the purpose of being able to generate and immerse the candidate for the final initiation with a certain type of energy *'to achieve the supreme, divinely creative degree of consciousness, while at the same time increasing the resistance of the nerves to the supreme degree in order to be able to endure this divine condition.'*

Initiation

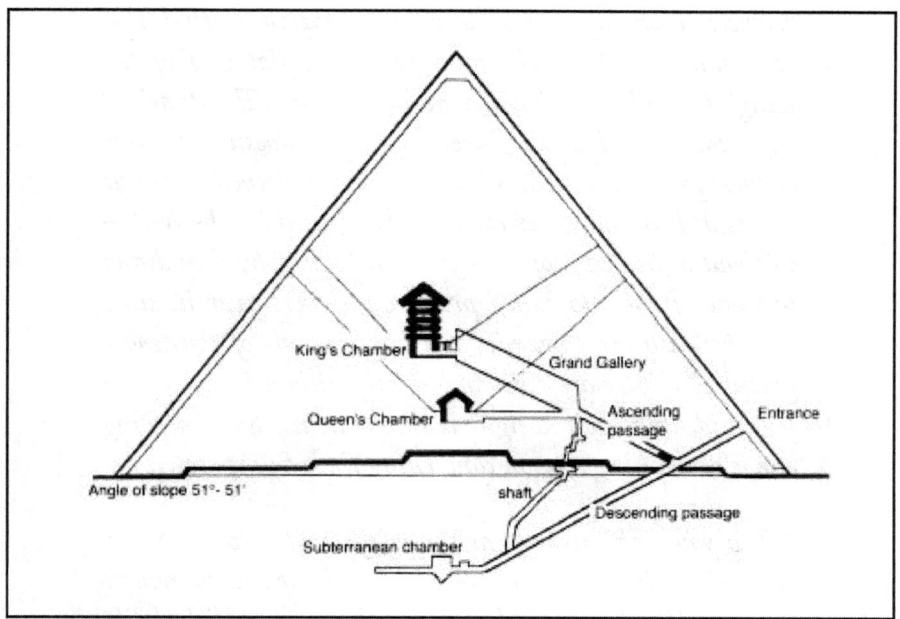

Figure 47: Cross-section of the Great Pyramid: Source: David Furlong- Keys to the Temple.

We need to understand that the level of knowledge held by the ancients was in many ways far superior to our current knowledge, as we remember the characteristics of the Satya Yuga and also from the many other examples that I have provided so far in this discourse. The true purpose of the Great Pyramid as a chamber/temple of initiation is hard to imagine based upon the lengths of false indoctrination that the world has been subjected to, which attempts to convince us it is just a tomb.

Consider the strange massive arrow-shaped silo at the roof of the King's Chamber. Let us look at some clues, and further insight, given in Drunvalo Melchizedeks '*The Ancient Secret of the Flower of Life – Vol. 2*' as to the specifics and true purpose of this construction.

> "The immediate ceiling of the King's Chamber is made of nine huge stones... and over it is a series of stone layers, as shown in the drawing (Figure 48), with an air space

between each layer. The usual explanation is that this was built to relieve the pressure on the flat roof of the King's Chamber so that it doesn't cave in...The standard explanation is that the Queen's Chamber doesn't need one of these pressure-relievers because it has a pitched roof. But there's at least one other room in the pyramid—the Well—without a pitched roof, and you could ask, why they didn't put one of these so-called pressure relievers over it, since it is beneath the Pyramid and has millions of tons more pressure? (There are two-and-a half million blocks in this pyramid, and their weight is tremendous). So something else is obviously going on concerning these five spaces...

When you look carefully at those layers, it becomes pretty clear that they are more than just air spaces to relieve pressure. The bottom sides of the blocks are polished like glass. The top sides are totally irregular and covered with about a quarter inch of black foam. Yes, foam! It looks like somebody sprayed it on with a spray can. I don't know what it is, but that's what it looks like. When you think about it, you've got these mirror-like surfaces facing downward and these irregular, foam-covered surfaces facing upward... it's designed to reflect energy coming from underneath and absorb energy coming from above. It's a separator... The spaces absorb the black-light energy coming from above and reflect the white-light energy coming from below. In this way they separate the two from each other. When you're lying in the sarcophagus, the male energy comes down, rises off the floor at a 45-degree angle and passes right through your head. That beam, about two inches in diameter, comes up through the back of your head and passes through your pineal gland, which is the hidden secret to all this work."

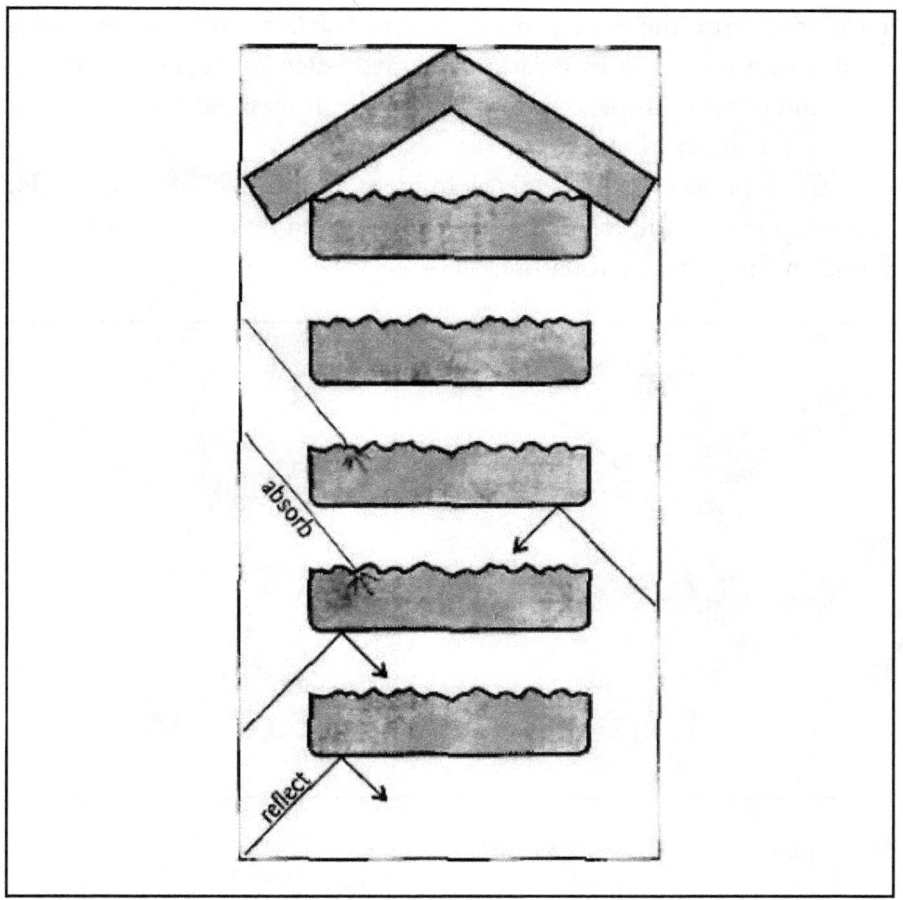

Figure 48: The five open spaces above the King's Chamber. Source: The Anceint Secret of the Flower of Life – Vol. 2, Drunvalo Melchizedek.

Drunvalo goes on to say that many tourists, when lying down in the sarcophagus, experienced strange and heightened states of awareness and had visions. So, the Egyptian government moved the sarcophagus from its original position (out of the energy stream) and the strange phenomenon stopped.

Remember the Egyptian Flower of Life? How this is sacred geometry from which universal patterns can be extracted? The golden mean and the Fibonacci sequence are also to be found in the geometries of the Flower of Life. For those of you who have not come across the term 'the golden mean' before I will briefly explain that it is an observable ratio in creation patterns, such as in shells and tree rings and other examples throughout nature; it was also captured in da Vinci's Vitruvian Man.

The Fibonacci sequence is as follows: 1, 1, 2, 3, 5, 8, 13, 21, 34. The proportions follow a curve known as the golden spiral which is found in the patterns of nature.

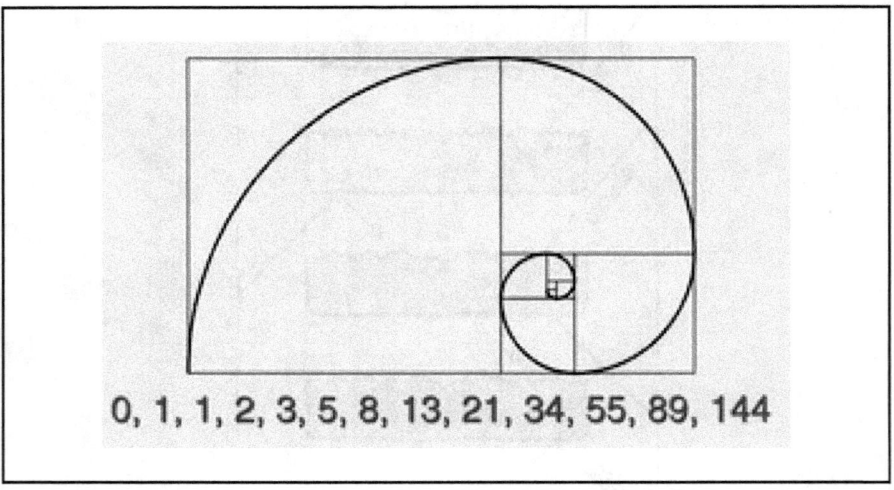

Figure 49: Fibonacci spiral. Golden ratio.

Drunvalo Melchizedek also demonstrates in '*The Ancient Secret of the Flower of Life, Volume 2*' that the Flower of Life geometry, along with the proportions of the Fibonacci spiral, is at work within the Great Pyramid, and this will be shown in Figures 50a and 50b. What is interesting, as you can see in the diagram on the next page, is that the angles of dark light (represented by the broken line) and white light spirals (represented by the solid line) show the path they take moving through space, and how the primary diamond at location 'A' is the same as the King's Chamber in the Great Pyramid, and the exiting angles are reflected in the angles of the 'air shafts' that actually align to specific star constellations.

Obviously, the calculations are much more complex than what is required to be investigated in this message, so if we wish to further look into this then it is best to grab a copy of *The Ancient Secret of the Flower of Life'* and read it all for yourself. You will, however, be able to see from the comparative diagram that I have put together below; with this, sacred geometry superimposes over the construction of the Great Pyramid, and the specific location and angles of air shafts and chambers designed exactly where they are for a specific purpose.

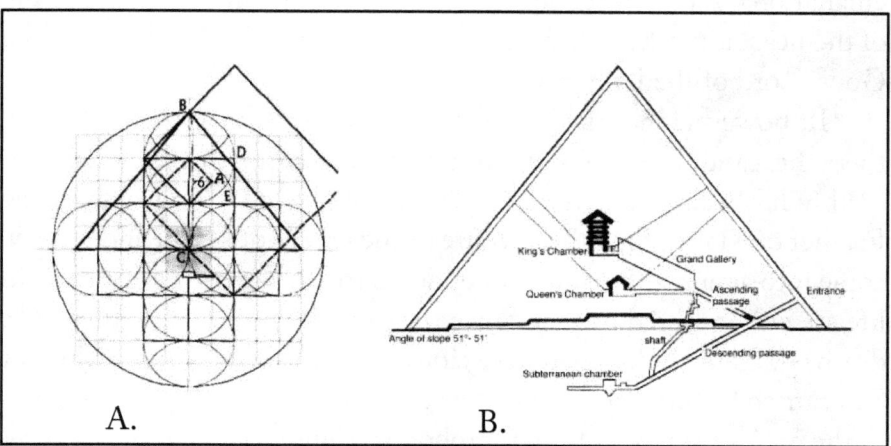

Figure 50: Figure 50a: dark-light spiral (broken line) goes through center (zero point) to the centre of the Earth. White Light spiral (solid line) travels to the centre of the galaxy. Source: The Ancient Secret of the Flower of Life, Drunvalo Melchizedek. 50b Cross section of the Great Pyramid showing explanation of the location of the chambers and shafts.

The Weighing of the Heart

So back to the 'Weighing of the Heart.' Partway through the Age of Taurus and before a great flood, we have a shift from initiation being physically taken in the Great Pyramid to a symbolic journey depicted in the 'Weighing of the Heart', where the candidate for initiation undertakes his tests in the very act of living. In this representation of spiritual truth, we have the candidate for initiation **dressed in white, being led by higher forces** (depicted as Anubis) on the spiritual journey of life. The candidate is presented with various tests, and if he passes them by his life's conduct then his 'Heart is weighed and measured against the 'weight' of the Feather of Ma-at' – the feather of truth. If his heart is lighter than the Feather of Ma-at, the initiate passes by the devourer (The forces of karma and rebirth – continuation in the wheel of Samsara) unharmed and passes out of the wheel of Samsara and is led into higher realms of knowledge to be closer to the divine emanations of the God-Head (Osiris). The outcome of the weighing of the heart is marked on the Akashic records by Thoth – Scribe of the Gods, Lord of the Universe, and Lord of Space and Time.

If, however, the trials of life weigh too heavily on the candidate, then the candidate's burden from suffering from the experience of earthly life weighs down his heart and his heart is heavier than the Feather of Ma-at, then the devourer – the 'forces of karma and rebirth' come into action at the moment of death (because verily, great trials in life are either passed or they prove too great leading to an individual's death) – and the individual's consciousness is put back into the wheel of Samsara to be born again. It is the very forces at work in the depiction of the ancient symbol of the Ouroborus; Figure 51 – the snake eating its own tail on and on into eternity.

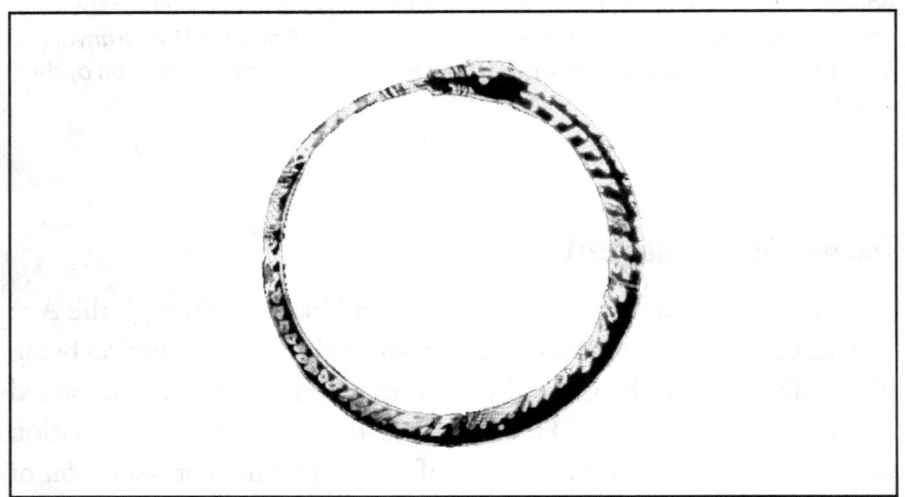

Figure 51: Ouroborus – ancient symbol of the perpetual rebirth/transformation of energy/consciousness.

Initiation

The ancient teaching being of the *Egyptian Mysteries**:

"My Son, the universe originates from two tremendous forces which touch, cross, and join together without becoming confused, without losing their own character, without losing sight of their goal. These are the Force of the Spirit and the Wave of Life. The Force of the Spirit originates from the heart of God; each spark – the human spirit – must descend into matter, assume a material form and then conquer this so that it can continue to develop as a result of this fight. In the Kingdom of Death they cleanse themselves of impurities they have acquired and rise, purified, up to the Kingdom of Life. They stay there until they are once again dragged down by matter: in reincarnation in matter they gain new strength by overcoming difficulties. In this way spirits rise and descend, but always in ever-higher circles of the divine spiral. The higher they go, the more love they radiate, and they exude so much warmth that all selfishness burns away until they finally reach the top. Burning with love, they unite with the primeval fire – the so-called Great Leap.

"By descending into matter, the spirits are not only forced to develop themselves, but they also exert an ennobling influence on the material form in which they are temporarily accommodated. These material forms are actually manifestations of the Great Wave of Life, which is constantly developing higher forms of life.

"The Wave of Life originates in the Lap of God and permeates space and time. The mineral world is created over thousands of years, from deposits of air and water, from myriads of invisibly small impurities. Slowly, life moves through this heavy matter, and in the core of the Earth crystals form, while on the surface the primeval rocks are weathered. On these weathered rocks, mosses and ferns will grow.

"The rocks continue to weather and the vegetation becomes increasingly luxuriant. Animal life now also developed, from the lowest to the highest forms. Thus the Wave of Life passes through the animal and plant kingdoms, as well as that of man and the spirit, creating new and consistently higher forms until it returns to the lap of God. These two spirals, the Force of the Spirit and the Wave of Life, which exist side by side, together promote the evolution of the universe.

"However, my son, there is a shorter, steeper path for reaching the top than this natural path, and that is through Initiation. You can attain the highest point by following a path that gradually ascends – but you can also climb more quickly up a steep, narrow and extremely difficult path.

*"**There are spirits which are driven to take the path of Initiation. These are the chosen who wish to attain the goal faster so that they can help others onward. They lead a difficult life, full of sadness and problems, but it is also rich in insight and silent joy.** In one lifetime, they experience the content of many lives, for they wish to go on, even at that price. These chosen ones have been called by the Gods. They are the ones who wish to know, who seek the answer to the question: 'Where do we come from and where are we going?' **They are prepared to subject themselves to tests and undergo trials – and you are one of them. They reach maturity sooner than others, and will find peace and joy even in this life through giving help, support, comfort, service, care and love.** This is your path. Now go and thank the Gods."**

In the ancient teachings, the weighing of the heart is overseen by forty-two karmic lords and each of them asks a question to the initiate, the answering of which determines the measure of the weight of the heart against the feather of truth 'Ma-at.'

* See Bibliography

Initiation

In Dolores Ashcroft-Nowicki's book, *'The Shining Paths – An experimental journey through the tree of life'*, there are forty-two questions asked of the forty-two assessors at the weighing of the heart. Now, when you read the questions that follow please go easy on yourself. A realisation will come upon you of where you may have been living out of integrity, where your work lies ahead of you, and a very real picture of your heart weighing more than the feather of truth – of Ma'at – will be presented to you.

Remember, go easy on yourself and allow yourself to feel. The good news is, there is still time to make corrections in your life.

Forty-two questions at the Weighing of the Heart against the Feather of Ma'at

> "1 – *Hast thou given due thought to the body inhabited by thee?*
> 2 – *Hast thou lived the fullness of the time allotted to thee?*
> 3 – *Hast thou refrained from being unclean in body and mind?*
> 4 – *Hast thou loved with the body, only where the heart is also?*
> 5 – *Hast thou had knowledge of those forbidden to thee?*
> 6 – *Hast thou kept thee only to the sword or the distaff?*
> 7 – *Hast thou respected the bodies of younger brethren?*
> 8 – *Hast thou stolen?*
> 9 – *Has thou taken food and drink to excess?*
> 10 – *Hast thou killed?*
> 11 – *Hast thou spoken unjustly in anger?*
> 12 – *Hast thou looked upon the goods of another with envy?*
> 13 – *Hast thou known jealousy?*
> 14 – *Hast thou spoken ill of any man or woman in anger?*
> 15 – *Hast thou been indifferent in work?*
> 16 – *Hast thou profaned the mysteries?*
> 17 – *Hast thou known pride in thyself that is false?*
> 18 – *Hast thou strayed from the path allotted to thee?*
> 19 – *Hast thou lusted for precious metals?*
> 20 – *Hast thou been too worldly?*
> 21 – *Hast thou been just in thy dealings in the marketplace?*
> 22 – *Hast thou repaid all debts promptly?*
> 23 – *Hast thou been generous to the needy?*

24 – *Hast thou lived to gain from others?*
25 – *Hast thou tongue been as a viper to cause laughter in others?*
26 – *Hast thou been a friend?*
27 – *Hast thou hated another to the exclusion of all else?*
28 – *Hast thou lent thy body to any form from the other side?*
29 – *Hast thou been thy parent's joy?*
30 – *Hast thou honoured all faiths that are of the light?*
31 – *Hast thou given time to be at peace with the gods?*
32 – *Hast thou turned aside from wisdom given in love?*
33 – *Hast thou listened for that which is not for thy ears?*
34 – *Hast thou lived in the light?*
35 – *Hast thou been a sword for the weak?*
36 – *Hast thou enslaved any other life?*
37 – *Hast thou faced the mirror of self?*
38 – *Hast thou taken the words of the mouth of any other man as thy own?*
39 – *Hast thou known that all journeys end but to begin?*
40 – *Hast thou remembered the brethren of the Earth and been compassionate to those younger brethren who serve thee as beasts in the field and home?*
41 – *Hast thou ever worked man or beast beyond its strength in thy greed?*
42 – *Is there one upon the Earth who is glad thou hast lived?"*

Initiation

Figure 52: Weighing of the Heart

When I went through this list, I could answer positively for half of them, if I was lucky. So, I know the work that lies before me this lifetime. When the heart is heavier than the Feather of Ma'at then the heart is eaten by the Devourer – the forces of death and karma. The challenges of life become too much and we die of some cause, the divine atoms burn out and have spent their fuel, and we are reborn on the wheel of Samsara.

With every little life being like the attendance to a new class and the learning of a new lesson, albeit unconsciously for the most part, with the astrological conditions at the time of the entities' death being the exact same positioning at its rebirth, the entity is reborn at a time that the planetary conditions of the solar system reflect those of its last life. And so the baby human that is born is imprinted with the signature vibratory frequency, to work through the karmic consequences of cause and effect, not as a punishment but as the opportunity for the soul qualities to be developed through that hardship – on Earth, which is the school for the soul.

Esoteric Astrology

In Esoteric Astrology, the soul travels around the wheel of the zodiac in an anti-clockwise direction, working through the lessons of the signs in a largely unconscious fashion, until through many lives of suffering and torment, it gets an inkling of the point and the reason for its existence. At this point it starts to travel back through the signs of the zodiac in a clockwise direction. It is very much necessary for the youth to understand that 'you only live once' (YOLO) is inaccurate. The very position of YOLO is fabricated so that your divine essence can be siphoned off by those that know how; those that have the power behind the scenes. We will get to them in Chapter 8.

In Alice Bailey's 1974 book *'Labours of Hercules'*, page 2, she writes:

> *"The Great Presiding One says about the aspirant that is becoming the disciple: 'Tell him from me to return the other way and then to travel round the circle. Then will he find the object of his search. Watch over his steps and when he has an understanding heart, an eager mind and a skillful hand, bring him to me... again the centuries past. The great wheel turned, and in turning carried all the sons of men, who are the sons of God, upon their way. They found the way. They passed the gates and struggled towards the mountaintop and towards the place of death and sacrifice. The teacher saw a man emerge from out of this crowd... demanding deeds to do, service to render unto God and man and willingness to travel the way to God, he stood before the Great Presiding One who works within the Chamber of the Lord and a word goes forth: 'Obey the Teacher on the Way'. Prepare the last tests.* **Pass through each gate** *and in the sphere which they reveal and guard, perform the labour which befits the sphere. Learn thus the lesson and begin with love to serve the men of Earth."*

Initiation

When the soul has lived countless lifetimes, it progresses through the signs in a clockwise direction and progressively learns to master its body's lower nature. At this time, in Aries, the soul learns to kill the negative seed thoughts that keep it paralysed as it learns to deal with the fiery explosive energies of creation; its sacred and guiding mantra is *'I come forth and from the plane of mind I rule.'* In Taurus, it learns to control its desire nature, somewhat realising that the good of the group outweighs pleasure for itself, and its sacred and guiding mantra is *'I see, and when the eye is opened, all is illumined.'* In Gemini, it learns experience and it exhausts the exploration in following both the good and the bad, and light and darker impulses, in order to gather information through experience hence its signet being the 'twins'; its sacred and guiding mantra is *'I recognise my other self, and in the waning of that self, I grow and glow.'* In Cancer, the soul then retreats into its shell and digests its experience where it learns to follow the fleeting impressions of its sensitive intuition, its sacred and governing mantra is *'I build a lighted house and therein dwell.'* The next step, in Leo, the soul has found courage to come out of its shell and journey forth towards the mountain that it sees in the distance but in order to get there, it must overcome its personality.

The lion exerts himself/herself too forcefully and is hypnotised by its own roar. It has much to learn about its relative unimportance and its sacred and guiding mantra is *'I am that I am.'* In Virgo, the soul must learn that it is not in control and through the surrender of its need to control and just let things be, it embodies the mother/virgin, and can give birth to the divine child – and its sacred and guiding mantra is *'I am the Mother and the Child, I, God, I matter am.'* In Libra, the soul seeks balance. It is in a constant battle with itself to find balance and tame the wild boar of reckless abandon – the sacred and guiding mantra is *'I choose the way which leads between the two great lines of force.'* In Scorpio, all of the darker traits of the soul come forth and must be transmuted under the strength of the rock of the will, and it must die to itself, sting itself to death, in order to move forward transformed as the eagle Aquila – and its sacred and guiding mantra is *'Warrior am I and from the battle I emerge triumphant.'*

In Sagittarius, the half-man-half-god creature, the 'centaur', and the resurrected phoenix, must recognise the need to overcome the devastation of abuse of power and spiritual pride and arrogance before being permitted to close the gate behind it that lies at the foot of the mountain of initiation. Its sacred and guiding mantra is *'I see the goal. I reach that goal and then I see another.'*

In Capricorn, the soul's mettle is tested, and in this sparse and hostile wilderness the soul must find its own strength and stand in its true essence. At the same time, it must learn to bend its knees and surrender to a higher power and become the initiate – this is a journey of immense loneliness and terrible trial, in which the spiritual man becomes the *'Signature of God.'* Its sacred and guiding mantra is *'Lost am I in Light Supernal, yet on that light I turn my back.'*

In Aquarius, the soul has traversed the mountain of initiation (well at least it thinks it has, it is only really one peak of the mountain range). It stands visible on the summit and looks far down into the valley and plains below and sees the whole road that led to its current position of glorious revelation and insight. Here, it hears the 'word' of that power that it has learned to humbly bow to, and the word says, *'You must now go back down the mountain and share with others you meet that are on the way up what it is you have seen and heard, to help them if they are lost.'* At this stage, the soul is the true server of the race and despite the conditions of the way that ensure and guarantee that he will be misunderstood, and shunned and criticised and perhaps hated and killed, he happily carries that burden for the sake of the salvation of his brothers and sisters in humanity and for the grander heavenly plan; and the sacred and guiding mantra is *'Waters of life am I, poured forth for thirsty men.'* The lights of humanity such as Mahatma Ghandi, Nelson Mandela, Mother Teresa, Dalai Lama, Krishnamurti, Martin Luther King, Helena Blavatsky, Gautama Buddha, the Prophet Muhammad, and Jesus Christ were all initiates of varying degrees.

In Pisces, the soul melts into the universal mind and becomes a saviour of humanity and the Earth. It is rapidly approaching the culmination of its terrestrial individual physical existence on Earth, and its need for re-birth through the turning of the wheel of Samsara is coming to an end. This is providing that the soul heeds its lessons and does not regress through abuse of power (thereby setting up conditions for a negative karma that will need to be atoned for, transmuted, and worked through in another lifetime) before it is free of the trammels of earthly life. Its sacred and guiding mantra is *'I leave the Father's House and turning back I save.'*

The zodiac is a blueprint, a map, with stations that show the journey and path of the development of a soul, an individual spark of divine consciousness that has separated itself from the whole to go through myriad lifetimes to experience pain and suffering. And thus, by way of its dark struggle, it remembers its divine origins, transmutes the darkness into light and transmutes the matter of the vehicle of its consciousness (the body) into spirit, successfully **spiritualising matter.** In Alice Bailey's book *'Initiation Human and Solar'*, pages 103-104, she describes the difficulty of walking this path, read and apply it back to what you know of the lives of the people I have listed on the previous page.

> *"The Path of Discipleship is a difficult one to tread, and the path of Initiation harder still; an Initiate is but a battle scarred warrior, the victor in many a hard-won fight; he speaks not of his achievements, for he is too busy with the Great Work in hand; he makes no reference to himself or to all that he has accomplished, save to deprecate the littleness of what has been done. Never the less, to the world he is ever a man of large influence, the wielder of spiritual power, the embodier of ideals, the worker for humanity, who unfailingly brings results which succeeding generations will recognise. He is one who, in spite of all this great achievement, is seldom understood by his own generation. He is frequently the butt of men's tongues and frequently all that he does is misinterpreted; he lays his all – time, money, influence, reputation, and all that the world considers worthwhile – upon the alter of altruistic service, and frequently offers his life as a final gift, only to find that those he has served throw his gift back to him, scorn his*

renunciation and label him with unsavoury names. But the Initiate cares not, for it is his privilege to see somewhat into the future and therefore he realises that the force he has generated will in due course of time bring fulfilment to the PLAN."

What must also be understood is that, as we live our life, we actually move into the influence of other signs by the way we learn our soul lessons; our sun sign does not remain fixed. In Astrology the 12 signs of the Zodiac are categorized into Cardinal, Mutable and Fixed signs. The Cardinal Signs are Aries, Cancer, Libra, Capricorn; Mutable Signs are Gemini, Virgo, Sagittarius, Pisces; and the Fixed Signs are Taurus, Leo, Scorpio, Aquarius.

However, at the point where we make the jump to the seventh octave of vibration – then we actually become 'cause', and this is what is meant in the first symbol of The Book of Thoth that I have revealed to you, The Magician. At this level, we are no longer affected by the planetary influence of the zodiac. At the seventh octave of vibration, because divinity has recognised itself within us, we become a potent centre for the expression of the working out of the plan on Earth – we actually become cause as a conscious co-worker. This is the coded message preserved in the Great Pyramid in Egypt – using the square base, the material form, divinity can manifest itself! The golden capstone to the White Pyramid – the Great Pyramid – is the model of man, Adam Kadmon. All DNA activated.

Six Initiations on Earth – where the candidate becomes the Path

The path of the initiate, where the candidate is holding the hand of Anubis, is comprised of six stages, for there are six major initiations for a human being to go through before they succeed in the task of the elevation of their consciousness to the divine, and the spiritualisation of the matter of their bodies.

According to the book, *'You Can Avoid Physical Death: Physical Body Ascension to the New Earth'*, by Robert E. Pettit PhD, there are six temples that the candidate (from which I said was depicted in white being led by Anubis in the Weighing of the Heart frieze) must progress through in order to achieve the goal of the spiritualisation of matter and become an ascended master. These six temples are as follows:

1. *Temple of God/Goddess: Here the candidate for initiation brings all thoughts and feelings into alignment with their divine self.*
2. *Temple of Learning: Here the candidate receives information about the universal laws in operation on Earth.*
3. *Temple of Love: Here the candidate learns to achieve a state of harmony and unconditional love for all creation.*
4. *Temple of Ascension: Here the candidate has to discern their God/Goddess within and then become aware of their past negative (thought) creations and transgressions against the Holy spirit so that they can face and overcome the tricks of the ego and transform everything into white light.*
5. *Temple of Consecration: Here all of the body systems of the candidate are cleansed and purified in preparation for the ascension.*
6. *Temple of Service: Here it is that the candidate is guided towards giving service to others by putting aside their worldly pursuits. They are expected to volunteer some of their time to give service on a planetary level. This service usually manifests as becoming a teacher.*

This six-stage Initiation process is the very same one that Jesus Christ went through himself, and the reason why we don't hear from him until he is thirty-two years of age in the Holy Bible, as he had to undergo his training and he had to pass his tests. And the accounts of the person Isa throughout India are the accounts of Jesus before he returns to his homeland. Remember Christ's words, 'These things I do, you can also do and greater.'

This is what he meant, as one becomes the Path or the Way.

The six-stage initiatory process up the Mountain of Initiation.

1. The Birth of Christ – TEMPLE 1
   The heart centre 'Anahata' is vivified (birth of Christ in a manger).

2. The Baptism of Christ – TEMPLE 2
   The throat centre 'Vishudda' is vivified (John the Baptist- baptising in the Jordan).

3. The Transfiguration – TEMPLE 3
   The 3rd eye centre 'Ajna' is vivified (forty days in the desert).

4. The Crucifixion – TEMPLE 4
   The Crown Chakra or 'Sahahsrara' is vivified.

5. The Resurrection – TEMPLE 5
   The soul Chakra (8th Chakra) is vivified (rising from the dead – the empty tomb).

6. The Ascension – TEMPLE 6
   The goal is almost complete, matter has been spiritualised (translation into white fire on the mountain).

Seven Mystical Gates – Seven Golden Keys

In esoteric teachings, there is mention of seven fabled mystical gates that must be passed through if one is to attain 'Christ or Buddha Consciousness or Nirvana.' In the book, *'Voice of the Silence'*, by Helena Blavatsky, originally published in 1889, she outlines these gates and tells us that the gates are locked by the passions incarnate. One must possess the golden keys in order to pass through them and move into higher states of consciousness. A vital link that Blavatsky does not mention is that each passing through of a 'gate' indicates the successful passing through of the next stage of initiation. Sometimes the trial proves too great and it leads to death. Then the soul must pick up from where they left off in the next life.

1 – Birth of Christ.
Golden Key – Dana – Key of charity and love immortal.

2 – Baptism of Christ.
Golden Key – Shila – Key of harmony of word and act.

3 – Transfiguration.
Golden Key – Kshanti – Patience sweet that naught can ruffle.

It is here that Christ spent the forty days in the desert. It is here that the disciple faces the '*Dweller of the Threshold*', it is here that is the beginning of the *Dharma* – the work that the soul is meant to do. It is here that the soul comes to know that the terrifying bridge of swords lies ahead.

4 – Crucifixion.
Golden Key – Virag – Indifference to pleasure and pain and the illusion conquered. The Gate of Woe.

The walking of the bridge of swords, the path of 10,000 snares, the path of the terrible Tau. The Bodhi Tree lies just beyond.

5 – Resurrection.
Golden Key – Virya – Dauntless energy that fights its way to truth.

The disciple/initiate who rests at the foot of the Bodhi Tree is now walking the path of true knowledge on the way to becoming the Diamond Soul.

6 – Ascension.
Golden Key – Dhyana – Diamond Soul.

The initiate must saturate himself in Pure Alaya – the Holy Spirit – and be as the flame in the pure white alabaster vase.

7 – The Paramita Heights.
Golden Key – **Prajna – The key that makes of a man a god. (The achievement of the 7th octave of vibration.)**

Buddha, Christ, Krishna, Horus, OSIRIS.

It is at the 7th Gate that one attains full Christ or Buddha consciousness, and it is here that the five ornaments of the Buddha are bestowed to the initiate and adept, verily upon the master. Each attainment is done through overcoming a total of ten defilements. This can be achieved through the practice of specific Jnanas (see appendix). The Five Wisdoms of the Buddha are symbolised as the following ornaments:

1. Wheel-like crown ornament — *mirror like pristine awareness* (Adarsa Jnana).
2. Earrings — *pristine awareness of discernment* (Prateyaveksana Jnana)
3. Necklace — *pristine awareness of total sameness* (Samata Jnana)
4. Bracelets — *pristine awareness of the ultimate dimension of phenomena* (Tathata Jnana)
5. Girdle — *the accomplishing of pristine awareness.*

So, we have the Buddha with:

Mirror-like pristine awareness; Pristine awareness of discernment; Pristine awareness of total sameness (foundation for unconditional love); Pristine awareness of ultimate dimensional phenomena; and the accomplishing of Pristine awareness. These are the same qualities exhibited in the life of Jesus the Christ and of Krishna and Horus.

It is also important to note that the seven portals/gates are spread out across three different hallways, the walking of which is the 'road less travelled' and will be the focus of the next chapter.

Using symbolism again, we come to a point in the journey of the spiritual seeker/disciple/initiate where they have a very specific, very hard, existential decision to make. They must choose a *vestment*. But before we get to that, I have something special to share with you.

True Interpretation of Biblical Revelations

Remember in Chapter 2, I presented a picture of the precession of the equinoxes to you and I assigned dates to the commencement of each of the ages? The dates of the ages were calculated based on astronomical phenomena being prophesied in the Bible in revelations. Although, up until now, this relationship has not been well understood as it requires an initiate to the mysteries sacred cosmic knowledge to understand.

The journey from the Age of Leo (10880 BC) to the Age of Aquarius (2020 AD) is 12,900 years. 12,900 years is one half of the 25,800-year full processional cycle or Great Cosmic Year, and a period where man will evolve to achieve the spiritualisation of matter or evolve to the 7th octave of vibration/consciousness.

The ancient initiates of Egypt left this knowledge preserved for us in the symbolism of the sphinx and the Great Pyramid. The Great Pyramid tells us that we have the potential to spiritualise matter, using the 'square base' material 'human body' as the vehicle. The sphinx tells us when this process will begin and how to get there to achieve it. The sphinx is an enigmatic creature comprised of four animals: the lion, the bull, the eagle and man.

The lion symbolises courage. It is the primary manifestation of the energy of fire – the fire element – and is fatherly in nature. The bull represents will. It is the primary manifestation of the energy of earth – the earth element – and is motherly in nature. The man represents knowledge. It is the primary element of energy of air – the air element – and is spiritual in nature. The Eagle symbolises spirit/silence, it is the primary manifestation of the energy of water – the water element – and is emotional/feeling in nature.

Astrologically, lion is to Leo, bull to Taurus, man is to Aquarius and a scorpion eagle to Scorpio. The goal of the human life is to spiritualise matter and the microcosm will always be 'by Hermes Law' reflected in the macrocosm – *As above, so below, so below, as above.* In other words, as in the heavens so on Earth, so on Earth as in the heavens.

So the sphinx constructed just before the age of Leo, in approx. 10880 BC, is a coded message and a marker that tells us that this current round of human evolution began approximately 12,900 years ago, and is due to culminate and begin again in the beginning of the Age of Aquarius circa 2020. In the heavens we have the macrocosmic representation of this as the fixed cross, Figure 53 (next page).

Revelation 4:7 *"The first living creature was like a lion, the second like an ox, the third had the face of a man, and the fourth was like a flying eagle."* – Leo, Taurus, Aquarius, Scorpio-Eagle.

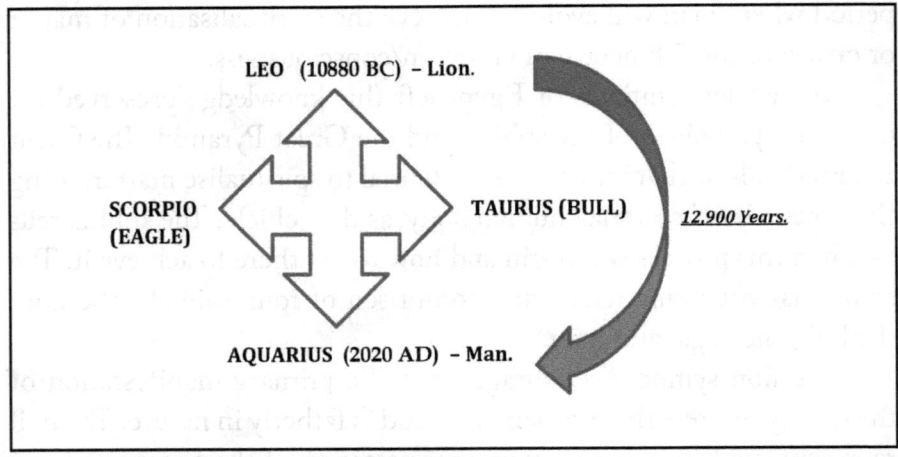

Figure 53: The fixed cross in the heavens. The 12,900 journey from the Age of Leo to the Age of Aquarius. Source and Copyright: N. S. Elijah 2016.

Revelation 4:8

> *"Day and night they never stop saying: 'Holy, Holy, Holy is the Lord God Almighty, who was and is, and is to come."*

Whilst the North/South axis (the vertical arm of the fixed cross) gives us the 'time of beginning' in the Age of Leo and 'time of ending' in the Age of Aquarius, the East/West axis (the horizontal arm of the fixed cross) gives us the method and the consequences of our choices of the use of our free will and creative life force. If we follow the lower nature of the animal and regress back to the 3rd octave of vibration, then we are the vile scorpion. However, the spiritually self-initiated man has learned to transmute his sexual urges and energies and guide them to higher channels, and thus the scorpion stings itself to death. Through exercising the will 'Taurus influences correctly', it transmutes and becomes the eagle and uses the creative forces to progress into the 6th and 7th octaves of vibration.

As the vernal point was moving into the Age of Taurus, we had the 'Sons of God', the 'priests/followers of Horus' who reigned for 13,400 years, preparing to leave the earthly plane. But they first made the great sacrifice and identified themselves more fully with matter, through breeding with our jungle-dwelling ancestors – under the motherly energies of the Age of Taurus – and planted the divine seed into our DNA around 6,000 years ago. This is the missing link that evolutionary scientists have not been able to understand!

The 'Sons of God' did this so that over time, from the astrological Age of Taurus to the astrological Age of Aquarius (soon beginning), the race of man, without visible guidance, would be given the opportunity to learn to spiritualise the matter of their physical bodies. They were given the opportunity to learn to open the seven chakras and function at the 7th octave of vibration:

Revelation 5:1

"Then I saw in the right hand of him who sat on the throne a scroll with writing on both sides and sealed with seven seals (Chakras)."

5.2 "And I saw a mighty angel proclaiming in a loud voice, "who is worthy to break the seals and open the scroll?" – The scroll is the locked DNA of mankind.

5.3 "But no one in heaven or on earth or under the earth could open the scroll or even look inside it.'

5.4 "I wept and wept because no one was found who was worthy to open the scroll or even look inside it."

5.5 "Then one of the elders said to me 'Do not weep! See, the lion of the tribe of Judah, the root of David, has triumphed. He is able to open the scroll and its seven seals."

At the beginning of the Age of Pisces came a 'Son of God', incarnated in a human body and taught the way to spiritualise matter (open the scroll) by being unconditional love in mind, body and spirit – love incarnate. That son of God was Jesus the Christened one, and Jesus succeeded in shifting his consciousness from the 4th to the 5th to the 6th to the 7th octave of vibration/consciousness and opened the seven seals (chakras) thereby achieving the goal and spiritualising matter, at the age of thirty-three.

And Christ gave a message that he would return and harvest the kingdom and punish the wicked.

Revelation 6:17 *"For that great day of their wrath has come, and who can withstand it?"*

7.3 *"Do not harm the land or the sea or the trees until we put a seal on the foreheads of the servants of God."*

7.4 *"Then I heard the number of those who were sealed: 144,000 from the tribes of Israel."* (12,000 masters from each sign of the zodiac).

7.9 *"After this I looked, and there before me was a great multitude that no one could count, from every nation, tribe, people and language standing before the throne and before the lamb. They were wearing white robes and were holding palm branches in their hands."*

7.13 *"Then one of the elders asked me, "Those in white robes… who are they, and where did they come from?"*

7.14 *"I answered, "Sir, you know." And he said, "These are they who have come out of the great tribulation; they have washed their robes and made them white in the blood of the lamb."*

7.15 *"Therefore, they are before the throne of God and serve him day and night in his temple* (their own bodies); *and he who sits on the throne will shelter them with his presence."*

7.16 *"Never again will they hunger, never again will they thirst. The sun will not beat them down; nor any scorching heat."*

Those who have heard the message and learn to spiritualise matter, submitting their personal will to the higher will of God-will, at the appointed time, gain the ascension and will not have to reincarnate into the denser energies of Earth again (unless they choose to). However, those that do not listen and continue as the vile scorpion, worshipping the false god of materialism and selfishness will be punished (the Earth will be subject to a cleansing).

9.20 *"They did not stop worshipping demons, and idols of gold, silver, bronze, stone and wood."*

9.21 *"Nor did they repent of their murders, their magic arts, their sexual immorality or their thefts."*

Then from Revelations 10-21, there is an account of the ramifications of not heeding the *true* meaning of the instruction of Christ. Remember that in Chapter 2, I brought to your attention the ancient understanding of the four elemental triangles of astrological signs that comprise the zodiac. Pay attention now, as we add this to the fixed cross, and explain the true meaning of the next passages of Revelations.

Revelations 21:10 *"And he (the last of the seven angels) carried me away in the spirit to a mountain great and high and showed me the **holy city Jerusalem – coming down out of heaven from God**."*

Revelations 21.11 *"It shone with the Glory of God, and its brilliance was like that of a very precious jewel, like a jasper clear as crystal."*

Revelations 21.12 *"It had a great, high wall **with twelve gates**, and with twelve Angels at the gates. On the gates were written the names of the twelve tribes of Israel."* (Which we know are the twelve signs of the zodiac).

Revelations 21.13 *"**There were three gates on the East*** (the earth triangle), ***three gates on the North*** (the fire triangle), ***three gates on the South*** (the air triangle) *and **three gates on the West*** (the water triangle)."

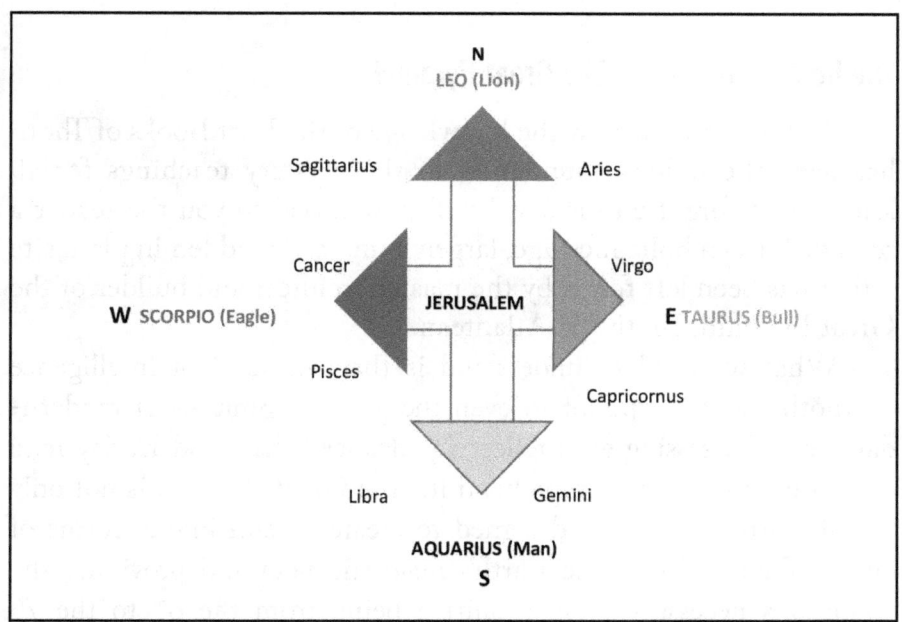

Figure 54: The Four Faces of God, The Twelve Gates of the Fixed Points. The High and Holy city Jerusalem coming down out of heaven from God. Source and Copyright: N. S. Elijah 2016.

In Malachi in the Bible it mentions this:

"Lo, I will send you the prophet Elijah before the great and terrible day of the Lord comes. He will turn the hearts of parents to their children and the hearts of children to their parents, so that I will not come and strike the land with a curse."

– Malachi 4:5-6

The 12,900-year period written in the stars that began about 12,900 years ago, is due to culminate at the beginning of the Age of Aquarius in approximately 2020AD.

Amongst others, I am here to assist in the externalisation of the heavenly hierarchy on Earth and to help in the awakening, so do not miss this unprecedented time. Don the white robes spiritualise matter. The pages you are reading are part of the fulfillment of this prophecy!

The Book of Thoth and The Great Pyramid

To further show how the knowledge of the Lost Books of Thoth has been the hidden foundation to the mystery teachings for all known and forgotten history, I will now reveal to you the reader a remarkable symbolic message, largely remaining hidden in plain site – that has been left for us by the master architect and builder of the Great Pyramid, Thoth the Atlantean.

What we need to understand is that the level of intelligence of Thoth was far superior to even the greatest geniuses of modern-day man. Possessing an intellect so advanced that modern day man cannot even begin to comprehend it. The Great Pyramid is not only a multipurpose machine designed to create certain higher forms of energy for stabilizing the Earth's magnetic field and providing the conditions necessary to help shift a being from the 6th to the 7th octave of vibration, but contained in its construction it holds the measurements of the size and weight of the Earth, the distance of the stars, the distance of the Earth to the Sun. And if that is not enough, there is also contained within its very construction, a map for the evolution of human consciousness. It symbolically reveals the steps taken from a human in their first incarnation and all the way through their long journey of incarnations, to the point of becoming a realised divine being. Nothing in its design has been left to chance. It is in the viewing of the cross section of the Great Pyramid that 'with eyes to see', we are shown the journey of mankind from their first incarnation, to the last one where they no longer need to re-incarnate on Earth, as they reach the goal of achieving the 7th octave of vibration and become Divine.

If we examine the cross section from figure 47 page 151, we will note that the entrance into the Pyramid (triangle = divinity) is on a downward slope. This depicts how the spirit of man descends into matter and journeys for a time through many incarnations, learning and assimilating at the 3rd and 4th octaves of vibration. However, a time will come in his personal evolution where he has after many incarnations reached a crossroad. He can at this point of decision, choose to follow the voice of his lower nature and thus continue to descend further and further into matter, becoming grosser and coarser in consciousness until he descends into 'Hell'.

Or he can take his lower nature in hand, turn from the path that he has walked blindly for many incarnations, and begin to listen to the promptings of his divine over self, become a disciple and begin the journey up the mountain of initiation (the upward sloping path). This point of decision in the Lost Books of Thoth is depicted in the Major Arcana tarot card VI of *The Lovers*: on the one hand, one choice – sensuality. On the other hand, the other choice, wisdom. And at the point of decision, choosing wisdom – the seeker becomes the Hermit, withdrawing from life to come into closer contact with the voice of their soul.

After lifetimes of struggle further into light, learning to purify his character and development of an all-encompassing love, he comes more and more into contact with his soul and is led to discover many hidden treasures and gifts of his spirit – represented by the secrets hidden in the Queens Chamber. Then after lifetimes symbolically dwelling within the Queens Chamber, being immersed in the spiritual gifts and insights and wonders – the time will come for the Initiate to reach a yet higher level. And it is then that the sacred walk to the Kings chamber begins – whereby, the Initiate in full contact with the Heart of the Mysteries, with assistance of Divine energies channeled through the portals to Sirius and Orion (the shafts leading out of the sides of the pyramid), a man becomes Divine.

The 7th Octave of vibration is achieved, a man becomes more than man – walks unencumbered on the physical plane, holding the blue light codes of Sirius awakened in his DNA (the central spiritual sun) – becomes in himself the Sun of Osiris, all seven seals opened, a master of time and space – like *Jeshua Ben Joseph* – The Christed one.

Chapter 7

THE ROAD LESS TRAVELLED

"Two roads diverged in a wood, and I took the one less travelled by, and that has made all the difference."
— **Robert Frost**

Remember the circumpunct ⊙ (from Chapter 2) being the symbol for God? Recall that from the point of origination in the middle, vibrations are sent forth in all directions and eventually slow down to become matter. It is on the journey to the spiritualisation of matter that the other levels of reality become apparent to the candidate for higher initiations.

The Gate of Sagittarius lies at the foot of the mountain of initiation. The man or woman working through the lessons of Capricorn climbs the mountain, comes down the other side and enters Aquarius, shines their light and nourishes with the waters of life and finally immerses themselves back into the universal ocean of consciousness, overcoming the challenges and lessons by working through the sign of Pisces.

The initiations of the way to Christ or Buddha consciousness are not ritualistic set formalities, but rather the passing through of experiences and intuited tasks that are designed to test the strength of certain soul qualities of a disciple. Once passed through, they allow heightened cosmic energies to flow into the initiate and the natural unlocking of the bandhas (energetic blocks in the body linked to achieved states of consciousness).

You may think that the experiences of Jesus Christ and Gautama Buddha and the depiction of the candidate on the wall being led by Anubis are different, but they represent the same thing; Jesus and Siddhartha Gautama also wore that white robe and 'had their hand held' by Anubis (the higher forces). You must remember that the ancients relied upon symbolism to depict deep spiritual truths.

The Four Stages of Enlightenment

The stages of initiation are also represented in Mahayana and Theravada Buddhism. They are known as the four stages of enlightenment – or Ariyas. However, their teaching also does not specify the concept of initiation. I will draw a very clear link to this now for you.

At the first initiation (The birth of Christ consciousness):

The seeker/pupil/aspirant/disciple/chela/initiate has an uprooted wrong view but still has other defilements to overcome; at this stage he is known as *'Sottapatti'* or 'one who has entered the stream' or 'stream-winner.' He has seen Nirvana but as yet cannot reside there. Interestingly, in the Buddhist teachings of Ariya's they say that one who has become *'Sottapatti'* will attain *'Arhatta'* (full enlightenment) within seven more lifetimes.

However, if they are diligent then they may awaken fully in their present life. It is at this stage that the *Sottapatti* (the one who has gained Sottapanna and entered the stream – pranava) has an intuitive grasp of their Dharma. The Dharma is the work that their soul is meant to do in this lifetime, they have the *Dharmacakku*; the opened eye to Dharma.

After the first initiation and at the second initiation (The baptism of the Christ):

The *'Sottapanni'* becomes the *'Sakadagami'* or 'The Returning One.' According to the Buddhist teaching, the *'Sakadagami'* will have but one more lifetime at most on the wheel of Samsara. However, if he attains the next stage of enlightenment in this lifetime through diligence then he will not return to this world again (karmic consequence). The *'Sakadagami'* is free of three of the ten chains:

1. Belief in the separate self
2. Attachment (ritual and rites)
3. Sceptical doubt (for he sees the truth). He has also considerably weakened the chains of
   a. Sensuous Craving
   b. Ill Will or Dislike.

According to Wikipedia, the mind of the *'Sakadagami'* is very pure. Thoughts of greed, hatred and delusion do not arise often and if they do they are not obsessed over.

At the third initiation (the transfiguration into Christ), the *'Sakadagami'* becomes *'Anagami'* or a 'non-returner.' This is the third stage of enlightenment, the third Avidya. The *'Anagami'* has cut five of the ten chains that bind the ordinary mind:

1. Belief in a separate self.
2. Attachment
3. Sceptical Doubt
4. Sensuous Craving
5. Ill Will (Dislike)

But the five higher chains still remain, the *'Anagami'* is not yet free of:

6. Craving for material existence
7. Craving for immaterial existence
8. Conceit
9. Restlessness
10. Ignorance

Remember the Seven Principles of Thoth/Hermes: *All is mind, the universe is mental.*

Remember too that we are made in the Father's image as creator beings in consciousness. It is at this level of *'Anagami'* that the mind is very pure. Also remember Christ's admonition: *'The things you do in the mind you have already done.'*

The fourth stage of enlightenment is where one becomes *Arhat* or *Arhant* or '*one who is worthy.*' The Arhat has gone through the fourth initiation and through this crucifixion and great renunciation the last of the chains are broken: craving for material existence, craving for immaterial existence, conceit, restlessness, and ignorance.

It is here, the Buddhist instruction is, the first four **Jhanas** assist with the overcoming of the craving for material existence and the last four Jhanas assist with the overcoming of the immaterial existence. **Remember the Ornaments of the Buddha** (see Appendix for information about the Jhanas).

In the mystery school teachings, it is taught that where we stand on our personal journey of evolution is a private affair. It is not something that should be boasted about or advertised etc. Despite this being an anonymous treatise, all I will say on this matter, is that I identify as *Sakadagami* on my way to becoming *Anagami*, as I am in possession of *Dharmakaccu* – I have the opened eye to my Dharma and I understand very clearly my life's mission – my life's work..

My life's mission has been to remember and figure all this out, to start in the valley with the mountain in the distance. Born with a state of amnesia, a state that is maintained by the deliberate manipulation of society to ensure that the level of consciousness remains repressed; and to seek the truth. A journey to truth in which man becomes the path. I would become the path the hard way; through suffering encountered via the ignorant abuse of the noble eight-fold path, and encountering the exacting measure of karmic consequence for living with the wrong view – the wrong intention, the wrong speech, the wrong action, the wrong effort, the wrong livelihood, the wrong mindfulness, and the wrong concentration.

In order to reorient my life and live by following the noble eight-fold path of:

1. Right View
2. Right Intention
3. Right Speech
4. Right Action

5. Right Livelihood
6. Right Effort
7. Right Mindfulness
8. Right Concentration.

I chose this path to be able to show the way, to be able to point out the pitfalls along the way, by documenting the stages of my transformation through direct experience in this very message you are reading. In order to show the 'truth' of the messages of the previous messengers that the five major religions are built upon; in order to illustrate that it was indeed the same message that they each come to deliver. However, without 'eyes to see' and without 'ears to hear', these messages were misinterpreted and subjected to thousands of years of historical distortion.

It is in the 'Following of the Path' by the 'becoming of the path', that the bridge is built, from the 'Fathers of the Spiritual Doctrines' to the Son's that taught to the best of their ability what they understood to be the meaning of their spiritual experiences. It is in the becoming of the path that the truth of Jesus Christ's message is finally seen "I am the Way (The Path), The Truth and the Life" and "These things that I do, you can also do and greater."

Will I become *Arhat* in this life? I do not know. All I can do is follow the 'noble eight-fold path', work with the Mystical Kabbalah Tree of Life, seek the remaining three keys over the bridge of swords, surrender my individual will to the will of God, Allah, Yahweh, Jehovah, and The Divine Singer – Brahma.

The Three Hallways

These six Initiations on Earth are encountered over what is known as three symbolic hallways.
The first hall is the hall of ignorance –
– the physical reality and associated challenges. First initiation.
The second hall is the hall of learning –
– the astral reality and associated challenges. Second initiation.
The third hall is the hall of wisdom –
– the mental reality and associated challenges and blessings. Third initiation.

THE THREE HALLWAYS – THE THREE PLANES OF INITIATION.

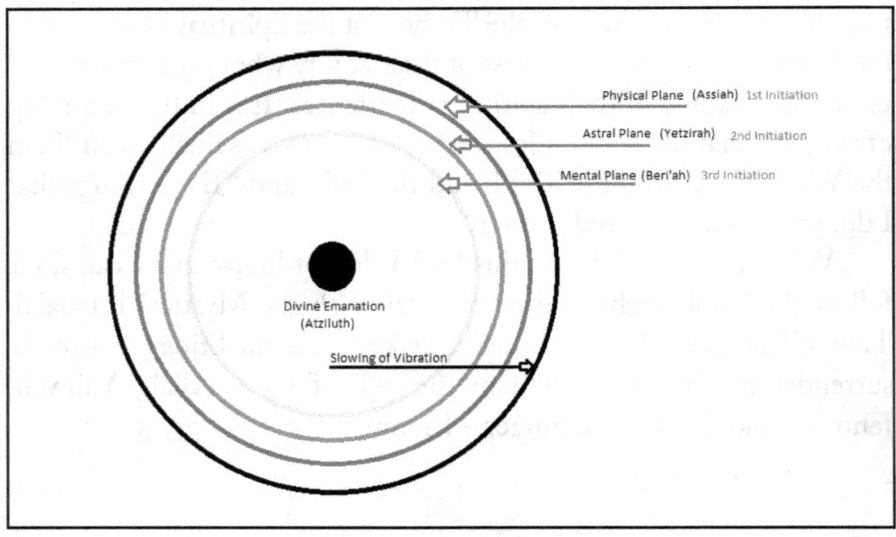

Figure 55: The Three Hallways, the three planes of Initiation, showing the slowing down of divine emanations/vibration and the corresponding Jewish Kabbalistic worlds. Source and Copyright: N. S. Elijah 2016.

At the first initiation, the birth of the Christ; the lures of the pleasures of the physical body are controlled. Gluttony, licentiousness, lust, getting drunk; all these impulses are no longer listened to (as they are at the 3rd level of vibration). It is in the Hall of Ignorance upon the physical plane that the first initiation is taken.

At the second initiation, the baptism of the Christ; the initiate enters the Hall of Learning, and here the initiate learns to navigate the astral plane and go through the difficult 'hour' known as the *'Tearing of the Veil – the Dragon of the Threshold.'* The astral body and the astral plane are his training ground. Long and hard must this struggle be in order to learn control of the energetic centres of the body and the astral forces.

At the third initiation, the transfiguration; the initiate knocks upon the door of the hall of wisdom, and here the initiate learns to control things on the mental plane. It is here that the initiate faces the *'dweller of the threshold'* and here that the victor transmutes their lower self. Here the initiate is given access to more 'cosmic-energy' and his whole being is flooded with light from his christed self, his divine over-self – think of the auras of Christ, Buddha, Krishna, Horus and the halo of the saints.

As one progresses on this spiritual journey, overcoming the different challenges and discovering the various keys of ascent up the Mountain of Initiation, with every step they are further spiritualising the matter of their physical vehicle.

Every renunciation, every overcoming of the lower nature, the passions incarnate, serves to activate hidden aspects of our genetic code; and man moves from the 6th octave of vibration or consciousness of the prophet/seer, into the 7th octave – that of the God Man, or a Son of the Higher Light, the Son of the Stars. In the treasured teachings and instruction in J. J. Hurtak's *'Keys of Enoch'* ®, reproduced with permission, he explains this phenomena in Key 104 as follows:

42. And so in the Prajnaparamita Sutra we have the mathematical star coding of how the son of Man, the son of human flesh, rises to orders of the stars to become a son of the stars.

43. This evolution from the physical body of creation to the higher intelligence involves a deeper understanding of life as multidimensional evolution where individuality does not count, only the continuity of the human species. To this end, the physical body must be initiated into the light before it can receive the 'over-self' body of light which is the true *I AM* identity.

(The third initiation: the transfiguration).

44. This means that all seven chakra centres must first be working in perfect harmony and completely aligned with the template of light, the eighth chakra, the connecting link with the over-self, working with the Christ body of Light.

45. And once man has gone beyond his physiological limitations of self and desires only to serve his fellow creation and the Father – he has purified himself from his carnal predilections and manifested love sufficient to receive the outer garment of light.

At the fourth initiation, the crucifixion; the initiate is walking through the Hall of Wisdom, denounces everything that is held to be of importance in the eyes of his fellow men and aligns his will with the will of the divine. He walks upon the path known as The Path of the Terrible Tau (the tau is another word for cross), he becomes the path, navigates across the bridge of swords and 10,000 snares, and if this trial does not kill him, he passes through the Gate of Woe to the Vale of Bliss and sits under the Bodhi Tree. At this stage, the initiate is in possession of five Golden Keys:

DANA – *The key of charity and love immortal*
SHILA – *The key of harmony of word and act*
KSHANTI – *The key of patience sweet that naught can ruffle*
VIRAG – *The key of indifference to pleasure and pain*
VIRYA – *The key of dauntless energy that fights its way to truth.*

The Initiate has at this point used DANA to pass the first gate (the first initiation), SHILA to pass the second gate (the second initiation), KSHANTI to pass the third gate (the third initiation) and VIRAG to pass the fourth gate (the fourth initiation). The initiate finds himself holding VIRYA and searching for the final two keys: DHYANA – the key of the diamond soul, and PRAJNA the key that makes of a man a god.

Because a picture says a thousand words, I have put all of this into a representative diagram, Figure 56 (next page), of the journey up the spiritual mountain of initiation. Take five minutes now to study this, reading from the bottom up.

Figure 56: Mountain of Initiation – 7 Noble Gates of Virtue. The Journey up the Mountain of Initiation: paralleling the ancient Egyptian teachings of the Weighing of the Heart, The 7 mystical gates of Theosophical teaching, the four stages of Enlightenment of the Buddhist teaching, the Four stages of the Cross of the Initiatic Journey of Christ, the Culmination of the Working with the Kabbalistic Tree of Life and the correct interpretation of Esoteric Astrology. Source and Copyright: N. S. Elijah 2016. This diagram cannot be reproduced in any format without prior express written permission from the Author.

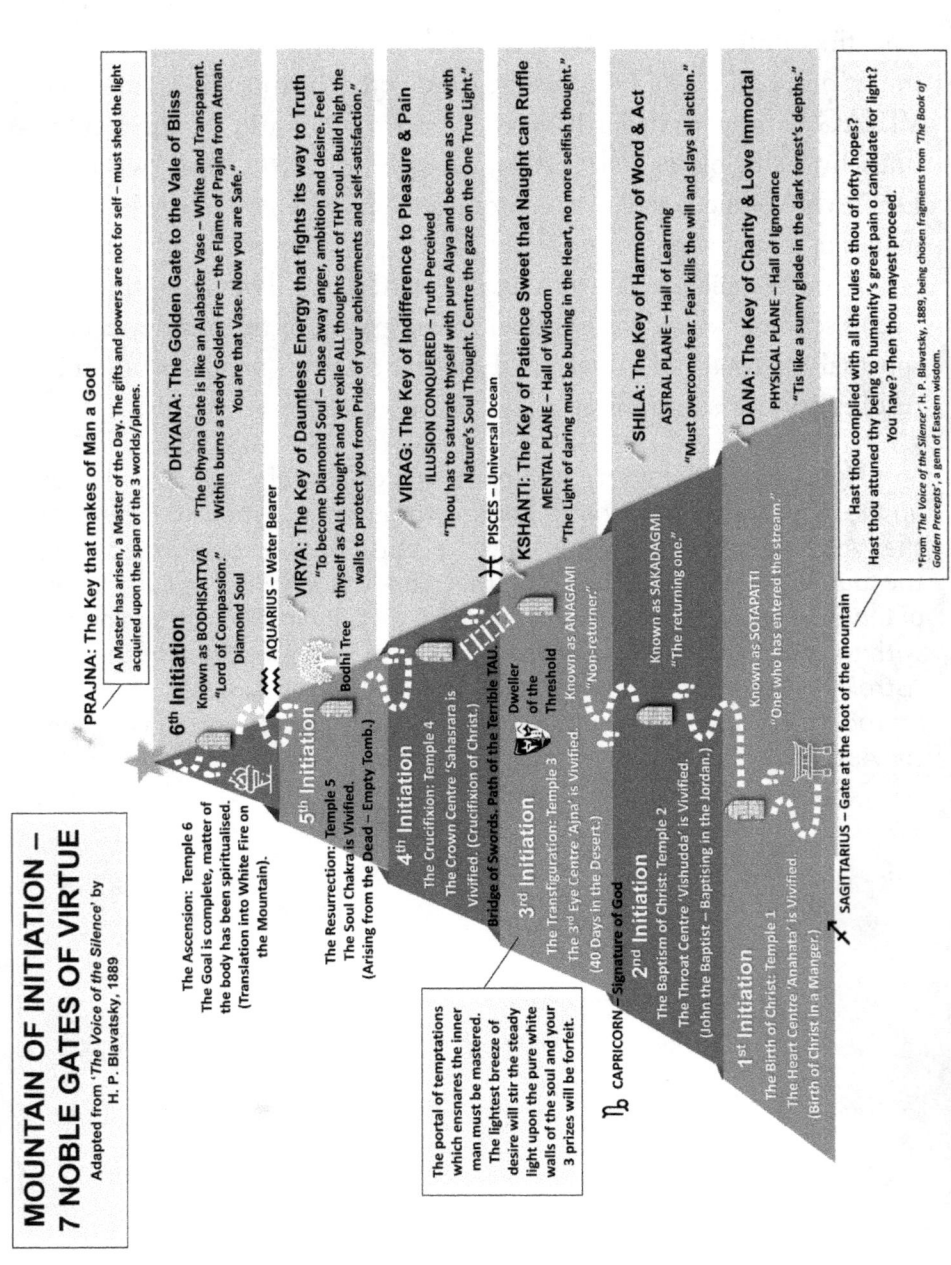

Figure 56: Mountain of Initiation – 7 Noble Gates of Virtue (Adapted from *'The Voice of Silence'* by H. P. Blavatsky, 1889).

The Path – Buddhist Instruction – The Dharma.

Buddha taught the four noble truths:
1. The truth of suffering
2. The truth of the origin of suffering: The ignorance that gives rise to twelve links of dependent origination and rebirth on the wheel of Samsara.
3. The truth of cessation of suffering.
4. The truth of the path.

Great blessing and solace can be found in the realisation that *'the seed of enlightenment'* – Tathagatagarbha – is latent in all of us; although generally, through our present circumstances, we cannot directly perceive it.

According to the instruction of Kalu Rinpoche in his 1986 publication *'The Dharma that illuminates all beings impartially like the light of the sun and the moon'*:

> *"Part of the fundamental process of turning our minds away from Samsara (the wheel of rebirth) and towards enlightenment is understanding Samsara for what it is. Understanding suffering and recognising the limitations of our present situation, we begin to seek a way out. This initial turning of the mind is the foundation of the path in its aspect as a causal factor leading to enlightenment."*

Existential Quandary

The initiate is climbing the mountain of initiation and a very real existential question comes upon him: Do I wish to go on?

And If I wish to go on, do I do so for myself or to assist others?

So according to the ancient book of Golden Precepts: an initiate must choose a robe to wear. Now this decision does not come lightly and as you can probably deduce in the language of symbolism, it is not an actual wardrobe selection of a physical garment of clothing but rather the conscious choosing of a pathway, represented as a vestment. Do they choose the robes of *Dharmakaya*? Or do they choose the robes of *Nirmanakaya*?

According to the Golden Precepts of Blavatsky's Voice of the Silence, 1889:

The choice of Dharmakaya vestment is known as *'the open way'* where the Arhant enters the thrice glorious state: the Nirvana of destruction of the personality that kills compassion, as it is the end of rebirth as they have ascended for themselves. This is the way to selfish bliss shunned by the bodhisattvas of *'the Secret Heart.'* The thrice glorious state which is the oblivion of the world and men forever.

The choice of the *Nirmanakaya* vestment is known as *'the Secret way'* where the Arhan chooses to wear the humble robe and forego eternal bliss for self, to help mankind with salvation. This choice is to reach Nirvana's bliss but to renounce it and it is the Supreme path. For the golden precepts teach:

"The path is one, Disciple, yet in the end, twofold. Marked are its stages by 4 and 7 portals. At one end – bliss immediate and at the other bliss deferred."

To choose the *Dharamakaya* vestment – the open way – is to choose bliss immediate and to choose *Nirmanakaya* vestment – the secret way – is to choose the supreme path of bliss deferred. The first will see the Arhan immersed in Nirvanic light, but it is the lesser path, the second will usually see them bleeding over the path of woe but is the greater path.

Hence the existential quandary: do you, who has found the way take the selfish path of self-realisation claim your prize, forgetting and forsaking humanity? Or do you forsake your prize, take the path of the Bodhisattva of compassion and remain in the limitations of suffering in the physical life to aid humanity with their plight?

To renounce the individual state of Nirvanic bliss, to help ones brothers and sisters in humanity, is to willingly walk over the bridge of swords or 10,000 snares with bare feet knowing that your feet will bleed. To willingly work for mankind, knowing full well the conditions of the way mean that you will most likely be misunderstood, abused, and possibly even killed. And so, it is known as the Path of the Terrible Tau, the Gate of Woe, the Crucifixion, and the great renunciation. Verily, it is the road least travelled by.

And so, it is that the existential question comes, **do I wish to go on? Do I actually possess the metal and strength of spirit to willingly face what awaits?**

Remember, in the desert, Jesus knew the path that lay before him (because he was functioning from the 6th octave of vibration/consciousness and his third eye, spiritual vision 'Ajna' was fully open), he knew he was to be betrayed by someone close to him and that he would have to carry the very cross he was to be crucified upon up the mountain of Golgotha (as he was the way, the path; his life was the path). And yet he willingly went forth to this fate because he was in possession of the **Golden Key of VIRAG – 'indifference to pleasure and pain'**, because his little life was not important. If by his life he could aid his younger brothers and sisters of humanity on their journeys to hasten the evolution of their souls, if by his life he could light the way, and be the light, then he would give his life, as it was verily the working out of the plan.

You see, it was never meant to be that for 2,000 years we exalted the personality of Jesus 'as the only son of God', it was that **we were supposed to live at the 6th level of vibration – Love of the Prophet/Seer;** a state of unconditional love, with the gift of supernatural appreciative love and through our achieved elevated state of consciousness, spiritualise the matter of our bodies and recognise ourselves as both the creator and the created, and move into the 7th octave of vibration. For we are all sons and daughters of God!

I have come to realise that my life's journey over the last 38 years has come down to choosing one robe, walking three halls and finding seven golden keys.

Four Dharmas of Gampopa – Kalu Rinpoche

The dedication of Kalu Rinpoche's book speaks volumes of the character of the man that wrote it, and so I would like to share that dedication with you to set the tone of the instruction that follows:

"May all beings who see, hear or read this book in this life and all successive lives, obtain the precious human body and meet with friends of

virtue. Having completely perfected the paths and stages of Boddhisattva conduct may they complete the Two Objectives: benefiting themselves and others."

Continuing on now to the four Dharmas of Gampopa:

1. The mind turns towards the Dharma

"The first teaching invokes a thorough understanding of our situation in Samsara and the different destinies within the cycle, the six states of rebirth…through this teaching we learn the consequences of virtuous and unvirtuous action, which tendencies lead to these various rebirths and the sufferings which the beings in these realms undergo. We come to understand that although a particular karmic process may lead from higher to lower or lower to higher rebirths, Samsara itself provides no means of escape, and if we rely on it we can make no progress towards enlightenment. At the beginning of the Path, this understanding of Samsara is necessary to turn the mind towards the Dharma…and to do this we contemplate the four ordinary preliminaries 1- the unique value of human life, 2 – impermanence, 3- karma and 4 – unsatisfactory nature of suffering of Samsara. By contemplating these preliminaries – the potential of a precious human existence, impermanence and inevitability of death, the karmic process of cause and effect and sufferings and limitations of Samsara – we turn our minds to the Dharma and thus fulfil the first of the four teachings of Gampopa.

2. The Dharma becomes the path

"The teachings of the Dharma become our way of life, our path. We realise that in Buddhahood one is omniscient and omnipresent, endowed with infinite capabilities we see that the teachings of Dharma, which proceed from this enlightened state, are the path that every being can follow to enlightenment.

When the Dharma becomes our path we develop the second attitude: compassion… when compassion develops we see that all life is the same, and that every single being wishes to be happy: in every form of life a fundamental search for happiness goes on – but usually in a way that contradicts and defeats the aim of the search. Few beings understand that real happiness is the result of virtuous conduct. Many are involved in actually destroying their chances of happiness through confused and harmful actions and thoughts. When we see this we develop real affection and compassion for other beings. This infinite compassion for all forms of life is the second attitude involved in making the teaching our path.

(Beginning to function at the 6th octave of vibration – The Prophet/Seer).

3. The path dispels confusion

"By travelling the path our confusion is dispelled. The experience of emptiness – the realisation of the ultimate nature of mind. This realisation of emptiness is known as ultimate Boddicitta.

Realised mahasiddhas, such as Tilopa and Neropa of India, or Marpa and Milarepa of Tibet, were able to perform miraculous changes in the phenomenal universe. They could do so because they had realised the entire phenomenal world as essentially empty and a projection of the mind. This allowed them to manifest miracles and actually change the phenomenal world. Such transformation is not possible when our mind clings to what we experience as ultimately real and immutable."

(Functioning at the 7th octave of vibration – The God Man – such as the Buddha or Christ and the miracles attributed to them).

"In Mahayana sutras (The Great Vehicle*), it is taught that everything we experience is like a reflection, a mirage, a rainbow in the sky or the moon shining on the water's surface; everything we experience has only conventional reality and is ultimately unreal. We experience the third Dharma of Gampopa when first we must dispel our confusion through understanding and experiencing the essential emptiness of mind, and, second, when this reveals the illusory nature of all phenomena, then the path dispels confusion.*

4. Confusion arises as primordial awareness.

The transformation of confusion into primordial awareness.

Remember the ornaments of the Buddha, which symbolise the attainments of pristine/primordial awareness.

In the 'Secret Heart' tantra, called in Tibetan 'Sang way nying po' and in Sanskrit 'Guhyagarbha- tantra' we find a prayer to the mind itself:

"I pay homage to the mind, which is like a wish fulfilling gem. Through which one can realise ones aims. Mind-nature is the basis of everything. There is nothing in Samsara or Nirvana that does not come from it"

And we are reminded of the first of Hermes Principles from Chapter 1:

Order – The universe is mental – all is living mind!

To paraphrase Atisa, who brought transmissions and teachings from India to Tibet:

The field of knowledge is incredibly vast and life is very, very short. Thus, the most important approach is to practise what is most relevant to one's situation. If we can extract the essence of the teachings and directly apply it to our lives then we have a valid approach to Dharma.

The fundamental nature of mind is three-fold – Emptiness, Clarity and Unimpeded – and is *'Tathagatagarbha'*, 'the seed of enlightenment' possessed by every living being. Guarded by the seven gates, locked by the passions incarnate, each key is found in the overcoming of one of the passions incarnate. It is said that there are 84,000 teachings of the Buddha, broken down as follows:

Desire: 21,000 emotional afflictions arise from the root poison of desire. Antidote: Vinyana Collection – prescription for ethical behaviour.

Hatred: 21,000 emotional afflictions arise from the root poison of hatred. Antidote: Sutra Collection.

Ignorance: 21,000 emotional afflictions arise from the root poison of ignorance. Antidote: Abhidharma.

The remaining 21,000 emotional afflictions address desire, hatred and ignorance together. Antidote: Teachings of Vajrayana.

"The teachings of the Buddhas are not intellectual speculation but based on their personal experience of absolute enlightenment."

To follow now is the mantra of perfection of wisdom. A mantra which pacifies all suffering. It condenses the experience of emptiness into a verbal formula. The mantra signifies the experience of emptiness.

TAYATA OM GATE GATE PARAGATE PARASAMGATE BODHI SOHA x 7

Before beginning the next chapter, I would like to include a passage of writing that I wrote in a moment of inspiration a few years ago, that I think highlights the power of finding guidance within and the power of faith and service in one's dharma.

"The Masters Apprentice" –

The walking of the spiritual road is never easy. Always will the aspirant encounter difficulties designed to develop the missing qualities within the soul. It would be nice to sit on a mountain side and think nice thoughts in the Sunkissed grasses for all of ones existence but that does not really help the world.

Action is what helps the world and right now the world needs action. It does not require lip-service, it does not require halfhearted measures or luke-warm service. What it requires are spiritual warriors that are not afraid of getting their hands dirty and doing the work necessary to help shift the planet and planetary consciousness into a higher level, a greater level of existence and way of being.

The primary challenge that faces Earth and its inhabitants at this time is that people do not know what they do not know. People have had the wool pulled over their eyes by the established controlling powers – so much so that they seem happy and content to live with technological distraction. This is sad. You see, what people do not understand is that the technologically advanced society is a direct reflection of the evolution of man's consciousness. As we are able to achieve more with technology, we are also able to (by redirecting our focus within) reach marvellous heights in our own consciousness. This is one of the primary observations that is so important to be recognised by the masses. As above so below, so below as above – is an ancient adage , but it still rings true today as it did many thousands of years ago when it was first coined – and it will continue to ring true as long as there are galaxies expanding and contracting in the vast cosmos. For the great cosmic governing laws are immutable. As above, so below, so below as above, as within so without, so without as within.'

It can be difficult to remember to live with this wisdom of ancient days past especially in a world that has largely forgotten this sage knowledge. But dear brothers and sisters, we must remember! Our society is proliferated by the idea that we only live once – and this is a dangerous idea, as it creates a mass of self-seeking individuals. For if we hold the belief that we only live once – there is no consequence for wrong action, right? It is a clever agenda that has been injected into the psyche of humanity to create a pleasure seeking, self-seeking, epicurean, hedonistic society that live for pleasure and material luxury at any expense.

The radio is filled with catch lies of 'only live once, only live once, only live once' – and everywhere the deluded masses are losing themselves in intoxication and pleasurable pursuits. I was no different – I to had been a sensitive, susceptible young teenage human exposed to the mass media influence of the 'gloriousness' of drinking lots of alcohol and having lots of sex and partying. I lost myself in intoxication for many years and I thought that it was normal…but it almost killed me. And I have had a bitter struggle bringing myself back from that path of destruction that had almost thrown me over a cliff to total annihilation.

The effects of this seemingly harmless belief of we only live once are insidious. One of these effects of great concern is the deterioration of ethics and values as they are sacrificed to the perceived advantages of receiving a large monetary gain. As I write these words I am in despair. I am 37 years old now and things have not turned out as I had planned them. At this point in my life I had had a picture in my mind of how my life should be…but the reality of where I am vastly distances itself from this mental picture…and I feel like a boat without oars drifting on the oceans waves – with no control of where I am going and no visible means of gaining such control.

But as I write these words with sheer unmasked naked honesty – a funny thing happens…clarity. I understand why

I am where I am and how to view this in a position of light. The universe is teaching me surrender. I must surrender to something greater than myself, for I have been a poor architect. I have been a poor architect because I held myself in lofty esteem as a Master Architect and I realise right at this point of writing these words…Cause and Effect.

We cannot build on untruth; it is not possible. Foundations will collapse and buildings will crumble – especially when the vision of the building is of great lofty purpose. The master architect builds for the glory of the vision of creation itself and not for the glory of himself.

And I realise that I have been trying to build a vision of lofty purpose not for the glory of the creation itself but for the glory of myself – and this realisation is as humbling as it is terrifying. And I am at a critical point in my personal evolution. If I try to deny this hypocrisy, the self-serving motivation for wanting to create then I will continue to live a life of blind delusion. If I accept that I have been overindulgent and selfish in my striving, then it means I may be at risk of total collapse through the weight of recognised failure. However, I am reminded of the ancient wisdom of the Eastern Sages, those giants of the human spirit that say "Our greatest glory is not in never falling, but in rising after every time we fall."

And the message of this moment is… surrender. You are not in control N.S. Elijah, you are not the Master Architect, God is the master architect and you are but his apprentice. So I am in the boat without oars drifting. The master's apprentice. The master architect's apprentice.

As I write these words, I go within….

I smell the salt on the air, and I hear the seagulls calling as they circle overhead. I feel the sea spray cool against my face and the sun beating down overhead…to the present… the waves are still, there is a small ripple as the water laps gently against the side of the boat. I look over the side and peer into the clear waters of unimaginable depths...and the funny thing is I see light. That is strange, there should not be light coming from the water. I look again, sure enough it is there... the light... is it an invitation? For it sure feels like it is beckoning me. Strange again – a full diver's wetsuit and breathing gear has appeared in the boat when a minute ago there was nothing there. The sky is starting to change colour and the clouds are beginning to close in and cover the sun... a storm is coming; I must change quickly.

I don the wetsuit and breathing apparatus and throw myself overboard just as the wind picks up and skies blacken, and the waves begin to rise... now where was that light?

I find myself in an alien environment, there are hundreds of different coloured fish and turtles and stingrays, I swim through them all unafraid. Some look at me curiously, others just swim away, and I move my legs in rhythmic kicking action to dive down deeper, deeper into the ocean towards the light.

The light is suddenly everywhere and it is accompanied by the most beautiful angelic music...I sit in the water in suspended animation and let the light and the sacred music seep into all the aspects of my being – I feel it penetrating to the very DNA in my cells... healing me. So this is what divine healing feels like.

I close my eyes and bask in the feeling, I feel totally replenished, full of light. My heart is at peace and deep serenity washes over me. I dare to open my eyes and I see bright Angelic-like mermaid beings swimming and playing in the light. They are, as mermaids are, naked at the tops and their perfect breasts show the glory of divine creation – the divine mother, nurturing the growth of humanity and growth of planetary consciousness. Then this image is replaced by golden light and all I see is fleeting movements of golden light accompanied with a great unquenchable joy.

This is what has been missing from my life for so long…Joy. I have been so serious that I had forgotten to live. I have been a seeker to the power of X and I had forgotten the gift of the physical life. I realise that I have been living out of balance and right at this moment I know exactly how to remedy it.

A flash of the enlightened one's surges through my mind's eye – Maitreya Buddha, Jesus the Christed one all of them were happy, they lived with joy…but what was the source of this joy? I am humbled as I realise it was a deep knowingness of who they really were and where they fit within the Great Master Architect's plan. And as this thought permeates my mind I begin to see apparitions of the images of the great personages surrounding me:

Melchizedek, Buddha, Maitreya, Christ, Lao Tzu, Confucius, Egyptian and Atlantian High Priests and Priestesses and they all smile with the unspoken light… Service. They were happy because they realised the great joy in service to something greater than themselves. They all had their difficulties, struggles and trials but they lived in a greater joy because they had surrendered into service.

I understood the message, it rang so crystal clear and penetrated right to the depths of my DNA…joy in service to something greater than yourself… I the master architect's apprentice understood.

Still floating in suspended animation...

Still immersed in the light...

Still with the divine music playing in my mind...

Still with the mermaid angelic creatures playing and swimming in immense joy...

Still with the Masters of wisdom of bygone days as apparitions surrounding me...

Still with the cool of the water against my wetsuit...

Still with the bubbles of my breathing through the diving gear...

Still with the great depths below me offering unimaginable revelation...

Still with the sky black 200 metres above me...

I make my decision.

I express deep gratitude and love in my heart to the angelic mermaids, the golden light, to the angelic music, to the apparitions of the divine personages. I bring my hands to my heart in prayer and bow my head softly and then turn my head up and begin to swim back to the surface, back up towards the blackened sky...

When I resurface, after passing by the stingrays and the turtles and the fish I am met with a shocking sight... The sky is no longer black and by some miracle the boat is still there. I climb aboard the boat, the sky back to its sparkling blue, the water calmed to a gentle ripple… I remove my clumsy diving gear and lay back in the boat looking up at the beautiful sky and reflect on what I had just experienced. But no sooner that I lay my head down that I feel it hit something hard…I am amazed to find that in the boat are two beautiful wooden oars wrapped with a gold and red bow and a message 'You have earned these – The Master Architect.'

With childlike wonder and joy, I put the oars into position… where will I go now? What lay in any direction? I search the sky above me; I search the vast ocean around me, I close my eyes and search my heart…I feel a prompting… then I begin to row. And a song from my childhood springs into mind… "Row, row, row your boat gently down the stream, merrily, merrily, merrily, merrily life is but a dream"… swish, swish, swish.

Chapter 8

EXITING THE MATRIX – THE RED PILL

"This is your last chance. After this, there is no turning back. You take the blue pill – the story ends, you wake up in your bed and believe whatever you want to believe. You take the red pill – you stay in wonderland and I show you how deep the rabbit hole goes."

– Morpheus, The Matrix

The second hallway of learning – astral plane

There is something that our world does not truly understand, and which it becomes paramount for it to recognise now. Up until now, the notion has been rejected and denied and laughed at because of disbelief. Well, I am here to tell you now, through direct experience, I have experienced the reality of this, and because of a lack of resources available to guide one through the swamps of this curse, I am driven and compelled to account to you, the reader, as an act of service, to speak plainly and offer what guidance I can.

What I am going to talk about concerns itself only with those that have passed from the first hallway – *the physical hall of ignorance* into the second hallway – *the Astral Hallway of learning*. However, to those still walking the first hallway, I urge you to pay attention so that you do not cause yourself seemingly irreparable damage, and set yourself back several lifetimes of intense struggling and suffering to rectify the misgivings made from ignorance or laziness or apathy in this lifetime.

Like I said, I will speak plainly, and I urge you to pay attention now:

The world-view we are taught as we grow up from a babe to a child to an adolescent to an adult is only a partial truth. We are brought up to believe that the physical is the 'be all and end all', that we are our bodies – perhaps there may or may not exist a soul. We have intellect and this is the result of conditions at birth and genetic disposition, we breathe oxygen in and breathe carbon dioxide out, we have to eat food and drink water to survive – as we are born on the Earth and live out our time in accordance with the workings of biological physical laws and processes with a life span of 100 years.

And, whilst we navigate this reality, we are convinced that the feedback from our five physical senses will convey to us an accurate representation of the conditions of reality. However, we would be incorrect. For the five physical senses of the human being are limited in their functionality. Our vision can only detect visible light in the spectrum of 380nm to 780nm, and visible light is a tiny portion of the bandwidth of the electromagnetic spectrum. Our hearing can only detect sounds and vibrations ranging from 20 to 20,000hz, and we know that other animals on Earth have a greater sensitivity – dogs, cats, bats, dolphins, whales, and so on.

So, what it all boils down to is that our physical senses lie. They depict to us a snapshot of reality but they are limited. It would be more accurate to suggest that the reliance upon our physical senses alone to navigate this existence is like wearing ear-muffs and a blindfold. We are deaf and blind to reality. There exists so much more.

What we understand about the circumpunct and the Sri Yantra is that spirit vibrations sent out in all directions have to slow down to become matter. So, mankind exists somewhere near the perimeter of the circumpunct, vibrating at a certain vibratory frequency detectable on the physical plane, within the range of physical senses.

However, other beings vibrating at a higher vibration that are non-corporeal exist outside of that normal range of human detection in a plane that we will call the astral plane. So, we have as follows:

Point of undifferentiated consciousness → mental plane (hall three), → astral plane (hall two) → physical plane (hall one) → solid inert matter.

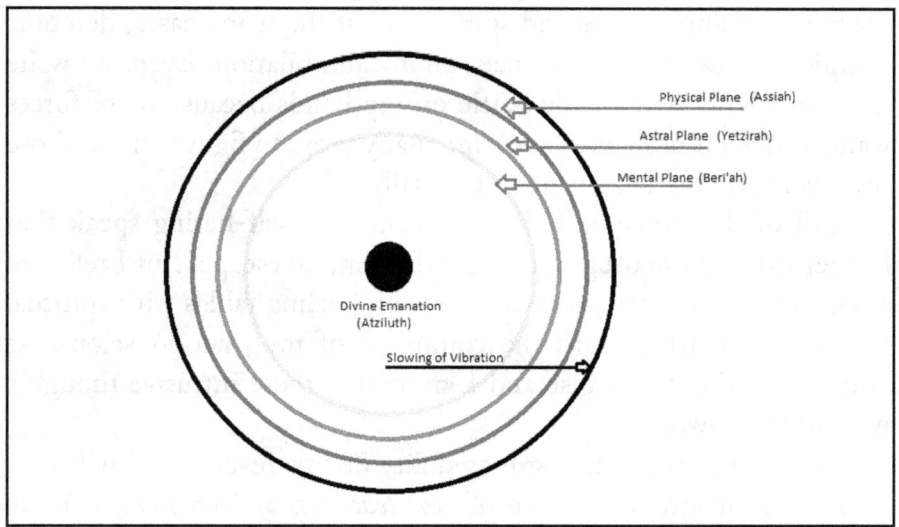

Figure 57: Three hallways, showing parallel mystical Jewish knowledge.

Is that clear to you? Going back to the teachings of the chakras or spinning wheels of energy. Each chakra in normal functionality has a protective sheath that prevents the intrusion of other energies. However, substances like drugs and alcohol strip away the protective sheaths, forcing the chakras to be blown open unnaturally. When this happens repeatedly, the protective sheath is destroyed and people that have done this become '*hot- spots*' for all the beings and entities of the lower, baser, debased levels of consciousness that are stuck without a physical body. It is these obsessing entities that make it so hard for people to overcome alcohol and drug addiction.

People are ignorant to the fact that these entities even exist on this astral plane, so they do not know the danger they open themselves up to when they drink alcohol or take drugs. Now, you may be scoffing in disbelief, but believe me or don't believe me, that is of course your prerogative, you can take the blue pill now and stop reading – you can wake up in your bed and believe whatever you want to believe.

I have battled long and hard with this for several years, as I paid the price of too much alcohol and too much marijuana through my late teens and early twenties. I unconsciously stripped away the protective sheaths to my chakras, leaving me open to possession, to be the host to many possessing entities and spirits and, at the worst cases, demonic energies and demonic forces bent on my annihilation. Even as I write these words, I have a daily battle on my hands because these forces want to remain hidden. It took me many years to figure out all those scary voices in my head were not actually me.

All of the ridiculously self-negating and self-hating speak that further led to more drugs and more drinking to escape. But I tell you, after many hours battling these forces on healing tables with spiritual healers and battling with the command of my own consciousness fading in and out, I realise and I know that these intrusive thoughts were not my own.

Because of the seeming incredulity of this revelation I will now bring to your attention some of '*The teachings of Don Juan, a Yaqui Way of Knowledge*', from the writings of Carlos Castaneda 'The four enemies of knowledge.' The four enemies of knowledge are: fear, clarity, power, and old age.

> *"When a man starts to learn he is never clear about his objectives, his purpose is faulty and his intent is vague. He hopes for rewards that never materialise, for he knows nothing about the hardships of learning. He slowly begins to learn, bit by bit at first and then in big chunks and his thoughts soon clash. What he learns is never what he pictured or imagined and so he begins to be afraid. Learning is never what one expects, every step of learning is a new task and the fear the man is experiencing begins to mount mercilessly, unyieldingly. His purpose becomes a battle field and thus he has*

stumbled upon the first of his natural enemies... fear. A terrible enemy. Treacherous and difficult to overcome. It remains concealed at every turn of the way prowling, waiting. And if the man, terrified in its presence runs away, his enemy would have put an end to his quest. If he runs away however, nothing bad happens to him accept that he will never learn. He will never become a man of knowledge.

So what can a man do to overcome fear? The answer is very simple... he must not run away. He must defy his fear and in spite of it he must take the next step in learning and the next and the next. He must be fully afraid and yet he must not stop – that is the rule. And the moment will come when his first enemy retreats. Once a man has vanquished fear, he is free from it for the rest of his life, because, instead of fear... he has acquired clarity. A clarity of mind that erases fear. By then he knows his desires, he can anticipate the new steps of learning. And a sharp clarity surrounds everything. The man feels like nothing is concealed and thus he has encountered his second enemy... clarity."

Castaneda, Carlos, *The Teachings of Don Juan: A Yaqui Way of Knowledge*, © 1969 by the Regents of the University of California, © 1998 by Carlos Castaneda. Published by the University of California Press.

There are lots of people that are convinced that they are people of knowledge. They are convinced that their clarity is the 'be all and end all' and as such, they are extremely arrogant. But underneath that arrogance is fear... the fear of being wrong. So, they will fight tooth and nail and hang on for dear life to their assumptions and to the ways that they have put the pieces of their existence together with their logical minds, based entirely upon observations of *the hall of ignorance*. They may think they are clear, but in fact they are afraid, and if they are afraid then they will never learn and never become a man of knowledge. So, if you are afraid, you do not have to continue reading, stop now and continue living your life as before. But if you are afraid and you don't want to run away then continue reading for the next step in learning.

I will here reference a gem of wisdom spiritual guidebook, written in 1926 by F. Homer Curtiss, called *'The Voice of Isis.'*

Now, to clarify – I am talking about the personification of the **holy mother aspect of divine trinity Isis** – not the more recent seeming appearance of forces of terrorism I.S.I.S. The fact that this book, *'The Voice of Isis'*, is not widely found today is because a lot of effort by the powers behind the curtain has gone into the suppression of such manuals – so they can evince a design that keeps mankind enslaved in fear. Also, it brings to your attention, well at least it should, **that the design of control and fear is at work with the use of the holy word ISIS to be related to horrors of terrorism.** This is not the first time such a travesty has occurred – look at the Buddhist sacred symbol of the Swastika, which is the ancient symbol for the equal arms of the radiating spiritual fires of the heart, and how it is now primarily associated with Nazism. Open your eyes, pay attention. **Words and symbols carry power, and the powers behind the curtain know this very well. So, this strategy to defile sacred words and symbols serves to shift the sacred power inherent in them, so that they are robbed of their spiritual purity and potency and twisted to their own designs.**

Chapter IV – Narcotics Alcohol and Psychism *'The voice of Isis'*

> *"The human body is the temple of the living God. Within it are certain vital centres comparable to doors (chakras) which open into inner shrines. Using these centres as points of contact, the life forces from the higher planes flow into the physical body through them as an electrical current flows through a wire. And it is through these centres that the Christ force must flow to reach and spiritualise man's various bodies before their redemption or resurrection can take place. By resurrection we mean the ultimate building up of a spiritual body within the physical by a process of*

gradually raising the vibrations of its particles to respond to the keynote sounded by the Divine or Higher self.

These centres or doors are normally protected by nature with oily coverings or sheathes (composed of both astral and physical matter), which permit the flow of normal life forces and protect them from all others. These doors should be opened only by gradual purification and development of the protecting sheathes. Normally this takes place as a natural growth resulting from a life of mental and bodily purity and intense spiritual aspiration. It should not be a forced or hot house growth, for each door must be opened and closed under the absolute control of the will. Each individual has been given these doors to safeguard and is held responsible for their keeping. Only as he can master them and in full knowledge open them to the knock of the Christ and close them to his enemies can he hope to conquer. It is only after long training and great spiritual growth can the entities of the Astral world be mastered and held at bay when these doors are opened. In fact the first and most important work of the advanced disciple is to stand faithful watch over these doors.

*The Holy Ghost or mother principle or the power of bringing forth – hence, the destruction of these sheathes prevents the bringing forth or manifesting of the Christ force within you. The sin against the Holy Ghost "The unpardonable Sin" (unpardonable only because irreparable) is the **separation of the personality from the guidance of the Higher Self through the destruction of the means of contact**. This takes place through the breaking down of the doors or the destruction of the oily sheaths that protect the centres leading from the physical into the astral and psychic bodies. Once these sheathes are destroyed, the person is no longer able to close the doors and so becomes an easy prey to the* *denizens of the astral. Such a one becomes a helpless victim to any and ALL sorts of Psychic imposition and deception.*

There is no such thing as a lost soul, but it is possible for the personality to persistently refuse the guidance of the Higher Self and ultimately break away from it and become a lost human – animal. The animal life force of such a soulless entity may incarnate several lifetimes, each time growing more and more degenerate, until it has finally exhausted the force obtained during its contact with the soul and the aggregated atoms disintegrate and return to the elements from which they were gathered. The soul in such cases is not lost but is indrawn to await the new opportunity to gather up the materials necessary to clothe itself in a personality.

There are several abnormal ways in which the oily protective sheaths (of the chakras) can be broken down and the doors thrown open. Chief among them are the uses of alcohol and narcotic drugs. **Chemically speaking ordinary alcohol is ethyl-hydroxide. The ethyl (the spirit) vibrates to the highest rate reached by mere physical matter, the point where matter transcends the physical and enters the astral, the ethyl actually functioning on both planes.**

Narcotic drugs also contain an ethyl element. The ethyl when taken into the body immediately seeks to escape into the astral, and it naturally follows the usual avenues of communication between the two planes. But in escaping it passes through the centres in a reverse direction to the normal current and gradually burns off the insulating sheathes until in time they are utterly destroyed, just as an electrical insulation might be burned off by interference with the normal flow of the current.

This breakdown may be very rapid, as in the case of a habitual drunkard or drug fiend or it may be insidious and not show markedly for several incarnations, but the result is certain and every indulgence in the substance mentioned is a step towards the end.

Ultimately this leaves the doors unguarded and open for all the horrors of the lowest astral plane to rush in and take possession of the 'Temple of the Living God'... The drunkard and drug habitué open the doors while in a state of debauchery and in such a condition, being particularly unable to defend themselves, they practically invite all the fiends of the underworld to enter and take possession!

It is our duty to give our sympathy and help to this class of sorely afflicted ones. For since it took many lives to breakdown the protective sheathes, it will require a long hard fight to rebuild them. Hence do not let such unfortunate ones become discouraged. No matter how many times they may fall back into old habits, every effort to conquer aids in the rebuilding and the very fierceness of the struggle will ultimately strengthen the soul."

Maybe take the time to read that passage again and sit and take it in. It is heavy, but if you are walking in the second hallway or about to, it may well save your life.

This reality of different planes of existence and different energies and entities existing on different planes has been known since antiquity. Just look at the picture of Buddha on the next page. The obsessing entities, tempters, and demons are trying to get to him but cannot penetrate his spiritual aura.

Figure 58: Wall painting Bodh Gaya – Mahabodhi Temple. Depicting Gautama Buddha's aura keeping spirits and demons at bay, they cannot penetrate his spiritual purity. Source: www.cluboasis.net/uploads/1/4/0/8/14087890/1049775_orig.jpg?0

This is not all nonsense, it is very real and it is largely unacknowledged. We have mental wards and hospitals and prisons full of possessed individuals and skyrocketing levels of suicide. However, this system of control of humanity has attempted to stack the deck after centuries of deliberate historical distortion, and the driving of a design that ensures we are focusing on lower desires and 'needs.' And so, just by mentioning this, something so far from the focus of your normal state of consciousness – no doubt your first response will be to shout 'bullshit' or 'all nonsense.'

But as the deliberately distorted picture begins to come into view as to who the divine messengers were and what their message actually was, then I hope you will see at least a hint of truth in the ancient annals of sacred scripture of demons, and possessing spirits, and the great initiates being able to heal people and rid them of their afflictions and Earth-bound spirit attachments. Verily, it is indeed the taking of the red pill and being unplugged from the matrix.

Sacred Scripture – records of subtle world.

Buddhism

Some modern followers of Buddhism try to convince themselves that the demons and spirits depicted around him in the ancient images, such as in Figure 58 from Bodhgaya, are only a personification of the Buddha's personal fears and doubts, and yet, in the Buddhist tradition, the universe can be looked at in terms of three realms:
1. The realm of desire.
2. The realm of form.
3. The realm of formlessness.

The realm of desire has six kinds of beings:
1 – hell beings, 2 – hungry ghosts, 3 – animals, 4- humans, 5 – asuras (demons), and 6 – gods.

How is it then that some devotees of Buddhism can continue to deny the actual literal interpretation of the reality of these forces and existences? The answer is to be found in the concept of cognitive dissonance. It is right in front of them, but it is too painful to accept, so therefore they attempt to explain and rationalise it.

Christianity – The Holy Bible: King James version

Matthew 12:43-45

"When the unclean spirit has gone out of a person, it passes through waterless places (Astral Plane) seeking rest, but finds none. Then it says 'I will return to my house from which I came' (The body of the person it left). And when it comes, it finds the house empty, swept and put in order. Then it goes and brings with it 7 other spirits more evil than itself, and they enter and dwell there, and the last state of the person is worse than the first. So also it will be with this generation."

Ephesians 6: 10-18

"Finally be strong in the Lord (Christ consciousness) and in the strength of his might. Put on the whole armour of God, that you may be able to stand against the schemes of evil. For we do not wrestle against flesh and blood (Physical plane), but against rulers, against authorities, against the cosmic powers over this present darkness, against the spiritual forces of evil in the heavenly places (human hearts). Therefore, take up the whole armour of God, that you may be able to withstand in the evil day, and having done all, to stand firm. Stand therefore, having fastened the belt of truth and having put on the breast plate of righteousness."

Luke 4: 33-36

"Now in the synagogue there was a man who had a spirit of an unclean demon. And he cried out with a loud voice, saying, "Let us alone! What have we to do with You, Jesus of Nazareth? Did You come to destroy us? I know who You are—the Holy One of God!"

But Jesus rebuked him, saying, "Be quiet, and come out of him!" And when the demon had thrown him in their midst, it came out of him and did not hurt him. Then they were all amazed and spoke among themselves, saying, "What a word this is! For with authority and power He commands the unclean spirits, and they come out."

Matthew 17: 14-20 A Boy Is Healed

"And when they had come to the multitude, a man came to Him, kneeling down to Him and saying, "Lord, have mercy on my son, for he is an epileptic and suffers severely; for he often falls into the fire and often into the water. So I brought him to Your disciples, but they could not cure him."

"Then Jesus answered and said, "O faithless and perverse generation, how long shall I be with you? How long shall I bear with you? Bring him here to Me." And Jesus rebuked the demon, and it came out of him; and the child was cured from that very hour. Then the disciples came to Jesus privately and said, "Why could we not cast it out?"

"So Jesus said to them, 'Because of your unbelief; for assuredly, I say to you, if you have faith as a mustard seed, you will say to this mountain, 'Move from here to there,' and it will move; and nothing will be impossible for you.'"

Mark 9:20-21

"Then they brought him to Him. And when he saw Him, immediately the spirit convulsed him, and he fell on the ground and wallowed, foaming at the mouth. So He asked his father, 'How long has this been happening to him?' And he said, 'From childhood.'"

Luke 8:2

"And certain women who had been healed of evil spirits and infirmities—Mary called Magdalene, out of whom had come seven demons."

Mark 9: 26

"Then the spirit cried out, convulsed him greatly, and came out of him. And he became as one dead, so that many said, 'He is dead.'"

Mark 1: 32-34 Many Healed After Sabbath Sunset

"At evening, when the sun had set, they brought to Him all who were sick and those who were demon-possessed. And the whole city was gathered together at the door. Then He healed many who were sick with various diseases, and cast out many demons; and He did not allow the demons to speak, because they knew Him."

Mark 5: 1-20 A Demon-Possessed Man Healed

"Then they came to the other side of the sea, to the country of the Gadarenes. And when He had come out of the boat, immediately there met Him out of the tombs a man with an unclean spirit, who had his dwelling among the tombs; and no one could bind him, not even with chains, because he had often been bound with shackles and chains. And the chains had been pulled apart by him, and the shackles broken in pieces; neither could anyone tame him. And always, night and day, he was in the mountains and in the tombs, crying out and cutting himself with stones.

"When he saw Jesus from afar, he ran and worshiped Him. And he cried out with a loud voice and said, "What have I to do with You, Jesus, Son of the Most High God? I implore You by God that You do not torment me."

"For He said to him, "Come out of the man, unclean spirit!" Then He asked him, "What is your name?"

"And he answered, saying, "My name is Legion; for we are many."

Also he begged Him earnestly that He would not send them out of the country.

"Now a large herd of swine was feeding there near the mountains. So all the demons begged Him, saying, 'Send us to the swine, that we may enter them.' And at once Jesus gave them permission. Then the unclean spirits went out and entered the swine (there were about two thousand); and the herd ran violently down the steep place into the sea, and drowned in the sea.

"So those who fed the swine fled, and they told it in the city and in the country. And they went out to see what it was that had happened. Then they came to Jesus, and saw the one who had been demon-possessed and had the legion, sitting and clothed and in his right mind. And they were afraid. And those who saw it told them how it happened to him who had been demon-possessed, and about the swine. Then they began to plead with Him to depart from their region.

"And when He got into the boat, he who had been demon-possessed begged Him that he might be with Him. However, Jesus did not permit him, but said to him, 'Go home to your friends, and tell them what great things the Lord has done for you, and how He has had compassion on you.' And he departed and began to proclaim in Decapolis all that Jesus had done for him; and all marvelled."

The Seal of the Prophet

The Prophet Muhammad's (peace be upon him) birth is generally given as April 20, 571AD, and tradition teaches that when his father died he inherited five camels and a slave girl. At age six, Muhammad lost his mother 'Aminah' and the orphan was taken care of by his grandfather 'Abdul Muttalib.' After two years, 'Abdul Muttalib' died and Muhammad was placed in the care of 'Abdul Muttalib's son 'Abu Ta lib.' At this time, Muhammad had to tend the sheep and goats of the Meccans to support himself.

At age twenty-four, he was employed by a rich widow named 'Hagidah' to drive caravans of camels and at the age of twenty-five, Muhammad married 'Hagidah' who was then forty years old. In the Oxford 1880 publication of 'The Quar'an – Part 1 Chapters I to XVI', by E.H Palmer, it advises:

"All that is certain is that he was an honest upright man, irreproachable in his domestic relations and universally esteemed by his fellow citizens who called him 'El Amin' – meaning 'the trusty.' He was a man of highly nervous organisation, thoughtful and... possessing an extreme sensibility, being unable to endure even the slightest unpleasant odour."

Muhammad was forty years old when his first revelation came to him. According to history:

"From youth upwards, Muhammad suffered from a nervous disorder which tradition calls 'epilepsy' and he began to wonder if he was possessed by a Ginn, one of those dread supernatural beings. Person's afflicted with epilepsy or hysterical symptoms were supposed by the Arabs, as by so many other nations, to be possessed, and we find the constant complaint in the Qur'an that he was regarded as such by his fellow citizens.

"During one of his solitary sojourns on Mount Hira, a wild and lonely mountain near Mecca, an Angel appeared to him and bade him 'READ.' 'I am no reader' Muhammad replied in great trepidation, when the angel shook him and again bade him 'read.' This was repeated three times, then the angel uttered the five verses which commence the 96th chapter of the Qur'an as:

"Read in the name of the Lord, who did create man from congealed blood. Read! For thy Lord is most generous who has taught the use of the pen has taught man what he did not know."

"The thought that he might be, after all, mad or possessed was terrible to Muhammad. He struggled for a long time

against the idea and endeavoured to support himself by being in the reality of the Divine Mission which he had received upon Mount Hira; but no more revelations came, nothing occurred to give him further confidence and hope, and Muhammad began to feel that such a life could be endured no longer. The Fatrah or 'intermission', as this period without revelation was called, lasted for two-and-a-half to three years.

"Dark thoughts of suicide presented themselves to his mind… at last the angel again appeared in all his glory and Muhammad in terror ran to his wife 'Hagidah' and cried 'daththiruni', 'wrap me up!' and lay down entirely enwrapped in his cloak as was the custom when attacked by the hysterical fits (which were always accompanied, as we learn from traditions with violent fever)… partly to screen himself from the gaze of evil spirits.

"As he lay there the angel again spake to him 'O thou covered! Rise up and warn! And thy Lord Magnify! And thy garments purify; and abomination shun! And grant not favors to gain increase; and for thy Lord await!'

"And now the revelations came in rapid succession, he no longer doubted the reality of the inspiration, and his conviction of the unity of God and of his divine commission to preach as it were indelibly impressed upon his mind."

*"Muhammad believed that he was sent as an apostle to both men and Ginns and Surah LXII contains an allusion to a vision in which he beheld a multitude of Ginns bowing in adoration and listening to the message which man had disdainfully refused"… "There was however another sect who professed to have found the truth and who preached the faith of their **father Abraham, nothing more no less, in fact, than the doctrine of the unity of God…and Muhammad***

> *first adopted the title of Hanif – as expressing the faith of Abraham but subsequently changed it to Muslim."*

In Jewish we have the Shedim or Mazzikim – the harmers and the Ruhin – the spirits.

In Islam we have the Jinn and Shiatan.

Ad –Dhariyat 51:56 – *"I did not create the Jinn and mankind except to worship me."*

If we review what we know of the six spiritual initiations taken on Earth by an aspirant, disciple, initiate, we find some interesting similarities.

1. The first initiation is taken on the physical plane, and it is here that the initiate's disposition aligns to unconditional love and good will. Here the initiate becomes aware of the wisdom of exercising willpower over bodily pleasures and lusts, and following the higher voice of their guiding spirit/soul. Here it is also that an initiate's senses are awakening into higher levels of functionality and it is such that he/she becomes much more sensitive to the physical world.

> *"Possessing an extreme sensibility, being unable to endure even the slightest unpleasant odour."*

An initiate at this stage must possess Golden Key 'Dana' – key of charity and love immortal. And we have the Prophet Muhammad (peace be upon him) being called 'El Amin' – 'The Trusty.'

2. The second initiation is taken on the astral plane, and it is here that the initiate must live through the hour known as the 'dragon of the threshold' or the 'tearing of the veil.' Not only do spirits and jinn exist as detectable on the astral plane, but also angels.

An initiate at this second level must possess Golden Key 'Shila' – key of harmony of word and act. And to achieve this, he must overcome fear. Fear kills the will and stays all action:

> *"Muhammad in terror ran to his wife 'Hagidah' and cried 'daththiruni', 'wrap me up!' ... And now the revelations came in rapid succession, he no longer doubted the reality of the inspiration, and his conviction of the unity of God*

and of his divine commission to preach as it were indelibly impressed upon his mind."

In order to make it through the tearing of the veil, the disciple must purify his vehicles (garments) – physical body, astral body, mental body:

Rise up and warn! And thy Lord magnify! And thy garments purify; and abomination shun! And grant not favors to gain increase; and for thy Lord await!

3. The third initiation is taken on the mental plane, and it is here that the initiate must possess Golden Key 'Kshanti' – key of patience sweet that naught can ruffle. Remember, we have the period known as the intermission – two-and-a-half to three years – where there was no outward sign of having a divine mission, and dark thoughts of suicide came over him:

"But no more revelations came, nothing occurred to give him further confidence and hope, and Muhammad began to feel that such a life could be endured no longer. The Fatrah or 'intermission', as this period without revelation was called, lasted for **two-and-a-half to three** *years."*

"Dark thoughts of suicide presented themselves to his mind."

For remember in the Bible, Jesus teaches that when a man cleans up his act then the possessing demon/spirit will leave but come back with seven more, and the state of such a man is worse than the first. Here it is that my journey aligns with the trials of Muhammad and also with our shared stage of development. At this level, the dark forces do not want you to succeed in being a vessel for divine loving consciousness. They will do everything in their power to have you try and end your life. Dark thoughts, indeed, are the realm of the darker forces.

And so, it is that the Prophet Muhammad (peace be upon him) was indeed a prophet. And he was a man that lived largely at the 6th level or octave of vibration/consciousness progressing from the 3rd octave of the animal, through the 4th level of the normal man, through the 5th level of human genius. Over his lifetime, he achieved the first two initiations and worked solidly towards the third initiation of the transfiguration into the 7th octave of vibration/consciousness into the God Man. He learned to submit his individual will to the higher will of 'God' – which is what happens through the trials of the second initiation. And so, we understand the mechanism of the truth of his experience that formed the bedrock of Islam – 'he who submits to the will of Allah.'

Jesus Christ was the master that progressed further past the third initiation on the mental plane, overcoming the temptations of the darker forces (represented in the Bible as the temptation of the devil) who promised immense powers for his own right and thus, in his surrendering of his individual will to the divine will, underwent the transfiguration after the dark night of the soul in the wilderness.

As he had undergone this transfiguration, a stronger divine energy worked through him, and so, he was able to cast out the spirits and demonic possessors of those afflicted in the accounts in the Bible. Jesus then underwent the fourth initiation – the crucifixion, as he was the path – his life lived as he became the path. Christ willingly underwent the journey over the bridge of swords, because he was armed with the Golden Key Virag – indifference to pleasure and pain – and the illusion of separation and physicality was conquered. The initiate undergoes the crucifixion not always literally, as did our elder brother Christ, but in being misunderstood, mistreated, and even killed as they work as vessels for the working out of the divine plan.

Jesus was then reborn, resurrected as the divine man, as he underwent the fifth earthly initiation, saturated in pure Alaya (holy spirit) as the flame in the white alabaster vase he possessed the Golden Key Dhyana – the diamond soul – and ascended this physical reality, back to the heavenly realms of superluminal light.

Heart

From my direct experience and being guided on my own journey through the Hall of Learning, I can here offer some very valuable, in fact priceless, advice that will save you many hundreds of hours of suffering; namely, that the underlying reason for possession to occur is **a weak heart**.

Now, as we look back to the teachings earlier on in this discourse of the aura and the chakras and the 72,000 energetic centers in the body, we remember that as a human being we are energy. The Director of Research at the Heartmath Institute, Dr. Rollin McCraty, explains in his chapter 'The Energetic Heart', that "*The heart generates the largest electromagnetic field in the body. The electrical field as measured in an electrocardiogram (ECG) is about 60 times greater in amplitude than the electrical field of the brain measured in an electroencephalogram (EEG).*" McCraty, R. in *Bioelectromagnetic and Subtle Energy Medicine*, Second Edition (ed Paul J. Rosch) (2015).

Also, what is of interest is that their studies at the institute have identified that the heart generates a series of electromagnetic pulses. These pulsing waves of electromagnetic energy create fields within fields and give rise to interference patterns when they interact with magnetically polarizable tissues and substances. So, the heart also generates a powerful and measurable pressure wave that "*travels rapidly throughout the arteries much faster than the actual flow of blood that we feel as our pulse. These pressure waves force the blood cells through capillaries to provide oxygen and nutrients to the cells and expand the arteries, causing them to generate a relatively large electrical charge.*"

What they have found also is that there is a measurable relationship between the heartbeat's evoked potential, which is measured on the scalp of the head. They have found that "*changes in these evoked potentials associated with the heart's different neurological input to the brain are detectable between 50 to 550 milliseconds after the heartbeat. Gary Schwartz and colleagues of the University of Arizona believe… that this cannot be explained by simple physiological mechanisms alone and suggest an energetic interaction between the heart and brain… they have confirmed that heart focused attention is associated with increased heart-brain synchrony, providing further support for energetic heart-brain communications."*

So, we have the heart proven to be the largest generator of the electromagnetic field in human bio-field. And we have the importance of the heart at the centre of all mystical traditions. We also have a proven heart-brain link that shows; with our focused attention, we can manipulate the pulsations of our hearts energy, and we are reminded of the ancient mystical adage "Energy Follows Thought" and now we come to the primary cause of possession – a weak heart.

If we only choose to look at the body with our physical eyes, from the position of the 'Hall of Ignorance', it will be impossible for us to see how the heart can be infiltrated and taken over by other energies, for the heart will just appear to be a 'blood bag' to such vision. If, however, we look with quantum vision or spiritual vision or multidimensional vision then we will see that the body, comprised of 72,000 Nadis or energetic points, can provide up to 72,000 places for these unwanted energies to hide!

Now, I know that this is a lot to take in, and at this point you must think I'm out of my mind, but I ask you to bear with me. You see, what happens is that with every emotionally distressing event in our lives that we experience, it puts undue pressure on our hearts and generally what happens over time is that the heart is hardened to the world. And with approximately 17,000,000 people dying each year worldwide from heart or cardiovascular disease, we need to pay attention to what is really going on!

We harden our hearts to the world because it is our last bastion of defense against feeling all of our accumulated pain and suffering. As divine beings, we are born with an inkling of our greatness, and yet typically our life experience gives us blow after blow; knocking us down, reducing us to a shell of our former selves as we lose the fearless authenticity that we are born with, as our divine consciousness is crucified on the crossbeams of time and space.

We were born into a manipulated and controlled system that drip feeds us 'knowledge-lies' of all the boundaries and limitations to what is possible; precipitated from the voices of our current system of education (developed from Napoleonic times because they wanted to teach people how to follow orders), our own parents, and the near and dear.

Our parents, a product of the propaganda of society, having given away their fearless authenticity, unconsciously communicate to us that this is what we must also do. That we are living in the world and in order to get along, we have to follow the rules and not upset the applecart because it is 'how things are done.' I am not pointing the finger of blame, just raising awareness as to what happens. Our parents, and our parents' parents, were also born into this vicious system of control so it is not their fault.

However, living in this fashion, feeling powerless to effect the changes to society that we feel in the depths of our beings, in the very core of our hearts, has the effect of breaking us down. As a result, we either are crushed and deemed weak or we harden our hearts to the world so as to be strong. Krishnamurti explained the idiocy of this in his words *"It is no measure of good health to perform well in a profoundly sick society."*

And he is right. All of this striving for material wealth – taking a small advantage of this person here and bending this moral, paying the price with our integrity over there; all of this is what allows the heart to be defiled. Every being in the universe knows very intimately the difference between right and wrong, and when we understand that we are a deeply interconnected organism, that we each contain the spark of God, then every selfish decision we make to advance ourselves at the expense of another sucks the light out of that spark. We not only take advantage of our brothers and sisters in humanity but we sabotage ourselves.

On the surface this may look like success. However, this is all founded in the Hall of Ignorance and is *not real*. And because it is not real, we make a sacrifice of the good, the beautiful and the true. We ignorantly close the doors to the divine within ourselves, and we foul the floors of the pure white alabaster temple of our hearts with selfish intention. With our unchecked greed, lusts, perversions and craving, all of these are based on the illusion of the Hall of Ignorance.

This, coupled with our buried pain and the likely substance abuse that ensues to deal with our pain, causes holes in our energetic field. We create a major imbalance in the bio-field. It is weakened at the source... the heart. The heart is the generator of the bio-field. And with a weak generator the doors of the heart are opened to all the horrors of the astral plane. Because the world is largely functioning from the Hall of Ignorance, these things on the astral plane, which are consciously encountered in the Hall of Learning, are not only unacknowledged by our society at large, but are completely rejected as having the possibility of existing at all.

So, I will now reference some invaluable words of guidance that saved me from total annihilation as I was thrown into the dark challenges of this astral world without a light and without a compass. These words that follow were my light and my compass! They helped me to navigate the seemingly uncharted and hostile terrain. I have included around 100 small stanzas from the 600 that form the book called '*Heart*' published in 1932 by the Agni Yoga Society, New York. **I have been given permission to include these verbatim from the director of this society** as the consciousness of the authors of the unseen guiding brotherhood of humanity – The Great White Brotherhood conveys a special energy and way of presenting these insights that aid in the lighting of the fires of the heart, increasing awareness of the hour that approaches and setting us to purpose.

AGNI YOGA - HEART- Second Hall Challenges - Guidance

9. Heartlessness is nothing but an uncultured state of the heart. Faint-heartedness arises from limitation of thinking. Intolerance belongs to the same family of abominations, all of which degrade the sacred vessel of the heart. You already know that a refined heart, whose energy is intensified, provides an impulse similar to that of an electrical generator; this shows that the heart is a vessel of universal energy. But the culture of the heart does not accumulate unless it receives proper nourishment. Likewise, the best accumulator will be inactive unless it is protected and connected properly. The heart demands constant nourishment; without it, the heart is deprived of the highest link and begins to decompose. In light of this, **let us not forget how the ancients symbolised ascent by depicting an infant on the bottom of the chalice.** (And Christ said, unless you are like little children then you will not enter the kingdom of Heaven).

13. Can you picture what a humanity with healthy bodies and uncultured hearts would be like? It is difficult even to imagine such a feast of darkness. All the illnesses and infirmities in the world are unable to restrain the rampant madness of the heart. Truly, so long as the heart remains unenlightened, illnesses and infirmities will not be eliminated; were that not the case, the frenzy of the heart coupled with powerful bodies would horrify the worlds. Long ago it was said of a righteous man that "he walked before the Lord," which meant that he did not violate the principle of Hierarchy, and thus had purified his heart. Through even the slightest purification of the human heart one can derive a cascade of Blessings. Nowadays it is all right to act, if cautiously, but only in cases where the heart has not decayed. You should not get depressed about it, **but you need to know that the darkness has intensified and many hearts are putrefying. The significance of the heart is an old truth, but this truth has never been so needed as now.** (Welcome to the 21st Century!)

45. The process by which energy is compressed or intensified is similar to the workings of a pump. Thus, the upward impetus of energy is sure to be conditioned by downward pressure. People usually regard this pressure as misfortune or failure, whereas it is the physical threshold of ascent. Oppression, of course, manifests in an entirely different way; **but any person who has attained ascent is able to determine moments of inner or outer compression. It is sad to see how uninformed people, not understanding the law of the pump, give way to compressive forces.** This situation is especially serious nowadays, when a mass consciousness is being moulded, when it is urgently necessary to harmonize thousands of consciousnesses that are disorderly, uneducated, and ignorant of the simplest and most unshakeable laws. It would be so easy for these masses to lose sight of the fact that intensification is the gate to ascent.

61. **One has to live through the difficult hour that is called "The Dragon of the Threshold." We call that hour "The Tearing of the Veil."** That is how We designate the time when darkness intends to tear the veil

but ends up only revealing the distances. But courage is needed; indeed, how else can the accumulation of courage come to light? (This is the 2nd Initiation – The Baptism of the Christ – into the Astral Plane).

62. *Just as the sun is the heart of the system, the human heart is the Sun of the organism. There are many sun-hearts, and the Universe represents a system of hearts; that is why the cult of Light is the cult of the heart. To understand this abstractly means to leave the heart out in the cold; but as soon as the Light of the sun-heart comes alive, the need for the magnet's warmth will make it shine forth like a true sun. It has been said: "Let your heart lead you in crossing Santana." That is how you can make the concept of the heart resistant to the cold. You can look upon the rhythm of the heart as the rhythm of life. The Teaching about the Heart is as bright as the sun, and the warmth of the heart speeds as swiftly as a sunbeam. Everyone has felt astonishment at how a ray of the rising sun can instantly insulate everything from the cold. The heart can do the very same thing! I am speaking of the warmth of the heart now that it is especially necessary.* **A thought surging forth in aspiration sets space on fire, while the warmth of the heart is a constant hearth. Courage dwells in the warmth of the heart—remember this!** *The manifestation of the dark forces acts like frost on a sown field. Only the heart's warmth provides a radiant shield.* **But just as we conduct tests on light waves with delicate care, we should approach the heart with caution and solicitude.**

63. *A heart that has dedicated itself to goodness radiates grace unceasingly, without depending on intentional transmissions. Likewise, the sun sends forth its rays without premeditation. A heart that has pledged itself to evil sends out arrows consciously, unconsciously, and unceasingly.* **The heart of goodness sows around itself health, smiles, and spiritual wellbeing. The heart of evil destroys warmth and, like a vampire, sucks away the vital force.** *And so the activity of hearts—whether it be good or evil—goes on without pause. The conditions of good and evil have a different meaning on the lowest plane of Being and in the Highest World. You can picture a radiant furnace of light and a yawning abyss of darkness.* **It is terrifying when the swords of the demons and the Archangels are crossed! Amid the flashes of battle, so many hearts are drawn to Light or to darkness!**

64. One needs to clearly visualize the ceaseless radiation of the heart. It is necessary to understand why the presence of evil hearts is so painful to good hearts. Neither the smile nor the forced grin of evil can conceal what the heart is radiating. The establishment of good in the heart in no way excludes righteous indignation, but irritation is the domain of evil. Only by striving to the Hierarchy can a person determine the boundary between many feelings.

69. Complaints about insufficient guidance are the usual thing. People are used to covering up their peculiarities with complaints. But if there is anything that has not been grudged to humanity, it is Guidance; **people just need to pay attention to everything that is being given! The multitude of impulses that spring from spiritual influences may vanish without benefit, but they also may work harm by remaining misconstrued in the pantries of a person's consciousness.** *It can be safely asserted that only* **a very small fraction of spiritual influences find a proper application; especially obstructive are the habits that drive the consciousness into conventional paths.** *They also enfeeble the faculties of the heart when it is ready to resound to the Highest Guidance. Precisely, it is the heart that knows the highest from the lowest; but when enfeebled and befogged, the heart itself will reside at the lowest level, where even the lowest will appear to be the highest.* **Purity of heart is the most essential possession. There is no room for wisdom, courage, and selflessness in a beclouded heart.** *But Guidance will whisper about deeds of podvig, and this advice should not seem terrifying or harsh.*

71. True solemnity is built upon the highest degree of tension. Solemnity is not rest, not satisfaction, not the end; it is, precisely, a beginning—that is, resoluteness and a march forward on the path of Light. **Hardships are inevitable, for they are the wheels of striving. Terrible pressures are inevitable, for without them the explosion lacks power.** *How could joy arise from frivolity? Only lust lies in frivolity, while joy abides in the solemn victory of the spirit.* **And the victory of the spirit lies in affirmation of the unshakeable principles from which everything begins. When the Banner of Peace is being raised, you should be full of solemnity.**

76. A very tortuous line runs between the worthy and the unworthy. Only the heart can find its way through all the folds of the brain. But now is the time to pass onward into the knowledge of spirit-creativity. **Perhaps it seems strange to many people that even the Subtle World is invisible to them, although in the gradation of the various worlds it is still rather dense. This means that the physical eye is so crude that it cannot even discern the next stage of bodily transformation.** If people are trying to improve even scientific instruments, then how desirable it is to refine the human apparatus itself! But unless the help of the heart is attracted, work on this achievement cannot move forward. A person who can feel through the heart is already able to advance beyond the limits of the body. An apostasy that renounces spirit-creativity retards a person for many lives to come. **It is inexcusable to enter a low state when your eyes have already been unsealed. Let us recall what work it is to break through the physical shell, what measures are used to move the consciousness forward after it has undergone tension! After all that effort, can you just turn back?**

77. **Many people are suffering from possession during humanity's transition to spirit-creativity; it is as if somebody had made spare keys to loose locks.** It is especially necessary to examine people with care. Moreover, you need to remember that the possessed have a peculiar way of thinking that is full of contradictions. Someone who wants to help them can use the power of suggestion to drive out the possessing agent, or he can leave such people in peace and even, if possible, completely isolate them. That works because **the possessor is in need not so much of the subject himself as the ability to exert influence through the subject on the people around him.** The worst thing is to pester the possessed person by urging him to show the good judgement of which he is incapable. It is bad to start showing pity for the possessed person out loud or begin finding fault with his contradictions. The expression of a command, strong and striking, or else isolation, can lighten the lot of a weak heart. **It is through weakness of the heart that possession sneaks in. The fire of the heart singes the fur on the shaggy visitors.**

Rejection of the Teacher puts an end to all possibilities, especially when the rejection has entered into the student's consciousness long before he or she is possessed. So it is that people often awaken dormant denials; of course, rejection of the Teacher is the primary consequence, **because anything chaotic is first and foremost outraged by creativity and cooperation.** In the chaotic *lurk the seeds of evil, which are crushed out only by hard experience.* **But nowadays an unprecedented number of people are possessed. Darkness also wishes to express itself.**

78. *Originally the boundary between the physical and the Subtle World was not so clear-cut. In the most ancient annals you can find fragmentary indications about the very close cooperation between these worlds. During the densification of the physical, the focus of the heart was needed to maintain a balance between the physical and the subtle energies. The corporeal world itself was necessary as a way of reworking matter and thereby increasing energies. But as you know, the intellect strove for isolation, which ended up impeding evolution... So let us agree to pay the proper attention to spirit-creativity. We can grow used to thinking about things from this perspective. Thus, we need to concern ourselves with what is most significant in giving life its direction. Whoever schools himself in maintaining a balance between the worlds is making his path a great deal easier.*

79. **Since the heart is an accumulator and transmuter of various energies, there must be more favorable conditions for arousing and attracting these energies. The most fundamental condition is work, mental as well as physical. In the motion of work, energies are gathered from space; but one must understand work as a natural process that enriches life. Thus, every kind of work is a blessing,** *while the vagaries of inaction are extremely harmful in a cosmic sense.* **Love for the endlessness of labor is in itself an initiation of considerable degree; it prepares you for the conquest of time. Being in a condition where you have conquered time guarantees you a place in the Subtle World, where work is an unavoidable condition, just as it is in the body. A complaint about having to work can only come from a slave of the body.**

89. *Be on your guard against senseless criticism. Not only does it contain a quality that causes decay, it also delivers a weak person who criticizes into the power of the criticised. A weak but cruel heart may give rise to a hostile reaction in the aura of the person criticised. Moreover,* **usually the person doing the criticizing is not strong himself, or else he would not find time to indulge in judging others.** *The unjust nature of criticism, like that of any other lie, weakens the already insignificant consciousness of the self-appointed judge, thereby causing him extensive harm; whereas*

the person unfairly judged only gains by strengthening his magnet with the attractive force of new auras. Readers might ask, "Why these ethical discussions in the book Heart?" First of all you should remind them about the hygiene of the heart. *The hygiene of the heart ought to be regarded as an absolutely necessary activity. You should discard all discussions about abstract ethics. Everything is good that is healthy in every aspect. We insist that anyone who has entered the path of the Teaching shall, first of all, be healthy in spirit. Can a person walk in evil toward the Light? Truly, the Light will detect every grain of evil.*

93. *One condition may be dangerous, even disastrous—irritation full of imperil opens up access to the dark ones. All sorts of uninvited guests head for wherever there is irritation, seeking to make the most of it and enhance the efficacy of the poison.* How much tissue is torn, how many tests and experiments are ruined, much to the joy of the malevolent entities! *Advise people to accept this not as a fairy tale but as a dangerous reality. The source of good and evil does not disappear.*

96. *"Sickness from sin"—so says Scripture. We say that illness arises from the imperfections of past and present. You should know how to approach illness.* **Much to the regret of doctors everywhere, the true preventative measure will be perfectment—the process of becoming perfect. People can understand that perfectment begins with the heart, and that it has not only a spatial meaning but also a strictly material one.** *Mothers carry their children close to their hearts as a panacea for calming them down, but they are usually unaware that holding somebody close to one's heart exerts a very powerful influence. That is why in the Subtle World we gather people close to the heart so they can be strengthened and healed. Naturally, the giving heart loses a great deal of energy through application of such a powerful remedy. Often a mother's heart has been depicted as pierced by swords and arrows, a symbol of the absorption into her heart of all the pains manifested.*

Treatment by the heart can heal illnesses with clear symptoms, but it is particularly effective with diseases at an early stage. Now this remedy is almost forgotten, but it is no less powerful than a blood transfusion, for the subtlest of energies is transmitted by the action of the heart—only without the admixture of blood, which is disagreeable and lower in its quality. In thinking about perfectment, one must not forget to be solicitous of the heart that gives.

97. **After two weeks of superficial striving and apparent effort, a person comes to the conclusion either that he is unsuitable or that the Higher World does not exist. Yet the very same man will tell a servant who has worked for him a year, "I can't promote you yet. You haven't been on the job long enough."** With commonplace worldly affairs people understand that the period of time matters; only when it comes to considering things of a higher order are they reluctant to learn what is essential for attaining mastery. **It is difficult to speak to people who have not matured in heart or those who have managed to extinguish its fires. It would seem that the fires of the heart are quite natural and simple in the way that they manifest; but long periods are necessary for the understanding of the heart to appear in the physical world—the understanding that links the lowest plane with the Subtle World.** Of course, the multitude of fires demand that one adapt to them, in order to bring what seems to be chance into a chain of rhythm. **Few are the people who strive to be citizens of the Universe. Earning this title requires a great deal of solicitude, keen observation, vigilance, and, first and foremost, indomitable striving.**

98. **How can you get across to people who are unprepared that the topic of the Higher World deserves a heartfelt attitude? It is hard when somebody does not know anything, but even more difficult with people who have swallowed the Teaching like a spoonful of gruel; from them you can expect a special degree of betrayal and distortion. There is no sign strong enough to persuade a consciousness gone astray that it needs to look more at itself than at the people around it. How can someone see any fires when his eye is searching for a wrinkle on his neighbor's face?** Someone with a cold heart may be surprised and harbor doubts about the achievements of other people, and thus cover each spark of the heart with ashes.

You are amazed that people can swallow poisons without harm; won't you consider where that immunity comes from? Not from the structure of the stomach walls, but from the innate fire of the heart.

99. To those who have not paid attention to the so-called "phenomena" that have been corroborated by photography, x-rays, and the testimony of

witnesses, it would seem that a new Subtle World could not possibly come into being. Let us recall: **someone responded to cosmic manifestations; someone heard distant voices; someone saw the Subtle World and took part in it; someone gave off light; someone levitated; someone walked on water; someone walked on fire; someone swallowed poison without harm; someone had no need of sleep; someone had no need of food; someone could see through solid objects; someone could write with both hands; someone could attract animals; someone could understand a language without having learned it; someone could read thoughts; someone could read a closed book with his eyes shut; someone did not feel pain; someone surrounded by snow generated the heat of the heart; someone could go on without feeling fatigue; someone could help by healing; someone could manifest knowledge of the future.**

In this way one can recount all the phenomena that have manifested and enumerate a multitude of instructive examples that actually happened. Gather, for a moment, all of these qualities into a single body and you will have the transfiguration of the old humanity into a new one, a process referred to in many Teachings. *The main thing to note about this transfiguration is that all its various parts have already manifested, even in the midst of an imperfect existence. This means that with a well-defined effort one can impart to humanity a powerful impetus to transfigure life in its entirety.* **Therefore, let us remember about the great Fire and the fiery citadel—the heart. This is no fairy tale—the heart is the dwelling of the Spirit!** *People want evidence, but there is plenty of proof right in front of them, which means that first of all they should call that to mind, and understand the power of thought and the power of the heart's fire. Think! Thinking shows a person the significance of Culture!*
100. Healers fall into two groups: one heals through laying his hands on the patient or looking directly at him, while the other sends a heart current over a distance. Naturally, in building the future the second method is preferable. When you use the heart's radiation, it is not necessary to impact many of the patient's centres; rather, you can just work on the diseased part without burdening his attentive powers, thereby supporting his organism in its battle to restore balance. *You know how intangible Our touches are, so that We can avoid infringing*

upon the person's ability to act independently. You also recall how We have avoided physical manifestations, allowing them only to the extent that was necessary in providing evidence of a particular step. We hurry beyond that as soon as We see understanding. We say that a lazy person is a violator of the laws of life. Those who heal through the heart are acting in the subtle body as well as the physical. Attention should be paid to the phenomenal side of life; it is far more substantial than it seems.*(This is what we need to be aware of as we review the account of Jesus' remote healing and healing by laying on of hands).

106. **Usually one of the main things that puzzle people is their inability to see the Subtle World with the physical eye. Naturally, it is because the eye is not yet able to master the transmutation of ether. Imagine taking a photo right up against the window of a room; you could never succeed in getting a clear image, whether of the objects inside or of the distant contours outside. Similarly, in going from a dark place into sunlight, we sometimes are blinded and struck by the force of the blue light. By intensifying these manifestations of light to an infinite degree, we obtain the light of the Subtle World, which appears as darkness to an unprepared eye.** *People sometimes are also puzzled as to why a seemingly limited person has visions of the Subtle World. First of all, although that person may have fallen to a lower level now, in the past he possibly performed some purifying action; in other words, there once was a time when his heart was awake. It is especially remarkable that the quality of the heart does not disappear; it may manifest in a very one-sided way, but it continues to exist as a potential force.*

Also, why is it that women are often awake to the Subtle World? It is because their hearts are far subtler, which makes transcendental perception easier for them. Truly, the Epoch of the Mother of the World is based upon the cognition of the heart. It is women, and women alone, who can solve the problem of the two worlds. And so you can summon women to understanding through the heart. That will also be beneficial, primarily because the quality of the heart is everlasting. Already women have performed heroic deeds of all kinds, but now they are being given the flame of the heart instead of the fire of the stake. Let us not forget that for every important achievement, the Feminine Principle is absolutely necessary as the foundation and essence. The heart cannot be open to the Subtle World if it is not understood through a special *podvig*.

111. Truly, the successful development of the heart rests entirely upon moral foundations. These foundations transform the physical nature and vivify the spirit. Of course, people may ask you, "How does this condition apply to the dark ¬forces, seeing that their hierophants possess certain fires?" It is correct to understand that the dark amorality is based upon a discipline of fear. You should realise the cruelty of this discipline! While We very cautiously take into account the law of Karma and value individuality, on the opposite side are disharmony and destruction, and their foundations rest on tyranny. Of course, on the lower steps fear appears to be a reliable approach. **Thus, the dark intimidator comes across as a stern creditor. But you need to keep in mind the solidarity of the dark, amoral destroyers. Ill-prepared warriors often do not want to know the enemies' strength, but the heart can be pierced as effectively through the breast as through the back. Therefore, be skillful in learning all about the enemies' methods.**

113. Humanity is terrified of everything "supernatural," forgetting that nothing can be supernatural—that is, beyond the real. Therefore, strongly insist that Agni Yoga and the Teaching of the Heart cannot contain anything supernatural. Be especially cautious with people under thirty, since they are still at an age when not all of the centers can function without harm to the heart. It is essential that you make clear that Our Yoga includes no coercive magic and would never generate chaos. You need to light the fires of *podvig* in the young, to kindle heroic achievements that will transform their essence and, imperceptibly to them, prepare their hearts for future perfectment. Thus, with as much joy and simplicity as possible you should set sail to the White Island, as We sometimes call Our Dwelling.

115. Do not reject, do not be horrified, and do not be surprised— these rules will make it easier for the phenomenal side of life to unite with the ordinary. Of course, you ascertained from your own experience that the phenomenal side could enter your life with perfect naturalness, in no way disturbing your productivity and even enhancing your ability to work. What I am saying has all the more significance inasmuch as it is commonly *thought that perceiving the phenomenal in daily life tears one away from productive activity. Quite the opposite,* **the manifestation of striving to the Infinite teaches the vastness of human possibilities. Likewise, there are many misunderstandings around the concept of testing. Certainly, people are familiar with the idea that even whole worlds are being put to the test, but their brains are accustomed to legal and academic tests, so they are always able to imagine examiners full of schemes and ruses whose sole aim is to convict the unfortunate who fall into their hands. Actually, there are no examiners, but there are observers who watch how a person makes use of his or her knowledge. Naturally, one should put the blame for failure not on the observers but on oneself.**

117. *Intolerance is a sign of ignobility of spirit. Intolerance contains embryos of the most evil activities. There is no place for the manifestation of spiritual growth where intolerance nests.* **The heart's potential is unlimited; how impoverished a heart must be to deprive itself of the Infinite! One has to eradicate every sign, every indication that might lead to the idolatry of intolerance. Humanity has invented all sorts of ¬obstacles to ascent. The dark forces are trying in every way they can to restrict evolution. Naturally, their first assault will be an action against the Hierarchy. Everyone has heard about the power of a Blessing, but out of ignorance they have turned this beneficial action into a superstition.** *And yet the power of the Magnet also lies in its ability to strengthen someone with a Blessing. Much is said about cooperation; thus, with every creative act it is necessary to assert awareness of the Higher World. And what strengthens the power with more immediacy than the Ray of the Hierarchy!*

A person who understands the essence of continuous labour, who grows strong through concentration on the Hierarchy, who frees himself of complicated formulas in order to transfer concentration to the heart—that person will understand the essence of the future.

118. *I affirm that because we human beings serve the transformation of matter into energy, nobody should belittle our significance or the importance of our passage through the lower strata. As the essence corresponds so little to the form that it happens to take in life, one might even think of the existence of human beings as that of envoys in disguise. Indeed, the essence may be very beautiful!*

I am affirming the striving to construct a temple of the heart. That is what we shall call the awareness of cooperation.

122. The world's convulsion is like a convulsion of the heart. Just as nothing can make the threatening forces abandon their assault, nothing can free the sensitive heart from quivering when something precious to it is subject to assault. **But you should tell everyone not to feel terrified, for as long as the formation stands firm, nothing can penetrate.** *However, the quivering of the heart is unavoidable on the Tower, as well as anywhere there is devotion. Let us distinguish this feeling from those caused by atmospheric influences, which even in time of tension cannot give rise to the sort of reaction that the psychic reflexes convey.* **I affirm that you should be as calm as possible, because We are keeping vigil.**

131. I am now advising that scientists pay attention to the organism's sensitivity to all sorts of inexplicable phenomena—the sensation of goose flesh is one example. Of course, this can be explained as a nervous contraction, **yet it is instructive to pay attention to whether or not there is something alien in the surrounding atmosphere. Such observations are quite useful when one is investigating psychic energy. Something makes the physical atmosphere tense and acts on the surface of the skin and the nerves.** *This physical reaction should be investigated from a chemical point of view as something that accelerates nervous contractions. Rays and currents are so close to the Subtle World! But the people conducting these investigations should first of all learn to pay attention to sensations. Doctors themselves pay less attention than anyone else to the great variety of sensations. They divide complex ¬organisms into primitive parcels, and that prevents them from making their observations more subtle.* (This Stanza refers to how you can detect entities/energies in your vicinity).

133. **Use every means to spread the Good. It is a shame to see how at times a speck of something brings a whole wheel to a halt. A great heart has a great capacity, while a petty heart mainly fills itself with petty things. Evil must not be allowed to spread unimpeded. The example of a garden and weeds makes this sufficiently clear. Invite the sweet-sounding singers for a walk among the weeds, and their mellifluent tunes will fade. But the ardor of the warriors of Good will not cool as** *they progress on the path! Thus, let the heart be the judge of where the Good begins!*

136. *If clairaudience and clairvoyance exist, there must also be clairalience—the ability to smell distant or subtle scents. Of course, in the manifestation of psychic energy it has a special significance; psychic energy is found in condensed form in the aroma* and, moreover, brings on the spasmodic inhalation that I have already mentioned. *It is helpful to recall the odd way in which the ancient wisdom was transformed, how it degenerated into absurd ceremonies. When you read about the customs of Egypt, China, and other ancient peoples, telling how they greeted each other by means of smell and inhalation, it may be difficult to discern therein a recollection about psychic energy, a memory passed down from vanished races. But even now, open straight-knowledge reveals the ¬essence of the surrounding atmosphere. It is not a question of smell but, precisely, of essence.* (For me this remains one of the strongest indications that there is bad energy nearby. Smelling smoke, when there is no fire, indicates demonic presence, so be careful, guard the heart, and keep your chakras closed).

146. *You should remember that while the spiritual battle rages there may be unusual vibrations, and of course you should not expect that they will all be in harmony.*

You may ask Me what I need of you right now. I need devotion, a devotion that is purified of all additives. When space shudders, we need to purify our feelings, just as an archer ¬removes the tiniest particle of fluff from the tip of his arrow. Our Battle is moving forward, so plant your feet firmly and cast aside every impediment.

What kind of help is possible when a battle is going on? First of all, it is possible to create new circumstances; therefore vigilance, and still more vigilance!

148. *Again someone will come up with the question, "Why is so little said about the Subtle World in all the scriptures?" You can be sure that a great deal is said everywhere, but people do not want to take notice of it. Upon ancient icons you can see green spheres that represent the earthly next to red spheres that represent the fiery realm—in other words, the Subtle World. On one image you can see a whole scene in green tones*

and next to it a red world of angels. What could be more graphic than that? The various prophecies are full of messages about the Subtle World. The Koran also makes mention of the Subtle World. You cannot name a single Teaching in which no place is given to the life of the Subtle World. Because they feel terror before everything invisible, people stuff their ears and close their eyes, preferring to remain in ignorance. But can a person think about the heart or ponder psychic energy without remembering about the Subtle World, a vast realm so inseparable from the dense world?

156. When the world becomes tense, the spiritual armor of the closest co-workers grows stronger, and their radiation grows purple and fiery. So the cosmic armor comes to correspond to worldwide conditions independently of personal feelings and day-to-day work. Thus, one can get a sense of the cosmic influence so long as things are unfolding according to the law of Hierarchy.

One should note how the spiritual armor is being forged at the same time that the consciousness is expanding. We can help make this armor stronger, but unless there has also been growth of the consciousness, such intervention will be tantamount to destruction. So the Mysterious Hand can be seen when people are acting according to the law of Hierarchy. This needs to be remembered especially now, for even a tempered heart may feel distress when sensing the unprecedented tension.

157. *The flaming sword is a ray of the spiritual armor.* **The symbol of a sword-like ray, which has appeared in every Teaching, is an extremely challenging sign. Even the most peace-loving images have affirmed a sword. This does not express a desire to coerce, but it does indicate a readiness to defend the most sacred.** So in the midst of the raging fire one can see a thin sword above the brow of a warrior of spirit. It is a shame that on the earthly plane the process of impressing the aura's radiation on film is still so imperfect. Clear evidence of rays and other fires could be presented. (Christ said, I did not come to bring peace but a Sword – the sword to defend the most sacred.)

160. It is right to remember that even the passing shadow of a person leaves behind an ineradicable trace. How, then, to describe the impact of thoughts and words! The light-mindedness of humanity is astonishing, for

with its every step it leaves behind the most frightening deposits. Humanity supposes that words can wipe away the traces of past thoughts. But who, then, creates the impassable labyrinths that bring on the destruction of destined manifestations? **When you realise that the fiery sphere retains the remnants of all the thoughts carelessly cast into space, you may recall the old riddle: "What cannot burn away?" — "A thought."** Humanity generates thought that is lodged firm in the strata of space. You should know with what complexity space resounds when it is shot through with thoughts, often ones that are insignificant and filthy. But if you start talking about the chemical reaction of a thought, people will consider you mentally unsound. Neither threat nor fear nor counsel will help unless the traveller in the Subtle World runs up against his own thought barrier. **As an inscription on an ancient stele reads, "Traveller, do not stand in your own way!"**

*(And this is the guidance given as you prepare for the 3rd Initiation- Energy follows thought, do not send out harmful or gross thoughts into space for then you will be standing in your own way and blocking your ascent).

162. It is not enough to firmly establish the consciousness; one also has to get used to guarding it under various circumstances. You need one blade for cutting paper, another for wood, and a completely different one for metal. You might liken the physical, subtle, and fiery worlds to the resistance of paper, wood, and metal. Truly, one has to constantly accustom oneself to being conscious of the Subtle and Fiery Worlds; various exercises can develop that consciousness. So one must get used to a state of constant work, endless and untiring. There is no substitute for such tension of the consciousness in its usefulness for the Subtle World. **People usually work only for rest, not for the limitless process of perfection; so when they find themselves in the Subtle World, before the very face of Infinity, they fall into confusion and fog. Likewise, to approach the Fiery World you must accustom yourself to going forward without fear, as if walking on the edge of an abyss. Only the highest self-mastery and readiness for danger can prepare a person for the fiery spheres.**

*164. Dissatisfaction is a characteristic suited to the Subtle World. In it one can discern eternal motion, for without this motion it is impossible to go forward in the higher worlds. You can satisfy and satiate the stomach and muscles, but what will satiate the heart? Though it may fill you with rapture, even contemplation of the Highest Light will not give you satiety. **Flaming heart, insatiable heart, only the very pain of the world will propel you forward!** The mist that obscures sated eyes will turn into the radiance of the kindled heart's flame. So let us guard the fiery treasure. **Let us help the people to understand the precious heart. And in doing so, let us call to mind all the milestones needed on the path.** Let us not forget the wise words, "And this, too, will pass." An impetuous motion will never bring one back to the same place.

168. **It is impossible not to notice what strong opposition every conscious movement toward Light encounters. Besides the usual counteractions from the dark ones, the work of Chaos may also be noticed. In being aware of this law of the opposition from the Unmanifest, we find self-consolation and experience in cultivating patience.**

*(As the White Sphinx, forces of good-advances, so too must the black sphinx, forces of Evil, in order for man to choose correctly and build his strength by fighting the dark and darker impulses within themselves!).

169. *People may be so savage in spirit that they can only exist by criticizing one another. This is not an inspection of someone's armor for the purpose of helping him out; quite the contrary, criticism becomes the very meaning of life. If one were to deprive such a critic of his tongue, he would wither away like a plant without water. Such a phenomenon could be examined from a medical point of view. One can find in this criticism a sort of vampirism involving possession, in which obtaining more active, vital fluids is necessary to nourish the possessor.*

170. *If you wish to make a speech in a language you do not know, it is unwise to start preparing the night before you deliver it. If you wish to perform on an unfamiliar instrument, it is unwise to start practicing the night before you go on stage. If you wish to cross into the Subtle World, it is unwise to begin preparations the evening before you depart. It is horrible when a person who has turned away from thought about the Subtle World his whole life behaves like a negligent student and only on the eve of his crossing begins in confusion to repeat words he has never really understood.* **The time of crossing is sure to come—this is an unavoidable fact that**

every Teaching proclaims. It has been said, "We shall not die, but change." Is it possible to speak more concisely, to speak with a greater sense of affirmation? It means that one must know the language of the Subtle World. It also means that one has to acquire the right of entry with full consciousness, but all this is impossible to attain on the eve of departure. There are those who instil terror, instead of joy, in the person about to cross over, and this violates the law of life. *But as you know, the best guide forward is the flaming heart. When you have such an inextinguishable lamp, there is nothing terrifying about crossing the skies and meeting the Guiding Ones. This phenomenon of life can and should be investigated with a scientific purpose. Of course, it is difficult to overcome possession, especially because after possession the gates remain open to visitors for a long time. With someone who has admitted a possessor, very intense observation is necessary to protect him from irritation, which leaves the door wide open. The heart is the best guardian against possession, but you have to make sure that the heart does not fall asleep!*

176. **Armageddon has already begun—the end of 1931 saw the start of the Great Battle, and I did not conceal it from you.** *So the Battle cannot end now, but must reach a victorious conclusion…You should not be surprised that events are piling up, for the earthly battle is following the heavenly. A great deal has been said about the Heavenly Host, about Michael the Archstrategus, the Supreme General, about the manifestation of the affirmed Leader, and about all the perturbations. That is why I say,* "Caution!"

177. **Do not neglect anything. In neglect lies the cause of many misfortunes. Advise people to understand that even the greatest of manifestations may be the least visible. Cosmic significance is not dependent on physical dimensions. A seed provides the best example of this.** *Now especially we are pointing out the need to respect the diverse manifestations that have filled life.* **Does a messenger necessarily have to be a giant? And must a ray be nothing less than blinding? And wouldn't a voice of deafening volume be harmful? Right now a multitude of manifestations, insignificant in appearance, are traversing the world. Every seeker needs to sharpen his attention. A person who can train his attention to observe the smallest will also understand the greatest.**

178. *The ability to have respect for even the smallest will help you to acquire the ability to be patient as well. And what patience is necessary when facing Infinity, especially when we realise that it is unavoidable!* Besides, we know how much every murmur of protest impedes the path. The burden created by disrespect for the small should be replaced with the joy that is found in observing the multiformity of creation. We can help each other by speaking the very simplest words. (3rd Key – KSHANTI – Patience sweet that naught can ruffle).

179. *Who, then, will help out when the Battle is raging? A person who, having acquired patience, accepts the armor of courage. You know what courage is necessary to go forward on a dangerous course. Two paths can be offered, a dangerous path and a safe one, but a flaming heart will choose the former.*

180. *No sooner is the beginning of the Great Battle mentioned than someone starts to feel tired. What will he have to say, then, when he confronts countless hostile warriors? Every Yuga has a preparatory phase of considerable length, but there may be periods of acceleration when all the forces must be intensified to an unusual degree. People should not understand the great, decisive Battle as just a war. The manifestation of the Battle is something far deeper. Its torrent will flow through the entire Subtle World as well as the earthly. It will express itself not only in armed conflicts but also in unprecedented clashes among peoples. The boundaries between the belligerents will be as tortuous as those between good and evil. The earthly eye will not have access to many of the decisive battles. The ominous clashes in the Subtle World will express themselves as catastrophes on the earthly path. Similarly, earthly courage will have an impact on the Subtle and Fiery Worlds. The Great Battle will be the first link in the unification of the worlds.* Thus, one can expect quick actions to arise from every direction. Cooperation has enormous significance in this Battle. *Even now the star of the flaming heart is bringing tremendous help.* Since this help may not always be visible, you can illustrate it by citing the example of an author who exerts great influence even though he does not know his readers. The same may be said about cooperation between the two worlds. *One has to maintain a high degree of tension in the days of the Battle. Of course, this does not rule out doing all kinds of*

everyday work, **but in performing each job you should remember to send it off with a thought for the benefit of Light. Likewise, whenever you are pierced by a hostile arrow, you should be conscious and receive each blow in the name of the Great Battle.**

*182. **The golden light that fills the inner essence is a characteristic sign that the heart is being armed. Just as the outer reaches of the aura turn from purple to ruby, the silvery Lotus of the heart flashes with a burst of red and gold when the spirit dons the ultimate armor.** That is how an inner condition is attained that allows participation in the fiercest battles without harm or risk of the subtle body being severely wounded. The results of this armoring of the heart were already evident when the warrior stood up to the dark forces and, in spite of their overwhelming numbers, made them tremble. She left them with their threats,* **and the empty threat of an enemy is in itself a victory.** *Naturally, the pure golden light is not easily attained; it requires a lengthy achievement.*

*183. **Although many conditions of the heart, ranging from soft-heartedness to hard-heartedness, have been noted in people's observations, fiery-heartedness has hardly ever been mentioned. But it is precisely this quality that ought to attract our attention and occupy it. It is hard to be unafraid of the black assembly, but no one can overpower the fiery heart. Let them come up with all kinds of threats; one pillar of Light will put all the darkness to flight!***

*188. **The immediate duty of everyone who knows about the Subtle World is to affirm the existence of this invisible but real world every time the opportunity presents itself. Some people may respond by getting angry, but it will give them an opportunity to think about reality.** If research on human physiology were supplemented by the study of the Subtle World, which connects all the various conditions of existence, our world would at once enter into a distinctly new era.* **I can affirm that the commotion arising from the present turmoil has attained unprecedented proportions, because the bond between the worlds is totally ignored. Let nobody claim that he has not been warned in due time. Let the traveller not forget that he cannot return to the house that he left behind, that it is only by his own efforts that he can reach the Luminous City to which he has been summoned.** *Let the traveller remind everyone he meets at the crossroads that paths are irreversible.*

189. The appearance of Our trusted messengers can be accepted as a sign that the New World is now being born. I admonish all those who are failing to notice the myriad of signs appearing everywhere in the world. The Teacher can tell a person to look, but He cannot force him to see. Do not be surprised that in the mosaic of the book Heart so much is included about the Subtle World and the Great Battle. Many hearts sense both of these realities, but often they cannot express them in words. Yet the thought born in the heart with the swiftness of light will express itself in words. Remind your friends that there is a good reason why their hearts are aching.

191. I want to accustom you to the scales of Infinity. Understanding of these scales develops slowly, as does the ability to use them in commeasuring events. A neophyte cannot grasp the universal context and dimension of various events. To him it is difficult and unusual even to rearrange his room. How, then, is he to think about universal wings! He is also held back by his concern about the pettiest possessions, and he does not see the stage at which any condition is acceptable because it has been weighed on the scales of Infinity.

192. A disease may nestle inside a person for a long time, but if it does not manifest in gross physical form, no ordinary physician will recognize it. Ten prophets and clairvoyants may testify to the existence of a hidden disease, but they will be looked upon as liars because it has yet to appear at the grossest level. Similarly, **humanity has schooled itself in the coarsest forms of everything, having banished refinement and straight-knowledge.** *Even the most importunate signs of the Subtle World have been consigned to oblivion. Nobody wants to know about or count up the multitude of words that speak quite definitely about the Subtle World—words found in every language. Let us take, for example, a favourite word, 'inspiration.' It means that somebody "breathed into" or "instilled" something; that inspiration came from somewhere else. With perfect clarity the word presupposes that something came from without, but people go on speaking about inspiration without any awareness that what it refers to is a manifestation of the Subtle World. Just think of all the signs scattered everywhere in the world, yet something shuts people's eyes to them. What is it, if not darkness?*

196. Imagination is the result of the accumulation of experience. This is quite well known. Yet there may exist a tremendous accumulation (of good deeds karma and energy from many incarnations on the path of light), *and instead of imagination only lust and irritation are in evidence.* **Affirm that the imagination cannot be developed without the participation of the heart. That is why the creators, both inner and outer, will be those who have wisely combined accumulations with a manifestation of the heart's fires. This should be explained to all the children in every school, so that not a single tenet of the Teaching remains an abstraction.** *You yourself also see how the manifestation of the spirit unfolds in a logical progression. You know how at first the fiery sword begins to shine and completes the aura, but later it penetrates one's entire being. The symbol of a sword is especially appropriate to the Great Battle, when all the spiritual forces are gathering under the Banners of the Lords of Light. The golden light also grows stronger at this time and thereby grows closer to the golden deposits of prana. All of the forces are expressed in the flaming heart.*

197. Isn't it amazing that in the days of the Great Battle we can still speak about the imagination? For the Battle is not a work of imagination but already the clash of hordes. **So, one more page has been turned. I insist on great caution, great care, for the time is a great one. We are also gathering in the Tower in order to oppose all the evil ones. You ought to be ready for great battles, for only the inconsequential are not called to battle!"**

The primary battle is fought within yourself as you test the lighter and darker promptings in your chosen action/thoughts. I will include at this point an illustration of Christ with his Sacred Heart, and Mother Mary with her Immaculate Heart, to illustrate the sacred significance of heart at this juncture.

Figure 59a & 59b: Source – Images of Sacred Heart of Jesus and Mother Mary – of the Fratelli Bonella™ used with permission from WJ Hirten company.

205. *It is commendable to defend the Sign of the Lords. It is useful to train oneself in understanding how close the Lords are. Just as it is impossible for a person to do without food, he cannot live rightly without holding close to the Hierarchy. Let the seeker not resemble a log that just lies there, leaning on something else for support, but rather be like a vigilant guard who increases his powers by being ready to rise up in defence at any moment. Though you are sufficiently aware of the One Light, I am speaking about it again, so that you can increase your powers. Even the cross itself is powerless without the heart. Even the purest prana will not penetrate a spiteful heart.* **Even Aum (Om) will amount to nothing in the face of a deceitful, treacherous heart. Let us keep this in mind, so that no form of possession may penetrate the heart. Having examples of possession right before you, you see what is being lost during these days of shameful weakness.**

213. Possession must be very clearly defined. You should not be surprised to find a number of possessed people near the hearths of spirituality. The reason for this is that the dark forces are seeking to shore up their guard. Who, if not the possessed, is best able to assist the dark forces? Moreover, there are countless varieties of possession. First of all, you need to look into the essence and discern where there is Good and where harm. *That is how the flaming heart will immediately discern where possession is concealed.*

Spiritual teachers that hold themselves in lofty esteem that do not abandon harmful habits such as drinking more than a rare glass of alcohol or practicing sexual frivolity etc thinking that they are above the laws that govern normal people, are caught in a very strong ego glamour. They are actually slaves to the body. It is exceedingly difficult to penetrate this glamour as spiritual teachers such as this cannot see their blind spots, blinded by their misguided perception of Earthly power. And because they hold this superior opinion of themselves, they will rarely listen to outside advice as their rampant ego will not let them stoop so low as to listen to others.

Consequently what happens is that this excessive spiritual ego attracts powerful dark entities to take possession and they continue to sink lower and lower in light quotient, but believe that they are actually getting stronger in light. All one needs to do is compare an older photograph of the same person and a new photo and it will be evident how their spiritual light has diminished. The spiritual teacher of course may try to rationalize it away as being a product of old age. But here is the kicker – the spiritual being that has activated the light codes in the DNA and lives in divine purity at the 6th and 7th octaves of vibration actually can reverse the aging process. The mind body spirit connection is real. Pay attention to your inner bearing, pay attention to your subtle emanations. The divine is in every person, we may be at different levels of conscious awareness – but we are all equal.

214. The guarantee given by the Forces of Light is the most powerful foundation for the New Life. **I can assure you, the dark ones have a dreary road ahead. I am affirming the Light of the future, which through various voices will kindle fires all over the world. I am affirming that the**

Teaching is a manifestation of the New World. I am affirming that the most precious concepts are steps on the path of life. I am affirming that there is no darkness that could extinguish Our signs. I am affirming that something beneficial can be obtained from the turmoil. I am affirming that the forces of the Subtle World are striving to approach the earthly plane. I am affirming that this difficult hour is a clarion call. I am affirming that everyone who follows Us will attain salvation. I am affirming that the many scattered members will be united. I am affirming the path to the sunrise, a path on which there is but a single decision. I am affirming the date of happiness, a date that brings a promise of salvation to the world.

219. *There is tremendous tension; you should understand how closely the world situation is connected with the work. It is impossible to divide the two, when the overall situation is tantamount to a battle of unprecedented proportions. That is why I emphatically command that you stay undivided, that you be imbued with the tension of the moment.* **You must not retreat, but rather join together in putting pressure on the possessed. If a jest be permitted, one might call this phase of the conflict "the battle against possession." The dark ones try to strengthen themselves through possession, but such methods cannot last very long, for it is precisely through possession that they bring on their own disintegration.** *You know how possession gradually destroys the organism, for it inevitably causes the paralysis of certain nerve centers. In fact, doctors could do a great deal of useful work by directing their attention to possession. Ask Dr. L. whether he noticed certain peculiarities in the eyes of the possessed, for one can judge the duality of existence by the eyes. After he replies, I will make corrections in response. I do not have in mind just superficial manifestations, such as lackluster eyes or a shifting glance, for attention should be paid to other symptoms as well.* **One can also observe symptoms in the gait, the voice, and even in a change of weight. Do not ask psychiatrists about it, because their conclusions are already set in stone;** *but physicians like Dr. L. are able to observe without preconceptions.* **How urgent such observations are now that possession is reaching epidemic proportions! Sensing the weakness of human hearts, hordes of spirits, shrewd and ferocious, are rushing to capture the earthly odour!**

222. **We constantly insist that you learn to overcome every sort of**

*fear. **This requirement is not something abstract, but has in mind your immediate ascent.** Once it has grown stronger, fear, like many negative features, forms itself into a sort of negative magnet. During the lifetimes that follow, this magnet will impel the personality toward the object of the fear that has been instilled. If someone is afraid of something, he will inevitably be compelled to cross the path of that very horror until he has freed himself of fear. That is why it is beneficial if a person, having realised the invulnerable nature of his spiritual essence, goes on to liberate himself from all fears, because all the objects of fear are really insignificant. **Even an encounter with a powerful dark entity is not dangerous for someone who maintains a firm bond with the Hierarchy.** Other negative qualities can also be terminated if a person is aware that reverting to them would be worthless, since he would have to experience their return blow.* (Overcome fear in order to pass through the second Gate – to do so you need the second Golden Key – Shila)

228. It is no honour to be enticed by the dark ones. It is no honour to find oneself at a loss for words in speaking against the dark stratagems. Let us not imagine that the devices of our attackers are going to decrease. It is wrong to believe that someday a state of undisturbed rest will arrive. Every shock is but a touchstone. So you should look forward to each act of oppression as a source of the tension preceding a leap. ***If a depth of spirit exists, who can exhaust its depths? And who could measure the fullness of the heart, and with what measures? Truly, the heart answers for itself. Truly, only the language of the heart can convey the essence of existence.*** *Therefore, we shall not be afraid when the oppression intensifies.* ***Doubt may undermine every intensification, which is why doubt is rejected and its progenitor is called the father of lies.***

The details of what is happening now correspond to the great significance of what has been destined. You may rejoice in these details, for they remind one of some glorious pages.

234. ***When the world is deep in confusion you may expect frightening whirlwinds that, like waterspouts, will pierce through the lower strata of the atmosphere and totally twist the way people think. You must be ready for assaults quite unlike anything undergone before, but to pass through them means to go forward on the path of knowledge.***

236. *If we look at a deodar tree, the tallest and most powerful, we will find many marks on the trunk where former branches have fallen away. Far from weakening the deodar, the departing branches leave the most powerful evidence of the tree's strength—even steel will break against these spots. No Teaching feels frightened about those who fall away. The Teaching knows that the lower branches must fall. In fact, when carried off by the wind, those that have fallen away may end up carrying out what they have been assigned to do. They may even give birth to new deodars. And their resin will have curative properties, all the same. Later, when they are joined together to support the corner of a house, they will unite in bearing the overall pressure. So do not be frightened when people fall away. They cannot go far from the resin of the heart.* **And if you observe from above, looking down upon the multitude of crossroads that intersect, you will even smile upon the travellers who are meeting. When you realise the length of the infinite path, you will come to apply different standards of measurement. There is nothing frightening about people wandering; it is only immobility that is chilling.**

237. *A guarantee will make a good shield, but let us distinguish between falling away and betraying. Falling away may be due to some karmic cause or some peculiarities of the physical body, but there are no circumstances that justify betrayal. I can assert that the consequences of betrayal are the most impossible to avoid. Nothing can free the traitor from the fate of being betrayed himself. A betrayal of the Teaching is considered to be the most heinous of all. Human beings cannot blaspheme the Highest Spirit. In studying the activities of the heart, you can see what physical shocks are brought on by betrayal of the Highest. The disintegrative force that issues from a betrayal is not limited to the boundaries of the personality; it acts ceaselessly over vast expanses.* **Just as the highest spheres sense every benevolent ascent, every betrayal resounds like the stones of a crumbling tower. Following up the analogy of the deodar, one might say that betrayal is like a hollow tree in which bats have nested.**

239. *If a mother does not attend patiently to the first wishes of her baby, she is no mother. If a Teacher does not show patience in dealing with the first steps of a disciple, he is no Teacher. If the Teacher does not understand the path of a disciple, he is no Teacher. If a Teacher does not lay*

his hand upon the eyes of his disciple, he will be the one who deprives him of sight. So let us guard the path of the heart. Any form of oppression is foreign to the heart of a Teacher. The Teacher keeps an eye on what the student is experiencing, and will gently remove his hand if it touches fire. **Patience is a gem in the Crown. It is evidence that one is drawing near to Infinity.**

242. Regarding the various qualities of love, let us note the love that holds back and the love that impels forward. Essentially, the first type is earthly, while the second is heavenly. What a multitude of creations have been destroyed by the first, and what a similar number have been winged on by the second! The first is aware of all the limitations of space and consciousness, but the second has no need to measure things by earthly standards. It is unimpeded by distances or considerations of death. While the first views the world as a planet, the second is not hampered even by the possibility that the planet may be destroyed, because all the worlds lie before it. Actually, the second love extends to the physical world as well as the Subtle and Fiery Worlds. It kindles hearts, giving them the highest joy, and is therefore indestructible. So let us expand the heart—not for Earth but for Infinity.

243. **Let us accept love as the motive force in the expansion of consciousness. The heart will not be aflame without love; it will not be invincible, nor will it be self-sacrificing.** *So let us bring gratitude to every receptacle of love, for love lies on the border of the New World, where hatred and intolerance have been abolished. The path of love unfolds with the intensity of cosmic-energy.* **So on this path everyone will find his place in the Cosmos. Not as dried leaves but as lotuses aflame will people find kinship with the Highest World.**

244. Where does the boundary of personal gain begin? The heart knows such boundaries, while the intellect is unable to pull apart the petals of the fiery lotus. **When the guard is entrusted with protecting the entrance, when he is given a shield, and when he accepts in his shield all the arrows aimed at the Teacher, this will also be a personal action, but it will be the very opposite of personal gain.** *The heart is well aware of these beautiful personal actions in which every enemy arrow grows into a new petal of the fiery lotus. These personal actions—compelled by no one, ordered by no one, disproved by no one, but condemned by all the evil forces—will be the true rays of podvig. Precisely such a condemnation, arising from malice* and anger, will serve as genuine evidence of podvig. **You should note that darkness does not condemn genuine selfishness; this also provides a true criterion. Not only should you know the standard that leads upward, you should also know the one that draws people down. That is the only way you can fully appreciate the shield of podvig.**

251. *Some people deny everything invisible. Not only savages but also many "educated" people are unwilling to even think about the stars. The Teachings offer hints about countless heavenly dwellings, but evidently people do not wish to speed up their journey. It is just as in the theatre where spectators sob with pity one moment, but the next thing are ready to go back to their grudges and pounce on each other.*

255. *You know that living fire is the best means of disinfection, but the nature of fire is the same in all of its manifestations. The fire of the heart will be a lofty manifestation of fire, which means that it will be the best purifier and protector. So instead of using all kinds of dubious, often poisonous antiseptic medicines, it is much better not only to have the fire of the hearth but also to kindle the fires of the heart. One can find out for oneself how effectively the fires of the heart fight serious illnesses. Sooner or later our contemporary physicians will have to pay attention to the various states of the fires.* **Doctors will not make much progress in finding a panacea if they go on barking at truths that have been known for ages.**

Your thoughts about the Vedic deities are perfectly correct; indeed, the microcosm resembles the Macrocosm. **I affirm that the fire of the heart purifies the densest darkness. But along with this ability to purify, the heart is full of the qualities of a magnet, which is why it is the natural link with the Macrocosm.**

256. **One should understand the fiery path as a path to the Highest. Not words, not fear, not habit, but the communion of the heart is the most enduring manifestation,** *the one transmitted from time immemorial. So it is the rainbow bridge that will bring us closer to the other shore.* **How many controversies rage on regarding that shore, but it does exist, and one must find the path to it.** *Not dried up autumn leaves but the flaming heart will cross every bridge.* **A person who does not think about the birth of the heart's fire is ignorant of the upward path; he is unwilling to look upon it in a luminous way.**

259. **People should not think that lofty attainments will make them safe from the monsters of darkness. On the contrary, the Light will reveal new monsters whose fury is fathomless. We shall not grieve over this, for it is the monsters that provide the legs for the throne.** There is a good reason why sacred objects are depicted as mounted upon animal-like pedestals. But this consideration does not mean that people need not be vigilant.

260. Since the so-called state of Nirvana is not rest but rather the highest tension of energy, one might ask whether rest even exists. Indeed, how is it possible to imagine rest if everything is in motion and exists on account of motion? The very concept of rest was invented by people who wished to flee from existence. They preferred immobility, forgetting that there cannot be a moment without motion. Equilibrium is the concept needed. The seeker should think not about rest but about how to maintain equilibrium in the midst of the whirlwinds. The silver thread is made taut by the power of striving, and for that very reason one should know what equilibrium is, so as to avoid burdening the thread of the Hierarchy by faltering. The thread will not break when it is tautened, for even a straw holds out so long as it is not bent. The silver thread is based on the very same law of connection, but if a person does not refrain from fluctuating in a disorderly manner, he usually cannot hold fast to the link. So let us not bemoan the lack of rest, since rest does not exist in the first place.

261. Nobody in the wrong will be able to hold out against equilibrium, which is why the stroke of the sword must be delivered in accordance with the law. **So let us understand the way in which both the physical and the higher laws are focused in the heart. This centre was called the crossroad, and was represented by an equilateral cross; the dorje, like the swastika, indicated the rotation of the heart's fire.** Rotating and having arms of equal length are signs of equilibrium. In childhood someone tried to stand on a ball, unaware that this is a great symbol of equilibrium.

262. The external must not conceal the fundamental. That is why humanity should not litter up the path to ascent. One has only to let in a little dust and the most resonant trumpet will lose its tone. **It is this tiny pinch of dust that is more dangerous than all the swords and knives put together. The same must be said about the fluctuations: they arise not**

from great works but from the same speck of dust of the spirit. Thus, a person who is successful in the great also keeps his eye on the small. And a heart destined for the great senses even the smallest. It is wrong to suppose that the great is blind to the small. Quite the contrary, **the great eye can see the smallest, and the flaming heart detects the inaudible rustle.** *If we understand the sensitivity of the great heart, then we will also be well aware of the significance of the world's structure. Let us not soar with intoxication, nor wilt away with lofty pride.* **Pridefulness struts in shoes of stone; intoxication flaps wings of wax. But the dignity of the spirit is the fire of the heart, the wings that ascend to the sun.**

268. Uriel is the Lord of powerful action. One can turn to various Leaders according to the nature of the help needed. **If Michael joins hands with Uriel, it means that a powerful offensive is necessary.** *With rigor and severity did Uriel master the elements on Venus. So it is possible to steel the power, tempering it by accepting the blows of the elements.* **These mighty Forces should be understood as realities.**

274. Because of the earthly attraction, the shells of the Subtle World are especially close to dense, physical existence. **It is precisely these shells that roam the entire world in the form of phantoms, and all sorts of evil spirits love to take over these free lodgings. Great is the responsibility of those who pass over into the Subtle World while still harboring earthly passions!** *It is horrible to litter up the beautiful expanses of Space, for Space leads to Light and can resonate with the higher knowledge.* **How hideous is the husk of petty carnal desires, from which it is so easy to free oneself— one has only to think of the Hierarchy of Light.**

The heart, the heart, the heart—the heart is what will always remind you about the Light!

276. Naturally, it is neither spring nor autumn that brings on fatigue; rather, **it is the growing density of the currents, which is pressing upon the centres. It cannot be otherwise when legions of people, possessed and raving in rage, are rushing forward. So there is no reason to be surprised when possessed people on distant continents begin to utter the very same formulas. This is one more proof of an Invisible World Government that issues from a common Source. After all, both Light and darkness are monarchical. It is extremely helpful to follow the trend of world thought.**

Looking at both sides, one can see a definite division, since each side will make its own efforts and adopt its own decisive measures. So even from the perspective of the earthly plane one can observe this division of the forces and understand the movement of the armies.

277. *A person can think with the heart or think with the brain. There was perhaps a time when people forgot about the work of the heart, but now is the era of the heart, and we must focus our efforts in that direction. Thus, without freeing the brain of its work, we are ready to recognize the heart as a motive power. People have thought up a thousand ways to place limitations on the heart. The works of the heart are understood in a narrow sense, and not even always in a pure sense.* **We must bring the entire world into the sphere of the heart, because the heart is the microcosm of everything that exists. A person who is not inspired by the great concept of the heart will end up belittling his own significance. We tell people to give up getting irritated, but only greatness of heart will save a person from the poison of irritability.** *We speak about the ability to embrace, but where is there an all-embracing ocean outside of the heart?* **We remind people about the distant worlds, but it is the heart, not the brain, that can remember about Infinity. So let us not belittle the organ that has been bestowed upon us to be a receptacle of Grace.**

283. **Pure thinking is the best disinfectant. It is high time that thinking was accepted as a chemical process.** *Likewise, the manifestation of Armageddon should not only be understood as a war in the conventional sense but should also be viewed in terms of all the events in life.* **The epidemic of possession is a phenomenon that characterizes the time of the Great Battle. Certainly, our convulsed planet is overrun with suicides as well as physical and spiritual calamities. Amidst humanity can be found unusual diseases of the brain and nerves, as well as every sort of perversion. The vacillations of the spirit may be truly astonishing. One may feel indignant about the way in which the finest people are greeted with threats and hatred. It is as if the soil itself were speeding to destruction! Of course, the mad ones do not see all the luminous warriors, and they allow the dark forces to drag them into the abyss.** *So every seeker must summon up all his strength in fortifying himself on the foundation of the Hierarchy. Even on an ordinary battlefield a warrior must not let*

his communications get cut off. In this way, one should realise the Great by turning to the simplest examples.

292. Whoever keeps watch on the manifestations of subtle energies knows how the heart is linked to them with unbreakable bonds. He knows how hard it is, when surrounded by tigers, to rise up and carry others on into the higher spheres. But this is the labour that must be performed by those who are launching the New World. Yes, even the very beginning must be tangible.

300. Today is a good day for good thoughts. If thought contains creative energy, how useful it is to send a good thought out into space. **Once humanity agrees to send forth good thoughts simultaneously, the infected atmosphere of the lower spheres will clear up right away. Even if it is only a few times a day, you should make a point of sending forth thoughts not about yourself but about the world. In this way you will get used to aspiration that is free of selfish motivation.** You should not regard the transmission of thought as some sort of supernatural activity. Rather, let it be the food of the spirit, just as fuel is food for a fire during the night. Also, you should simply follow the higher example. The heart will act as a trustworthy timepiece that calls one to thought about everyone and everything. **There is no need to sit in tiring meditations; thought about the world is short and reflects the renunciation of self so simply: 'May good things come to the world!'**

302. It would be helpful to compile a book about the harm brought on by evil thoughts—helpful for oneself as well as for others. These thoughts are the source of a great many maladies. In the past only mental illnesses were thought to be connected with evil thoughts, **but it is now time to discern the vast number of extremely diverse physical illnesses that arise from thought. Not only heart disease but also most afflictions of the stomach and skin are a consequence of destructive thoughts. Similarly, the transmission of infectious diseases may be a result not only of predisposition but also of thinking.** This is not simply a matter of autosuggestion, for one finds cases in which a disease was spread by one person to many. One can see how physical effects run entirely in tandem with spiritual manifestations. In this regard it has been noted that certain organisms unintentionally spread a specific infection without being subject to it themselves. In ancient times people already

knew about such carriers of infection, but later that scientific knowledge was forgotten, and everything was attributed to the so-called evil eye.

303. **This means that even when dealing with purely physical illnesses one needs to search for the cause in the quality of thought.** *Therefore, gradually direct the thoughts of the people around you toward good. You already have an example that shows how much pain is caused by maledictions and swear words, even at a great distance. In order to really pay attention, one has to turn one's heart toward the essence of what is happening.* **Possessed people who contact the aura may especially have an effect, even if the contact is slight. So it is essential to pay close attention to one's very first impression of people, for it is then that the heart is able to convey its sign. It is easy to imagine how possessed people may spread infection quite efficiently, which is why one ought to avoid them.**

311. *The Teacher affirms that a warrior can expect complete victory if only unity in consciousness is maintained. On the other hand, he cannot expect success if he harbors the slightest suspicion of the Teacher.* **So we have to work together, knowing that everything allowed by the laws of the Universe will be done. Is there anyone, then, who will regard this period as a time of rest?** *No one will deny that this time is unprecedented, not even someone who does not see far ahead. The warrior has to stand watch as if there were no one to replace him. The Teacher understands that your hearts are also burdened. Every day the world situation grows more complicated. From the perspective of Armageddon, this is entirely natural. A consciousness which insists that Armageddon must be nonsense is just raving, because it fails to see the path ahead.*

313. *The consequences of the Great Battle's beginning first of all affect the heart of humanity. Affirmation of the heart is especially needed now, for without it the unaware heart will not be able to withstand the hurricane of elemental confusion. Therefore, think of the heart as a mediating principle that connects you with the distant worlds. You should be aware of just what it is that burdens the heart most. It is not dramatic events that burden the heart so much as the chain of small* **specks of everyday dust.** *It is very important to remember this, because great events may even lead to a special influx of psychic energy. But Armageddon does not just consist of great events. Quite the contrary, during Armageddon*

a multitude of small events are evaluated, **and the poor heart must get used to this downpour of small currents.** *I say "poor," because in essence the heart already knows the great fiery realms, but for the time being it must be dashed against the rocks of the Earth.*

320. *In ancient times certain mechanical methods were used to strengthen the connection between the heart's activity and the distant worlds.* **For example, one method was to clasp hands above the head with fingers interlocked—that was how a magnetic circle was formed. People also used to place their hands at the Chalice with fingers interlocked so that the edge of the left palm would lie on the heart. That was a way to strengthen magnetic waves. But now, of course, when we are teaching the expansion of consciousness,** *we will avoid external, mechanical methods. It is far subtler to act through the inner consciousness.* **We should sense how a transmission of the consciousness touches the substance of the heart, sending its motion upward, as if drawing it into Infinity.** *Of course, many of our sensations depend on atmospheric conditions. We may feel depression or sense solemnity, but let us be aware that at these moments the heart has opened the supermundane gates. Only enmity or fear uses the subterranean passages.*

328. **The preparation for contacting the higher strata first of all entails purification of one's consciousness and development of the life of the heart.** *But these conditions need to be kept in mind. Usually people recall them only in times of idleness or rest; but when these conditions need to be met, they are forgotten and replaced by irritation—and the stench of irritation is dreadful.*

329. **Who will think of attaining success in the Subtle World if no one is allowed to speak or think about it? A teaching that is ignorant of the Subtle World is no guide, because existence on the earthly plane is not even a hundredth part of the life in the Subtle World.** *This means it would be beneficial to know about the conditions in the lengthier state of existence.* **But now a battle is going on in the astral world, and conditions are still more complex.**

335. *A person who thinks deeply about the heart even amidst the horrors of anarchy shows that this thought has dwelt with him for a very long time. One can place a great deal of trust in him, because he has come in*

contact with knowledge and thereby already safeguarded his spirit from the filth of treachery. **You can be sure that a person who carries an embryo of treachery does not know about the treasure of the heart.** So build up the subtlest understanding layer by layer amidst the horrors of darkness. Great is the heart's ability to hear and see!

352. **The persecuted leads, with the persecutors trailing after him; so says the ancient truth about the superiority of the persecuted. To understand it means to enter the path of the persecuted. Many persecutors turned to the path of those they persecuted, for the pursuit upon that path ended up attracting them to it. That is why We prefer the path of the persecuted.**

356. There is a story of how one Yogi, in a moment of tension, lifted up a container full of water and shattered it. When he was asked the reason for this destruction, the Yogi replied, "If I hadn't done that, my heart would have burst." Similar discharges exist under all conditions. **The tension of the heart may become so great that one has to perform some kind of action in space to liberate the necessary conditions from the condensed sphere that is holding them back. Such condensation may occur externally due to outside causes, but it may also arise from within—that is exactly what happens during cosmic disturbances. That is why we should follow the dictates of our hearts with such careful attention. The heart senses and reflects invisible processes to such a degree that one could use it as the basis for writing an entire history of the Invisible.** It is difficult to correlate the causes of seismic events with the cataclysms that take place in the Subtle World, but the heart resonates to them as well.

367. If someone were to collect in a single book all the forms of behaviour harmful to perfectment, he could easily ascertain how simple it is to overcome them. He could see from what small actions this evil accumulates. **Is it difficult to give up trivial habits in one's daily life? Is it difficult to suppress the small destructive acts that poison the body? Doesn't a child feel ashamed after his first feeble attempt to lie? Only by habit does a child harden his heart.** That is why We call habits the calluses of the soul. Who is unaware of the warnings the heart gives every time an unworthy act is about to be performed? Such actions of the heart transmit the best calls, **but often people force the heart to be silent. This is a grave**

crime, as serious as cutting off the current that is bringing salvation to someone near and dear.

380. Of course, the battle of the past does not bear comparison with the battle of tomorrow. **No one should think that Armageddon is just a commotion in the kitchen. No, the biggest guns are in action, and the swiftest cavalry is taking part.** *If we compare the recent Great War with Armageddon, it is like comparing Europe with the entire world, as it were. I offer this comparison just in case anyone is thinking that the present time is ordinary and easy. People need to summon all the imperturbability of the heart that they can, in order to find themselves among the ranks of Rigden's forces. Nobody should forget the nature of the time that we are going through.*

Right now there is no one who can get by without courage. Only utter madness whispers that everything will fall into place of its own accord—that cannot happen! Being unable to govern by the basic principles, the dark forces have violated them; therefore, we must close ranks and go forward undivided in everything. The warriors should understand that the spiritual tension of the present time is no longer at the level of the Subtle World, but is already approaching the Fiery World. The Teacher is reminding us: not terror but a sense of the majestic should fill the hearts of the warriors of Armageddon.

389. Rather than regard the heart as personal property, **it is preferable to convince oneself that the heart is not entirely one's own organ but has been granted one for attainment of the highest communion.** *Perhaps if people began to think of the heart as something on loan from Above they would handle it with greater care.*

A certain hermit emerged from his solitude with a message, saying to everyone he met, "You have a heart." When he was asked why he did not talk about mercy, patience, devotion, love, and all the beneficial foundations of life, he replied, **"Just so long as we don't forget the heart, the rest will come." Indeed, how can we turn to love if there is nowhere for it to dwell? Or where will patience lodge if its dwelling is closed?** *So to avoid torturing oneself by seeking virtues that find no application, one has to build a garden for them, a garden that will open up thanks to an understanding* *of the heart. Let us stand firm on the foundation of the heart, and let us understand that without the heart we are no more than discarded husks.*

390. **Whoever loves flowers is on the path of the heart. Whoever knows the striving to the heights is on the path of the heart. Whoever thinks with purity is on the path of the heart. Whoever knows of the higher worlds is on the path of the heart. Whoever is ready for Infinity is on the path of the heart.** *So let us summon these hearts to realisation of the Source. It is right to understand the essence of the heart as something that belongs to both the Subtle and the Fiery Worlds.* **One can perceive worlds through the heart, but not through the intellect. So wisdom is contrary to the intellect, but there is no ban on adorning the intellect with wisdom.**

403. **People should understand that a boundary runs between Light and darkness. True, it is a tortuous line, but by following the heart one can unerringly discern the adherents of darkness. Can a person whose heart is dark strive upwards? Will that person reject falsehood and self-love as his life unfolds? Will he overcome fear when facing the future? So recognize that whoever is afraid of the future belongs to darkness—that is the surest touchstone.**

405. *The flow of events is carrying away the decrepit old world. Although this period was indicated in all of the scriptures, people are not thinking about what is taking place. They cannot even begin to think about the future.* **So one should not issue a book unless it indicates the Teaching of the period that has already arrived. One should not assume that something will change the course of the current that people have created. On the distant worlds there is already a feeling of horror about the fiery inevitability, yet the Earth continues to shroud itself in a dark mantle. What once required a century now takes place in five years; a law governs the progression of this acceleration. That is why when I speak of the heart it means that salvation can be found by following this channel. Do you hear? I am speaking again about salvation! Not deliberations, not doubt, not vacillation, but salvation will be the sign of this hour. People need to understand still more firmly just how inappropriate the old measures already are. Only one bridge remains to the higher worlds—the heart.** *Let us approach the source of the feeling of Light. Let us understand that*

even the youths in the fiery furnace were not consumed when they ascended by way of the heart. **This time is a difficult one! We shall go on repeating this, not fearing the derision of the ignorant. They lack the slightest notion of the heart's significance.**

407. In a fit of hatred someone ailing from a horrible disease attempted to harm humanity by touching as many objects as possible. That is how the mobility of evil expresses itself. **Evil requires no definite personalities, just a general desire to inflict harm. If only goodness would distinguish itself by showing a still greater mobility! If only each person filled with goodness would sow it with every touch! What a multitude of beneficial sparks would be cast into Space and how much easier the battle with evil would become!** It is true that human goodness can be quite profound, but it often lacks mobility. This happens because the heart has not been cultivated or educated. **The potential of the good heart usually works spasmodically and is far from being always open in readiness. However, it is precisely this spasmodic quality that allows the many assaults of evil, which works like a winnowing fan, blowing out in every direction. Only by donning the impenetrable armor of goodness can a warrior protect himself. It is hardly commendable to have armor that is very solid in back but leaves the heart, of all places, unprotected.** (As Mother Theresa said: 'We cannot all do great things, but we can all do small things with great love.)

412. Even the Highest Beings must be filled with spirit in order to act. The expression *be filled* is quite precise, for indeed one needs to be filled. This means filling oneself with an abundance of the spirit. But does this not also mean that we must enter into contact with the Hierarchy? Only by drawing the spirit from the Highest Source do we receive renewal and intensification of the fiery energy. That is why it is not indicated anywhere that a person should withdraw in spirit; on the contrary, **seekers should be filled with the power of the spirit that leads to Light. You correctly recalled the experience of standing on the edge of an abyss, recollecting how you contacted a boundary that intensified your energy. Only such crests of the waves will uplift the spirit to a point of fullness. But a person who is focused on himself and thinking about self-assertion will never draw from the Eternal Fire.** Let us aim our efforts at carrying out spatial

measures. I can welcome you resolute warriors who know of the Phoenix that rises from the ashes.

426. Development of the power of observation will lead to fearlessness. We should not be afraid of what is around us. So by making observations, we ourselves will bring to light new structures that only yesterday were imperceptible or invisible. And in doing so, we will be able to accustom ourselves to things that once seemed extremely unusual. What yesterday was forbidden out of ignorance will tomorrow become a participant and inspiration in life.

427. **Nobody would believe that you knew so much about what is happening now, nor would anyone believe in the signs that you are accustomed to discerning. However, should one pay attention to people who desire neither to understand nor to accept? You know many followers of the Higher Teachings, but do they carry them out? Quite the contrary, their cruelty of heart and self-adoration are astonishing. It means that reasoning has drowned out the voice of the heart!**

444. Among the various sacred pains there is a certain type that is called the "Vina of the Creator" after the Indian lute. The pains of the centers in the throat, shoulders, elbows, extremities, knees, and elsewhere speed out like chords reverberating on a musical instrument. That is how the heart is tuned. Without question, the heart's bond with the Highest remains the sole refuge of humanity. The other forms of Yoga were connected with other cosmic conditions. Now the heart is being cast forth like an anchor in a storm, and it is not difficult to approach the fiery Yoga of the Heart. **First, the seeker should sense the great battle and the ominous cloud of destruction that is gathering over the Earth. Second, the seeker should look upon his heart as a refuge. And third, the seeker should be firmly established upon the Hierarchy.** It would seem that these conditions are not so hard to meet, but so often we humans prefer side-paths and would even rather practice deceit than turn to the simplest means. Of course, **tension of the heart is needed. With good reason the heart was called the "Great Prisoner".**

446. People should firmly understand that the development of spiritual forces, which formerly took decades, is now being accelerated to the highest degree by means of the heart. They can accept Agni Yoga as the rapid evolution of forces. Where whole years were once devoted to the refinement

and tempering of the body, now the heart can move the spirit almost immediately. **Naturally, the education of the heart is necessary, but this lies in the sphere of feelings, not mechanics. So let us swiftly summon the heart to service for the New World."**

-END OF SELECTED AGNI YOGA GUIDANCE-

While reading this, you will no doubt be filled with many emotions and have questions. Just sit with it for a time, perhaps re-read it a couple of times over the coming weeks and take note of how the love, power, and urgency speaks to your spirit. You are needed at this time. Self-pity and self-doubt will sabotage your efforts. Sit in the silence of the heart and have a conversation with your spirit. Quieten the thoughts in your mind, breathe, and generate prana – the vital life force – deep into your body, and relax and feel with your heart.

There are many thousands of people on the planet who have taken the first initiation, and many more than we realise are dealing with the challenges of the second initiation. So it is, my brothers and sisters, that I hope you find solace and guidance from the 1932 publication *'Heart'* and the passages I have chosen to include to assist you.

> *"When a well-packaged web of lies has been sold gradually to the masses over generations, the truth will seem utterly preposterous, and its speaker a raving lunatic."*
>
> – Dresden James

To speak of such things as the astral plane, spirits, demons, witches, fairies and angels is, I realise, to speak of things that are not generally seen with the naked eye. Consequently, the mere suggestion of them actually being real may result in derision, shouts of *'all nonsense'* and shouts of *'he is a raving lunatic.'*

We have to realise, however, that we have been indoctrinated for so long that the gulf from the general consensus on 'reality' to what is 'actually real' is so great that the man who speaks the truth will appear as a raving lunatic. And that is why I chose to open this book with the quote I did:

> *"Those who see a vision that is withheld from those lacking the necessary equipment for its apprehension are regarded as fanciful and unreliable. When many see the vision, its possibility is admitted, but when humanity itself has the awakened and open eye, the vision is no longer emphasised, but a fact is stated and a law enunciated. Such has been the history of the past and such will be the process of the future."*
>
> — The Tibetan

Navigating the Subtle World

Revelation of newly perceived truth goes through a process: first, it is hostilely rejected and then after some time it is generally accepted. It has always been that way and it will always be that way. The world was flat – until it was not. The Earth was the centre of the universe – until it was not. The physical plane is all that exists – until it does not. And life can only exist on the physical plane – until it does not.

As you are walking the second hallway, your experience of what constitutes reality will change. And without a guide or credible resources, it can be damned scary and overwhelming. As your higher senses of perception come online, the world that you thought you knew crumbles to dust. You have to build a new world-view based on the foundation of your experience, and you realise your previous world-view was merely the tip of the iceberg.

So, you have to exercise caution and wisdom in your life. You must learn to discern between the things you have a right to speak of in certain company, and the things that you cannot. You encounter the ancient mystical rule and universal law of 'silence' or the 'covenant of the tongue of Abraham.'

A man or a woman is a centre of force – a spark of God consciousness and a powerful generator of thought and energy. However, a man or a woman is a centre of force within a larger centre of force. Every thought and feeling will not only impact the state of the originating entity, it will also have an immediate impact on that originating entity's (the man or woman's) environment. The people around them will consciously or unconsciously pick up the thought force emanating from them.

Further, the act of speaking, as a being conscious on the divine plane, is the act of exercising the creative power – *'In the beginning there was the word and the word was with God.'* You see, our words are imbued with creative power, and that is one of the first universal spiritual laws that the probationer/aspirant/disciple will encounter on the path of 'becoming the path.' Every word one speaks carries power, and should only be spoken if imbued with the love force or wisely withheld from being spoken at all.

If our words cannot be imbued with the divine love force, and for some reason we allow emotion of the 3rd level or octave of vibration, at the animal level of being, to react – then it is that we recognise where our immediate work lies ahead for us.

As the astral world starts to become familiar, as our weird and seemingly inexplicable experiences start to accumulate, we learn to trust our intuition. We learn to listen to our heart's truth and this helps us to recognise that we are not losing our minds, we are not going insane, we are simply encountering levels of reality that few human beings have encountered consciously in their lifetime and had the courage to speak of.

Remember, all of our medical professions and fields of mental health, such as psychiatry, are entirely based on the physical plane – the Hall of Ignorance. How many poor souls have been put into mental asylums because these professions do not have instruments sensitive enough and systems and knowledge accurate enough to identify the real issues? In a world that has had the response of locking up what they fear and don't understand, and loading these people with sedatives and drugs; it takes extreme courage to speak of such things.

We have to let go and forget the 'knowledge-lies' taught to us about our history – who we are and where we are going. We need to listen to the still silent voice of divine guidance within our hearts. Indeed, we are all the same in this regard – we can all hear the voice of God within our hearts, and if we listen to it and trust it, it will not lead us astray.

God wants us to remember who we are. God wants us to realise that what appears to be unfair suffering is in fact a grace in disguise, as it allows mankind the opportunity to choose – the good, the beautiful and the true – as we recognise the Law of Cycles at work in our life. Sometimes the wave lifts us to great heights, and then after a time it crashes on the shore. Then it begins to gather its forces and is sucked back out and clears the sand of the debris of the previous actions. So, it is with life, and if we recognise this law at work in our lives we will understand that this is also in accordance with the seasons of the Earth – Summer, Autumn, Winter and Spring, which are all necessary for the growth cycle.

With every decision made thusly, where we choose the good, the beautiful and the true, we compound and strengthen our energy; this gives us access to greater knowledge, abilities, power and presence. For God is inside of us, and when God recognises himself/herself within a form of creation, we then have an entity functioning at the 7th level/octave of vibration/consciousness.

God is characterised by three traits – omnipotence, omniscience, and omnipresence. All powerful, all knowing, and everywhere. However, the prerequisite to making the jump from the 5th octave of vibration to the 6th and the 7th octaves of vibration – is unselfish and unconditional love for all creation. For that is the source of the omnipotence of God.

After the first initiation, you have understood the wisdom of no longer defiling the temple that is your body. You are no longer drawn to the lures of licentious behaviour, or gluttony, or drinking to excess, and you have somewhat achieved some measure of control. Your higher self-overrides the desires of your lower self. Then it is that we enter the Hall of Learning and undergo the challenge of the tearing of the veil and meeting the dragon of the threshold.

And so, as an initiate tackling the challenges of the second initiation – baptism into the astral waters – and as walking the second hallway of learning progresses, it is important for them to understand practices of energetic cleansing and psychic defense.

If you have made progress on your journey of purifying your vehicles and you notice a strong thought or suggestion to go to a pub for a drink or go to a sex worker for example, stand firm. Exercise your will, for this is a time where the swords of the archangels and darker forces are crossed – will you be led to the darker gate or will your light triumph? Remember, many hearts are putrefying and darkness also wants to express itself. These alien thoughts and suggestions and feelings are coming from disembodied entities around you, or temporarily in you, which are stuck in the grosser level of consciousness and tied to the earth plane.

They want to inhabit your body and thus vicariously partake of the experience of the pleasures and lusts that it liked so much during its last Earth life that has kept it Earth bound. Be careful visiting lands abroad and having traditional tattoos – you do not know what the real meaning is of the ancient symbols that you are having put onto your body. Sometimes the energy of the tattooist and the ancient symbols carry an energy not conducive to your evolution into the light. Discernment is paramount!

An individual's writing will always carry the energy of their consciousness – blessings or ill health. Because we are creator beings – that is why Sadhus of India send leaves or twigs or simple remedies to the sick and they get better! These simple things are imbued with the pranic vitality and divine consciousness and pure intention born of the 6th and 7th octaves of vibration. This is something that modern science and medicine is yet to recognise – but it is a lost ancient understanding, based on the application of the scientific principle of energetic entrainment.

When a man, initiate, bramacharaya, 'holy one' has reached a certain level of consciousness that of the 6th octave of vibration, they are vibrating closer to vibrations and consciousness of God. Thus, God is working more powerfully through them. So, they become a more potent centre of force within a larger centre of force.

You will realise that the next step to living a holy life is **purification**. It is in this purification of your body, thoughts, and heart that the challenges of the astral plane come to pass. A command strong and striking will come from your higher self and say to you, 'Turn off your body!' For it is on the astral plane that the battle for your soul is fought, and I will give you some advice:

Before you put one foot on the holy ladder to climb up the mountain of initiation, ensure that you have allowed your desire nature to run its course. This does not mean reckless overindulgence but a measured self-assessment of where your soul is on its path of evolution. You must quell the desire body, for if you do not and you attempt to climb the holy ladder, then you will encounter the black sphinx and a gale force wind of astral debris will glue your feet in place and stop you in your tracks.

If you have ignored these teachings and attempted to climb the ladder with slimy feet, and slimed the steps with your impurity and your lust for knowledge, power, and bodily flesh, then woe to you. If you have attempted to steal the fire of the gods without the necessary purification then you will have to figuratively burn in the karmic fires before you are allowed to continue! Ingrain these words just given on the very fabric of your souls. The key to the quelling of the desire nature is to be found in the image of the 'High Priestess' or the Kabbalah teachings of the Tree of Life; the balancing of the pairs of opposites from Chapter 2.

The balancing of the pairs of opposites

Remember the High Priestess sitting on the throne in a state of balance of the masculine and feminine aspects of herself from Chapter 2? To ascend the holy ladder, you must balance the pairs of opposites within yourself. You must investigate and recognise the animalistic drives and urges of your body at the 3rd octave of vibration, and you must take stock of where you are on your evolutionary journey. To that end we come now to the subject of spiritual sex, divine union and the balancing of the poles.

In 2003, a book called '*Spiritual Sex: A treatise on the creative life force in you and the spiritual expression of your creative life sex force*', by the late Robert Wall Crary, was published by the Rishis Institute of Metaphysics. On the very first page of this book there is a symbolic diagram of the Rishi Institute of Metaphysics that outlines the journey of evolution of the sexual nature in a human being from a normal animal man, through to a neophyte (a beginning seeker), a disciple, an initiate and finally an adept or arhan. This is the diagram reproduced with permission, Figure 60 (below):

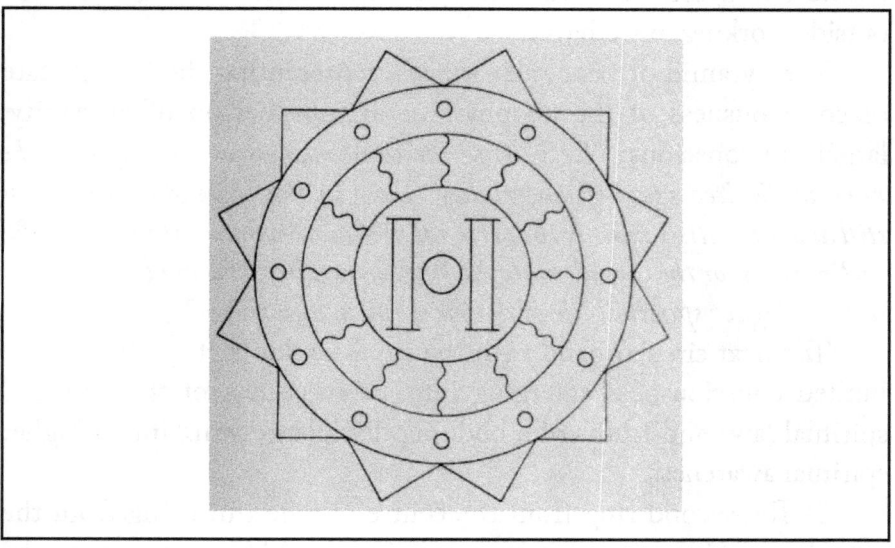

Figure 60: Symbolic diagram of the Rishis Institute of Metaphysics. Source: Rishi Institute of Metaphysics.

You will see that it is comprised of five layers. Now remember our symbol for God being the circumpunct?

Superimpose this over the top of the Rishis Institute diagram. In the centre of the diagram you will see the smallest inner circle which symbolises God, whose centre is everywhere. The two pillars portray the positive and negative pillars (Boaz and Jachin) in the Kabbalistic Tree of Life, and the High Priestess symbol from the Lost Book of Thoth, from which it is derived. When balanced, then there is 'divine energy' or 'divine light' in perfect equilibrium. Crary's book says: *"This light which is God's creative power in perfect, infinite expression, is the eternal, positive, harmonious action of Divine Love, the perfection of all being."*

The other circles surrounding the inner one depict the various states of consciousness that *all* souls progress through on their spiritual journeys to union with God through their Christed selves. From the outside working in we have:

The pyramid or triangular shapes, representing the lowest state of consciousness of the neophyte or average person of humanity, largely unconscious: *"Represents the consciousness of the self and the narrow, limited view of materiality. Those in this state of consciousness still desire to satisfy mainly the personal needs and wants with their lustful inclinations for the carnal, material world, but they now are beginning to seek the higher spiritual life of divine wisdom and truth."*

The next circular band with the small circles in it symbolises the limited consciousness emerging into an awareness of the universal spiritual laws and truths of a budding disciple growing into a higher spiritual awareness.

3. The second ring from the centre (or the third ring from the outside working in), with its wavy lines within it, represents the state of consciousness of the initiate. Crary explains: *"The wavy lines illustrate the heights and the depths that the human soul experiences, as it travels its path of self-discipline and self-mastery into the initiations and consequent illumination. It is in the process of this illumination that the soul enters into the higher frequencies of light that gradually lift it into its Divine destiny of spiritual mastery, the highest attainment humankind can achieve on this planet Earth."*

The inner circle, Crary explains: *"In (the centre) which the pillars stand, exemplifies the state of consciousness of the Adept. To become Adept, it is necessary to balance the two poles of positive and negative electromagnetic energy into perfect, positive, physical, mental, emotional and spiritual expression. This equilibrium must be achieved in order to gain total mastery of the self and the material plane. It is accomplished by lifting and unfolding the lower phases of the body and mind into ONENESS IN CONSCIOUSNESS with the spiritual phase, the Christ Within.*

In other words, it is achieved from the lifting of consciousness from the 3rd octave of vibration of the animal, through the 4th octave of regular human being, on through the 5th octave of the genius of humanity, further through the 6th octave of vibration of the prophet/seer (characterised by the acquirement of universal selfless love) into the 7th octave of vibration – the God Man (the goal as explained in the first symbol of the Book of Thoth – The Magician) and achieving ascension. Crary continues: *"The Ascension is the process of uniting in consciousness with one's own superconscious phase of mind and spiritual phase of body, the Godself within. In this accomplishment, the mortal mind becomes One in consciousness with the universal divine mind, which is present everywhere in every point of existence throughout Infinity and Eternity. It is the ultimate goal and destiny of all souls. Thus every soul, through its evolution of human awareness, returns to its source from which it came. Though, in this achievement, it returns on a higher plane into its heritage of spiritual consciousness as a perfected spiritual being- A Master of Light."*

Such as Jesus the Christ, Gautama Buddha, Krishna, Horus etc.

However, to get there it is imperative to strengthen the heart. To strengthen the heart, we must first cleanse the heart. To do this we must first heal the heart. One of the most effective ways to do this, to open the doors to healing, is to write yourself a letter. Below is the one that I wrote myself to assist in my own healing.

Now at the time of writing this manifesto before you – I have walked through this life for thirty-eight years and dedicated my life to finding the truth under the amnesia that we as humans are mostly born with, and the journey has not been an easy one. I consciously recognise myself to be a Starseed being of Light, and this is what I said in a letter to myself to help myself to heal.

Healing the timeline

A letter to my 15-year-old self from my 35-year-old self.

> *Dear N. S. Elijah,*
> *You are so amazingly perfect just as you are. People are not ready for the love that you carry in your heart. It scares them – but love them anyway. For it is better to be misunderstood than to lose your fearless authenticity. The world generally only knows about love between a man and his wife, boyfriend or girlfriend or partner or family and friends. The world has rarely experienced the unconditional love you hold in your heart for all life and for all creation. Therefore, know that you will be misunderstood and learn to love that feeling. Don't change who you are or mould or adapt yourself to 'fit in', for you were born to stand out. You are a sword and you were born to defend the sacred and cut down the established outdated misaligned paradigm. You were born to make waves.*
>
> *You have come back to this planet to bust this system wide open. This system that is based on greed, competition, fear and lack. Do not play small just so others don't feel small around you.*
>
> *It is important to remember to avoid drugs and alcohol, your chemical makeup is refined and these substances will affect you more than usual people. They will quickly take you into a downward spiral and having you testing every element of your strength to rid yourself of their effects.*
>
> *You are a son of God. A divine being and you are meant to be heart-centred. Dear N. S. Elijah, do not be afraid to show the world the immensity of your love. Because despite what you may think, the world needs it more than you know. With an all-encompassing great and unconditional love, 35-year-old, N. S. Elijah."*

If my 15-year-old-self had known this, then my mid-twenties self would not have gone off track so much, and would have helped so many more people, and his conscience would be clearer. But if that was the case, you would not be reading these words, for we are the sum total of our experiences and whilst we may not be able to see "the way of things" when "bad things" happen to us, we must trust that there is a grander plan and a grander design that is beyond our ken.

Writing a letter to oneself is extremely healing and it heals the timeline. Because you deeply understand that you did the best you possibly could with the available resources at the time. That is all any of us can ever do and it is most important to forgive yourself unconditionally.

For you see, with this understanding comes peace, inner peace. We realise very deeply that we are a spiritual being on a human journey, and we allow ourselves to be really strong by being vulnerable to feel our feelings. As we open our hearts more and more to love and to the world, a blessing is bestowed upon us. When we let go of the selfish striving, a blessing is bestowed upon us – a supernatural appreciative love. In Lakesh – you are another version of me. Namaste – the divine in me recognises and honours the divine in you. Shalom.

You see, God is the beautiful, the good and the true... God is love. Love is an energy, the deeper and more unconditional the love, the higher the energy; the higher the energy, the more light that emanates. Love begets light. And so, it is that the Father, The Son and the Holy Spirit takes on a new more accurate meaning: Love, Light and Holy Spirit. It is verily the ancient code, the Law of Three – The Holy Trinity.

So, when the Christed one, known to us as Jesus said, "I am the Light of the World," this is what he meant. When Jesus said, "I am the Way, the Truth and the Life," this is what he meant.

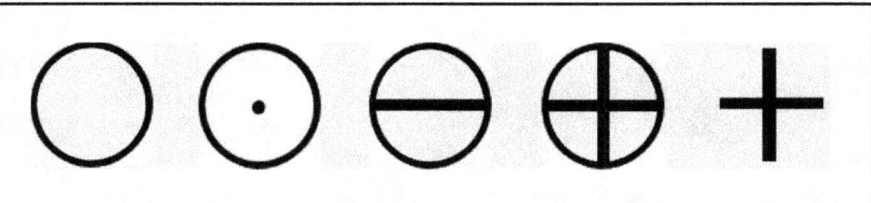

Figure 61: Secret doctrine

Take up your cross (the crucified divine spirit on the cross beams of time and space) and follow me (live by my example). Live, as love incarnate, and surrender your individual human will for the Will of the Spirit of God that emanates through you. For the Kingdom of Heaven is near and it is indeed good news… The Kingdom of Heaven is in your heart. But he always added, "For those that have ears, let them hear."

Are you listening? Do you hear now?

Chapter 9

THE JEWEL OF GREAT PRICE

"The heart of the world is a crystal marked by 21 paths and one narrow road thin as a flint blade that the fool walks."
— The Egyptian Book of Coming Forth By Day
(Book of The Dead)

When you consciously start to become aware of the world of energy, possibly observing alien self-debilitating thought patterns, and possibly being invaded by entities and energies in your body and in your aura (for this is not the same for those who have not engaged in actions that have damaged their auras protective sheath), or perhaps you may be experiencing euphoric energies or subtle flickerings of light or powerful warm and nurturing energies of Angels, know then that you are beginning to tread down the second hallway – the Hall of Learning.

It is important that I give you a clue to assist you with these challenges and how to surmount them. The universal adage *'energy follows thought'* will help you to walk out onto the bridge of 10,000 snares. As you realise the quality of your thoughts attracts certain higher or lower energies to you, take this warning seriously now. If you attempt to be like the black magician of the left-hand path and you mistake the fires of lust for the light of life, then mark my words you are in for a fierce battle and you will probably die.

Thoughts of lust, greed, and material avarice will sow a barren crop, and you may become prey to dark forces that want you for your acquired light so far. On the other hand, aligning yourself to the higher voice of the Christ consciousness within you, you will find yourself in the company of angels and other spiritual marvels of light.

But why is this the case? Remember the Chariot card from the Book of Thoth that I have revealed to you the original interpretation of? It is because as human beings we have the potential to become divine, but the only way that that happens is through overcoming tests and trials that ensure we learn to choose the good, the beautiful, and the true, no matter what is put before us in our life. In order for us to demonstrate this we must fight evil, and in order to be strong we must practice. It is the yin and yang – the light in the dark – and the dark in the light. We have the potential to make choices that lead us down a dark road or we can choose to make different choices that lead us down a light path, even if we are walking in the brightest light we still have to face darkness, but the stronger we are the easier it is to overcome their influence.

Another one of the greatest, most special works of the ancient world attributed to Thoth, the God of Wisdom, is the translated works of *The Emerald Tablets* of Thoth by Dr Michael Doreal. In this works there are fifteen tablets that have been published, and two that have not been published because of the explosive content that mankind is not yet ready for. These tablets were unearthed by instruction from The Great White Brotherhood in 1925 and translated by an initiate to the mysteries. Their antiquity dates back some 36,000 years, and they are made from a material that defies the laws of physics – there are twelve in number and are emerald green in colour, formed of a substance through alchemical transmutation. They are imperishable, resistant to all elements, and the atomic and chemical structure is fixed. It cannot be altered. They violate the laws of ionisation.

And Doreal advises that if there is light in you, then the light in you will respond as recognition of truth to their content. One of these

The Jewel of Great Price

tablets I have chosen to share with you is Tablet VI. It is Called the Key of Magic, and it explains that the mindscape is the battlefield of light and dark and if you have eyes to see you will quickly see the true reason behind the epidemic of mental-health issues such as depression that are sweeping the planet. First printed in 1939, it has now been 81 years and the works now belong to the public domain.

Hark ye, O man, to the wisdom of magic.
Hark the knowledge of powers forgotten.
Long ago in the days of the first man,
warfare began between darkness and light.
Men then as now,
were filled with both darkness and light;
and while in some darkness held sway,
in others light filled the soul.

Aye, age old in this warfare,
the eternal struggle between darkness and light.
Fiercely is it fought all through the ages,
using strange powers hidden to man.

Adepts has there been filled with the blackness,
struggling always against the light;
but others there are who, filled with brightness,
have ever conquered the darkness of night.
Where e'er ye may be in all ages and plane,
surely, ye shall know of the battle with night.
Long ages ago,
The SUNS of the Morning
descending, found the world filled with night,
there in that past, began the struggle,
the age old Battle Darkness & Light.

Many in the time were so filled with darkness
that only feebly flamed the light from the night.

Some they were, masters of darkness, who sought
to fill all with their darkness:
Sought to draw others into their night.
Fiercely withstood they, the masters of brightness:
fiercely fought they from the darkness of night
Sought ever to tighten the fetters,
the chains that bind men to the darkness of night.
Used they always the dark magic,
brought into men by the power of darkness.
magic that enshrouded man's soul with darkness.

Banded together as in order,
BROTHERS OF DARKNESS,
they through the ages,
antagonist they to the children of men.
Walked they always secret and hidden,
found, yet not found by the children of men.

Forever, they walked and worked in darkness,
hiding from the light in the darkness of night.
Silently, secretly use they their power,
enslaving and binding the soul of men.

Unseen they come, and unseen they go.
Man, in his ignorance calls THEM from below.

Dark is the way of the DARK BROTHERS travel,
dark of the darkness not of the night,
traveling o'er Earth
they walk through man's dreams.
Power they have gained
from the darkness around them
to call other dwellers from out of their plane,
in ways that are dark and unseen by man.
Into man's mind-space reach the DARK BROTHERS.

Around it, they close the veil of their night.
There through its lifetime
that soul dwells in bondage,
bound by the fetters of the VEIL of the night.
Mighty are they in the forbidden knowledge
forbidden because it is one with the night.

Hark ye O man and list to my warning:
be ye free from the bondage of night.
Surrender not your soul to the BROTHERS OF DARKNESS.
Keep thy face ever turned towards the Light.
Know ye not, O man, that your sorrow,
only has come through the Veil of the night.
Aye man, heed ye my warning:
strive ever upward,
turn your soul toward the LIGHT.
The BROTHERS OF DARKNESS seek for their brothers
those who traveled the pathway of LIGHT.
For well know they that those who have traveled
far towards the Sun in their pathway of LIGHT
have great and yet greater power
to bind with darkness the children of LIGHT.

Listen ye, O man, to he who comes to you.
But weigh in the balance if his words be of LIGHT.
For many there are who walk in DARK BRIGHTNESS
and yet are not the children of LIGHT.

Easy it is to follow their pathway,
easy to follow the path that they lead.
But yet O man, heed ye my warning:
Light comes only to him who strives.
Hard is the pathway that leads to the WISDOM,
hard is the pathway that leads to the LIGHT.
Many shall ye find, the stones in your pathway:
many the mountains to climb toward the LIGHT.

SACRED ALIGNMENT

Yet know ye, O man, to him that o'ercometh,
free will he be of the pathway of Night.
For ye know, O man,
in the END light must conquer
and darkness and night be banished from Light.

Listen, O man, and heed ye this wisdom;
even as darkness, so is the LIGHT.
When darkness is banished and all Veils are rended,
out there shall flash from the darkness, the LIGHT.

Even as exist among men the DARK BROTHERS,
so there exists the BROTHERS OF LIGHT.
Antagonists they of the BROTHERS OF DARKNESS,
seeking to free men from the night.
Powers have they, mighty and potent.
Knowing the LAW, the planets obey.
Work they ever in harmony and order,
freeing the man-soul from its bondage of night.

Secret and hidden, walk they also.
Known not are they to the children of men.
Ever have THEY fought the DARK BROTHERS,
conquered and conquering time without end.
Yet always LIGHT shall in the end be master,
driving away the darkness of night.

Aye, man, know ye this knowing:
always beside thee walk the Children of Light.

Masters they of the SUN power,
ever unseen yet the guardians of men.
Open to all is their pathway,
open to he who will walk in the LIGHT.
Free are THEY of DARK AMENTI,
free of the HALLS, where LIFE reigns supreme.

The Jewel of Great Price

SUNS are they and LORDS of the morning,
Children of Light to shine among men.
Like man are they and yet are unlike,
Never divided were they in the past.

ONE have they been in ONENESS eternal,
throughout all space since the beginning of time.
Up did they come in Oneness with the ALL ONE,
up from the first-space, formed and unformed.

Given to man have they secrets
that shall guard and protect him from all harm.
He who would travel the path of the master,
free must he be from the bondage of night.
Conquer must he the formless and shapeless,
conquer must he the phantom of fear.

Knowing, must he gain of all of the secrets,
travel the pathway that leads through the darkness,
yet ever before him keep the light of his goal.
Obstacles great shall he meet in the pathway,
yet press on to the LIGHT of the SUN.

Hear ye, O Man, the SUN is the symbol
of the LIGHT that shines at the end of thy road.
Now to thee give I the secrets:

now to meet the dark power,
meet and conquer the fear from the night.
Only by knowing can ye conquer,
Only by knowing can ye have LIGHT.

Now I give unto thee the knowledge,
known to the MASTERS,
the knowing that conquers all the dark fears.

Use this, the wisdom I give thee.
MASTER thou shalt be of THE BROTHERS OF NIGHT.

When unto thee comes a feeling,
drawing thee nearer to the darker gate,
examine thine heart and find if the feeling
thou hast has come from within.
If thou shalt find the darkness thine own thoughts,
banish them forth from the place in thy mind.

Send through thy body a wave of vibration,
irregular first and regular second,
repeating time after time until free.
Start the WAVE FORCE in thy BRAIN CENTER.
Direct it in waves from thine head to thy foot.

But if thou findest thine heart is not darkened,
be sure that a force is directed to thee.
Only by knowing can thou overcome it.
Only by wisdom can thou hope to be free.
Knowledge brings wisdom and wisdom is power.
Attain and ye shall have power o'er all."

Because the world has largely been operating from the Hall of Ignorance (the physical plane) for the last 2,000 years, these things I bring to your attention, that exist in the subtler planes, will be a hard pill to swallow. It is verily the red pill. But if you look at this world and you can see that it has the potential to be such a beautiful place filled with love and with Mother Nature thriving in pristine glory, what is it if not unseen forces of darkness that are responsible for the current horrific state of affairs? Once this is seen as the cause then we can fight it – as long as it hides in the shadows and convinces mankind that it does not exist then we will never confront it, but it must be confronted for the survival of this planet.

Remember that energy follows thought, energy follows thought, energy follows thought! And at this level – the tearing of the veil of the physical plane – you are vibrating at a higher frequency than you were walking down the Hall of Ignorance. Consequently, your thoughts carry more power. When these other senses come online, when your astral senses awaken, know that your lower self will rebel at being transmuted. You will encounter the dark night of the soul, the forty days in the desert, but you will make it through if you listen to this guidance.

Know that the well-worn path of all masters that have walked before you is marked by the conditions of loneliness and immense suffering. It is the law. It is through this suffering that one learns to transmute matter into spirit. As I have said, suffering is necessary to strengthen the soul, and you will need every ounce of your strength to face the 'Dweller of the Threshold.' The Dweller of the Threshold is the sum total of all your ill deeds and thoughts across countless lifetimes. Remember that human beings are creator beings in consciousness 'made in the divine image.' The thoughts and misuse of divine creative energies does not go away, it congregates and coalesces into an ugly form of your own creation, and it remains until you are strong enough to face it, accept it as your own creation, and transmute it with love.

For, as a human being, you are a duality – and you must transmute darkness into light. The brighter the light you shine on yourself, for a time – the bigger the shadow. In order to spiritualise matter and have the voice of the serpent silenced, the scorpion must sting itself to death and rise from the ashes to be reborn as the phoenix, transforming into Aquila – the golden Eagle of the Spirit. And so it is you will face an existential quandary… do I want to go on? For if I go on it is certain that I will lose touch with my fellow humanity, but like the tireless words in Kahlil Gibran's *'The Prophet'*:

> *"The mole is comfortable and warm in his burrow, the eagle is chilled in its flight, but alone it must fly towards the sun."*

The Way, the Truth, and the Light

You are divine. A radiant being of light! Your consciousness is eternal. If you identify yourself as being your body then you are unconsciously eating of the 'Tree Of Knowledge' – of 'evil', and you will travel the round of Samsara (reincarnation) through all twelve signs of the Zodiac (the twelve Tribes of IS-RA-EL – Isis-Ra-El) until you learn the lessons the energetic signature of each sign is there to teach your soul. If, however, you identify yourself as being your consciousness, then this is a game changer. You realise that you have a body, but you are not your body, and then you are living your life eating of the fruits of the 'Tree of Knowledge' – of 'good', and this is wonderful.

Your task then becomes to learn to distinguish the human and the animal from the divine, and learning to first identify the effects of 'fifth force' (subtle energies) in your life and, secondly, how to use these forces in the integration of the feminine and masculine elements of your consciousness until you are able to unify them within yourself. This path is not easy. It is the road less travelled.

This is an ancient truth, and please do not let it deter you or upset you. It is okay to simply be a 'regular human' and live in accordance with the existing societal paradigm and following the natural flow of forces in your body leading you to couple and marry and beget children. No one is going to judge you for it – for we are all individual frequencies of divine consciousness and everyone and their chosen use of their free will is essential to the whole, and everything is always right on time, for there are no coincidences. Hermes Law states, *'There is no such thing as coincidence – only effects of the Law not recognised.'*

For we must realise that we are 'a part of something.' We are a part of God, and I am not better than you and you are not better than me. Our individual soul journey is our own to own, and no one else's.

Ultimately, then, we are reconciling that all religious faiths are based on the one truth:

'That we fall from paradisiacal unity into matter and then we journey long through time in many lifetimes to realise this and redeem our consciousness back into divine unity by spiritualising matter.'

That is the goal of human life – to spiritualise the matter of our bodies through the evolution of our consciousness by attaining a living embodiment of the seventh octave of vibration – and then spiritualise the matter of Earth, which indeed we are not separate from. Christianity, Islam, Buddhism, Hinduism, Taoism, and Kabbalistic Judaism are all fundamentally the same. And I hope that you all can see this now.

This was the veiled message of Christ, Krishna, Muhammed, Buddha and of Thoth –

'The divine is within, you are divine.'

It is the message and not the messenger that is of importance. But sadly, humanity has the tendency to glorify the messenger and misinterpret the message.

It is my hope that this recognition on a wider scale will help to shift the accepted paradigm, as people start to come together, understanding truly that we are all brothers and sisters in humanity and in God.

You see, once the individual intellectual brick walls of 'belief' are dismantled by the recognition of this simple truth of understanding the governing dynamics, then things will begin to change on a societal level quite rapidly on a global scale, because we are no longer talking about belief, but universal truth, and from this place we can build upon a solid foundation and we can achieve the spiritual and cultural transformation that Gus Speth mentions in my introduction, that is *'beyond the ken of scientists.'*

After all of this, you can choose to carry on with the preconceived ideologies that you sat down with before reading through this discourse, that may have differed from this understanding. It may be easier for you or more comfortable for you to do so and that is absolutely okay. It's your soul journey, so live it how you must to be true to yourself.

Now there is one final *Egyptian Mysteries** symbol that I would like to show you from the 'Lost Book of Thoth' that I hope you will ingrain on the very fabric of your soul. It is the Major Arcana Card marked '0' (and simultaneously it is the 22nd card of the Major Arcana) – the beginning and the ending. The Fool – The Madman:

Figure 62: Major Arcana Tarot card 0/22 – The Fool/Madman. Rider Waite Tarot deck.

"When the young priest appeared before the High Priest the next day, the High Priest said: "You have received the Initiation and now have the knowledge. You have received what was promised in symbols II and VI. You have seen behind the curtain, and worlds which are invisible to mortals have been revealed to you. You have been shown what human understanding is capable of.

"The essence and motives of the gods are unfathomable, the secrets of the universe are infinite, but you are on the correct path. Proceed from insight to insight, from one good deed to the next, and your power will increase accordingly. Nothing that could be revealed has been kept from you. You have received an answer to the questions: Where do we come from, where are we going, what do we live for? The symbols of the Book of Thoth make all this clear. There is nothing beyond these twenty-one symbols which is worth studying. It would be madness to seek further. That is why the last symbol is the number 0 and is called: The Madman (The Fool). I do not really have to explain this symbol to you. You can understand it without my help. It represents the man who lacks his vocation because he does not hear or see!

"Instead of developing his skills and allowing the spirit to take possession, he unknowingly carries the talents he has been given in a sack over his shoulder. He leans on his staff – on knowledge, convictions and teachings – which neither help, support, nor save him because he stumbles through the sands of the desert with difficulty towards his downfall. For this reason the crocodile is stalking him. The Passions symbolised by the dog (symbols X and XVIII) to which he surrenders without restraint, persecute him and his impoverished nakedness is visible to everyone!

"The High Priest raised his hand in a blessing and said solemnly:

"Knowledge, will, courage, and silence have always been the guidelines of the wise. And remember, your strength will grow through silence, and thus your power to act.

"Like us, the gods were once mortal. But a time will come when mortals like you, will become gods. Therefore, my son, go towards life with strength so that you will end where you began in the fullness of life. Now go my child, peace be with you."

* See Bibliography

Figure 63: Chosen four revealed arcane symbols of the Lost Book of Thoth on the Path of Osiris.

Light on the Path

For a long time I was following what Blavatsky calls 'the eye doctrine' of the spiritual path (the intellectual position rather than the heart), and I realised the error of my ways, after recognising that I was falling over the very laws that I should have been adhering to. I have experienced the walking of the path as The Fool for more years than I care to admit.

It was my ego driving the show, trying to draw attention to myself, to point out to others my intellectual grasp of deep hidden universal truths – highlighting the advances of my intellect in decoding the messages of signposts and the ways of spirit, indeed how man relates to God and God to man.

It is quite funny, and I have to laugh at myself, to think how naive I was. I deluded myself into thinking that because of my perceived advances in spiritual understanding that it would be okay for me to lapse from purity every now and then, as I felt I deserved to be rewarded, to receive a pleasurable respite for all the hard work that I had been doing and all of the things I had thus far endured.

But you see, what I found was of my own making. I had either in this lifetime or those that have come before it, set up the conditions for these adverse effects to be placed in my way. I encountered the unyielding law of the universe. I had to reconcile that I was responsible. I had called into being all of the negative attributes of my soul and spirit, and thus had to face the sum total of these known as *'The Dweller of the Threshold.'* I could not run from it, for it was my very own creation. All of the misuses and abuses of the creative essence and thought force from lifetime to lifetime over thousands and countless existences, it was my abandoned and unloved hell spawn child. All I could do was recognise it was a part of myself and love it into light.

I had to stand in the midst of the karmic fires – it was not a punishment, it was a purification, where all the inessentials of my being were being stripped and burned away. I know that my body in this life is of the masculine polarity and it wants to fulfil its nature of joining with its opposite. It seeks union with the polar opposite feminine expression. I recognise the desires within myself, these animal attractions at the 3rd octave of vibration, and so it is amidst these spiritual heights that there is 'evil' or darkness present, whilst there is a will to do good.

And this is what St. Paul meant when he spoke in the Bible:

> *"For the good that I would I do not: but the evil which I would not, that I do.*
>
> *Now if I do that I would not, it is no more I that do it, but sin that dwelleth in me.*
>
> *I find then a law, that, when I would do good, evil is present with me.'*

And so it is that here I stand looking at the Dweller of the Threshold and it is my duty to superimpose a higher order of love over the promptings and urgings of its lower voice. This is something that is not always easy to do. In fact, it has been downright hard and I have succumbed and fallen many times.

If I am to pass through the 4th gate – the bridge of 10,000 snares – I steel my will and make pure the children of my mind – my thoughts. I constantly and consciously stamp out thoughts of separation, lust, anger, selfishness, and greed. I align myself with 'All Thought' and then become 'No thought'. The All in one and one in the All.

I conquer the great illusion, the illusion of separateness. I am aware and remain vigilant to the fact that my physical senses lie. I remain vigilant and strike the lower thoughts from my mind and impose a higher order over my lower nature. And I take full responsibility for all conditions that surround me, for it is at this gate – all the conditions, the reactions of the physical world to me – are a reflection of the thought force that I send forth. If I send out doubt and suspicion, I receive doubt and suspicion. If I send out trust and unconditional love, then I receive the same. Thought is projected through the eyes. At a great distance it can be detected and is transferred instantaneously. Thought is like lightning; it strikes as quick as a flash and it leaves a mark. This is what is meant by Patanjali with the commandment 'Thou shalt not kill' – thou shalt not kill with thy thoughts!

And it is what Christ means when he admonished, "The things you do in your mind you have already done."

What does the superimposition of the higher order over the lower look like? It is a deep recognition of the following, that:

I have a body, but I am not the body.
I have intellect, but I am not intellect.
I have emotions, but I am not emotion.
I am divinity that is always manifesting itself in all ways, always.
And yet, paradoxically, I remain a part of God.

The divine is in each and every one of us, whether or not you recognise this, it is so. Whenever I speak with someone in everyday conversation, it is always a communion of spirit. It is always a soul conversing with another soul, one aspect of divinity in conversation, in silence sharing itself with another aspect of divinity. It is the truth in Lakesh – you are another version of me and I am another version of you.

Indeed, I am humbled by the divine universal law – not the laws made by man. As the grace of God bestows upon me all these realisations, I am reminded of the eternal wisdom preserved in the little gem of a book '*Light on the Path*'

"Before the eyes can see they must be incapable of tears.
Before the ear can hear it must have lost its sensitiveness.
Before the voice can speak in the presence of the master's it must
Have lost the power to wound.
Before the Soul can stand in the presence of the Masters, its feet must
Be washed in the blood of the heart."

We are all individual frequencies of God. We all come in with a specific purpose and under certain conditions, designed to teach us the next lesson, to strengthen and develop any lacking soul quality. There are of course myriad paths up the mountain, just as there are myriad individual journeys returning from separation, and we are all different because for different tasks, God requires different tools.

As Einstein says, "God does not play dice with the universe." What this means is that chance or coincidence are just other names for a law not realised. Remember to be gentle with yourself if you choose to integrate these teachings in your life.

However, to force the growth, to try to tear the petals open to get to the jewel in the lotus, to attempt to steal the fire of the gods, like Prometheus, you will only serve to damage or destroy the flower, cause yourself and those around you great injury, and create for yourself additional karma to be worked through at a time when the soul is strong enough to do so, perhaps in this lifetime or perhaps in many lifetimes hence.

So, let it be the eternal that draws forth your love force, not the striving for growth or power. And like the rose or lotus, in its time the petals will open, the flower will bloom with a sweet perfume and a steady **light revealing the glory of God and the jewel of great price within. If you choose this path, know well that all of the dregs of the bitter cup of suffering must be drunk, and that for good reason the masters are known as 'the receptacles of grace and earthly poison.'** Without the divine grace it would be impossible to take the earthly poison, and yet it must be taken if evolution is to carry on to other worlds, and for the heart to be weighed less than the feather of Ma-at, the feather of truth.

And so it is verily known as **the Jewel of Great Price**.

And this is why in the ancient teachings of Thoth it instructs the initiates thusly:

'Know how to suffer, so as to remain unaffected by suffering.'

The opening quote from the Egyptian book of the dead, should now be better understood: The heart of the world 'the jewel of great price' is marked by 21 paths (the intertwining paths of Osiris, Isis and Horus – represented by the 21 Major Arcana of the Tarot) and we are all Fools walking the path as narrow as a flint blade (holographically through all 21 stations – at the same time) which at any moment a challenge may be encountered so severe that it may result in us slipping off of the mountain to our deaths. Only to be born again and pick up from where we left off in our last incarnation (represented by the pouring of the waters from one vessel to another grander vessel in part of the true interpretation of the Major Arcana Tarot card XIV 'Temperance').

Our destiny – reaching the jewel of great price – the crystal heart of the world (becoming one with divinity), i.e. the Major Arcana Tarot card XVII 'The Star'– is determined by our own actions and willingness to pass through the fabled ancient mystical gates that are locked by the passions incarnate. We pass through these gates (initiations) by facing ourselves aided with possession of the 7 ancient mystical golden keys:

1- **Dana** – Key of charity and love immortal.

2- **Shila** – Key of harmony of word and act.

3- **Kshanti** – Patience sweet that naught can ruffle.

4- **Virag** – Indifference to pleasure and pain and the illusion conquered.

5- **Virya** – Dauntless energy that fights the way to truth.

6- **Dhyana** – Diamond Soul.

7- **Prajna** – The key that makes of a man a god.

Within these two paragraphs are contained the entire ancient mystical mystery of human existence, its goal and means of reaching it. Blessings to you all.

And this knowledge was something that Christ was in possession of and tried to get people to understand and how this is so will be further explained below. I will explain some of the words of Christ, using this foundation of knowledge presented in this discourse as the key to correct interpretation of his original meaning.

True meaning of the words of Jeshua Ben Joseph

The narrow gate

"Enter through the narrow gate; for the gate is wide and the road easy that leads to destruction. And there are many who take it. For the gate is narrow and the road is hard that leads to life, and there are few who find it."

The words of Christ in this instance for the aspirant are self-explanatory. It is easy to follow the whims of your body – do what you want, say what you want, to the detriment of others. It is easy to be spiritually lazy and ethically lazy and strive for selfish gain at the expense of others, and a lot of people live this way and suffer the consequences of their actions through karmic balancing (I too, learned this the hard way).

To live and to learn from one's mistakes, to seek and accept what is least accepted, to dedicate oneself to the higher work, to sacrifice one's personal desires for the demands being asked of them from the current state of world affairs, to deny oneself selfish pleasure-seeking activities, to serve selflessly, to humble ones personality, to pick oneself up from falling over the very laws that one has ignored, to strive, to suffer loneliness and being misunderstood, and being criticised, ridiculed, and laughed at in the name of service to the higher work – is hard. It is a narrow difficult road that ends in the finding of life – in the finding of God, and there are few who possess the courage and the dedication to follow this path.

These words of Christ come from the instruction of the Egyptian Mysteries, from the Egyptian book of 'Coming forth by day' (The Book of the Dead).

"The heart of the world is a crystal marked by 21 paths and one narrow road thin as a flint blade that the fool walks."

Do you see? Understand now.

Not peace but a sword:

"Do not think I have come to bring peace to earth; I have not come to bring peace, but a sword. For I have come to set men against his father, and a daughter against her mother and a daughter against her mother-in-law, and one's foes will be members of one's own household. Whoever loves father or mother more than me is not worthy of me; and who ever loves son or daughter more than me is not worthy of me; and whoever does not take up the cross and follow me is not worthy of me. Those who find their life will lose it and those who lose their life for my sake will find it."

The meaning – remember the first symbol of the Book of Thoth – The Magician – Swords wound, but they also change circumstances and stand as a symbol of courage and strength. The strength and courage to defend what is holy, even if that means to go against the established grain of society and pit father against son and mother against daughter, in terms of their different levels of conscious understanding, and in terms of seeing the truth of how man relates to God.

The one that loves their physical mother and father more than God – the recognition of the God that dwells in their hearts and therefore themselves – is not worthy of finding God. The one that takes up the 'cross' of their spirit crucified in matter on a cross of time and space and follows the example and message of the Christ – the example and message of selflessness, unconditional love and complete recognition of the divine spirit within at the 6th octave of vibration – will lose their personality (the goals and dreams of a selfish personality) that has protected them throughout the ages as the truth of the soul emerges. And when the soul does reveal itself in following the example of the Christ, they will find their life in selfless service to humanity and in recognition of their divine nature in humility.

In order to be free of this suffering he must surrender the little 'I' that is crucified on a beam of time and space, pick up its crucified consciousness and follow the way pointed by 'Christ consciousness.' In doing this, you will lose the little 'I' of individual consciousness, and those that do so for the revelation of Christ principle – the spiritualising of matter – will find true life in their divine self that is hidden within the human being. If man does not follow the true instruction of Christ consciousness within – which is the way to finding God – then those persons are not worthy of discovering the divinity that is concealed within their very hearts.

Concerning almsgiving

"Beware of practising your piety before others in order to be seen by them; for then you have no reward from your father in heaven. So, wherever you give alms, do not sound a trumpet before you, as the hypocrites do in the synagogues and in the streets, so that they may be praised by others. Truly I tell you they have received their reward. But when you give alms do not let your left hand know what the right hand is doing, so that your alms may be done in secret; and your Father who sees in secret will reward you."

Beware of practising your piety before others in order to be seen by them. Wherever you give to people or charity or a cause, do so as quietly and secretly as possible so that your intention remains pure – remains 'holy.' Namely, the intention is to be of service to others and ease the struggle and pain of those around you, by giving with no thought of rewards for yourself through perceivable offshoots of increased/improved public standing and the good opinion of your person through such action. If you do this, give quietly and in secret, then by natural law you will be rewarded with the gifts of spirit, by way of embodying high spiritual attainment, becoming closer to the nature of God, coming closer to spiritualising matter, but you must not seek the reward.

If, however, you make a fuss and announce to the world how generous you are, your intention is only that of self-elevation of the little 'I' in the eyes of the public and is thus not pure. In fact, it is a reflection of pure selfishness and you will have received your reward of increased public standing, but you will not be rewarded further with spiritual gifts by such a selfish act.

The sound eye

"The eye is the lamp of the body. So, if your eye is healthy your whole body will be full of light; but if your eye is unhealthy your whole body will be full of darkness. If then the light in you is darkness, how great is the darkness?"

Lamps shine light. In this case what shines in the eye is consciousness, is soul light. Because of the mind, body, and spirit connection, if your eyes are bright and shining then your whole body will be full of pranic vitality because you are living your life in accordance with the directions of your spirit and not your personality or ego.

But if your eyes are unhealthy then you are living your life in conflict to the higher promptings of your higher self and the troubles and trials of life have caused your spirit to be dampened, and consequently your ethics are relaxed due to the pressures of these trials and troubles. And if the soul is oriented towards the light and yet still succumbs to the temptations of the flesh and the material world without learned restraint (at the expense of the higher promptings – so that the darker inclinations are followed), then the dark is much stronger in that vehicle of expression because of the greater struggle that soul has gone through in order to reach its current level of light!

If the dark can still influence the one who has reached a level of higher attainment (usually through glamour) then it has found a much more potent spirit to work through. Often the ones that look to be in the light do not recognise the darkness in themselves, or they relax their standards as a reward for all the good work they are doing (I have been guilty of same) – but desire for recognition is a desire of the lower ego and not of the selfless serving soul. So be wary and be brutally honest with yourself about where you are living in accordance with the selfless promptings of the spirit, and where you are living in accordance to the selfish promptings of self-gain and elevation. It is your intention that you must scrutinise. And how well you are doing will be reflected in the light of your eyes.

I will offer a word of warning here that I hope you will listen to and thus save yourself from needless suffering and wasted time and wasted money. With all the hundreds and thousands of so-called 'light workers' at work in the world today, you can bet your bottom dollar that some of them are charlatans and subtle deceivers (some are conscious of this and some are unconscious of this).

How do you tell the difference? Appearances can be deceiving, as you well know. The way you tell the difference between those who are motivated by selfless planetary service, in true spiritual integrity and those that are motivated by more selfish reasons, will be shown in the clarity and condition of their eyes. If they are in any way advocates of the lower desires then they are not in alignment – they are operating from selfish personality, despite what their silver-tongued words may convey. For to follow the slight deviation of the truth as it is expressed as the 'sum of the truth' by them, ensures that you do not reach the top of the mountain, as you take an unexpected detour, and it simultaneously increases their power to influence you! The eyes are the lamp – and they shine the spirit. They are the window to the soul and they do not lie!

Look closely to the condition of the eyes you seek advice from before you pay for it or receive it freely. Use discernment – if they are cloudy or lack that clear shining quality then that is the surest indicator to seek assistance elsewhere, as their judgement and thus their advice is also cloudy! You have been warned. Jesus the Christed one revealed this truth 2,000 years ago! I bring it to your attention again now. In some cases, they will be consciously aware of this and in other cases they will be ignorant to this truth of their misalignment, which is limited by the confines or current ceiling to their level of conscious understanding and willingness to face themselves.

Profaning the holy

"Do not give what is holy to dogs; and do not throw your pearls before swine, or they will trample them underfoot and turn to maul you."

What Christ means here is quite self-explanatory. For the spiritual man, it is easy to detect the conscious level of evolution of the persons on your path. And to those that exhibit the desire to be led by carnal passions, violence, cruelty, and selfishness, it is pointless to try and save them by speaking to them of spiritual truths that you feel may be of assistance to them. If you go about throwing pearls of wisdom before such men, they will more than likely resent you and threaten physical violence to your person for presuming to give them advice. Only a man that has learned by the error of his ways is receptive to the subtleties of spiritual wisdom that may help to add the next piece of understanding or add to the foundation of his worldview to help lessen his current burden and move closer to salvation.

True kindred of Jesus:

"While he was speaking to the crowds, his mother and his brothers were standing outside, wanting to speak to him. Someone told him, "Look, your mother and your brothers are standing outside, wanting to speak to you." But to the one who had told him this, Jesus replied, "Who is my mother? And who are my brothers?" And pointing to his disciples he said, "Here are my mother and my brothers! For whoever does the will of my Father in heaven is my brother and sister and mother."

This is what was intended by Jesus when he said the above statement – "In the eyes of eternity we are born into subjective individual consciousness, indeed we separate from the collective consciousness. But the process of reunification is not measured by one human life. It is through thousands of lives. Thus, our spirit, housed in a physical vehicle for a 'lifetime', has a biological mother and father and brothers and sisters for that lifetime. However, over the course of thousands of incarnations, the soul will have many biological parents and siblings. The achievement of unity in consciousness with divine mind comes with the realisation of the divine father being the divine mind and the divine mother being mother earth (the means of birth of material being in order for that consciousness to experience itself as being separate). So when Jesus asks rhetorically, "Who is my mother and who are my brothers?" he is actually expressing deep occult wisdom. Those that know themselves to be one with the divine mind, subordinate their individual will, the will of the personality to the higher will. And in doing so, they become one in consciousness with all other subjective manifestations of consciousness – essentially brothers and sisters and mothers in consciousness to all of humanity.

Here ends the interpretation of the selected words of Christ.

The beginnings of Islam

During my investigations and study of the inception of the five major religions on Earth, I found an 1880 Oxford scholarly presentation of the beginnings of Islam by E. H. Palmer in his book '*The Quar'an*', published by Clarendon Press, Oxford. What the reader may find of interest is that, according to this source, at the time of the Prophet Muhammad's (peace be upon him) death:

> "*No collected edition of the Qur'an existed. Scattered fragments were in possession of certain of his followers, written down at different times… but by far the greater portion was preserved only in memories of men whom death might at any moment carry off. The death of many Muslim warriors at the battle of Yemamah opened the eyes of the early Caliphs to the danger the 'Book of God' might be, ere long, irrevocably lost. They accordingly provided, to the best of their power, against such a contingency. Abu-Behr, or rather Omar, during his reign, was the first to take the matter in hand and employed Zaid ibn Thabit, the Ansari, a native of Medinah, who had acted as amanuensis to Mohammed, to collect and arrange the text. This he did from palm leaves, skins, blade bones and the 'hearts of men', and presented to the Caliph a copy of the Qur'an.*
>
> "*The whole was strung together without any reference to chronological order, and with very little regard to the logical connection of various passages. The longer surahs were placed at the beginning and the short ones at the end, although the order of their revelation was, for the most part, just the reverse.*"

Then, due to a number of factors such as different Arabic dialects and people still being alive that remembered the words of the Prophet Muhammad differently to how they were presented, various interpretations arose. For example, *I'hfa'un* means *'to conceal'* in the dialect of one tribe and *'to display'* in that of another. And this... *"could not fail to give rise to disputes as to their interpretation. At length, some twenty years afterwards, the Caliph Othma'in, alarmed at the bitter feelings and open quarrels which these differences of reading and interpretation had already engendered, determined to prevent the Muslims from differing among themselves in their way of reading the word of God as the Jews and Christians did.*

> *"He accordingly appointed a commission, consisting of Zaid, the original editor, with three men of Qurais (Mohammed's own tribe), to decide once and for all, upon the text and to fix the reading definitely according to the Pure Quarais idiom. When this edition was completed, Othman sent copies to all the principal cities in the empire and caused all the previous copies to be burned."*

Othmans version of the Qur'an has **"remained the authorised text and has been adopted by all schools of Mohammedan theologies from the time it was made (AD 660) until the present day."**

Remember how I said that the one thing that we cannot overcome is the misinterpretation of the original teaching, due to human fallibility? Two things come to mind:

Firstly, that if in the example of a single word I'hfa'un can mean both 'to conceal' and 'to display' which are polar opposites, then what is to prevent other misinterpretations?

And secondly, Muhammad is also called 'The Seal of the Prophets', and the saying *'there is no prophet after me'* is traditionally attributed to him and makes it unlawful in Islam to expect the advent of another prophet.

If the interpretation of the 'Book of God' in the beginning was disputed and fought over, so much so that a holy edict had to be given to decide on the correct interpretation, at a time when the Earth was in the Kali Yuga and human intellect was at its lowest point, then what is to prevent the misinterpretation that Muhammad actually called himself the last Prophet?

In the beginning Muhammad was a Hanif, and professed belief in the faith in the covenant of Father Abraham – which was no more or no less than the doctrine of the unity of God. In the beginning, Muhammad approached the Jews but they would not recognise him as a prophet – and apostle of God. The Jews were 'the chosen people' and could not lower themselves to accept a gentile. The same thing happened with Jesus.

The Jewish people were stuck in their rituals and strict adherence to their doctrine and were blinded by their arrogance as being the 'chosen people of God.' The mystics of Islam, the Sufis, say that love is the emanation of God in the universe. And the Jewish people in the mystical Kabbalah have an identical position. It is because of the arrogance of the Jewish priests at the time of Muhammad that there was this break away and the foundation stone was laid for Islam. If, in the beginning, they accepted Muhammad as the 'apostle of God' history would have been very different.

Judaism, Christianity, and Islam all share the same father – Abraham. And as has been shown in this discourse, Abraham's covenant with God was built on the foundations of Hermeticism. I have no doubt that the historical personages existed. And since time immemorial, there have been men that have been the voice of God, known as prophets.

> The chief prophets recognised by Islam in the Qur'an are:
> Adam, Zafiy allah – which means – the Chosen of God.
> Noah, Nabiy allah, – which means – the Prophet of God.
> Abraham, 'Halila 'illah, – which means – the Friend of God.
> Jesus, Ru'ha ' illah, which means – the Spirit of God.
> Muhammad, Rusul allah, which means – The Apostle of God.

The evolutionary ability of man to move through the seven octaves of vibration does not stop hereafter because one man at the level of the second initiation is believed to proclaim such. One of the challenges of the second initiation is the overcoming of the personality. Having satisfactorily developed the love nature and recognised ones mission to help in the unfolding of the divine plan, sometimes the trap of the prophet is being overzealous and overstating their importance in the part that they are to individually play in the unfolding in the plan. Thus, they mar the work that could have been carried out in a better fashion.

From all of the teachings of the mystery schools of ancient Egypt, that go back many thousands of years before the time of Abraham, it should be evident to the reader that the best way to interpret the original covenant with Abraham is through the lens of this ancient mystical knowledge.

At the centre of the Islamic faith is the Ka'aba ٱلْكَعْبَة, which is a giant black cube in Mecca. Considered by muslims to be Bayt Allah (Arabic: بَيْتُ ٱللّٰه, the 'House of God'). Ka'aba is Arabic for Cube and Most famously this cube was rebuilt by Ibrahim (Abraham), and under instruction from Allah (God), Ibrahim was to perform the rite of the Tawaf.

Every year thousands of pilgrims travel to perform the tawaf. The *tawaf* is a ritual counter-clockwise circling of the Ka'aba seven times. The most significant practice of this is during Ramadan and the *hajj*, when millions of pilgrims gather for *tawaf*. A couple of interesting things spring to mind.

What have we learned in this discourse that is the most simple but profound revelation? It is the symbol at the beginning of each chapter. The Triangle within the Circle within the Square – the Sacred Alignment. Where the Triangle represents God or Divinity or Allah or Jahweh, The Circle represents the eternal passage of time, and the Square represents matter. Divinity for eternity within creation. Where by matter is represented as existing within 7 octaves of vibration as explained in Chapter 2.

So armed with this ancient seemingly lost sacred knowledge we can better understand the true meaning of this sacred site – The Ka'aba in Mecca and the sacred rite – the Tawaf.

The black cube is the representation of the house of God. Divinity for Eternity within Creation – The cube of matter.

The rite of tawaf the 7 x counter clockwise circling of the cube of matter is done once in recognition for each of the 7 octaves of vibration: mineral, plant, animal, human, genius, prophet, godman.

We can more accurately understand the seemingly lost but original accurate interpretation as to why the Ka'aba and its circling 7 times is at the heart of the sacredness of the Islamic faith. This revelation by itself is extremely powerful and I hope that my Islamic brothers and sisters can find the openness and willingness to see the deeper seemingly lost meaning. And there arise not even for a moment, a hint of anger. *Al Salamu Alaykum.*

Furthermore, as we are clear that Abraham was the author of the *Sepher Yezirah* – '*The Book on Creation*' at the heart of the Jewish faith, as explained in Chapter 5 – we have identified the effulgent light behind the clouds of higher source of wisdom behind this book as being the instruction of the lost books of Thoth.

This revelation is also extremely powerful in healing the division/conflict between the Jewish and Islamic faiths. It is evident that the knowledge of instruction from the lost books of Thoth lays at the heart of all Abrahamic faiths. Both the Jews and Muslims claim to share the same father Abraham as the point of origin of both their religions.

The ancient kabbalistic adage of *"Man becomes a stone, a plant, an animal, a spirit, and finally a God"* is the knowledge of the 7 octaves of vibration at the heart of the mystical dimension of the Jewish faith and is the same thing as the 7 times counterclockwise practice of the Tawaf around the Ka'aba – the heart of sacredness of the Islamic faith in recognition of the 7 sacred octaves of vibration existing within the cube of matter.

The tree of life of the Jewish Kabbalah, contained within the geometry of the ancient flower of life, is represented in the hidden symbolism of the Major Arcana of the High priestess card (symbol 2 of the 22 symbols of the lost books of Thoth). Whereby the high priestess is the embodiment of the 7th octave of vibration balancing all the pairs of opposites and sitting in perfect Sacred Alignment between the positive and negative, divine masculine and feminine pillars of Boaz and Jachin.

Perfect, divine atomic, all dna activated, all 7 scrolls opened – Divine being. Do you understand – be at peace now my brothers and sisters in humanity, please stop the unnecessary conflict - for now the light of understanding shines greater upon this ancient religious feud between the Jewish and Muslim faiths highlighting centuries of misunderstanding and unnecessary bloodshed.

The understanding of this sacred knowledge will serve to be a great unifier. The extension of which will also serve to unify the Hindu religion whereby the knowledge of the 7 Chakras in the body and the pranamayakosha will be seen to be the same understanding of the sacred 7 octaves of vibration and the progression through which leads to awakening of the buddha nature in the buddhist tradition and the awakening of the Christ consciousness of the true interpretation of the words of Christ – the true Christianity not 'Churchianity', by living as he lived as the divine instrument on earth as love incarnate. A supernatural appreciative love for all creation – serves to be the vehicle for achieving the Sacred Alignment. The shared mystical heart of all these great faiths in the world.

Do you understand? Blessings be upon you all.

Sacred knowledge in symbolism – Vedic Brahmanism – Hinduism

One of the key things you should take away from this discourse is that the ancients preserved deep occult and sacred wisdom in symbolism. This is what was generally misunderstood during the ages of the Earth in which there was a regression or involution in mental capacity, and from then on has been taught by those with perceived spiritual authority, incorrectly, by the same degree.

The entire pantheon of the Hindu Gods are merely representations of an aspect of divinity. As mentioned before, Ganesha is the elephant god of strength and wisdom, and if we look at all aspects of creation, they merely have a separate deity representing a different aspect of the Godhead. Take Vishnu, for example. Figure 64 (next page) is an image of Krishna/Vishnu.

Figure 64: image of Krishna/Vishnu By Ramanarayanadatta astri – http://archive.org/details/mahabharata06ramauoft, Public Domain, https://commons.wikimedia.org/w/index.php?curid=21175732.

Krishna is known to be an incarnation of Vishnu. And remember, Vishnu is a part of the Hindu Trinity: Brahma, Shiva, and Vishnu. Krishna is always coloured blue, which is symbolic of his divine state of consciousness, and he always carries a number of objects: the Golden Chakra, the Conch Shell, the Lotus Flower and the Mace.

The objects carried in his hands are symbolic of aspects or attributes of Vishnu. The Chakra in the back-left hand of the picture is known as the 'Sudarshana Chakra', and it is depicted as a weapon with 10,000,000 spikes in two rows, moving in opposite directions, that give it a serrated edge. The Conch Shell in the back right hand of the picture is known as 'Shanka/Panchjanya' and is symbolic of the giver of fame, longevity, prosperity, the cleanser of sin, and the abode of Lakshmi, who is the goddess of wealth and the consort of Vishnu. The Mace or Gada is called 'Kaumodaki' and is the symbol of strength. It symbolises the intellect – the power of knowledge, power of time, primordial knowledge (being in the left hand – denotes individual existence). It is described to sound like a lightning striking and is capable of slaying demons (daityas/ Asuras). Lastly, in the front right hand, Vishnu is holding the Lotus Flower, symbolic of purity:

In the Gopal-Uttar-tapani Upanishad it says in the voice of Vishnu:

"In my lower right hand, which represents the revolving or creative tendency, I hold the Conch, symbol of the five elements." (Vishnu's Conch Shell is called 'Shanka/Panchjanya' and produces the sound 'Om' – the primeval sound of creation).

"In my upper right hand, which represents cohesive tendency, I hold the discus/chakra, shining like an infant sun, symbol of the mind." (Vishnu's Chakra/Discus is called 'Sudarshana')

"In my upper left hand, which represents the tendency towards dispersion and liberation, I hold the Lotus, symbol of the causal power of illusion, from which the universe rises." (Vishnu's Lotus is called 'Padma' and it is the symbol of purity). It represents unfolding creation and the wisdom of non-attachment – advising we can partake in life's pleasures but must not become ensnared by them. It is the truth (Sathya) from which rules of conduct (Dharma) and knowledge emerge.

"In my lower left hand, which represents the notion of individual existence and it is the symbol of primeval knowledge." (Vishnu's Mace/ Gada is called 'Kaumodaki' and represents the elemental force from which all physical and mental powers are derived).

Do you see now how this symbolism runs throughout the entire Hindu religion? As we remove the layers and reveal the underlying veiled meaning we come into alignment with an understanding of the ancient sacred science, known as 'Gupta Vidya.'

Gupta Vidya

Over 120 years ago, in 1888, Helena Blavatsky, the founder of Theosophy wrote in *The Secret Doctrine, Part I – Cosmogenesis* that:

> "The said key must be turned seven times before the whole system is divulged. We will give it but one turn, and thereby allow the profane one glimpse into the mystery. Happy he, who understands the whole! The same may be said of the whole esoteric system. One turn of the key, and no more, was given in 'Isis.' Much more is explained in these volumes (the secret doctrine parts I and II). In those days the writer barely knew the language in which the work was written, and the disclosure of many things, freely spoken about now, was forbidden...
>
> "In century the 20th some disciple more informed and far better fitted, may be sent by the Master of Wisdom to give final and irrefutable proofs that there exists a science called 'Gupta Vidya'; and that like the once mysterious source of the Nile, the source of all religions and philosophies now known to the world has been for many ages forgotten and lost to men, but it is at last found."

So we have five major religions: Vedic-Brahmanism-Hinduism, Judaism, Buddhism, Christianity and Islam. And we have the patriarch Abraham/Ibrahim as the founding father of three – Judaism, Christianity, and Islam. From the words of Blavatsky (above) we see the source of the Nile – the source of all religions and philosophies – in the region of Egypt. And we have Hermes Trismegistus/Thoth – The Lord of the Universe in Egypt, as a teacher and instructor of Abraham, who taught Abraham/Ibrahim the wisdom of the Lost Books of Thoth and called him 'friend', as evidenced in the oldest Jewish text known to man, 'Sepher Yetzirah', ascribed to the authorship of Abraham himself. And we have the arrival of the awaited messiah, Jesus Christ, 2,000 years ago.

Then we have the Prophet Muhammad (peace be upon him) claiming that Islam is the one true religion descending from the original teachings of Abraham, with all Arabs descending from the line of Ishmael – the son of Abraham.

But when Christ came he pointed out where the Jewish people had lost their true direction from the original teachings of their founding father Abraham. And the Priests and Rabbis at the time did not want to hear that they were wrong, so they failed, or refused, to recognise him as the messiah – which simply means 'anointed one.'

Christ could clearly see the misguided direction that the Jewish religion had taken since the time of Abraham – based on his soul's wisdom:

Luke 2:40 King James Version

> *"And the child grew, and waxed strong in spirit, filled with wisdom: and the grace of God was upon him."*

Christ was also instructed in this ancient wisdom in Egypt from the mystery schools. And we know that Christ was in Egypt for a number of years, as he was hiding from the wrath of King Herod. Herod, who on the words of the three wise men, in fear of the coming king, issued an edict to kill every child two years old or younger, so Joseph and Mary took Jesus to Egypt:

Matthew 2:13 King James Version

> *"And when they were departed, behold, the angel of the Lord appeareth to Joseph in a dream, saying, 'Arise, and take the young child and his mother, and flee into Egypt, and be thou there until I bring thee word: for Herod will seek the young child to destroy him.'"*

Yet we do not know how old Jesus was when they had to leave for Egypt, but we do know that Herod wanted every child two years old and younger to be killed:

Matthew 2:16-18 King James Version

"Then Herod, when he saw that he was mocked of the wise men, was exceeding wroth, and sent forth, and slew all the children that were in Bethlehem, and in all the coasts thereof, from two years old and under, according to the time which he had diligently inquired of the wise men."

Obviously, historians are aware of the error of dating of the birth of Christ, and generally it is accepted that the birth of Christ was actually around 6 - 4 BC. According to historians, Herod died around 4 BC in his 37th year of reign as king. But if Herod reigned for a further two years after having all the children killed that were two years old or less, then we know that this order was given around 6 BC – two years before Herod's death in 4 BC. We do not know how old Christ was when he left Egypt. All we know is that he left sometime after Herod died, when an angel appeared to his father again in a dream.

Matthew 2:19-23 King James Version

"But when Herod was dead, behold, an angel of the Lord appeareth in a dream to Joseph in Egypt, saying, 'Arise, and take the young child and his mother, and go into the land of Israel: for they are dead which sought the young child's life.' And he arose, and took the young child and his mother, and came into the land of Israel."

It is not possible to know how much time passed between the death of Herod in 4 BC and when the angel appeared to Joseph in a dream to say they could return to Israel. It could have been a few years. So if Jesus was close to two years of age when he was taken into Egypt and Herod died two years after that, when Jesus was around four years of age, he could have been in Egypt for a number of years before his father had the dream that Herod had died. We know that Jesus was still a child when he left Egypt, so he could have been anywhere from six to twelve years old.

The current practice of Buddhism is that when the Dalai Lama dies, the other Lamas use their spiritual gifts to ascertain where he will be born again, and then they attend various locations with items that belonged to him and items that are very similar yet did not belong to him. The reincarnated Dalai Lama chooses without hesitation the items that belonged to him and so it is that the other Lamas can confirm that they have found the right child.

Now, similarly – ancient Egyptian priests and mystery schools aware of the knowledge of the Book of Thoth, and also aware of processes by which to spiritualise matter, would have been able to detect the soul accumulations of the child Jesus, and it is quite likely that he would have been instructed in this from very early on. Today it is believed, in the Buddhist tradition, that incarnations of great souls are preceded by wonderful and unusual events in nature, such as a sky filled with rainbows. The birth time and places of these great incarnations are known as 'Tulkus', and are spiritually detected by Lamas, and they visit the households of the parents before the birth to tell them that their child is a Tulku (such was the case with Kalu Rinpoche – see appendix). The Tibetan Buddhist belief is that a child that is two years old or less has full access to their soul memory over many lifetimes. After the age of two, the conditioning of the current reality sets in and this memory begins to fade, unless of course there is a large accumulation of wisdom from many lives, which was definitely the case with Jesus:

Luke 2:40 King James Version

> *"And the child grew, and waxed strong in spirit, filled with wisdom: and the grace of God was upon him."*

We have Christ recognised as a divine personage in the Christian religion, and in Islam he is known as Isa – a great prophet – the Spirit of God. In order to correctly understand the premise of all Abrahamic religions, it is therefore essential to view every original recorded word and teaching of Abraham and Christ through the lens of the Hermetic Wisdom of the Ancient Books of Thoth. ***And all of a sudden, we have*** *the Master Key for reconciliation for which humanity has been searching for thousands of years!*

What was the primary teaching of the Lost Book of Thoth? Remember the Major Arcana Tarot card I – The Magician:

"There is only one creator and his children are a part of him. They are the 'conscious' – therefore listen: Men are immortal gods and gods were immortal men."

This is why Christ called himself a Son of God, for we are all Sons and Daughters of God. We have the Holy Trinity in Christianity as **Father, Son and Holy Spirit.** However, its original teaching was **Osiris, Isis and Horus.** We also have the Divine Trinity in Hinduism of **Brahma, Shiva and Vishnu. It is** *all the same*.

Remember, also, how in the first chapter I gave you all the accepted definitions of the FIVE major religions, and that the primary characteristic of Buddhism was that they did not believe in an external creator? *"Buddhism has no creator God and gives a central role to the doctrine of Karma."* Well, the reason for that – and the unspoken primary foundation to Buddhism – is that when enlightenment is achieved then the enlightened person realises that they are Divine (their Buddha Nature) and that there is no separation of themselves from divine/God/creator.

However, with the limitations of language and the state of involution of consciousness/intellect of man on Earth 2,500 years ago, at the time of the Buddha, in the Kali Yuga, human beings only had the intellectual capacity of comprehending things at the gross/material level – *"The mental virtue is then in its first stage and only ¼ developed. The human intellect cannot comprehend anything beyond the gross material of this ever-changing creation, the external world."*

So Siddhartha Gautama Buddha, with his 84,000 teachings, did his best to instruct others on how to achieve enlightenment, but many could not grasp the deeper meaning of what was said. And so we have Buddhism today that leads that boat close to the shore, but many followers don't want to get out of the boat. And they seem to place too much reverence on the manifestation of Buddha himself (as being separate from themselves) and not on the true meaning of his teachings.

Denouncing his royal station would not have been easy for Siddhartha Gautama. As a prince he would've suffered challenges and heartache from a family who did not understand him, and that this renunciation of his royal responsibilities at age twenty-nine was where he undertook his initiations. He 'found enlightenment' under the Bodhi tree at age thirty-five, but in order to get there he would have to have first gone through immense suffering, characteristic of the journey up the mountain of initiation. The journey that all must take if they are to reach the goal set forth in the original lost teachings of the *Book of Thoth*, as they become the path.

We have Vedic-Brahmanism-Hinduism, the oldest religion on the planet. The Vedas are the original teachings of when there were many mortal men/women that spiritualised matter and lived at the 7th octave of vibration consciously, from the previous Satya Yuga. A pantheon of gods that represented different underlying characteristics of the Godhead – Brahma. But this teaching came from Egypt (which came from Atlantis before that), with its own pantheon of gods – from the Godhead Osiris and the different ways of representing divinity, but again this connection was lost or not understood.

The link is as follows: Hinduism developed from the Vedic religion; the Vedic religion is the ancient religion of the Aryan peoples who entered North Western India from Persia, circa 2000-1200 BC, Persia borders Egypt – Brahma means **'the ultimate reality underlying all phenomena.'** And from the Lost Book of Thoth we understand the correct meaning of Osiris to be the same as Brahma – ***"Osiris is the great one, who produces infinite series of numbers but is not descended from anyone himself"*** – which equates to being the ultimate reality underlying all phenomena.

In Hinduism today we have the sacredness of the cow, but due to the phenomena of the involution of consciousness/intellect of man through the effects of the different Yugas, once again the original meaning was lost. The divine bull, Apis, was sacred to Osiris because it was symbolic of the age of Taurus, where the divine radiations manifested on Earth and shaped and effected human beings and earthly events due to the magnifying nature that our Sun had on these radiations. Hence the bull Apis being Sacred to Osiris!

The Hindus misunderstood at that early time. Instead the Hindus literal interpretation of their legends/sacred stories fail to recognise the analogy of the Cow/Bull carrying the Gods as being identical with the zodiacal shift in the heavens, and so the cow became holy (as it was a vehicle that carried the Gods) and has remained thus ever since, rather than have the holy symbol shift to the Aries ram and then the Pisces fish as the vernal equinox shifted from one age to the next.

> *"Gupta Vidya can be translated as 'Secret Knowledge' or 'Secret Doctrine.' This hidden body of Knowledge is in the safe keeping of a relatively small number of individuals. They have been called the Masters of the Wisdom. They are adepts and initiates belonging to a hidden esoteric brotherhood which guides and watches over the spiritual evolution and advancement of humanity."*
> – www.theosophywisdom.wordpress.com

The science of the Gupta Vidya: the source of all religions and philosophies known to the world that has been for many ages forgotten and lost to men, is now at last found and is the sacred alignment.

Take a moment to look at the emblem at the beginning of each chapter or Figure 14 on page 49. Stop. Feel very deeply in your psyche and in your heart – for this is the meaning on the cover. My eternal gift to you: *"There is only one creator and his children are a part of him. They are the 'conscious' therefore listen: Men are immortal gods and gods were immortal men... That is the goal to which you must aspire from this day forth. Now go in peace."*

Divinity for eternity within creation.

The Great White Brotherhood

In the last paragraphs where I mentioned that Guptya Vidya can be translated as a hidden body of knowledge belonging to a hidden esoteric brotherhood which guides and watches over the spiritual evolution and advancement of humanity, I hope that you did not glaze over its importance. I also mentioned The Great White Brotherhood as being the vehicle for the rediscovery of Doreal of the Emerald

Tablets of Thoth as well as the vehicle of expression for the Agni Yoga guidance in Chapter 8.

As you are consciously spiritualising the matter of your body and consciously moving to higher octaves of vibration, at some point along the way your higher faculties will start to come online. And when they do you will be able to be aware of the existence of the guiding fraternity of humanity on the spiritual plane – The Great White Brotherhood.

I will mention that The Great White Brotherhood is comprised of beings – both male and female and of all skin tones; white does not denote ethnicity but *purity*. Purity, purification of the animal nature – that is why they are referred to as such. Brotherhood does not denote gender but *inclusivity*.

What the powers that be prefer that you never comprehend is that there is an overarching planetary governance of a synthesis of degrees of intelligence belonging to the personalities who have triumphed over matter and incurred greater responsibilities – to be responsible for the unfolding of the great plan on Earth.

> *"The International Government never has denied its existence. It has proclaimed itself, not in manifestos but in actions that were recorded even in official history. One can site cases from the French and Russian revolutions, as well as in the history of Anglo-Russian and Anglo-Indian relations, when an independent outside Hand altered the course of events. The Government did not hide the existence of its envoys in various countries. Naturally, in accordance with the dignity of the International Government, they never hid themselves. On the contrary, they showed themselves openly, visited various governments and were known to many. Literature preserves their names and adorns them with the fancies of their contemporaries. It is not secret organisations – of which governments are in such fear – but actual persons that are sent out by decree of Invisible International Government.*
>
> *Inimical to international tasks is each perpetration of*

fraud. But the unity of peoples, the appreciation of creative labour, the growth of the consciousness, are affirmed by the International Government as undeferrable measures. And if one traces the measures of this Government, it will be found that it cannot be accused of inactivity.

The existence of this Government has entered the awareness of humanity repeatedly, under various names. Each nation is warned but once. Envoys are dispatched but once in a century – this is the law of the Arhats. The acts of the Invisible Government conform with the process of world evolution, hence the results are based on natural law. No personal desire is here, only the immutable laws of matter. I do not desire – I know! And therefore decisions, even amidst the turbulent currents are firm. One may climb a mountain from the north or the south, the result is still the same. "

– Agni Yoga 1929

Dear brothers and sisters, what is helpful to understand and to hold in your consciousness at this significant time of Earth turmoil and tension, is that all is not lost. The members of the planetary government are watching closely and when necessary they intervene to influence the course of events. Know well that their forces and resources are mighty and they will not abandon us to the dark fate that our oppressors would wish for us. This planetary International Government is one and the same as The Great White Brotherhood. By our individual efforts for spiritual advancement and aligning every fibre of our beings to commit to help with the realisation of 'The Great Plan' on Earth, we gradually become more and more conscious of them. We learn to work in harmony with them, progressing through the stages of Solar and Planetary hierarchies as we earn greater responsibilities.

The Lucis Trust (who hold copyright) have graciously granted me permission to include the following diagrams of the solar and planetary hierarchies. The first, Figure 65, is the pictographic representation of the solar and planetary hierarchies, and the second, Figure 66, is the key to interpretation of Figure 65 as a written list.

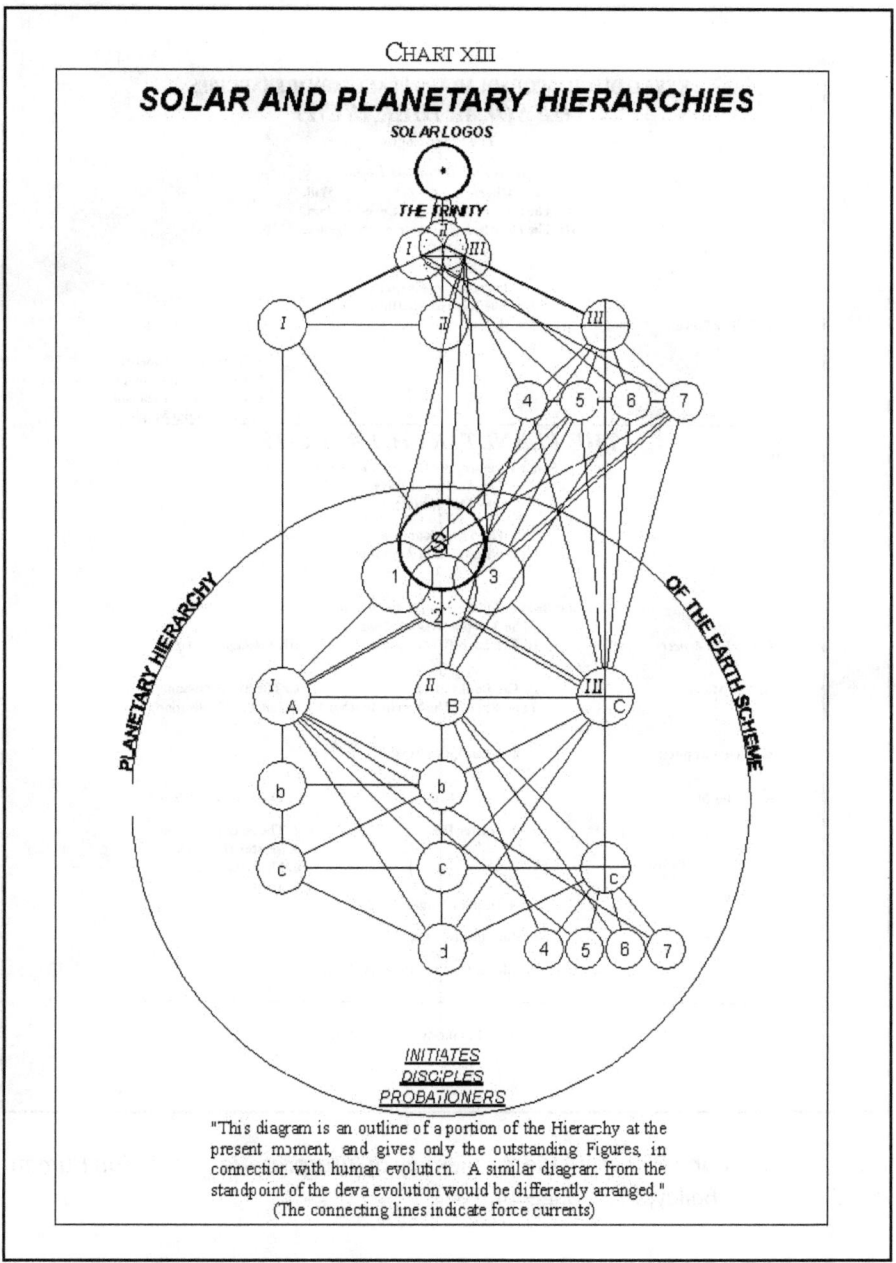

Figure 65: Solar and Planetary Hierarchies, Initiation Human and Solar, A. A. Bailey, 1959, page 48.

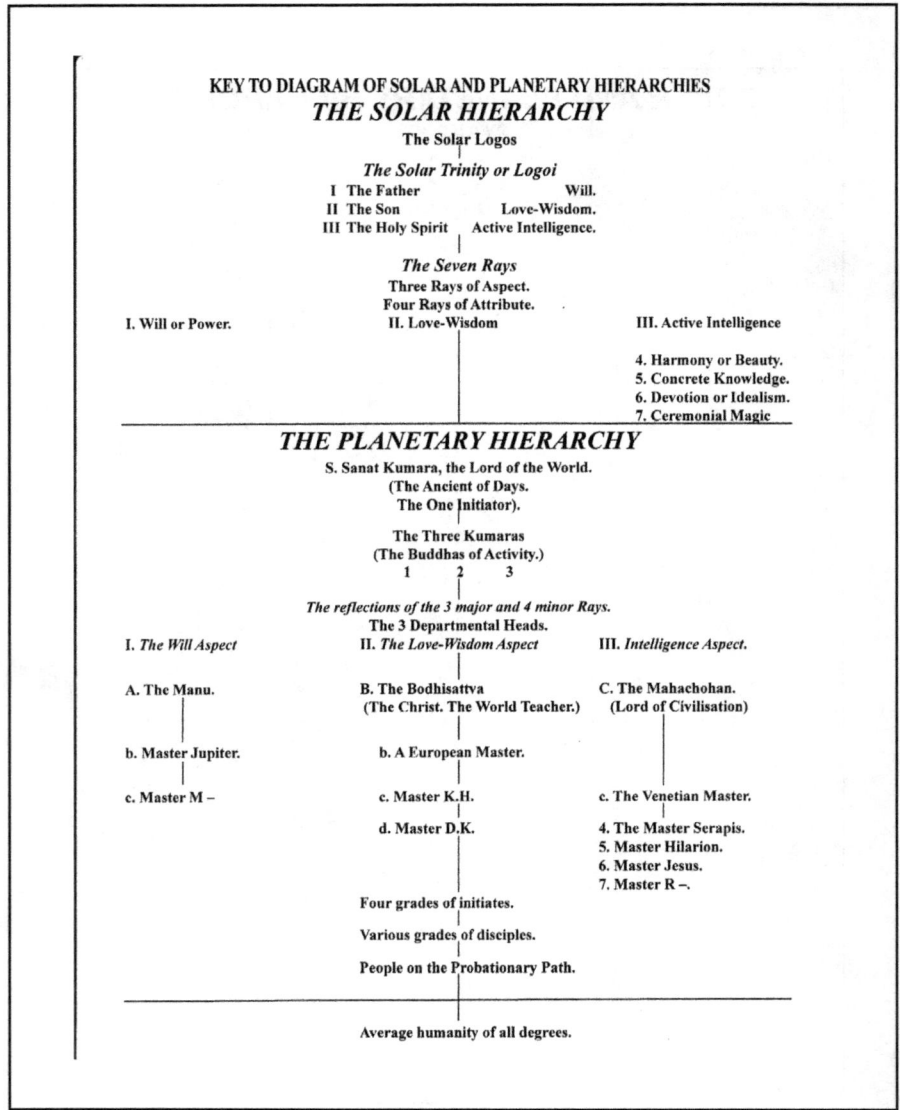

Figure 66: Solar and Planetary Hierarchies key of interpretation, Initiation Human and Solar, A. A. Bailey, 1959, page 49.

Though the subject of the planetary hierarchy is of such a profound interest to the average man (more so in the mid-1900s than today, due to manoeuvres to shift the focus of the consciousness of mankind onto more material physical pursuits) according to the teachings of A. A.

Bailey, its real significance will not be understood unless men and women realise the following:

- The entire hierarchy of spiritual beings represents a synthesis of forces/energies that are consciously manipulated for the furtherance of planetary evolution.
- These forces, demonstrating through those great personalities, link it with the great solar hierarchy.
- The planetary hierarchy have four distinct lines of work:
   a. To develop consciousness of self in all beings.
   b. To develop consciousness in the three lower kingdoms.
   c. To transmit the will of the planetary logos.
   d. To set an example for humanity to follow.

This journey through the octaves of vibration brings with it a corresponding degree of what we call *attainment*. I will now reference some priceless words of instruction from the same book *'Initiation Human and Solar'* by Alice A. Bailey, published in 1959 – to elucidate further on these degrees/stages of development/attainment. Permission to use quotes from the Alice Bailey books has been given by the Lucis Trust who hold copyright.

"***Probationary path:*** *The probationary path precedes the path of initiation or holiness and marks that period in the life of a man when he definitely sets himself on the side of the forces of evolution and works at building his own character. He takes himself in hand and cultivates the qualities that are lacking in his disposition and seeks with diligence to bring his personality under control… (Page 63)*

'***Disciple:*** *A disciple is one who, above all else, is pledged to do three things:*

1. *To serve humanity.*
2. *To co-operate with the plan of the Great Ones as he sees it and as best he may.*
3. *To develop the powers of the Ego (Egoless), to expand his consciousness until he can function on the three planes in the three worlds and in the causal body, and to follow the guidance of the higher self and not the dictates of his threefold lower nature… (Page 71)*

'A disciple is one that is beginning to comprehend group work and change his centre of activity from himself (as a pivot around which everything revolves) to the group centre. He is one who realises simultaneously the relative insignificance of each unit of consciousness and also its vast importance. His sense of proportion is adjusted, and he sees things as they are; he sees people as they are; he sees himself as he inherently is and seeks to become that which he is...

'Initiate: *The word initiation comes from two latin words 'in', int; and ire, to go; therefore the making of a beginning, or the entrance into something. An entrance into the spiritual life, or into a fresh stage in that life. (Page 10)*

'It is the first step, and the succeeding steps, upon the path of holiness. Literally, therefore, a man who has taken the first initiation is one who has taken the first step into the spiritual kingdom, having passed out of the definitely human kingdom into the superhuman.

'He has entered upon the life of the spirit, and for the first time has the right to be called a spiritual man. He is entering upon the fifth or final stage in our present fivefold evolution. Having groped his way through the hall of ignorance during many ages, and having gone to school in the hall of learning; he is now entering university – the hall of wisdom. When he has passed through that school he will graduate as a master of compassion."

– Initiation Human and Solar, A. A. Bailey, 1959

The above passages from A. A. Bailey talks of the hall of ignorance, the hall of learning and the hall of wisdom. As mentioned previously in this discourse, these halls refer to the different initiations that the spiritual seeker will pass through on their way to the final goal of becoming a master of compassion. These halls are not halls as such, but rather subtler levels of reality – the hall of ignorance is the physical plane, the hall of learning is the astral plane, the hall of wisdom is the mental plane. Remember the first of the hermetic principles – the principle of mentalism – the universe is mental. Energy follows thought, reality is shaped by consciousness directed under the powers of the will.

The idea of an unseen guiding brotherhood on the spiritual plane may be hard for you to get your head around because of the efforts taken by the powers that be to keep this knowledge from the populous. If you don't believe it, I can't make you do so. All I can do is present this information to you for you to weigh and measure and apply in your life, and perhaps over time your levels of awareness and perception may expand to the degree to which you are able to detect them.

The Buddha said that our conduct in life should be that every day we should strive to go to the ocean of human suffering and take out a soup ladle (spoon), thereby reducing the amount of human suffering with consistent effort. And of course, when you think of trying to reduce an ocean with a soup ladle, you very quickly understand the immensity of the work that lies before us as a race.

That is why the bodhisattvas are revered. They willingly choose to reincarnate back into this Earth school to help with the task of emptying the ocean of human suffering with a soup spoon. And they are fully conscious of the conditions of the way – they know that by doing so, most likely they will not be understood and may even be persecuted, spat upon and perhaps killed – but they willingly accept that burden as they know that one day all of our collective efforts will pay off and we will witness the realisation of the great plan.

That is why they say the greatest among us are ones that leave last. The development of compassion is so rarefied in these beings that they will not leave to go onto other higher states of existence until the littlest among us is brought into the light. Only then, will they proclaim – *'It is done.'*

On my journey of self-remembrance, one of my spiritual teachers, who I will refer to as 'K'; instructed to me the following hierarchy of service:

> *'The Shadow feeds the ego, the ego uses the intellect, the intellect is in service to others, service to others is delivered with compassion, compassion is delivered by love.'*

As long as you strive to live by this and be of service to your fellow humanity as best as you can, then you will naturally align yourself to the work of The Great White Brotherhood and you will be more likely to have contact with them.

So that is all I will say on this matter. If it is that you are wanting and wishing to detect and comprehend the existence of the guiding brotherhood of humanity, the paradox is that the way to discover them through your own individual experience is to not look for them – but instead set yourself to task and strive to aid the work in the achievement of the unfolding of the great plan.

By doing this you will then naturally be seen and detected by their ray that scans humanity for able co-workers, and before you know it you will be in their presence on the spiritual plane… only to find that they are very busy and would rather that you learn to be more self-reliant and self-directed.

Dr J. J. Hurtak, author of *The Keys of Enoch*, recently wrote, *'God, then Others, then Self.'* And this is a good way to align our being and bearing in life to go about becoming a conscious co-worker in the divine plan.

Frequency Control

So by now you will realise that it has always been about frequency control. Keeping human beings limited, misinformed with deliberate false indoctrination. The powers behind the curtain know that the potential of mortal man is to spiritualise their bodies and become immortal gods, so they have maliciously and insidiously stacked the deck to keep us limited, to keep our frequency low – through fear, through orchestrating wars and outbreaks of diseases, and driving the direction of society in accordance with their own plans – with an overly materialistic sex-focused culture. Let us focus on the definition of the word insidious for a minute:

According to the Oxford dictionary, insidious is:
'Proceeding in a gradual, subtle way, but with very harmful effects.'
This plan is more than a thousand years old! Do you see? Because it is so old, it is difficult to see. But if one stops and looks closely, then one can see the design. It is clever, I will give them that, but the gig is up now. The 'people' pulling the strings behind the curtains will have to surrender their dark thrones to the returning children of light. But, of course, they do not want to give up without a fight. And so they are attempting to accelerate things. We must understand that this is orchestrated from the top down, and that the varying arms of the hidden agenda of control of people spread out into every sector – **control of world governments, finances, education, religion, medicine, and the military.** It is like a game of chess, and they have been patiently aligning all of the pieces for some time, and they are preparing to check our king, but I tell you – they will not win!

For whilst these dark ones are moving forward with their plan, they think they have won and they have become overconfident, and they do not see the strategy of the army of light! Nor do they see our splendour. The dark ones with their agenda of control evidenced by the soon-to-be compulsory vaccination of all newborns to shut down awakening DNA, the pushing of the agenda of mandatory microchipping of the population under the guise of it being for our security/safety (amongst the 'plannedemic' – that is, COVID-19) so they can track and control us, and the driving of an agenda of unhealthy fear and materialism – they have dropped their guard and now it is our turn.

Through these mechanisms the dark ones have revealed themselves and just as they were largely unseen before, **the forces of light were also largely unseen, but now this is a call to action**! This message is a mechanism of the light to help you to wake up and see what is really going on. For what the dark ones are afraid of is humanity, as a collective, waking up. And despite their accelerated agenda they cannot stop us from waking up. Many are awake. However, now we must be smart and beat them at their own game. **The key is not to be afraid.**

Trappings of Glamour and Illusion

People have been touching on some problems with technology, and the effects that technology have on dehumanising us. I have seen images on social media of jokes of people being glued to their smart phones and the zombie apocalypse already being upon us, as they coin that to a photo of people walking in a line with their heads down looking at their phones, but do they really see what is going on? It is the serpent of frequency control.

The moderate use of technology is of course essential to progress. However, we must be aware that all of these wireless devices such as phones, tablets, and so on, alter the brainwaves. They emit energy at a certain frequency that is detrimental to human beings, and from experience, this effect is pretty much hypnotic. If one is not careful one can be sucked into a vortex and lose many hours of one's life looking at a screen! And that is what they want, a bunch of hypnotised, comatose, non-thinking people that they can dupe into submission and blind with the bright shiny colours of materialism.

In 1981 there was a movie released called '*My Dinner with Andre*', and the dialogue in this movie is chilling in its accuracy of predicting our current world situation thirty years later. It points to the fact that we are unconsciously building our own prisons, and because we have built them, we do not know that we are in prison and therefore do not look to escape. Here is the dialogue from the movie which I ask you to contemplate that has been reproduced with full permission:

> *"Okay yes we are bored – we are all bored now. But has it ever occurred to you, Wally,* **that the process that relates to this boredom that we see in the world now may very well be a self-perpetuating unconscious form of brainwashing, created by a world totalitarian government based on money. And that all of this is much more dangerous than one thinks and it's not just a question of individual survival, Wally. But that somebody who is bored is asleep. And that somebody who is asleep will not say 'no'**... *Just a few days ago I met this*

man whom I greatly admired... and he told me that he no longer watches television, he doesn't read newspapers and he doesn't read magazines – he's completely cut them out of his life, because he really does feel that we are living in some kind of Orwellian nightmare now and that everything you hear now contributes to turning you into a robot.

...Then I met this extraordinary English tree expert who had devoted his life to saving trees. Eighty-four years old and always travels with a backpack because he never knows where he is going to be tomorrow, and he asked me, 'Where are you from?' and I said, 'New York', and he said 'Ah New York, that is a very interesting place. Do you know a lot of New Yorkers who keep talking about the fact that they want to leave but never do?' And I said, 'Oh yes' and he said, 'Why do you think that is?' And I came up with different banal theories. **And he said, 'I don't think it's that at all. I think that New York is the new model for the new concentration camps. Where the camp has been built by the inmates themselves and the inmates are the guards and they have this pride in the thing they have built – they have built their own prison. And so they exist in this state of schizophrenia where they are both guards and prisoners and as a result they no longer have – having been lobotomised – the capacity to leave the prison they have made or to even see it as a prison.'** *And he reached into his pocket and took out a seed for a tree and put it in my hand and he said, 'This is a pine tree... escape before it is too late.'*

...The problem is where to go, **because it seems quite obvious that the whole world is going in the same direction.** *You see I think it is quite possible that the 1960's represented the last burst of the human being before he was extinguished. And that this is the beginning of the rest of the future now.*

And that from now on that there will be all these robots walking around – feeling nothing, thinking nothing. **And there will be almost nobody left to remind them** *that their once was a species called a human being... and* **that history and memory are right now being erased** *and soon nobody will really remember that life existed on the planet."*

Pay attention to the differences of our history presented to you in this discourse, understand why comprehension of our real history is of vast importance to the trajectory and survival of humanity.

Uttashart, Arise, Awaken!

We need to wake up. If you are still reading this then you are either awake or awakening. Now when I say to you that the truth that the powers behind the curtain have worked very hard to conceal from us is that mortal human beings can become immortal gods – this must be better understood. There must be a conscious understanding about what this actually means, and it is not your person or your individual personality that is elevated to Godhood and undertakes apotheosis, but rather it is that the divine recognises itself within its creation and then speaks, then acts, and so matter becomes spiritualised, through submission of individual will to a higher will.

And that is why all those that have come before that have attained this state of being have said that they are divine or that they are the son of God. This distinction is very important. For if it is that you think your individual person is God and you elevate ego to the position where it squashes the Christ consciousness, then this is the listening to the voice of the serpent. And by not listening to the Christ consciousness within you, you will only cause yourself to regress in your next life through the selfish abuse of the use of your creative thought force and the divine universal laws! As further explained in J. J. Hurtak's *Keys of Enoch* ® Key 206:

13. Today within our Tree of Life, man is listening to the computerised technology of the snake that speaks to us and says: 'There is no life beyond, there is no life beyond. Do not quest for knowledge of the higher living God for it is all here. You are the living God. This is it; stop where you are.

19. As long as man thinks he is God, he will never acquire the angelic radiations of true creation.

20. **For this reason man remains locked in space and crucified to his body of relativity. His scientific consciousness tells him that he is the only life force in the tree of life, which is the galaxy, and that he is God. Hence, he does not have to humble himself to the higher intelligence which is there to create in him more godliness.**

It must be that you surrender your individual will to the higher will of the force that emanates from you and gives you life, it must be that you learn to listen to the higher voice of love and raise your consciousness from the 3rd octave of the animal up to the 6th level of the prophet and the 7th level of the God Man. For then it is that the necessary purity and qualities of the light will manifest in your person – **tolerance, patience, love, wisdom, compassion, grace, and fearlessness.** Then it is that you are listening to the voice of the dove and not the serpent. Then it is that you will find, when you least expect it, the jewel of great price hidden in the lotus of your heart.

We must begin to look at all of humanity as existing on a radio frequency bandwidth, an AM station, if you like. AM – Also Man, All Mighty, I AM. The grosser levels of mankind stuck in animalistic tendencies of violence exist at the 3rd octave of vibration – that of the animal. They have fallen backwards from the decency of the regular human being. The regular human beings that are living by the golden rule 'do unto others as you would have them do unto you', are existing at the 4th octave of vibration. All geniuses have awakened at some level the consciousness level of the 5th octave of vibration – and must guard against falling by abuse of their intellect and power. All prophets/ divine messengers that have awakened the selfless all-encompassing divine love force within themselves, exist at the 6th octave of vibration/ consciousness. And all masters of compassion and wisdom that have transmuted the lower self and won victory over the material form are existing at the 7th octave of vibration.

Imagine now a radio bandwith with every single human being

marked along it. Understand that there are no two that are identical, we are each our own individual frequency of the divine, each with our dominant thought forms and inclinations and the different weights of tragedy and various experiences and how we have handled these experiences. This radio bandwidth extends out into space, and whilst as we atune the dial to tune in on the individual frequency of existence of one human being, with every minor adjustment of the dial, we then tune in on the frequency of existence of another human being. We must understand that all are deeply connected, that all are inherently made of the same cosmic-energy, which is the entire bandwith of radio frequencies.

In the recognition that you are not your vehicles (physical and astral bodies), that your consciousness is temporarily residing in your body, then you will fight to overcome the loud voices of your animal nature. In this tremendous act of the will and of courage, you will as Christ said 'be born again', and then it is that you can 'enter the kingdom of heaven.'

It must be mentioned that all the messengers before me have left various instructions, but they were not the be all and end all, and to be rigorously followed because of the select value of each specific action or religious observance. No, it was that the act of repetition of such positive actions that served to purify the bodily vibrations and thus by way of this purification – more light would be channelled into the energy centres. The repetition of specific mantras or specific focus on spiritual thought forms of higher planes of being, the instruction to have set times for prayer and ritual are all only necessary in order to purify and increase the bodily vibrations along the octaves of vibration/consciousness.

For if we conceptualise a cup of crystal pure water and we muddy it with one drop of dirty water, then it will take hundreds if not thousands of individual acts (as individual drops of crystal pure water) to remove the stain of the one muddy act. So the underlying reason for all these methods and instructions of the previous divine messengers is to develop consistency of vibration. And this is what Blavatsky meant when she said, 'change is the enemy.' Change of our purified state of oneness with God, which takes us back to the individualised expression of the personality through the muddying effects of a lower nature not mastered! It is not the specific task, but the effect of the puryfying nature of the repetition of the task on the human being that is of importance.

Now, on this journey of evolution of consciousness, as we progress by our own efforts from the 4th, to the 5th, to the 6th octaves of vibration/consciousness, we must be very soberly aware of the effects of our presence and energy on others and on our surrounding environment. The further along we progress, the more potent we become, and the closer our vibrations are to the pure vibrations of the divine. We must guard against our thoughts and our lower nature, which could cause us to fall backwards and lose the attainments we have gained by our selfless devotion and struggle for self-mastery.

We must understand that with every advance, our vibration increases and so does our responsibility. As our vibrations become more 'attractive', and if by then we have found our way into a spiritual teaching/mentor/guru position of influence, then as spiritual teachers we must particularly guard against the negative effects of this divine power that may be felt by others as a strong sexual attraction. Because spiritual energy is sexual energy redirected into higher centres and transmuted.

Spiritual teachers must guard against taking advantage of their students sexually by the effects of the magnetic appeal of their bodies and minds through their spiritual attainment. If they consciously decide to abuse this then they are listening to the voice of the serpent at the 3rd octave of vibration, where love manifests as the desire to possess/have another for oneself. If they choose to give in to this temptation and take advantage of their position of responsibility then they are sowing seeds of misery for future lives, where they will have to return to the earthly plane at a lower level of consciousness and atone for the abusive use of their divine creative power through enduring the purifying effects of suffering.

They may not know it, but by such choice they are walking the left-hand path of the black mage, which is caught in the web of lust and power (that caused the fall of Atlantis) and will, by inescapable cosmic law, come undone. Lightning from the clouds will strike such a person's self-made tower and he/she will fall far and fast and lose their crown, and their tower will fall down around them into ruin.

And so it is that it becomes of paramount importance to better educate people of the larger plan working out on Earth, to understand that, in the end, we are in a free will universe and we each have a choice. Those who block or limit the light will experience the energies of chaos more and more, and those who are attuned to the light will have the light flow through them, and they will become the light, as the axiatonal lines connect back to the higher universe and ground the higher light into the earthly dimension in our physical form.

The Earth is going through a period of immense change, the magnetic poles are shifting and with this shift comes the ability to access greater spiritual energies. So whilst the old cosmology of Yukteswar Giri and the teachings of the Ages of the Earth, the Yugas, play a part in better understanding our history – **we are at a very special time in which we could – and are – as a collective, about to take a giant evolutionary leap.**

As I mentioned before, the more light you shine on yourself for a time, the bigger the shadow, and so it is that the battle of light and dark is being fought on Earth in our psyche and in our consciousness right now. We must understand, as the teachings of the Keys of Enoch further advise us, that at this crucial time lower intelligences will soon reveal themselves to the planet. Yes I am talking about extraterrestrials, and we may be inclined to marvel at their technology and feats, and there is a risk that we will not discern them as belonging to the lower hierarchy. We must not allow ourselves to be hoodwinked by their technological and seemingly magical displays – and thereby surrender our divine selves over to them as they appear to us as creator gods. We must discern those of the lower hierarchy from those of the higher hierarchy. This is the final temptation of this age of Armegeddon.

It is at this time that through the teachings of the light and the unfolding of the scrolls of the light, that right now, as you read these words, there is taking place the externalisation of the hierarchy of light on Earth. Many ancient souls and the master 144,000 are returning to the Earth at this time and awakening.

There are benevolent higher intelligences that are accessible to us if we align our beings to the vibrations of the Christed unconditional love. Beings such as the Elohim and the B'nai Or 'the Sons of Light', are ultra-terrestrial intelligences that are here to assist us. For we must remember that the mind can be influenced. Different sound vibrations and denser thought forms can cause us to fall into negative spirals, and there are beings that would prefer us to negatively spiral downwards. Therefore, it is essential – if one is aligned to the higher vibrations of unconditional love – to use holy and divine names as a means to energetically protect your auras and minds from this negative influence. The teachings of the Academy for Future Science, advise that we should say twelve times:

'Angeloi Christou'
'Melek B'nai Or'
'Melek B'nai Elohim'

Whilst focusing our consciousness on the Godhead YHWH (Yod Hey Vod Hey) as the best means of protection.

Right now there is a battle going on here on Earth, and the battle ground is largely unseen, and is symbolised in the ancient Bhagavad-Gita as a place called Kurukshetra, but it is representative of the consciousness of man.

This must not be something that we grieve over. We must recognise ourselves as **warriors of the light and our weapons are love, tolerance, peace, prayer, courage, fearlessness, faith, fortitude, and reslience. No matter how many times we get knocked down, 'forward' must be our motto.** Remember, like the initiates of old, the ancient truth is that as we ally ourselves with the higher forces of creation, we are looked over, watched, guarded, and guided – like Horus standing at the back of the initiate. **The mountain before us is not a trial but, verily, a mission!**

This journey to consciousness, to the raising of your consciousness to higher and higher levels also directs higher vibrations into your body, and as your vehicles begin to vibrate higher and higher, the more light you produce and the more the dormant aspects of your DNA begin to awaken as you begin to live in a way that activates the divine blueprint the Adam Kadmon. This journey to spiritualising the matter of your body through the evolution of your consciousness, the lifting of your crucified divine consciousness from the crossbeams of time and space, is the Sacred Alignment.

Chapter 10

BLAZING THE TRAIL & PASSING THE TORCH

"Do not go where the path may lead, go instead where there is no path and leave a trail."

– Ralph Waldo Emerson

Our whole current civilisation is currently based upon events of only 2,000 years ago. How naive and foolish is it to ignore the previous 10,000+ years of records and messages? What we are told of history is a blatant lie designed to keep us all fighting each other, and oblivious to the fact that we are divine beings. I have memories of lifetimes where I used the divine energies for healing and creation. I can tell you all this, but still people will think it is only words. They want proof. Well, listen to this voice in your heart as you read this, listen to my consciousness conveyed to you in these writings. What does it whisper of? What does it tell you?

I could tell you that I have been this embodiment or that embodiment in this or that lifetime over countless thousands of existences, yet in each of these incarnations I was a part of a group of souls – a spiritual brotherhood and sisterhood. So whilst I have been all these things, I am not alone. Many masters have returned and are returning now. I recognise my spirit family wherever I go. Some have chosen amnesia to these things, some will awaken at different times.

I am just a brother that has travelled a little farther down the road and fought my way further into the light. But there are others ahead of me, and others ahead of them, who are lighting and passing torches to point out the way. My individual journey has brought me to the place of being able to put these ancient pieces of the puzzle together so that you may now stand on my shoulders, heed the advice, and not deviate from your own mission due to the darkness of ignorance and the debilitating denseness of the earthly vibrations.

In order to pass the torch to my brothers and sisters that feel the soul urge to climb the mountain of initiation, or perhaps so that they may recognise they are already climbing, I offer now some words from an elder brother known as 'The Tibetan.' These words have served to keep me warm through many a hard battle and a bitter cold night. These words that follow have been reproduced with full permission of the Lucis Trust, which holds the copyright of the book *'Ponder on This'* from pages 1 to 14, under the heading 'Food for thought' from which these words have been gathered.

Message from The Tibetan – instruction for the disciple on the verge of becoming the path:

> *"The student must be sincere in his aspiration and must be determined to go forward no matter what may be the reaction of and upon the lower self. Only those that can clearly differentiate between the two aspects of their nature, the real self and the illusionary self can work intelligently…*

> *The student must have lived long enough and battled sufficiently with deterrent forces of life to have enabled them to develop a fairly true sense of values. They are not to be kept back by any happenings to the personality or by the pressure of time and circumstance, by age or physical disability. They have wisely learned that enthusiastic rushing forward, and a violent energetic progress has its drawbacks, and that a steady, regular, persistent endeavour will carry them further in the long run…*

- *Every religious faith holds out the promise that those who seek with earnestness shall find that which they are seeking; let us therefore seek! If by our search we find that all these statements are but visionary dreams and profit nothing at all and lead us only into darkness, then time will nevertheless not have been lost, for we shall have ascertained where not to look. If by our search, on the other hand, corroboration comes little by little and the light shines ever more clearly, let us persist until that day dawns when the light which shineth in darkness will have illuminated the heart and the brain, and the seeker will awaken to the realisation that the whole trend of evolution has been to bring him this expansion of consciousness and this illumination, and that the attainment of the 5th kingdom is no wild Chimera or Phantasm, but an established fact in consciousness...*
- *This each man must ascertain for himself. Each soul must find out within himself, remembering ever that the kingdom of God is within, and that only those facts which are realised within the individual consciousness as truths are of any value. In the meantime, that which many know and have ascertained within themselves serves to be truths of an incontrovertible nature for them, may be stated; to the intelligent reader will then arise the opportunity and responsibility of ascertaining for himself their falsity or truth.*
- *Most men do not as yet distinguish with accuracy between themselves as thinker, persistent in time and space, and the vehicle through which they think, which is ephemeral and transient...*
- *No man is ever put into circumstances which are insurmountable, once he has reached the point where he has intelligently put himself on the side of evolution or God. Prior to that he may and will, be driven by gales of circumstance; the press of the group and racial karma will force him into situations necessary for the process of awakening him to his own innate possibilities. Once he becomes the conscious builder himself, seeking to control the forces and builders of his lower nature, and to construct the 'Temple of Solomon', then he is no longer subject to the earlier conditions. He becomes a ruler, a builder, and a transmitter until the time he is one with the solar angels and the work of human evolution is accomplished...*

> *Those who see a vision that is withheld from those lacking the necessary equipment for its apprehension are regarded as fanciful and unreliable. When many see the vision, its possibility is admitted, but when humanity itself has the awakened and open eye, the vision is no longer emphasised, but a fact is stated, and a law enunciated. Such has been the history of the past and such will be the process in the future.*
> Every step of the way has to be carved out by a man himself, and there is no short or easy road out of darkness into light. Seek to equip your instrument, learn to function in quietness, fulfil your obligations and do your duty. Develop restraint of speech and that calm poise that comes from an unselfish life motive and forget the selfish satisfaction that might well up in the heart when recognition of faithfulness comes from the watching hierarchy.
> Each field of awareness in its boundaries constitutes a prison, and the objective of all work of liberation, is to release the consciousness and expand its field of contacts. Where there are boundaries of any kind, where a field of influence is circumscribed, and where the radius of contact is limited, there you have a prison. Ponder on this statement for it holds much truth.
> *That the inner vision may be ours, the eye see clearly the glory of the lord, and the voice speak only in benediction, and the hands be used only in helpfulness, may well be the prayer of each of us.*
> Peace will be the result of understanding and sharing, and not the origin of them, as the pacifists so often imply.
> When the pupil recognises practically all the time, that he is not his vehicles, but is indeed the divine dweller within them, then certain things will be imparted to him.
> Man stands midway between heaven and earth, with his feet deep in the mud of material life, and his head in heaven. In the majority of cases his eyes are closed, and he sees not the beauty of the heavenly vision. Or they are open but fixed upon the mud and slime with which his feet are covered. But when his eyes are lifted for a brief moment, and see the world of reality, and of spiritual values, then the torn and distracted life of the aspirant begins.

> *One of the most difficult things with which the Masters are today confronted, is to prove to man that the old and recognised values, and the tangible world of phenomena (emotional and physical), must be relegated to their right place in the background of man's consciousness, and that the intangible realities, and the world of ideas and causes must be, for him, in the immediate future, the main centre of attraction. When man grasps this, and lives by this knowledge, then the glamour which now holds the world will disappear.*
> **A mystery only remains a mystery when ignorance and unbelief exist. There is no mystery where there is knowledge and faith. Every step forward in evolution and, therefore, towards the spiritual goal, is always at a cost, and through the relinquishing of that which has hitherto been held dear.**
> *Human beings are innately kind, when their minds have not been distorted and their vision impaired by the false teaching of any selfish interest, political propaganda and racial or religious difficulties.*
> *The bulk of human beings are still too hungry, too devastated physically, too bewildered and distressed and too unsure of their future, their freedom and their security, to be in any condition to listen to 'Him.'*
> **We are passing through one of the great natural transition periods at this time. We are laying the foundation for the emergence of a new species of human being – a more highly evolved unit within the human family – hence much of our problem, and much of our present failure to meet the demands of the race and to measure up to human need for development.**
> *A brief period of organised effort and, at the end, death, is of more vital usefulness today, than a futile doing of the things a man feels like doing in a leisurely way, and then meandering feebly down the years.*
> *Go your own way with strength and silence and do that which your soul demands. Let not the lesser voices of the loved and near deflect you from your progress upon the path of service. You belong now to the world, and not to a handful of your fellow men. The reactions of others are not your responsibility. It is your responsibility to give them*

> *strength and detachment. Shoulder not, therefore, responsibilities which are not yours.*
> - ***Be not in any way discouraged, brother of old, if you find the upward way stiff and hard to climb. You are in good company and are not alone. You have much to give and I would urge you to give it, and in so doing I would urge you not to become unduly aware of your efficient giving.***
> - ***The cry of the neophyte is, 'Tell me, tell me. Then I will change, I will accept anything that is said, but tell me.' The cry of the disciple is: 'Aid the work, forget yourself. The world needs you.' So let your horizon be wide and your humility great.***
> - ***At the centre of a great tornado is a point of peace. Thus, does the story go. It can be found. And thus, with all the storms of life, they lead you to peace if you are not a leaf.***
> - ***Be not afraid of loneliness. The soul that cannot stand alone has naught to give."***

There is much that I have spoken of in this discourse that may be incredible to many. And that is because what has been revealed has been for so long the target of an insidious agenda to erase our true history and ensure that we are controlled more easily, because of deliberate measures to keep us ignorant as a collective.

Perhaps the most difficult thing to come to terms with for many will be the challenges of the second hall of learning – the astral plane, as mentioned in Chapter 8 – *Exiting the Matrix – The Red Pill*. Even if that is such a stretch of incredulity for you that your mind wants to defend you by rejecting the acceptance of it, please remember that the mind slays the real, and don't then dismiss the whole message of this book because your mind at this stage is unable to reconcile what has been revealed to you.

With regards to those that read this book, there will be largely four different types of people, as '*Leaves of Moryas Garden 1924*' explains:

> *"424. At present you encounter four types of people:*
> *The first is fighting under Our Shield;*
> *The second fights without protection, yet already is terminating the stream of karma;*

The third raves wildly, blinded by the dark veil of its fate;
The fourth comprises the enemies of the Light.

The first will understand the call
The second will quiver with expectancy
The third will stupidly turn the head away
And the fourth will answer arrow for arrow."

And if it is that you are reading these words and you belong to the first type, then as you are carrying out your higher work it is wise to keep in the forefront of your mind:

"435. Some will come and say, "We know."
You should reply, "Good! Since you know, return to your home."
Some will come more aggressively and say, "We know who stands behind you."
Say to them, "Good! If you know, you will not speak thus."
Some will come to play dice on the steps of the Temple and will cast lots about you.
Say to them, "Pass on, people, lest lightning strike you here."
But here comes one who says to you, "I do not know,
And here I have brought all of my possessions with me." What shall I do with them?
Say to him, "Cross the threshold. We will find a place for you at the long table; for if you do not know, then you shall know."

It will be of interest for you to pay attention to the possible level of intensity of retaliation of certain parties to these works, once it has started to circulate among the populous. Pay attention to the offices from which these possible attacks may come – and by that very act, the disproportional intensity of the return arrow, you will understand where darkness is at the helm under the veil of false light!

Concurrence

"Science has made only feeble attempts in comparison to what it should have done to restore humanity to its rightful place in nature. Relatively, it has just begun to reduce a portion of the Great Architects' plan to that form which we can understand and use in our daily life. It concerns itself only with certain aspects of the Divine Architects' plan. The immaterial aspects, those qualities commonly referred to as spiritual and psychic are but casually dealt with – or not at all. First causes, or what are generally known as metaphysical propositions, such as "Why are we here?" and "What are the ends which we should attain in life?" are held not to be within its scope.

Religion on the other hand, in its declarations, its dogmas, rites and practices, has often held it to be beneath the dignity of its traditions to make inquiry into divine causes. We therefore are obliged to have blind faith in many matters, or to accept only those truths which materialistically inclined science is capable of demonstrating.

It is plain, therefore, that our duty is to become the middle builders. As such, we must learn a great deal about what concerns both the material and immaterial portions of the Divine Architects' plan."

-Extract from a Martinist Manuscript. (Courtesy of the Ancient Mystical Order Rosae Crucis -A.M.O.R.C)

And so it may indeed come to pass that what I have written here may cause a stir. If people react out of fear and inflexibility, which is of course possible, this message may be subjected to scorn, anger, and miscomprehension from people. And the rebuttals and the denials and the shouts of *'all nonsense'* may come – especially about the challenges of the second hallway and the identification of divine personages with initiates, will more than likely come from people that will defend their beliefs to the end with bitter resistance.

However, I cannot deny the responsibility I have to my higher wisdom and soul guidance at the expense of the whims of my personal desires in this life. Even if what is written herewith resonates only with a few and causes them to build upon what I have built without them having to learn through unnecessary pain and wasted time and suffering, then my efforts here will not have been in vain. The love I have in my heart for all of you I cannot explain. It is not conditional, I do not care if you love yourself or not, or what you think about yourself at present. You don't need to convince me of your worth, for as you are, *I am*. Perhaps the tools in this discourse will provide you with what you need to be able to change how you feel about yourself and see what is really going on.

My concern is only for the establishment of brotherhood, where race, social status, gender, and sexuality does not discriminate. Where tolerance, patience, teamwork, sharing, and universality of mind and heart are the guiding force of future generations that serve to eliminate fear, selfishness, and corruption, and work to bring this planet back into a state of harmony, a state of equilibrium, where man achieves a natural equilibrium with our glorious host, Mother Earth – Gaia. I include now some words of guidance from an ancient intelligence. These are words of guidance for humanity:

> *"Remember that life is a series of what you may call challenges, but these are not in continuous motion. There have to be periods of quiet reflection. Time to think, breathe and feel and to understand how far you have travelled on this, your journey. Life begins with reason, it has purpose, but the greatest shame is that you forget these reasons almost as soon as you are born. For life on Earth, which is so full of complex issues of survival, causes us not to remember that there is indeed purpose behind the chaos I call life. However, as you are aware, from chaos comes order. There is purpose and there are opportunities for*

you to grow or stay in what I call a state of neediness. Life is full of many materialistic views and therefore occupies your mind more than the spiritual pathways you should be taking. When the time is right, change will occur. Take my blessings and prosper well."

– The Great Initiator

Source: Pathworkings with the Egyptian Gods, Page and Malique, page 96.

Seek and you will find. You will of course note that I have only revealed four of the twenty-two symbols that comprise the summary of the forty books of Thoth – symbols which further explain the mysteries: the great mysteries of this life on the earthly plane and subtler planes of reality and the deeper mechanics of their workings.

When your intention is pure, you will ally yourself with higher forces, which may in time open the door to further knowledge. Perhaps, in time, I may be led to reveal more of the symbols to help you on your path. At the moment, however, the four symbols given will suffice, for it is man's destiny to consciously spiritualise matter, and this has been the true teaching in all of the sacred scriptures of the world. It has just been misinterpreted – in some cases through innocent human fallibility and in other cases for reasons that are not so innocent. In the Keys of Enoch®: Key 308 further explains:

18. People will speak of the scriptures, but they will not understand the codes. Their consciousness will be crucified to the 'cross of time' so that the 'cross of transfiguration' will not be able to operate within them to reveal the 'revelation' of YHWH that must come to pass to break the seals of the Old Age.

19. They will not appreciate the scriptures of Light because they will understand scripture only in terms of mythology, from teachers who are teaching from a historical standpoint being oblivious to the higher spiritual truths.

And so it is that this **message is an outpouring of divine love,** is a restoration of the spiritual truths concerning God's original covenant with Abraham and Israel and through Jesus Christ. A restoration and a reconciliation achieved through correct communication and understanding of the governing dynamics of this reality; the true teachings of the scriptures of light, based upon the seven octaves of vibration/consciousness, the seven Principles of Hermes Trismegistus, and the sacred law of seven!

Like white light shining through a prism, so it is that your consciousness separates from the Father and becomes an individualised expression.

Figure 67: White light through a prism symbolising divine radiations branching into myriad expressions of life. Association Source: N. S. Elijah.

And so it is then, that the gift of a supernatural appreciative love is bestowed to us, through a deep recognition of 'sameness' of being one. Just look at our modern understanding of quantum mechanics. We are at the very core building blocks of life deeply connected. As Christ claimed to be the 'way' or the 'path', man also becomes the path, as we take up the cross of our crucified spirits and consciousness from the beams of time and space and 'follow him', live as he lived, and set out to climb the mount of initiation, forsaking the desires of our individual personalities, and listening to the higher self, surrendering our individual will to a higher will to live at the 6th and 7th octaves of vibration/consciousness.

The Three Appearances of Elijah

In the first embodiment, Elijah was a representative of God as Creator, in the house of Israel.

In the second embodiment, Elijah came and went unrecognised, baptising people in the river Jordan and was a representative of God the Father.

In the third embodiment, Elijah is to come to Earth to reconcile the first two missions of these two previous embodiments. And as the living bridge represent and have authority from both God the Father and our elder brother Christ.

The holy book of the Muslims – The Qur'an calls Elijah – Ilyas or Ilya. The Jewish holy text of the Haggadah calls Elijah, Eliahu – 'The Bird of Heaven', because like a bird he flies through the world and appears where a sudden Divine interference is necessary. And in the Bible there is mention that one day... he would return again.

For this is what is meant by the words in Malachi:

"Behold, I am going to send you Elijah the Prophet before the coming of the great and terrible day of the Lord. He will restore the hearts of the Fathers to their children and the hearts of their children to their fathers, so that I will not smite the land with a curse."

The Fathers are of course those Patriarchs that taught the true covenant of God, of how man relates to God and God to Man: Noah, Abraham, Isaac, Jacob, Moses and the previous divine messengers such as Krishna, Buddha, and Jesus. The 'hearts of the fathers', are the original teachings from direct experience – from the original covenants and experiential revelations of the Patriarchs.

The Son's refer to those who taught the righteous ways of God- the disciples, the priests and pastors that taught a long time after Abraham and Christ. The 'hearts of the children', refer to the degree of accurate comprehension of original instruction of the Patriarchs, by those that carried on the holy work thereafter.

For nearly 2,000 years the 'hearts of the fathers' have not been aligned to the 'hearts of the children'. The original message and instruction was misunderstood and mistaught, resulting in loss of comprehension of the original simple truths preserved in allegorical camouflage.

Because of the darkening effect of the Yugas (the ages of the Earth), on the level of man's intellect and consciousness at the time of these world teachers; well-meaning faithful disciples such as Paul, who was known as 'the rock of the foundation of the church', unfortunately tried to carry on the message of Christ to the best of his ability, however, somehow his efforts were not carried through in a fashion that honoured the original instruction of Christ. And this institution was built on a **misinterpretation of the original message of Christ**, and down through the centuries that have followed this error has yet to have been corrected.

Understand the teaching that Christ was a great initiate, that Krishna was a great initiate, that Buddha was a great initiate, that Muhammad was a great initiate, and that they achieved the goal of the spiritualisation of matter to varying degrees, and as they did so, they pointed out and tried their very best to communicate that their very achievement was also the potential for all of mankind.

Thus this message **is a call for all religious and civil leaders the world over to repent and to acknowledge the misinterpretation of Abraham, The Law of Moses, and Christ's original message,** and its deliberate twisting through a dark agenda of control over centuries of deliberate historical distortion to mislead and control and disempower the citizens of the Earth.

If you can open your hearts and empty the cups of your mind that are filled to the brim with the ideas 'they want you to think', a product of their propaganda, then it is in the pages of this message, that you will find knowledge and understanding of the true message of the gospels, as originally set forth by our elder brother Jesus Christ. This goal is attained through sacrifice, through the superimposition of a higher voice over the animalistic tendencies and of the surrendering of our individual wills to the divine will. Not my will be done, but *thy* will be done.

Keys of Enoch® 107 explains how it is possible for a master to return:

41. Those who are called the ascended masters have originally descended from the higher orders serving the heavenly hierarchies to teach in the lower worlds.

43. The manner in which the physical bodies are chosen to house the ascended masters depends upon their previous work in biological cycles.

As this message comes to a close, I ask you to forget me. Instead, the focal point should be the message itself. Listen to the message in the pages of this book, weigh its content in your heart, apply the message to your own life and see how this resonates with your own truth.

From this place of reconciliation and equality, ask yourself, *what is your divine purpose?* What is it that you have come to Earth to build or to witness? How have you intended to help humanity? How have you intended to advance humanity? Or to help heal the Earth? And then without further ado, get to work – with love. The true essence of work is love made manifest.

A Call to Inner Revolution

Now you are aware from where man has come and to where it is man will go, and why indeed we are here. With this knowledge then, you can build intelligently. For this was the message of Christ and should have been the original foundation stone of the Church. For there never need have been an intermediary between you and God. As I said at the beginning of this discourse in the dedication – **for all of humanity, may you rest and find peace in this knowledge and then set yourself to task, for the world needs you!**

Together, we are invincible, and we can shift the direction that the world is heading in. We can fix the environmental issues and the social issues if we unite and achieve that much-needed spiritual and cultural transformation. We must not listen to the loud voices of fear. Fear is the primary weapon of the dark.

Up until now, mankind has struggled with listening to the pure wisdom of their hearts because there was for them no visible agent of accountability for immoral actions. However, you must recognise that this planet Earth you find yourself inhabiting is like a transparent glass fishbowl, and there are many watching you in the subtle and fiery worlds, taking note of your choices and actions and how you choose to use or misuse your knowledge and power, and there is no escaping the consequences of apostasy.

I challenge all the world leaders of government and the multinational and Fortune 500 companies to do this simple exercise: find a picture of yourself as an infant. Look deeply into the eyes of a picture of yourself (for the eyes are the window to the soul). What do you see? When you connect to your true essence; an essence not tainted by the gradual abandonment of principles through life's challenges or in the pursuit of wealth at any cost, and not tainted by the forced silencing of the heart!

What do the eyes of your infant-self communicate to you? And as you look at that innocence, ask yourself: Do you think that younger you would be proud of who you have become? And if the answer is a resounding 'NO', then do something about it. It is not too late to right the wrongs. It is not too late for redemption.

For verily, as Christ said, we must become childlike to enter the kingdom of heaven, and it is easier for a camel to pass through the eye of a needle than for a rich man to enter the kingdom of heaven. The kingdom of heaven is to be allowed to pass through to Osiris, and not be devoured by the 'devourer', as understood in ancient Egypt as the forces of karma and rebirth. **How did you fare with the forty-two questions at the weighing of the heart in Chapter 6?** The earthly plane is an illusion. The physical senses lie. Your mind slays the real.

In understanding this, then perhaps decisions will be made not from the position of what is going to drive stocks up or make your shareholders get a bigger profit, but decisions will be made from the position of *what is right? What is in the highest integrity? What is going to be best for the Earth?* For as the Native Americans say:

> *"Only when the last tree has been cut down, only when the last river has been poisoned and when the last fish has died will humans realise that they cannot eat money!"*

For those of you in positions of power, whether state, corporate, or ecclesiastical, you carry a great responsibility – not only to this generation, but to the ones that come afterwards. Make your decisions not from the position of what is best for your pocket or the survival of your institutions, but what is best for your great, great, great grandchildren. Do you want them to have an Earth to live upon? For the way things are heading, this, at the moment, seems very unlikely.

The Earth is at a very crucial time now, and I know that there are lights hidden in the darkness. I know that there are so many souls that pray for a better way and know that a better way is possible, and yet they take the road most travelled, more easily travelled, and they make an unholy sacrifice of their integrity because it is deemed easier and delivers a faster material return. But at what price?

We cannot continue this way. All the mining and the raping and pillaging of the Earth of her life's blood, the deforestation and the under-the-table golden handshakes for the officials to turn a blind eye, the fracking of the land and the cruel factory production of animals for slaughter, the modification of the genetics of the foodstuffs and the wiping out, or rarity of being able to plant non-modified heritage seeds. The gradual relinquishing of our freedoms, the control of health measures with forced vaccination and a push for the microchipping of the population under the guise of security or safety or convenience. Open your eyes, take a good look and see what is going on. This is the work of darkness and a dark agenda of control.

As we remember from Chapter 8 the words of the guiding brotherhood of light – The Great White Brotherhood:

> *"Right now, there is no one who can get by without courage. Only utter madness whispers that everything will fall into place of its own accord—that cannot happen! Being unable to govern by the basic principles, the dark forces have violated them; therefore, we must close ranks and*

go forward undivided in everything. The warriors should understand that the spiritual tension of the present time is no longer at the level of the Subtle World but is already approaching the Fiery World. The Teacher is reminding us: not terror but a sense of the majestic should fill the hearts of the warriors of Armageddon."

You must work together from the position of you being each other's brother or sister, and then there is no such thing as a stranger under God!

I call to every member of the military and police forces now: if you can clearly see the corruption or evidence of a sinister hidden agenda being the mechanism at work for orders from your superiors and their superiors and so on, and you think that you are alone and you have no power to affect the change that you know in your heart is necessary, then remember that as the Dalai Lama says:

"If you think you are too small to make a difference, then try sleeping in a room with a mosquito!"

Now, this takes courage, this agenda of controlling and disempowering the people comes from the top down, this agenda is about frequency control. So, I ask you, brother and sister of great courage, to have courage to do what is right. It may mean that you take your own journey over the bridge of swords and it may mean suffering, or it may mean your death as the cost for the greater good. I am not asking you to be careless with your life. Only you know what is right in your soul.

And for that matter, I call for the revision of your religions, for they are all based on the governing dynamics that have been put before you in this message. **It is the same Divine Chair you are all looking at and worshipping – you just have your own interpretation about what your messengers told you of 'how to worship.' It is tired, it is dogmatic, and mostly it is completely inaccurate and unnecessary and only serves to force wedges of division and bitterness and comparison and superiority between you all. It is time to unite as** one race, as one brotherhood and sisterhood. **Stop the wars and the fighting and the religious discrimination. Stop the focus on the misinterpreted words of the messages of love of the messengers that have come before me!**

Understand very deeply the governing dynamics. Understand very deeply the fact that God is inside each of us, and that means women as well as men. Look at the Star of David. Look at the true meaning of the intersecting of the masculine and feminine principles (as upward and downward facing triangles) and see the natural equality inherent in this divine design and then be ashamed of the treatment of women all over the world.

Women never have needed to hide their faces – the true reason for this interpretation is because the misguided patriarchy found it easier to cover the faces of the objects of their lusts rather than develop the will-power to eradicate their unbridled lusts from their wicked hearts! Understand this now! Be deeply ashamed and repent. Repent and seek immediately to right your wrongs. Make it public and abandon your primitive religious laws and, for God's sakes, grow up, for your interpretation of the law and of the true message is wrong. Of course, you are not going to like hearing that, but the truth is hard to hear sometimes. Remember that love is not quick to anger. Remember the actual message of Ptah-Hotep, Krishna, Buddha, Christ and Muhammed from Chapter 2. Quell your anger, still your hearts, in humility accept your error, and repent.

For then you will see that by our decisions, made in accordance with the golden precepts of old, that God will become more visible inside of you and that light will just burst out from you. Stop thinking that you must evangelise people to Christ's message, or Krishna's message or Buddha's message or Muhammed's message. Because **for many thousands of years you have had the message wrong!** You have not understood the message. When you actually understand the message, you will see that it is all the same message!

The Dalai Lama, the Bodhisattva of Compassion, has it right: Kindness. Compassion. Tolerance. Non-violence.

This is the way forward. But, you see, we needed to intellectually understand how all of this fits together before we truly see the wisdom of this. Kindness and compassion, tolerance and non-violence – not from a position of morality or ethics, but from a **deep recognition of the governing laws of the universe and the recognition of what lies hidden within each human heart... God.** And with this recognition comes 'supernatural appreciative love.'

Final Thoughts

Growing up as a Christian, particularly in the Western world, a picture is painted for us of Jesus. A kind and remarkable man, walking the sands of Palestine two-thousand years ago and giving to his followers the Lord's Prayer:

> *'Our Father who art in Heaven*
> *Hallowed be Thy name*
> *Thy kingdom come, Thy Will be done*
> *On Earth as it is in Heaven*
> *Give us this day, our daily bread*
> *And forgive us our trespasses*
> *As we forgive those who trespass against us*
> *Lead us not into temptation*
> *But deliver us from Evil.'*

Whilst this prayer still engenders a sense of calm faith and adoration for God (whatever we conceive God to be), we generally tend to forget that the man that spoke these words of the Lord's Prayer, that taught the Lord's Prayer, did not speak English. And as we have shown in Chapter 8 that words, written and spoken, are imbued with a frequency of consciousness and energy. In order to understand the real Christ and his mission, it becomes vitally important, then, to understand the original Lord's Prayer in Hebrew and Aramaic – and thus be able to attune to the light codes in the power of the words, and awaken the dormant light codes within ourselves.

With the courtesy of Dr J. J. Hurtak and the Academy for Future Science, I reproduce now for your benefit, the Lord's Prayer in Hebrew and Aramaic. I ask you to bring these words into your heart as you speak each line, and imagine a effulgent light connecting you to the hierarchy of light as you commune to the God within yourself and realise that you are a part of something truly wonderful. You are not isolated as a lonely individual soul struggling to come out of darkness and trying to find a light. No, you, my dear brothers and sisters, are an outpouring of the Father's divine love, and when you take refuge in your holy tabernacle – your divine heart – you will come to realise that you are the living light, a part of a vast family of light that exists throughout the cosmos.

Hebrew translation (in brackets is pronunciation):

AVINU SHEBA- SHAMAYYIM (a-*vee*-nu sheh-ba sha-*ma*-yim)
'Our Father who art in the heavens'

YITKADASH SHEMAYCHA (yit-ka-*dash* sheh-*may*-cha)
'Let Thy name be sanctified (hallowed)'

TAVO MALKUTAYCHA (ta-*vo* mal-ku-*tay*-cha)
'May thy kingdom come'

YE ASSEH RETZONCHA (yeh-ah-*seh* rih-*tzone*-cha)
'Let your will take place'

K'MO BA – SHAMAYYIM KAIN BA ARETZ (koh-*moe* ba-sha-*ma*-yim kane ba-*ah*-retz)
'As it is to the heavens, so also upon the Earth'

ET LECHEM HUKAYNU TEN-LONU HA- YOM (et *leh*-chem chu-*kay*-nu ten *lah*-nu ha-*yome*)
'Give us today, our daily bread (of life) for this day'

U-SLACH LONU ET HOVOTHEYNU (oo-slach *lah*-nu et cho-vo-*tay*-nu)
'Forgive us our sins (debts)'

KA- ASHER SOLACHNU GAM ANACHNU L'HA-YAVAYNU (kah ah-*share* so-*lach*-nugam ah-*nach*-nu lih-cha-ya-*vay*-nu)
'As we also have forgiven our debtors'

VIH-AL TIVI-AYNU LI-Y'DAY NISA-YON (vih-*al* tih-vee-*ay*-nu lee yih-*day* nih-sah-*yone*)
'And lead us not into the hands of temptation'

KEE IM HAL-TZAYNU MIN HARAH (kee im chal-*tzay*-nu min ha-*rah*)
'And deliver us from evil'

Aramaic translation:

Aboon da-bash-ma-ya

neth-ka-dash shamakh

tai-tha mal-koo- thakh

neh-we tzev-ya-nakh

ay-kan-na da-bash-ma-ya af bar-ah

hav lan lak-ma de-soon-ka-nan yo-ma-na wash-book lan

ka-vi-ne ay-ken-na da-uf

hanan sha-booka-n el-hay-a-vine

u-la ta-lahn el-anes-ya-na

ela pes- on men bee –sha

When you let the holy vibrations settle over you, you will feel an immense sense of simultaneous peace and inner empowerment that will help to raise you off of the cross beams of time and space, as the light codes work their magic on your DNA and you begin to awaken the divine template – the Adam Kadmon. It is then that you realise where the voice of the 'serpent of frequency control' has held you trapped in materialistic lower consciousness in the past, and it is then you realise that you no longer need to be so trapped, as you embrace your divine birthright.

It is my hope that what has been revealed in this teaching will serve to assist people to break down the walls of the established societal prison, and through recognition of the flow of subtle forces and their effects in the body, that right human relations are established, **because with the force of light** – information and correct explanation – then **the force of love** – specifically love unconditional – a supernatural appreciative love – **is not misunderstood.** Let us all then, focus on the majestic, strive for beauty to be born in our hearts and to manifest in the depths of our spirit, and sprinkle kindness and goodness wherever it is we go.

The Sacred Alignment

In the movie, *The Matrix*, Morpheus says the following:

> *"People have become so hopelessly dependent on the system, so inured that they will fight to protect it."*

In my daily life I encounter such people that believe the mainstream media narrative so completely that they think that the idea of a covert operation to repress the consciousness of humanity is a stupid conspiracy theory. They spout that their opinions are based on empirical evidence, but they do not realise that that so-called evidence is manipulated to sound authentic, and that these powers censor the real information from being widely spread. Today, with our eyes open, we can readily observe some social media platforms and online video streaming channels actively shutting down anything that does not support this vicious mainstream narrative of attempted control.

For over 10 years I have planted seeds and attempted to plant seeds into people's consciousness with the hope that that light would show them another way, show them the underlying reality – but sadly it seems – largely these headstrong opinions have not wavered for them to be able to see clearly. Some arrogantly do not even look.

Their heart emanations are so negative and forceful that I prefer not to be in their presence. It is interesting to me because they have visible love for their immediate families, for their small close circle of the near and dear, but that is the limit of their love. It is locked down, and they do not know the treasure of the heart – that can hold a love that embraces not only all humanity but all of creation.

In my early 40s now, I have been led to some amazing insights and knowledge that I believe if people held in their hearts daily, that we would indeed be able to usher in the new age and be victorious over the covert dark agenda to repress human consciousness to keep us as slaves – dependent on the material, physical and economic models that form the current foundation to their plan/system.

In Chapter 6, *Initiation*, I unmasked the true interpretation of Revelations in the Bible of the meaning of the shining city of Jerusalem being created on Earth (through the correct redirection, channeling, and application of internal forces at work in humanity), this however was just part of the explanation. There is another level to this that is much more esoteric and far more beautiful, that I think is of inestimable value to the spiritual evolution of mankind and to the current trajectory of the planet Earth.

As a man takes himself in hand, holds himself to account and fights to overcome his lower nature, he is by the nature of the conditions of the way itself, conditioned to be an instrument of the outpouring of divine love. A love that is not self-seeking, a love that embraces all humankind and all creation – a supernatural appreciative love.

And these conditions of the way are founded upon four pillars of wisdom. Next to each pillar, or rather a part of each pillar, stands a mighty Archangel and inscribed on each pillar is a prerequisite/ commandment/ quality that the disciple/initiate must not only adopt, but embody before they can become a being functioning at the levels of the 6th and 7th octaves of vibration and achieve the sacred alignment.

I have put together *Figure 68* over the page to further unmask the esoteric wisdom hidden in the passages of Revelation from the Bible. It reveals how to become a true disciple of the Christ consciousness and how the New Jerusalem will be built on Earth.

And so I leave you here with much to ponder on, much to analyse and self-reflect, and if you catch a glimpse of a spark within yourself in your heart, nurture it into a flame and in time it will grow into an all-encompassing, protecting, and sustaining spiritual fire from which others can be brought in and sheltered from the cold and kept warm by your radiance, as you become the living light!

"For like the once mysterious source of the Nile, the source of all religions and philosophies now known to the world has been for many ages forgotten and lost to men, but it is at last found!"

May the light shine on your path and may you recognise that the light of the great fire is hidden within us. As Thoth – the Master of Space and Time – says, *"Man is a star bound to a mountain!"*

The star is of course our spirit, our innate spiritual potential our divine spark. The mountain is the limitation of the purveying consciousness stuck in matter at this time on this Earth in a physical body. And without *internal* revolution, the chains that bind you to the mountain, and that stop you from soaring and blazing brightly will ever remain. The choice is yours, dear friend. With the love, light, and life of my soul I hope that you ever strive to walk in the light, so that it may pass unto you its many blessings. It is united that we will realise the kingdom of heaven here on Earth – 'The New Jerusalem.'

As we look upon each man and woman as our fellow brother and sister in humanity, we realise that the effects of the falling of the Tower of Babel – dispersing language and limiting comprehension – which have in the past served to divide us, does no longer need to do so. It is interesting to me that the undercurrent of consciousness of my home nation expresses the stance we need to take from a worldly position with amazing clarity:

'We are one, but we are many, and from all the lands on Earth we come. We share a dream, and sing with one voice, I am, you are, we are... Australian.'

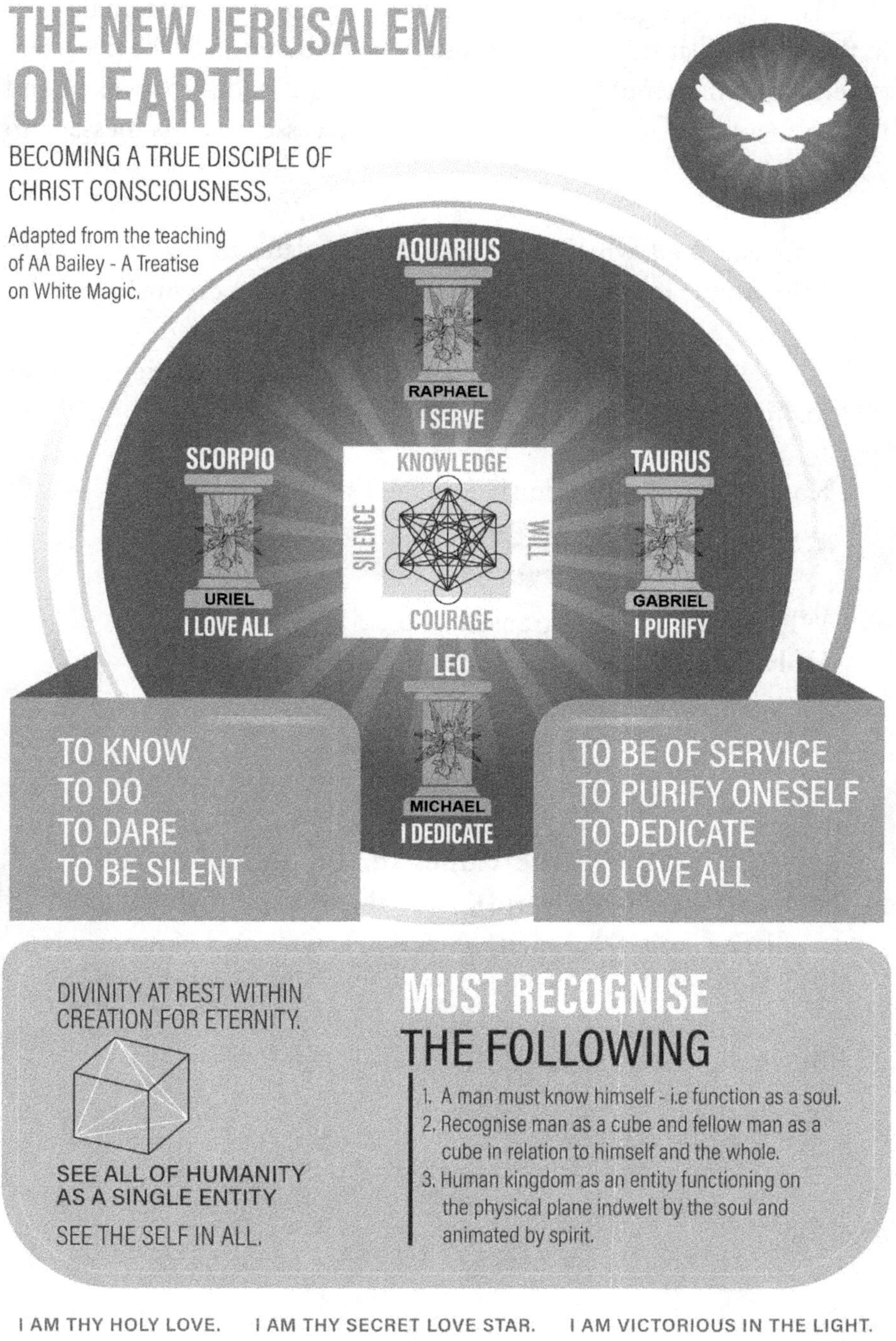

THE NEW JERUSALEM ON EARTH
BECOMING A TRUE DISCIPLE OF CHRIST CONSCIOUSNESS.

Adapted from the teaching of AA Bailey - A Treatise on White Magic.

AQUARIUS
RAPHAEL
I SERVE

SCORPIO
URIEL
I LOVE ALL

KNOWLEDGE
SILENCE · WILL
COURAGE

TAURUS
GABRIEL
I PURIFY

LEO
MICHAEL
I DEDICATE

TO KNOW
TO DO
TO DARE
TO BE SILENT

TO BE OF SERVICE
TO PURIFY ONESELF
TO DEDICATE
TO LOVE ALL

DIVINITY AT REST WITHIN CREATION FOR ETERNITY.

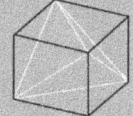

SEE ALL OF HUMANITY AS A SINGLE ENTITY
SEE THE SELF IN ALL.

MUST RECOGNISE THE FOLLOWING

1. A man must know himself - i.e function as a soul.
2. Recognise man as a cube and fellow man as a cube in relation to himself and the whole.
3. Human kingdom as an entity functioning on the physical plane indwelt by the soul and animated by spirit.

I AM THY HOLY LOVE.   I AM THY SECRET LOVE STAR.   I AM VICTORIOUS IN THE LIGHT.

Figure 68: The New Jerusalem.
Source and Copyright: N. S. Elijah

And so it is, I guess, I understand why I chose to reincarnate here in this country, at this 'time' in order to be coloured with the necessary experiences that would allow my dormant light codes to awaken and for me to awaken to my dharma and be the vessel for this message to you.

Namaste नमस्ते, which from Sanskrit translates to:
"The divine in me recognises and honours the divine in you."

Al-salamu alaykum السلام عليكم, which from Arabic translates to: **"Peace be upon you."**

Kodoish Kodoish Kodoish Adonai Tseybayoth –
קדוש קדוש קדוש יי צבאות מלא
כל הארץ כבודו:
Which from Hebrew translates to:
Holy, Holy, Holy is the Lord God of Hosts.

In nomine Patris et Filii et Spiritus Sancti
Which from Latin translates to:

In the name of the Father (divine thought), The Son (the divine word), and the Holy Spirit (the divine spirit). Amen, Amen, Amen, and Amen. (Amun-RA).

In cosmic service, now and always – Elijah.

The Great Invocation

"From the point of Light within the Mind of God,
Let light stream forth into the minds of men.
Let Light descend on Earth.

From the point of Love within the Heart of God,
Let love stream forth into the hearts of men.
May Christ (consciousness) return to Earth.

From the centre where the Will of God is known,
Let purpose guide the little wills of men –
The purpose which the Masters know and serve.

From the centre which we call the race of men,
Let the Plan of Love and Light work out
And may it seal the door where evil dwells.

Amen, Amen, Amen, and Amen."

('The above invocation or prayer does not belong to any person or group but to all Humanity' – Alice A Bailey)

The Eight Thoughts of a Great Person – by Kalu Rinpoche

"Through the power of compassionate truth of the supreme refuges, and through the root of virtuous action, and through pure noble motivation, may I alone, by my own efforts, dispel the sufferings, whatever they may be, of all beings who pervade space.

Through the excellence of virtuous activity in this world and beyond it, may I fulfil the hopes and desires of beings just as they conceive them.

May my body, flesh, blood, skin and all the rest of me benefit all sentient beings in appropriate ways.

May the sufferings of beings, who all have been my mothers, dissolve into me; may my happiness and virtue be obtained by them.

As long as the world remains, may there not arise in my mind even for an instant, the thought of harming others.

May I exert myself diligently in benefiting beings, not letting up for even a moment because of sadness or fatigue or anything similar.

May I be able to give effortlessly whatever enjoyment is desired to all beings who are thirsty and hungry and needy and poor.

May I take upon myself the great burdens, the difficult-to-bear sufferings of beings… and may they be liberated."

Wishing you blessings of Peace Profound, may you strive to walk in the light

www.thesacredalignment.com

APPENDICES

Elijah

**Page 582 of The Book of Knowledge: The Keys of Enoch®
explains:** *Jesus-Moses-Elijah as – "The Anointed Paradise Trinity sent into the world of Man to activate the Light thresholds of the Father's Program of 'Salvation' so that Man can ascend from world of Light to world of Light according to the blueprint of YHWH's Living Word. The Collective Messiah as a 'Collective transfiguration' which shows that Jesus did not work by himself, but within a 'Brotherhood of Light' which has its higher meaning, according to Enoch, in the three-fold giving of the star code to the human evolution. Moses gives man the "Torah Or" which he receives from the 'Living Light'; Elijah demonstrates oneness with the 'Vehicle of Light' which attaches our physical universe to other universes of messengers of 'the Living Light'. Jesus demonstrates the 'collective messiahship' with the "firstborn seed" of the higher overself worlds, whereby the 'Man of holiness' brings the garment of the Christ body to those appointed to be 'risen sons and daughters of Light' in the regeneration and resurrection of this world of intelligence. Jesus activates the Sonship of Yahweh for everlasting world dominion through his 'resurrection by Light'. Know then, that just as Moses-Jesus-Elijah came to the world through the transfiguration of Light (Matt. 17:3), so they will return together to quicken the saints in that day when the Earth shakes and Passover is not seen as the Passover of Man, but as the 'Sons of the Heavens' that will appear in the skies."*

The Parable of the Growing Seed

Mark 4:26-29

[26] And he said, So is the kingdom of God, as if a man should cast seed into the ground;

[27] And should sleep, and rise night and day, and the seed should spring and grow up, he knoweth not how.

[28] For the earth bringeth forth fruit of herself; first the blade, then the ear, after that the full corn in the ear.

[29] But when the fruit is brought forth, immediately he putteth in the sickle, because the harvest is come.

*Night and day refer to a single incarnation. The sickle being put to use represents death – the transition into the next incarnation.

Major Arcana Tarot Cards

Are by Arthur Edward Waite with Illustrations by Pamela Coleman Smith (1909). The illustrations of the tarot cards used in this book by all international laws are in the Public Domain from 1985 and 2012, and as this book is published in 2021, when the tarot cards are now part of the Public Domain, there has been no breach of copyright by their inclusion in this book.

The changes made to the images to indicate hidden symbolism by no means deface the original meaning of the cards, but rather reveal more of the hidden symbolism inherent in their design, known and unknown or lost at their re-conception in 1909 by Pamela Coleman Smith and by Arthur Edward Waite and Son – both of the Order of the Golden Dawn.

As revealed in this manuscript, the Major Arcana Tarot cards have changed over time, since their original conception, as they preserve in pictographic symbolism the summary of the lost 40 Books of Thoth as taught by the Ancient Khemitian/Egyptian Priests/Followers of Horus.

The additions made by the author have been done so to help remove the obscurity with which they were designed, in order to be a better aid of teaching and making the public more knowledgeable, and more readily understand the Sacred Truths preserved in this symbolism in this better form of instruction.

Janana's

Adarsa Jnana: Wheel-like crown ornament – *mirror-like pristine awareness*.

Mirror Knowledge – awareness reflecting the thing observed without alteration.

Prateyaveksana Jnana: Earrings – *pristine awareness of discernment*
Analytical intelligence, deduction in formal logic.

Samata Jnana: Necklace – *pristine awareness of total sameness*
Recognition of the similarities of things and grouping them/classification.

Tathata Jnana: Bracelets – *pristine awareness of the ultimate dimension of phenomena*
Knowledge of suchness – the end goal – becoming one with the thing observed.

Kalu Rinpoche

From the introduction of *"The Dharma That Illuminates All Beings Impartially Like the Light of the Sun and the Moon,"* By Kalu Rinpoche 1986. Pages 1 and 2.

"Kalu Rinpoche was born in the district of Tresho Gang chi Rawa in the Hor region of Kham, Eastern Tibet, in 1905. This mountainous area, bordering on China, is known for the independent spirit of its people. His father, Karma Lekshe Drayang [karma legs bshad sgra dbyangs], the thirteenth Ratak Palzang Tulku, was noted for his skill in the practice of medicine, as well as for literary accomplishments and mastery of Vajrayana meditation practice.

He and his wife, Drolkar Chung Chung [sgrol dkar chung chung], Rinpoche's mother, were students of Jamgon Kongtrul Lodro Taye ['jam mgon kong sprul blo gros mtha' yas], Jamyang Chentse Wangpo ['jam dbyangs mkhyen brtse dbang po] and Mipham Rinpoche, all founders and leaders of then may [ris med] movement which revitalised the religious life of Tibet towards the end of the 19th Century by minimizing the importance of sectarian differences and emphasizing the common ground of the lineages and stressing the importance of meditation.

Both husband and wife were devoted to practice, and immediately after their marriage undertook a religious retreat. They saw little of each other during this period, but one night together each dreamed that they were visited by the great meditation teacher and scholar, Jamgon Kongtrul, who announced that he was coming to stay with them and asked to be given a room. Not long afterwards Drolkar Chung Chung discovered she was pregnant. The dream had been auspicious; the pregnancy passed joyfully, without complications. Drolkar Chung Chung continued to work with her husband, and was gathering medicinal herbs with him one day when she realised the baby would soon be born. **As they hurried back to their house, they saw the sky full of rainbows. Such signs were interpreted in the neighboring countryside as portending the birth of a special incarnation.**

Conventionally, a tulku would have been taken to be raised in a monastery at the earliest possible age, but Karma Lekshe Drayang refused to follow this course. If the boy were not a high incarnation, he said, the training would be wasted; if he were, he would be quite capable of seeking the appropriate teachers and education for himself. That is just what he did.

'In his early years,' the young man, 'when he had awakened the excellent habits of virtue, and abandoned concerns for possessions and pleasures of this life, wandered at times in the wilderness of mountains and gorges, cliffs and crags. Spontaneously, uncontrived longing and resolution arose in him to nurture Dharma practice.'

Travelling freely in the mountains, Rinpoche would chant mantras, blessing the animals, fish or insects he might encounter."

MMR Triple Shot Vaccine

MMR Triple Shot Vaccine causatively linked to Autism – 2016 Movie '*Vaxxed – From Cover up to Catastrophe***':**

In the year 2016, a whistle-blower movie called '*Vaxxed*' was censored at a Major Film Festival. The reason: A senior scientist Dr

Thompson of CDC has come forth and said, according to Dr Andrew Wakefield, 'Dr Thompson said he was in charge of a study where we tested a hypothesis where MMR (Measles Mumps Rubella – Triple Shot) vaccination was causatively associated with autism and we hid the findings for 14 years. And we have known for 14 years that this vaccine is causatively associated with autism and we have concealed it, we have put millions of American children in harm's way and I can live with this no longer.'

Autism used to effect 1 in 30,000. Now it effects 1 in 58 and by the year 2032 it is predicted to effect 1 in 2!

Now everything that was revealed by Dr Thompson of CDC was not speculation, it can all be supported by facts, and these are the facts: *"Analysis plans, data outputs, meeting notes, internal correspondence – showing that the knowledge of this went to the very top of the CDC. They knew about it, they all knew about it and this was a huge crime. In terms of fraud they: 1. Changed the analysis plan, 2. decided to omit data on the very high risk in African American children – in particular boys and in all children of all races, children who would develop mentally normal to aged 12 months – children who developed normally and then lost skills! 3. They decided that they needed to destroy documents in order to get rid of anything that might lead back to the fact that they had committed fraud, but unbeknownst to them, Thompson kept his original records- which they thought were destroyed. 4. Then they went forward and mislead congress and the IOM – Institute of Medicine and IOM issued a report which said MMR vaccine is not causatively associated with autism, and no further funding shall be put into investigating this link. 5. On the basis of that, the vaccine court threw out 5,000 cases of children plaintiffs who were in that court seeking compensation for damages for autism following vaccination. So they were denied their day in court and this was a massive obstruction of justice."* – Dr Andrew Wakefield. www.infowars.com

If you want further information about the harmfulness of some vaccinations, watch the documentary '*Vaxxed*' and weigh and measure this for yourself. And also check out the links below.

127 studies of the autism link to vaccination:

https://www.scribd.com/doc/220807175/157-Research-Papers-Supporting-the-Vaccine-Autism-Link

You can also check out the below links for all these published studies that also show the harmfulness of certain vaccinations.

http://www.ncbi.nlm.nih.gov/pmc/articles/PMC3878266/
http://www.ncbi.nlm.nih.gov/pubmed/21623535
http://www.ncbi.nlm.nih.gov/pubmed/25377033
http://www.ncbi.nlm.nih.gov/pubmed/24995277
http://www.ncbi.nlm.nih.gov/pubmed/12145534
http://www.ncbi.nlm.nih.gov/pubmed/21058170
http://www.ncbi.nlm.nih.gov/pubmed/22099159
http://www.ncbi.nlm.nih.gov/pmc/articles/PMC3364648/
http://www.ncbi.nlm.nih.gov/pubmed/17454560
http://www.ncbi.nlm.nih.gov/pubmed/19106436
http://www.ncbi.nlm.nih.gov/pmc/articles/PMC3774468/
http://www.ncbi.nlm.nih.gov/pmc/articles/PMC3697751/
http://www.ncbi.nlm.nih.gov/pubmed/21299355
http://www.ncbi.nlm.nih.gov/pubmed/21907498
http://www.ncbi.nlm.nih.gov/pubmed/11339848
http://www.ncbi.nlm.nih.gov/pubmed/17674242
http://www.ncbi.nlm.nih.gov/pubmed/21993250
http://www.ncbi.nlm.nih.gov/pubmed/15780490
http://www.ncbi.nlm.nih.gov/pubmed/12933322
http://www.ncbi.nlm.nih.gov/pubmed/16870260
http://www.ncbi.nlm.nih.gov/pubmed/19043938
http://www.ncbi.nlm.nih.gov/pubmed/12142947
http://www.ncbi.nlm.nih.gov/pubmed/24675092
http://www.ncbi.nlm.nih.gov/pubmed/25198681

There is also a plethora of other material, federal cases of compensation awarded to impacted families. It is all right there in plain sight, do not accept what is presented to you by mainstream media and by the so-called 'experts' that have a vested interest to maintain a contrary position to this, there is a bigger agenda at play.

SELECTED BIBLIOGRAPHY

1. The Labours of Hercules, Alice A Bailey, Lucis Publishing Company, 2000.
2. Initiation Human and Solar, Alice A Bailey, Lucis Publishing Company, 1959.
3. Ponder on This, Alice A Bailey, Lucis Publishing Company, 2015
4. The Urantia Book, Urantia Foundation, 1955.
5. The Kybalion, The Three Initiates, Dover Publications Inc., 2009.
6. Poor Charlies Almanac: The Wit and Wisdom of Charles T Munger (Expanded 3rd Edition), PCA Publication, 2005.
7. The Holy Science, Swami Sri Yukeswar Giri, Self Realisation Fellowship LA, 1977.
8. The Four Loves, C.S Lewis, Geoffrey Bles, 1960.
9. The Secret Doctrine, H.P Blavatsky, Theosophical University Press, 1977.
10. The Instruction of Ptah-Hotep and of Ke'gemni: The oldest books in the world, London, John Murray, 1906.
11. The Orion Mystery, Robert Bauval and Adrian Gilbert, Arrow Books, 1994.
12. Fingerprints of the Gods, Graham Hancock, Three Rivers Press, 1996.
13. The Teachings of Don Juan: A Yacqui Way of Knowledge, Carlos Castaneda, Penguin Books Ltd., 1973.
14. The Dead Sea Scrolls Deception, Michael Baigent and Richard Leigh, Random House Group Ltd., 2001.
15. The Yoga Sutras of Patanjali, Swami Vivekananda, Watkins Publishing, 2007.
16. The Egyptian Mysteries, Samuel Weiser, 1991.

17. The Secret Teachings of All Ages, Manly P Hall, A & D Publishing, 1st Edition (October 31, 2007).
18. From Abraham to Paul, Dr Andrew E. Steinmann, Concordia Publishing (July 1, 2011).
19. Sepher Yezirah –A Book on Creation, Rev, Dr Isidor Kalisch, New York, L.H Frank and Co – Publishers and printers, 1877.
20. The Shining Paths, Dolores Ashcroft-Nowicki, The Aquarian Press, 1983.
21. You Can Avoid Physical Death: Physical Body Ascension & the New Earth, Robert E Pettid PhD, I-Universe, 2009.
22. The Voice of the Silence, Helena Blavatsky, Theosophical University Press, 1992.
23. The Dharma that illuminates all beings impartially like the light of the sun and the moon, Kalu Rinpoche SUNY Press, 1986.
24. The Voice of Isis, F. Homer Curtiss, B.S., M.D, The Curtiss Philosophic Book Company, 1926.
25. Bioelectromagnetic & Subtle Energy Medicine, 2nd ed, McCraty, R. (ed Paul J. Rosch), 2015.
26. Heart, The Agni Yogi Society, 1932.
27. Spiritual Sex: A Treatise on the creative lifeforce in you and the spiritual expression of your creative life sex force, Robert Wall Crary, Rishis Institute of Metaphysics, 2003.
28. The Emerald Tablets of Thoth – Dr M Doreal, Crystalinks website 2000 https://www.crystalinks.com/emerald.html.
29. The Prophet, Kahlil Gibran, Wordsworth Editions Ltd., 1996.
30. The Light on the Path, M.C, The Yogi Publication Society, 1903.
31. The Book of Knowledge, The Keys of Enoch, Dr J J Hurtak, The Academy for Future Science, 2004.
32. The Leaves of Moryas Garden, Agni Yogi Society Inc., 1988.
33. Path workings with the Egyptian Gods, Judith Page and Jan A Malique, Llewellyn Publications, 2010.
34. Extract from a Martinist Manuscript, A.M.O.R.C.
35. The Lords Prayer, Dr J. J. Hurtak, The Academy for Future Science, 1983.
36. The Tao of Leadership, John Heider/ Lao Tzu, Humanics New Age, 1997.

Holy Texts Used

The Holy Bible
The Torah
The Koran
The Upanishads
The Book of Enoch
The Dhammapada
Sepher Yezirah
The Bhagavad Gita

Video Content

The Fabric of the Cosmos – Brian Greene
https://www.youtube.com/watch?v=Zuedaptw73w

My Dinner with Andre
https://www.youtube.com/watch?v=68JLWyPxt7g

Understanding meditation requires Order, J. Krishnamurti
https://www.youtube.com/watch?v=bciKNE90kzU

Websites:

www.crystalinks.com/emerald.html
ancient-origins.net
Wikipedia.com
Oxford English Dictionary https://www.oed.com/
www.encyclopedia.com/science-and-technology/astronomy-and-space-exploration/astronomy-general/precession-equinoxes

N. S. Elijah, Silhouette, 2018.

"From time to time, I fly into Earthly existence and share my knowledge, gifts and love. For I have a great love for humanity and planet Earth, and I want nothing more than to see both flourish in the Creator's love. Like my Brother Christ – Sananda, I am a Sword – here to defend what is holy and stand up for the greater good, no matter the reactions of those around me whose vision may not be as far-sweeping.

When I venture forth to this planet to carry out a mission, largely I am not recognised – and so it has been also this lifetime, and yet – the work goes on, and to be given this opportunity to help as needed is such a great honour and joy.

Listen to the voice of love in your heart, it will not lead you astray. It is difficult to love as the masters do, with a great love that asks for nothing in return and yet that is the destiny of all mankind – to burn with the divine fire of love and ascend as a master of compassion. It is this sacred alignment that forms the fiery chariot to the Heavens."

— **Elijah**

Copyright Permissions.

Permissions granted in these works were originally obtained under the first changed (never printed) title of the book:
"*A Message for Humanity - The Golden Flight of the White Dove – A Journey to sacred knowledge.*"

Where the below works have been used, the permission has been granted under the following conditions:

Krishnamurti Foundation

Permission to quote the works of J. Krishnamurti or other works for which the copyright is held by the Krishnamurti Foundation of America or the Krishnamurti Foundation Trust Ltd has been given on the understanding that such permission does not indicate endorsement of the views expressed in this publication. For more information about L. Krishnamurti (1895-1986) please see: www.jkrishnamurti.org

Lucis Trust

Permission to quote from the Alice Bailey books has been granted by the Lucis Trust who hold copyright: *Initiation Human and Solar: Solar and Planetary Hierarchies* – pages 48, 49, 103-104; *Initiation* – page 10; *Probationary path* – page 63; *Disciple* – pages 71, 72 and 75; *The Labours of Hercules: Great Presiding One* – page 2; *Difficult to serve the species called man* – page 133; *Ponder on This* – pages 1 - 14.

Angi Yoga Society

Permission from the Agni Yogi Society has been given to "*Quote from the Agni Yoga books in whatever way you need to present the message.*" – Director of Agni Yoga Society.

Llewellyn

Pathworking with the Egyptian Gods by Judith Page and Jan Malique, 2010 Llewellyn Worldwide, Ltd. 2143 Wooddale Drive, Woodbury, MN 55125. All rights reserved, used by permission.

Penguin Random House UK

The Dead Sea Scrolls Deception, 2001, Michael Baignt & Richard Leigh. Pages 13, 21, 22, 28, 29, 39, 54, 58, 65, 66, 68-71, 72, 74, 75, 76, 93, 94, 101, 107, 169-171, 175-179.

Light Technology Publishing

The Ancient Secrets of the flower of Life Vol I & II, 1998 & 2000, Drunvalo Melchizedek www.lighttechnology.com

Aurora Press

Initiation, Elisabeth Haich, 2000, first published in 1953. Pages 146, 152, 153, 154, 258, 259.

Red Wheel Weiser

*Egyptian Mysteries, by Unknown Author, 1988 by Samuel Weiser, Inc. used with permission from Red Wheel Weiser, LLC Newburyport, MA. Pages 40-43, 51-53, 55-57, 65-67, 151-53.

State University of New York Press (SUNY Press)

The Dharma that illuminates all beings impartially like the light of the sun and the moon by Kalu Rinpoche, reprinted by permission, the State University of New York Press, 1986, State University of New York. All Rights reserved.

The Academy For Future Science

The Book of Knowledge – The Keys of Enoch®, 2004. Pages 65, 228, 230, 419, 582; and

The Lords Prayer, 1983, reprinted by permission of Dr J. J. Hurtak.

Green Dragon Books

John Heider, *The Tao of Leadership*, 1985, Humanics Publishing Copyright 2015 Green Dragon Books. (Quote on the back cover). Lao Tzu's Tao De Ching 5th Century BC.

Fair Use – Full Attribution

Dolores Ashcroft-Nowicki, *The Shining Paths* – From the Appendix page 229-230, "The Questions of the 42 Assessors" – total 351 words.

Robert Bauval & Adrian Gilbert, *The Orion Mystery*, pages 35-36 – total 111 words.

Robert E. Pettit PhD, *You Can Avoid Physical Death: Physical Body Ascension to the New Earth* – total 168 words.

Brian Green, '*Fabric of the Cosmos*' video series, 2015. Where content verbally presented was transcribed and placed into a diagram by the author and used to build Figures 2 and 3 in this book.

Image Copyright Permissions.

Ch 1 fig 1 pg 4 © schab 63815814 (Chairs).
Ch 2 fig 2 pg 29 © natros 67791583 (electromagnetic spectrum).
Ch 2 fig 12; Ch 4 fig 29, 30, 32; Ch 9 fig 64 Images used from the Rider Waite Tarot Deck are from the public domain.
Ch 2 fig 17 pg 51 © bodot 49196256 (Statue of Horus).
Ch 2 fig 18 pg 52 © Anne Mathiasz 50298533 (Sri yantra).
Ch 3 fig 26 pg 96 © basphoto 21271957 (Osirian dovetail grooves).
Ch 5 fig 44c pg 131 © Dirk Czarnota 58525500 (staff of hermes).
Ch 6 fig 46a pg 144 © styleuneed 45713423 (Flower of life).
Ch 6 fig 46b pg 144 © Anne Mathiasz 70937552 (Kabbalah tree of life flower of life).
Ch 6 fig 49 pg 150 © Ravennka 94228544 (Golden mean).
Back cover image Light © agsandrew 85905538.
Back cover image Dove © fotomaster 76005182.

"Behold, I will send you the prophet Elijah before the great and terrible day of the Lord comes. He will turn the hearts of parents to their children and the hearts of children to their parents, so that I will not come and strike the land with a curse."

– Malachi 4:5-6, New Revised Standard Version

www.ingramcontent.com/pod-product-compliance
Lightning Source LLC
Chambersburg PA
CBHW060050190426
43201CB00034B/635